D1074832

THE CRISIS IN HISTORICAL MATERIALISM:

Class, Politics and Culture in Marxist Theory

THE CRISIS IN HISTORICAL MATERIALISM:

Class, Politics and Culture in Marxist Theory

Stanley Aronowitz

Professor of Sociology
City University of New York

Foreword by Colin MacCabe

University of Minnesota Press · Minneapolis

Published by the University of Minnesota Press
2037 University Avenue Southeast, Minneapolis MN 55414.

Printed in Hong Kong.

Library of Congress Cataloging-in-Publication Data
Aronowitz, Stanley.
The crisis in historical materialism: class, politics, and culture in Marxist theory/Stanley Aronowitz; foreword by Colin MacCabe. — [2nd ed.]
p. cm.
Includes bibliographical references.
ISBN 0–8166–1835–6. ISBN 0–8166–1836–4 (pbk.)
1. Historical materialism. I. Title.
D16.9.A77 1990
335.4′119—dc20 89–20327
CIP

To Emily

Contents

Foreword

Colin MacCabe

The summer of '89 may seem an inauspicious time to write a foreword to a book about Marxism. The events in China, Russia and the whole of Eastern Europe are widely represented by the pundits of the press as the end of Marxism, the disastrous finish to a failed historical experiment. But it is one of the merits of this extraordinary book that it makes clear the very limited view of Marxism that has informed both that experiment and its critics. What is striking about Aronowitz's wide-ranging critique of existing forms of Marxism is that it does not limit itself to a well-understood criticism of the political and theoretical foundations of Leninism and Stalinism, indeed he takes those criticisms as uncontroversial starting points, but that the criticisms go right back to the roots of Marxism, to its fundamental conceptions of nature and science. Indeed so far-reaching is the critique that it might immediately pose the question of whether the book can be considered Marxist at all.

Aronowitz's own response to this is twofold. Theoretically his own project is to understand the logic of capitalist development and to explain how one is to understand the changing structure of economic production in its complex relationship to cultural and political life. That very intellectual ambition is to place oneself within the field of Marxism, to accept as fundamental, questions which Marx was the first to articulate. But there is also a political answer. Aronowitz's whole drive to understand is at the service of a profound commitment to the emancipation of humanity from the conditions of social domination. It is the belief that the political and cultural practices which will achieve such emancipation are crucially dependent on knowledge, which links Aronowitz to Marx politically. But this complex answer shows why Aronowitz's work is as much an heir of Weber and Simmel, who inherited Marx's theoretical questions, as it is of Luxemburg and Pannokoek, who attempted to further the political project.

But perhaps the most important way to indicate the importance of this work is the time and place of its production. The theoretical precursors and antecedents are important, vital, but many people have read these texts before to little effect. What is crucial is that this is a work (and the adjective here is riddled with historical ironies) of American Marxism. The irony is, of course, that the very adjective embodies the imperial project of the United States in the limited form of subsuming two continents to one of their constituent nations. But it is true to say that Aronowitz is the first working within the Marxist tradition to have treated the specific form of the development of the United States – the inseparability of capitalist development from questions of race and the appropriation of previously uncultivated land; the constitution of a work force from many different ethnic groups – not as anomalies to be explained away but as crucial to understanding the forms of contemporary global capitalism. In that sense it is no exaggeration to call this the first Marxist work to come out of the United States. Such a description is not meant to devalue the immense contributions of figures like Sidney Hook but it is to say that Aronowitz's first point of reference is always the political and economic development of the United States rather than those of Europe. Aronowitz also draws, as assumptions which are implicit throughout this work, on the best of the American democratic and libertarian traditions.

But if the place is crucial so is the time. When I first read this book in 1983 (two years after it had been published) I was immediately struck by the fact that this was the first work of Marxist theory which really came out of the political experiences of the sixties. This is, in many ways, a paradoxical if not a provocative statement. Is it not the case that one of the features that characterize that decade and its subsequent legacy was a re-flowering of Marxist thought? The names of Althusser and Marcuse, for example, are central to any account of the political and ideological history of the sixties. But if the thinking of the New Left was an essential part of the heterogeneous mix of economics, politics and culture which make up the sixties, that thinking was itself fundamentally unaffected by the heterogeneity of which it was a part. It is a historical puzzle (which in my own case is also a deeply opaque part of my own personal history) why so many students caught up in the turmoil of the sixties attempted to understand that turmoil with Marxist categories which fundamentally denied the heterogeneity of their own experience. The immense merit of Aronowitz's book is that it is a genuine attempt to produce a historical and social understanding which is fully adequate to that experience.

It is not surprising that the crucial categories that get recast are those of nature and science. On the one hand psychoanalysis and its attention to the forms of human sexuality emphasise that there are elements in the constitution of the human which cannot be reduced to history. On the other hand the very development of productive forces have reached a point where it is clear that if we leave our understanding of nature as simply material to be refashioned by those forces then we resign ourselves to the death of the world. Nowhere is Aronowitz's book more prescient than in its central placing of ecology for any future emancipatory politics. Such a statement may seem clearly obvious now but at the beginning of the eighties ecology was still seen by many on the left as a marginal single issue.

Indeed it is perhaps the most vital contradiction of our time that at exactly the moment that the definition of socialism in terms of centrally planned production for defined human need is most discredited, a new formulation which relates the planning of production to defined ecological need is most urgently needed. Aronowitz's book is the first stage in such a process and, as such, is of crucial importance to any future left politics.

It should go without saying that any such developments will once again place science at the absolute centre of political struggle. Much Marxist thought of the last two decades has been produced by people trained within the humanities. One of the results of this has been an unfortunate relegating of the importance of science which probably has as much to do with traditional academic prejudices as any weightier explanation. Aronowitz, by contrast, clearly sees the centrality of science both to the history of Marxism and to contemporary social development. Eschewing both the scientistic notion of objectivity and any of the burgeoning forms of anti-rational relativism, Aronowitz places science securely within the social process. The setting of research agendas is possibly one of the key political struggles of the forthcoming decade and, once again, it is Aronowitz's work which provides a theoretical context to inform such struggles.

Much intellectual work is so influenced by prevailing fashion that it is outdated even before it is published. Really original work has the feature of seeming ever more relevant. In the six years since I first read this text and in the complicated efforts to get an English version published I have several times returned and re-read it. On each occasion I have been astonished at its pertinence and its prescience. It is one of the very few really important theoretical works of the eighties and I am particularly delighted that the efforts to make it available to an English audience have led to its republication in the United States.

Colin MacCabe
London
21st September 1989

Preface to the Second Edition

When the first edition of this book was published in 1981, many readers wondered about the title. Shouldn't it be *Crisis of not in Historical Materialism*? I insisted the difference between the two was significant, that I believed Marx has asked the right questions, but that the tradition his work spawned, Marxism, had failed to carry on his most powerful motto: the relentless criticism of all received wisdom, although unfortunately not of historical materialism itself. This lapse has had the consequence of persuading many that Marxism has been surpassed by other social explanatory modes, and has already suffered its own historicity the more it cannot account for changes, or anomalies in terms of its scientific paradigm; Marxism is most successful, therefore, as a way of seeing the past, although recent developments in historiography tend to refute even the most sophisticated versions, determinations by the infrastructure in the last instance. I argue that despite the tendency of recent marxisms to fuse their tradition with others – phenomenology, structuralism, psychoanalysis of various sorts, and even liberalism – it remains tied to an outmoded conception of agency and has failed to follow the critical side of Marx himself, particularly his dialectical understanding of science. For Marxism has betrayed a tendency to privilege structural constraints over social movements; that is, to submit to a scientism for which "objective, historical tendencies" allow it to predict and control human action. As the reader will find in the pages that follow, I propose a different conception of agencies, the plural signifying that the proletariat, especially in advanced capitalist societies, no longer, if it ever did, occupies a privileged space in the social formation, and that this space has been radically displaced. This displacement has two distinct dimensions: the historical changes in all advanced industrial countries that have rendered manual labor subordinate to intellectual labor; and, perhaps more importantly, the theoretical displacement whose earliest manifestations were the critiques of Georg Simmel and Max Weber, but have been elaborated and deepened by both intellectuals linked to new social movements and various critiques of "essentialist" discourse, particularly the post-structuralist repudiation of the Hegelian intepretations of Marxism. My contention is that Marxism retains vitality but is no longer the master discourse about social relations. First, the historical: the working class in all advanced countries is progressively displaced by the globalization of capital and especially of industrial production which has now been effectively deterritorialized; the concentration of ownership is no longer matched by the centralization of production. Moreover, knowledge has become the decisive productive force and science the core of technological development. Far from constituting an oppositional social category to that of capital, science (to which Marxism aspires) has been both subsumed under capital and is a new site of power in all industrial societies, including those calling themselves socialist. While the leading capitalist powers still monopolize modern scientific and technical knowledge, the struggle of developing countries for autonomy entails developing their own knowledge centers. The working class of all countries faces not chiefly huge aggregations of physical capital symbolized in huge mills producing means of material production, giant cities that are the center of these facilities and the visible signs of class power and class struggle, but invisible power congealed in microchips, processed particles and molecules that are produced in the new knowledge factories – the laboratories. The signs of the new power-communications channels funnelling information inscribed on paper and preserved in artificial memory present an entirely new set of problems for those engaged in political and industrial combat. For even as the machines remain in place, they are increasingly driven by programs which occupy an inconspicuous space atop the machine. These programs direct the machine, handle materials and, in many instances, even perform repairs. And the identification of means of production with fixed places has given way to deterritorialization not only on a global scale but from public to private spaces.

These empirical transformations have had their theoretical counterparts: inspired by semiotics in its Foucaultian formulations, Ernesto Laclau has announced the "impossibility of the social" and insists that all we have left is discursive formations along which people occupy subject positions. Agency, argue Laclau and his collaborator Chantal Mouffe, has lost its fixed position in history. Even if it once could be said that a working class located in a definite position in something called a social structure, the social as such has disappeared. In any case, even in the nineteenth century it was a system of signs constructed in accordance with definite discursive rules, the totality of which is called historical materialism. For Laclau, interaction is constituted as discourse among shifting signifiers. Classes, social formations, historical agents – these are the categories of an old Hegelian essentialism the validity of which must be denied. A new post-Marxist discourse has emerged to explain the transformations, principally in spatial terms, which have rendered suspect many Marxist assumptions, especially Marx's argument that "we know only one science, the science of history". Now this tendency proclaims that we know only discourse analysis since language is the only possible object of knowledge. The "social", like nature, cannot be apprehended without the aid of constructed categories and exists in the interstices of language.

Jean Baudrillard has gone so far as to argue that politics itself, not just particular parties and programs, has been surpassed by the growing mass-refusal of participation in elections and civic duties of all sorts. For Baudrillard the power nexus provides absolutely no spaces for interventions of putative agents, except those which he calls a "silent majority" who have chosen, not only to refuse the rules of the game but to retreat from the simulations of difference upon which the political game depends. Anti-politics is a non-statement assimilated by executive authorities as apathy, a term employed to preserve the legitimacy of the game. So, while others bemoan the separation of the private and public which, for them, signifies an apalling triumph of rulers' economic and ideological hegemony, Baudrillard sees privatization as the most reasonable form of resistance available to many who will not legitimate the sham of politics in the contemporary era.

It is not difficult to see that in these two variants of post-Marxism, even if influenced by Saussurian linguistics, the historical materialist questions are still present, at least to the extent that the problems of (a) how it is possible to envision agency and (b) how it is possible to overcome the conditions of social domination stay at the core of the discourse. Moreover, even if their conclusions differ from those of Marxism, they are still in dialogue with it if only because there really is no alternative paradigm of capitalist development that embraces the scope of historical materialism. Sartre's remark that historical materialism is the theory of capitalist development, notwithstanding its weaknesses, becomes a late-twentieth century version of the eternal recurrence. Even when sharply criticized, historical materialism remains the referent of all theories and discourses whose object is human emancipation.

It may be safely remarked that unless we renounce metatheory as such, a plausible position, there are no current alternatives to Marxism which match its level of abstraction and historical sweep, only efforts such as Georg Simmel's to "construct a new storey beneath historical materialism such that the explanatory value of the incorporation of economic forms themselves into the causes of intellectual culture is preserved, while these economic forms are recognized as the result of more profound valuations and currents of psychological or even meta-physical preconditions." (*Philosophy of Money*, p. 56) Simmel follows this formulation by asserting that the relation between "ideal structure and economic structure" is dialectically infinite. By refusing the "economic in the last instance", Simmel inverts Marx's formula of historical causality to be found in the pristine determination in his famous Preface to the *Contribution of Political Economy* but does not thereby propose a new set of categories by which to understand social structure, historically considered.

In this respect, the criticism of Marx advanced by Max Weber, argues for the effectivity of ideal structures in historical change and for what Karl Korsch once called the principle of historical specification. In this mode of theorizing there are no transhistorical principles underlying social formations; the reasons for the appearance of the capitalist system differ from the transformations of early societies. Early capitalist development was fueled by a new rationality linked to Calvinism. Weber's comparative method distinguished feudal societies by whether the rational structure of traditional religion was displaced or by an ethic that privileged work, the path to salvation, and gave special status to savings/investment over the use of money for individual pleasure. In contrast his account of transitions in ancient European civilization depended upon an analysis that focused on different methods of the production of material life: "The pattern of settlement in the European occident contrasts with that common to the civilizations of East Asia. The differences may be summed up briefly, if somewhat imprecisely, as follows: in Europe the transition to fixed settlement meant a change from the dominance of cattle breeding (especially of milk) to an economy dominated by agriculture, with cattle-breeding continuing as a secondary element; in Asia, on the contrary, there was a shift from extensive, and hence nomadic, agriculture to horticulture without milk-cattle breeding." (*Agrarian Sociology of Ancient Civilizations*, (p. 37)

While capitalism is described as a new system of rational calculation, where instrumental reason replaces substantive reason, the fall of the Roman empire is ascribed to the collapse of its economic basis, particularly the shortages of slave labor upon which the Roman production system had become vitally and fatally dependent. Underlying these differences was, of course, a common thread of power, the appeal to which ultimately marked Weber's developmental history. Yet this hardly qualifies as a metatheory. Weber's whole point is to oppose metatheory as an unwarranted presupposition of historical change which undercuts the referent of empirical evidence as the arbiter of social knowledge. Put another way, Weber joins modern science in which the red thread of methodologies of inquiry replace transhistorical determinations as the common ground of natural and social investigations. On the other hand Weber is still preoccupied with the ramifications of the methodological starting-point of the "mode of production of material life". Transcoded into contemporary terms, Weber's theory of modern capitalism privileges the discourses of domination. Religion is a system of shifting signs subject to, but not determined by, "material" causes. Thus under the sign of "ideal structures" both Simmel and Weber prefigure later concepts such as episteme (Foucault), discourse (Pêcheux, Derrida) and *mentalité* (Annales school). Now, as before, the object of criticism is not necessarily Marx himself, but really-existing historical materialism that has transformed a critical science into dogma.

Despite Marx's own statements to the contrary, particularly the famous assertion of the *Communist Manifesto* that "All history is the history of class struggles" and the accusations of commentators such as Baudrillard of Marx's "economism", his empirically-based historical writings are as complex in explanations of concrete events as he was simple in his declarations. The evidence of pamphlets such as *The Eighteenth Brumaire, Class Struggles in France*, and the massive sections in *Capital* on the histories of the labor process, the process of capital accumulation, the history of ground-rent, and so on, show that there is no privileged term in the dialectic of labor and capital accumulation, that the logic of capital is not only mediated but also shaped by the spontaneous and organized working-class resistance to the impositions by capital. Perhaps the most familiar example in Marx is the correlation of the struggle for the eight-hour day by trade unions and the transformation of the form of exploitation from absolute to relative surplus value), the persistence of parasitism of the *rentier* class, which inhibits productive investment and may overdetermine capital-logic, and the autonomous actions of monarchy and state as well as political intrigues in France. One cannot read Marx without being struck by the variegated character of his historical understanding, one that easily confounded careless critics.

There is the other side, the side pushed forward by Marx's followers, especially in the context of turn-of-the-century Europe when the earlier "anarchy" of capitalist production seemed to yield to a world capitalism – highly organized, rationalized beyond Marx's expectations and able to offer to the working-class a new deal. As I shall argue in the last chapter, this arrangement was predicated, not on the crisis of the system as later, in the 1930's, but on the halcyon phase of central European capitalist development when, contrary to the "classical" English model, the integration of state with highly concentrated and centralized German capitalism was able to ameliorate the workers' living standards to an unprecedented level. The power of the economic seemed so absolute that even the anti-reformism of leading German socialists such as Karl Kautsky and Rosa Luxemburg singled out the question of the contradiction between productive forces and production relations as the main dynamic of history. Kautsky, in particular, became the major architect of these conceptions which were, without much amendment, adopted by Marxists the world over, not the least important of which were the Russian Marxists led by Plekhanov and his pupil, Lenin. (Except it is surely unwarranted to call Lenin an "economist" in the light of his voluntarism, particularly his celebrated theory of the party.) Actually, the charge of determinism, particularly the doctrine of socialist inevitability, is better affixed to the theorists of the Second International than to those of the Communist movement who adapted Kautsky's judgement that the working class by its own efforts could never achieve class-consciousness and required the assistance of revolutionary theory to achieve their socialist destiny. Despite this, turn-of-the-century Marxism was scalded with Kautsky's economism and has not managed to shake it ever since.

Weber, a somewhat younger man than Kautsky, was of the generation that came into its intellectual majority in Germany at the zenith of Kautsky's reputation as the chief legatee of Marx and Engels, the semi-official interpreter of their theory of history and surely the premier theoretician of social-democracy. A self-professed bourgeois liberal, Weber could be easily dismissed by orthodox Marxism. But his significance for the further development of Marxism could not be dispensed with so easily. Beginning with Georg Lukács, whose *History and Class Consciousness* attested to the value (or the danger) of merging Marx's analysis of the vagaries of the commodity form with Weber's theory of rationality, and extending to the Frankfurt School for which the category of instrumental reason became the very explanation for emergence of technological rationality and the consequent passing of historical agency as such, a spate of writing has grasped the significance of Weber's contribution to historical materialism, rather than comprehending his work as refutation, despite the many reservations to the universal claims of Marx's followers.

Notwithstanding the obvious linguistic turn in Baudrillard's work especially after 1968, the influence in his writing of his teacher Henri Lefebvre lingers to this day. Lefebvre's own reading of Marx is a creative combination of Hegelian dialectic and Kantian scepticism mediated by the same German influences that have informed the Critical Theory of Adorno, Horkheimer and Marcuse – not only Weber but also Heidegger and Husserl. For it is the concern with everyday life, with "lived experience", a category borrowed by the anti-Hegelian Louis Althusser as well, that marks the contrast between the marxisms that took account of the interwar destruction of the once-promising working-class movement and tried to offer an adequate explanation for its defeat, and the triumphalism of the marxisms of the Second and the Third Internationals (of which more below).

I will argue that the crisis in historical materialism is not to be discovered in the so-called failure of Marx's predictions concerning the transition from capitalism to socialism; nor does it consist principally in the economism of the majority of Marx's acolytes, however egregious this misinterpretation may be. What is at stake is the fate of those agents that, in Alain Touraine's terms, struggle over their own historicity and thereby form themselves and social relations. Historical materialism is incomplete, not surpassed. Now, as before, it is obliged to grapple with its own historicity in the wake of the sea-changes that have enveloped the modern world, particularly the fact that the domination of nature which Marx understood as the precondition of human freedom is no longer viable, if it ever was. The emergence of new unexpected agents in the theatre of history which have challenged the old Marxist assumptions have shattered Marxist ideological hegemony even in those countries where Marxism enjoys the status of official ideology. Today, historical materialism is obliged to enter a dialogue with other tendencies which claim theoretical and political validity. It can no longer subsume all competing world views under the rubric of 'bourgeois' to which it counterposes its own, proletarian worldview; it must face ecological, nationalist and feminist worldviews, each of which has its own competing camps and whose unity, as in the case of Marxism, is in doubt.

Pluralism has always, for Marxism, been equated with a struggle against liberal ideology. This view is no longer tenable if we understand alternative discourses as neither dominated by liberalism nor socialism. The question is, of course, whether the new discourses can be negotiated with socialist rationality or whether the crisis has gone beyond Marx's own understanding of the term: a profound rupture in the system but not necessarily fatal; in fact, for Marx the crises of capitalism are the necessary condition for renewal. Surely, ecosocialists and Marxist feminists have attempted to find common ground between the ostensibly competing paradigms with only mixed success. Nevertheless, the effort remains crucial, if only to determine whether historical materialism still offers an indispensable dimension.

Finally, I want to report on the progress of historical materialism since the latest crisis; say, the last decade. In general, the record is not particularly encouraging, from a theoretical perspective, although scientific Marxism – the work of historians, social scientists and literary critics influenced by Marxism – has made rapid strides, or to be more precise, continues in paths that were marked by their immediate predecessors. The new social history in the United States and Great Britain continues to contribute to our knowledge of the past, even if, in its desire to resurrect hidden histories of the marginalized, it frequently neglects important elements of economic and political relations. The Marxist hegemony over the study of feudalism and early capitalism has been little disturbed. In some respects, British sociology, including work in Australia and Canada, is marked by the Marx/Weber integration in the entire profession and in the United States Weberian Marxism, particularly in historical sociology, has earned a prominent place in the mainstream. (Although it is often confused with Marxism: I refer to the work of Immanuel Wallerstein and Theda Scacpol.) Although challenged by functionalism on the right and post-structuralism on the "left", Marxist anthropology in Europe and the United States remains extremely influential. And, largely spurred by Fredric Jameson and Terry Eagleton, Marxist approaches, laced, of course, with both French post-structuralism and German neo-Marxism that owes as much to Lukács and the Frankfurt School as it does to the new democratic movements that sprang up in the 1960's, if not dominant are, at least, respectable in the Anglo-American academy.

The situation is more complicated in economics. For, despite the growth of the political left among professional economists, the serious twenty-year-old crisis of world capitalism, combined with the decline of the hegemony of post-Keynesian doctrine and most importantly, economic policy, has produced a new birth of neo-classical paradigms that seem to have swept all opposition in its path, including Marxism. We discovered that, with few exceptions, notably Michel Béaud in France, the capital-logic school in Germany, James O'Connor and the *Monthly Review* group in the United States among others, that most Marxist economists are really left-Keynesians and have been unable to generate, with the exceptions noted, a coherent theory of the crisis. In any case, Marxist analysis is absent from the public debate, in contrast to the last great depression when, in England, for example, Marxism, despite its painful orthodoxy, enjoyed considerable currency, even in the midst of the implementation of policies of state intervention advised by Keynes.

However, the most serious challenge for Marxist economic doctrine is the discovery, yet again, that socialist models of planning have, for the most part failed, particularly in Eastern Europe, where in the past forty years they have dominated economic activity. In the wake of the world economic crisis, really-existing socialist countries have experienced its effects because, since the 1960s, their economic viability has depended in a large measure on loans procured from Western banks. Enriched with billions of dollars, Eastern European living standards rose, even when productivity slumped. For the joke that travels around the region contains more truth than its leaders care to admit, even in the Gorbachev era: "How do you like your job?" a visitor asks. "What job?" comes the reply. "They pretend to pay us and we pretend to work."

With the crisis came austerity. Suddenly, almost-forgotten queues formed for meat and many other goods. With the new Soviet regime, the word went out that efficiency criteria might be imposed to determine which enterprises should survive and which should be shut down, an approach that implied possible unemployment. And, for Yugoslavia, the situation was exacerbated by the effects of the crisis on employment in such countries as Germany and Switzerland; emigration was no longer possible on a large scale, a development which revealed the dark side of the country's economic "miracle"; it simply got rid of one million workers to maintain full employment even as it accumulates $30 billion in debts to western banks. In the wake of these disturbing developments, economists east and west, revived discussion of what became known as "market" socialism. The proposals to reform the economies of Eastern Europe and other countries characterized by central control over most economic activity have, to say the least, spanned the range of possibility. "Liberals" argue that enterprise managers should have more power to determine a wide variety of functions at the enterprise level including the choice of technology, setting wage and productivity norms, and should have a freer hand to sell products within the framework established by the plan. Further, privately-owned peasant plots should be encouraged and the market for agricultural commodities should be expanded. But in no case, according to this view, should central planning be dismantled. The "market" should be restricted both in definition and scope.

"Radicals", including Alec Nove, echoing the earlier work of Polish economist Oskar Lange, argue that only when consumer choice dictates production decisions can (a) social freedom be guaranteed and (b) efficiency insured. The function of state planners is to coordinate some decisions in a restricted sector such as utilities, and they may intervene to encourage new types of investment. But, for Nove, "social ownership" implies neither state ownership nor control, but only that private property is not restored on a large scale. But he does not exclude arrangements that resemble those of Hungary where many enterprises, although state-owned, are leased to private individuals who run them according to (principally) market criteria. Nove's indictment of the stultifying Soviet system of state control over all crucial economic decisions is, to say the least, devastating. However, his idea of consumer-driven rational (i.e. profitability) choices is by no means an inevitable conclusion from his critique. Despite his avoidance of the usual moralizing which too often accompanies such critiques, and his willingness to assign to the state considerable power in decision-making, Nove is arguing that the free market is the most effective site for achieving stability and growth, if not equality. On the contrary, Nove implies that democracy and freedom entail surrendering much of the ideology according to which justice is equated with greater equality. For despite the considerable evidence supporting the charge that Eastern European regimes are systems of privilege for party, state and managerial elites, when compared to Western counterparts their allegiance to relative equality is still powerful. However, even with the most stringent state controls, the Soviet Union is far from an egalitarian society; privilege and nepotism are rampant.

That the history of really-existing socialism has been marked by the extreme politicization of all social and economic functions is beyond question. At its worst, socialism has abolished both the bourgeois public sphere where issues may be debated and the instruments through which some version of the popular will may be felt (such as a freely-elected parliament) and the private sphere where individuals and groups may engage in the exchange of goods and ideas without the threat of surveillance and state intervention. So it has produced the worst of situations. It is neither democratic nor prosperous. And, when civil liberties are not broadly enlarged except for the political and technical intelligentsia, and market relations are severely restricted, we can expect to find a second political sphere where not only dissidence but refusal is rife and where a second economy undermines the official price structure and becomes a challenge to the fundamental premises of the regime. *Perestroika* may be viewed in this light as an intelligent political and ideological accommodation to what is already happening in everyday life, an illustration of the primacy of the social. Of course, restructuration is not so easy, if for no other reason than that the current economic and political system harbors vital interests – of the party elite, the technical and cultural intelligentsia for whom *glasnost* means more openness within and between elites, particularly the scientific and political. In any case, Marxism has been unable to successfully grapple, with some exceptions, with the problems raised by the partial breakdown of socialism as it has historically been constituted. As a result, not only the main features of the liberal state, civil liberties and representative democracy, are being introduced as solutions to the crisis of consent which has produced nationalist turmoil in Yugoslavia and the Soviet Union and profound popular alienation everywhere in socialist countries, but also markets and privatization are hot issues in the economics debate.

More can be said, and this report is, to say the least, incomplete, but I see no reason to support the view that Marxist "science" is alive and well. Marxist philosophy has never been more troubled. We are witnessing the palpable decline of Marxist metatheory that filled the intellectual landscape of all countries east and west, north and south, in the 1960's and early 1970's. Superficial judgements would ascribe this outpouring (structuralism, the Frankfurt School, Freud–Marx syntheses, phenomenological Marxism and several others) to the vitality of new student, anti-war, feminist and other social movements. Yet the 1920's produced considerable work of this sort in a period not only of left defeat but of rising right-wing movements that seized power within the decade. I submit that, after the decline of post-structuralism, social and cultural theory is experiencing its own crisis: having renounced master discourses of all sorts, the void is slowly being filled by a new call for ethics or to be more precise, a drift away from relativism. At the same time, there is a clear "political turn" to literary criticism parallel to the revival of political theory, signified by the slogan "bringing the state back in" to Marxist theory. Within these rubrics, Marxist criticism and theory are reexamined, precisely because other paradigms offer little more than liberal political ideas when they make room for the political at all. As a consequence, we are currently in the thrall of Marxology, which consists of close readings of classical texts and some of which is excellent intellectual history. Never before have the plots been rendered with such elegance and the preparation of the historians (or philosophers writing summaries and comments) so sophisticated. Some of these treatments (David Frisby's superb essay on Simmel, Kracauer and Benjamin, Martin Jay's admirable small book on Adorno, and Marshall Berman's discussion of modernity come to mind) are contributions to a Marxist understanding and clarification of the problem of modernity, particularly the sociology and social psychology of the modern world. Similarly, a strong Marxist tendency in feminist literary and philosophical studies has produced significant work. Nancy Hartsock's ambitious and brave treatise for a feminist historical materialism stands out in the

American context just as the wonderfully dense essays of Veronica Beechey, Meaghan Morris, and Jacqueline Rose among others, in the British debate. But these are a handful of instances where writers have taken on, from the perspective of a nuanced historical materialism, crucial aspects of contemporary metatheory. In doing so, all of them have been obliged to recognize the structural weaknesses of the Marxist paradigm and have hastened to shore it up rather than dispense with it. This attests to the intellectual power of the questions posed by historical materialism, which remain indispensable for the understanding of the new cultural contradictions of capitalism that seem to have been thrust to the forefront even as states and capital alliances fail to resume a brisk accumulation rate in most countries.

What all of these writers, above all Jurgen Habermas, have grasped is that for which Lukács and Gramsci are attacked, their insistence that the twentieth century has witnessed the persistence of capitalist social relations even in the midst of revolutionary upheaval precisely because they are not merely an economic system but have become a system for organizing consent as well, the results of which are not obliterated by changes in the structure of political power. The reproduction of the relations of production by means of cultural hegemony must be seen as analytically separate from the antagonistic production relations, and constitutes the sufficient condition for explaining the survival of capitalism even if the accumulation process exhibits all of the standard features such as frequent breakdowns, stagnation and deformations. However critical I remain of Habermas's solution to the perplexing issues raised by late capitalism, let me hasten to add that he is perhaps singular in attempting to reconstruct historical materialism in the light of some features of modern linguistics, Weber's work and recent history. This singularity only highlights the intellectual crisis. For the fate of historical materialism in the late capitalist epoch is marked by its fragmentation or, to be more specific, a high ratio of absorption by other discourses and paradigms within which Marxism is relegated to one way of seeing among others. In short, nowhere does Marxism retain its status as the master discourse it once enjoyed. Nor are most Marxists concerned with exploring how it may be restored, if not as a master discourse, then as a vigorous theoretical framework for comprehending the novelty of contemporary society and culture. Habermas has felt constrained, not only to return to Weber and Parsons in order to plumb the depths of the legitimation crisis because he has concluded that the sphere of economic relations has transcended ideology owing to the disappearance of class struggles as the structuring principle of capitalism. He has also drawn from developmental psychology and the philosophy of language, elements of a new moral theory, just as his studies of modernity have led to the conclusion that historical materialism is not an exhausted paradigm and that post-structuralism and post-modernism are premature if not destructive of the preservation of reason as the regulative principle of human affairs.

Under Habermas's influence, most left post-Marxists working on the problem of categories rather than time-bound historical or sociological issues, are theorists of modernity. The new rationality suggested by Weber and Marx, not only designs and engineers machines and consumer goods, but human souls as well. As Frisby demonstrates, Simmel is the theorist who shows that fragmented snapshots hide a coherent modernity that should be grasped as a unique totality. The problems of modern politics in both the West and Third World societies, are linked to the fact that capitalism, as Marx remarked in the *Manifesto*, not only destroys the old idyllic relations of feudalism, but creates a new world around the permutations of the commodity form where the material and symbolic are to be considered aspects of the totality not arranged in vertical order. This new world is not only a commodity-exchanging universe, but consists in a built environment constituted by the anonymity of its privatized inhabitants. As the production of signs dominates the production of goods, even the old working-class neighborhoods, from which solidarity was fashioned disappear or are recast as domiciles for the salariat. The "inner city" which was once a working-class political and industrial bastion, and even the red suburbs, have been transformed into appendages of the metropolis.

This is the most stunning contribution of recent Marxist and neo-Marxist criticism: to remind us that lived experience is the last frontier of contestation in the wake of the dispersal of the old agents. And this is what the present work is about.

Introduction

Theorists have interpreted Marxism in various ways; the point, however, is to change it.

The recent outpouring of social theory, social criticism and historical writing from a Marxist perspective is a development unparalleled in the history of the United States. Even the upsurge of radical and socialist *practice* in the first decades of the century and in the brief "red" decade, the 1930's, failed to produce the volume and sweep of intellectual activity that began to emerge in the 1960's and early 1970's. Certainly there were notable works during the earlier years: the translations by Daniel De Leon and Ernest Untermann of the writings of Marx, Engels, Kautsky and other European socialists; the pioneering *Theoretical System of Karl Marx* by an American lawyer, Louis Boudin; and finally, the monumental corpus of Thorstein Veblen, whose Marxism was always coded in a language that might be called specifically American. If Veblen was not a self-proclaimed Marxist, even a cursory reading of his *Theory of Business Enterprise* and *Absentee Ownership* would reveal his debt to the Marxist tradition.

In the wake of the rise of mass industrial unionism and the black movements of the 1930's, a new generation of intellectuals was attracted to the left wing, and some of them made significant contributions to the development of radical social and political thought. The greatest of these, W. E. B. DuBois, owed his Marxism to this decade, if not his intellectual formation. His pioneering *Black Reconstruction,* a path-breaking historical treatment of the post-bellum South, is perhaps the most influential study in the radical rewriting of American history from the point of view of the losers. DuBois placed himself squarely in the tradition of Marxist historiography, insisting that the underclasses are makers of society as much as the ruling classes.

During the 1930's and 1940's, thousands of intellectuals were influenced by Marxism in almost every field of the natural and human sciences as well as literature, visual arts and music. This is not the place to list the exciting and important works that emerged from this fecund era, or to explore this content. Suffice it to note that most of the influence of Marxism in America was not directly reflected in work that called itself by that name. For example, Robert Lynd, Robert Brady and C. Wright Mills[a] were not Marxists during most of their academic lives, but the stamp of Marxian modes of social inquiry is indelible on their writing. Similarly, historians such as Edward Kirkland, Charles Beard[b] and others who followed their so-called economic interpretation of American history were denounced for that orientation by Marxists who vehemently asserted that their theoretical system was not an "economic" but a materialist interpretation of history. The difference was mostly lost on Americans accustomed to the hero theory, according to which the psychological attributes of great men determined the course of U.S. history, or, alternatively, used to a political determinism in which the plan of parties and other power forces was held accountable for profound change. While it would be excessive to claim that Beard had "misread" Marx, or that Marxism is the decisive influence upon his account of the way in which the U.S. constitution and subsequent historical developments were framed by men with pecuniary interests, our common understanding of the unique contribution of Marxism is still, to this day, its insistence that the economic structure of society determines, in the last instance at least, the course of social change. Even if it can be shown that this view is a naive reading of "what Marx really meant," it cannot be denied that this is the way most Americans (and probably Europeans as well) understand Marx.

Of course, the Marxist revival of the late 1960's benefitted from two closely related developments: its force derived primarily from the reaction of the new generation of leftists to the repressive political and cultural environment of the 1950's. But its intellectual inspirations were as attributable to the development of German, Italian, and French Marxism as much as the teachings of those Americans such as Mills and Paul Sweezy, who were as deeply influenced by the American traditions of muckraking in economics and sociology as they were by Marxism.

American radical and Marxist thought has, in the recent past, been divided. On the one side, the main tendency of radical thought has applied a variety of theoretical perspectives within the Marxist tradition to concrete problems of American and world economic, political and social developments. Here the illustrations are virtually inexhaustible. From the writing of history (the traditional strength of American radical scholarship) to work in political economy, Marxists and others influenced by the elementary propositions of historical materialism have contributed an impressive body of research to the understanding of the course of U.S. capitalist development. The consistently interesting work of Sweezy, Harry Braverman,[c] members and associates of the Union for Radical Political Economics, sociologists like Maurice Zeitlin and James Petras,[d] and the cultural and literary criticism of Fredric Jameson and Stuart Ewen[e] have succeeded in making Marxism a respectable part of American intellectual life, especially in universities.

On the other side, Americans have contributed some interesting and valuable literature in the field of Marxology. Jameson, perhaps America's leading Marxist literary critic, is also a superb historian of ideas. His *Marxism and Form* has led a new generation of literary, cultural, and intellectual historians to explore the major European sources of twentieth-century Marxist thought. Martin Jay, Russell Jacoby, Paul Piccone, Susan Buck-Morse, Paul Breines and Andrew Arato[f] have, through the significant European-American journal *Telos* and their various books, made aspects of the German Marxist tradition after Marx a part of our intellectual legacy. Mark Poster and Ronald Aronson,[g] among others, have ably contributed to our understanding of the French neo-Marxist tendencies. The work of Marxist interpretation proceeds with some force and amplitude even today, when the political climate has changed so dramatically that those committed to a sympathetic treatment of Marxism may find their academic reception increasingly more chilling. The tendency to provide clear and coherent explanations of theoretical ideas is fully consistent with the American intellectual traditions of the current century. Americans are not fond of theory, even in the physical and biological sciences, but are good at application. We have brilliantly adapted European physics and chemistry to practical technology, but our contributions to the philosophical understanding of physical and life phenomena has been relatively undeveloped. We stand in the same relation to the social and human sciences. The American sociological tradition still relies on the scaffolding provided by Max Weber, Emile Durkheim, and Auguste Comte. The works of our most original thinkers, those who have argued for behaviourism or functionalist theories of various kinds, constitute merely an application of English empiricism (the most articulate expressions of which have no defined social theory, but reduce social phenomena to social psychology). American social psychology does not really draw upon gestalt, phenomenological or Freudian traditions, but derives in its principal aspects from the propositions that social life is an aggregation of individuals who behave like any animal. In turn, these individuals are merely the sum of their drives or instincts, upon which the social environment acts. Thus, consistent with the presuppositions of eighteenth-century English philosophy, American ideology or theory is uniquely individualistic, our Freudianism a degraded form.

Marxism in America has opposed the positivism present in even the most eminent radical theory with a rather rigid economism. Those in the contemporary Marxist community who refuse mechanical explanations have not yet succeeded in offering their own interventions in Marxist theory since, as I have already pointed out, we are still struggling to assimilate the less naive European traditions within social thought as well as older Marxism. The intellectual historians of Marxism in the United States have, to their credit, ignited some theoretical interest among students and their academic colleagues as well as a small number of political activists and intellectuals not in the university, but made few original contributions. This book is both an intervention into the debates that are still current within Marxism as well as an attempt to address various theoretical issues from a specifically U.S. standpoint. In this introduction I will try to locate my own work in the broad historical context within which Marxist theory has evolved.

Perhaps the most dramatic event that gave rise to the fissures within Marxist theory was the insistence by the Communist International in 1924 that Georg Lukács and Karl Korsch withdraw their respective contributions to Marxist debates under penalty of expulsion from the Communist party. (The other culprits, Bela Forgazy and Joseph Revai were, in historical retrospect, merely ancillary figures in the affair.) From the outset, there was never any doubt that Korsch and Lukács were the real objects of the condemnation of Zinoviev, the Chair of the International, and through him, the entire Communist movement. The charges levelled against the heretics were those of departure from scripture as interpreted by the political directorate of the International. And, in the lexicon of Marxist invective, they are conventionally accused, as petty-bourgeois intellectuals, of having harmed the workers' cause, the prospects for socialist revolution, and the strength of its leading detachment, the Communist party.

However, the common sin of Lukács and Korsch, the assertion that philosophical inquiry retained an important place in Marxist theory and could not be replaced by science until the proletariat itself made its abolition possible, has confused matters for the last sixty years. Although the criticism of the new orthodoxy that arose after the Bolshevik revolution became a convenient point of demarcation in the heat of political struggle, our distance from the conditions that characterised the theoretical and political fissure in the communist movement of the 1920's ought to be an occasion for reexamining the Marxist legacy. In this reprise, we admit our own partial vision, one that is profoundly influenced by current events.

A convenient starting point is to consider the term "Western Marxism" as the name for those who, between the two world wars, were constrained to wander from the prevailing social-democratic and communist interpretations of Marx. Although Perry Anderson acknowledges that the term "indicates no precise space or time," he does not hesitate to claim that a large number of writers as disparate as Lukács, Korsch, Benjamin, Gramsci and Della Volpe among others were part of a "mutation" of Marxism, "an entirely new intellectual configuration within the development of historical materialism."[h] We note the use of the term "mutation" to describe this tendency, a sign that implies the existence of a genotype that is normal. Further, Anderson's list is so inclusive as to embrace all dissenters from those within the parties of socialism who, owing to their hegemony over the means of ideological and theoretical production of Marxist discourse, defined orthodoxy and deviance, in the period between the two world wars.

My first encounter with "Western Marxism" was in Maurice Merleau-Ponty's attempt to distinguish Lukács's conception of historical materialism from that of the "Marxist-Leninists".[i] The concept (if indeed it may be considered so) is reported to have been coined by Korsch himself. Presumably "Western" meant that theory took its intellectual cues from the historical experience of the working classes of the advanced capitalist countries, rather than from the underdeveloped areas of the world. For Korsch, Lenin's affirmation of a rather naive realism, his tactical use of philosophy to affirm a particular politics, and the strategic considerations that informed his Marxism, may be ascribed to the concrete conditions of Russia, rather than constituting a new orthodoxy to which all revolutionaries were obliged to subordinate themselves. Lukács and Korsch held Lenin himself in high esteem, but were reluctant to grant his epigones the status of a new priesthood.

Curiously, Merleau-Ponty asserts this division in order to attack Leninism, while Anderson takes the same separation as proof that those who dissented in 1924 were a "mutation" from true Marxist science. Of course, the historical contexts within which the term "Western Marxism" was employed by Korsch, Merleau-Ponty and Anderson were radically different. Merleau-Ponty adopts Lukács and Korsch to excoriate Sartre for his turn, during the mid–1950's, towards the French Communist Party, after having been among the most implacable opponents of Leninist ideas in the first decade after the war. Anderson, a founding member of the new left generation of British intellectuals who rediscovered Marxism in the 1960's, uses "Western Marxism" as an epithet in order to affirm his own recently acquired scientific Leninism. However, in both instances, as well as in Korsch himself, the tactical employment of the term conceals more than it reveals. I would contend that the real differences in the Marxist tradition may not be made a function of the struggle between Bolsheviks and left oppositionists of the 1920's, Stalinists and phenomenologists in the 1950's or new leftists and Trotskyists in the 1970's. In fact, the term "Western" Marxism is a signifier that connotes no particular body of doctrine. Its historical function has been linked to the anti-Leninist movements of this century both as the object of accusation and, less often, a self description of a melange of dissenters. Its theoretical status is not only ambiguous, it is problematic.

How to determine what, if any, *theoretical* distinctions may be made in the history of Marxism? I assume that Marx himself provides the clue to all tendencies that arose after his death, including the tendency that may be ascribed to Engels. But, even as Marxists have consistently cited the master to support their particular interpretation, one does not discover in Marx a series of definite arguments that validate any specific position. Like any other theorists who frequently swam in political waters, Marx was forced to emphasize one or another aspect of the theory of historical materialism depending on the polemical conditions under which it labored. In this connection, it would not be difficult to show that Engels spent much of the twelve years he survived Marx "explaining" the theory, correcting excesses and trying to clarify why, at a particular moment, certain ideas were emphasized over others. So, we will find in Marx elements of economic determinism, subtle demonstrations of the relative autonomy of superstructures, a theory of multiple determinations that privileges the economic only in the "last instance" (which never comes), and – in the configuration of his whole work which presents itself, more often than not, in polemical form – an implicit focus on the production of ideology as material practice. There is Marx the historian, a commentator on the events that shook the nineteenth century such as the Paris Commune, speaking as a voluntarist, and the Marx of the eighteenth Brumaire for whom "politics takes command" in a concrete historical situation. We have Marx, the capital logician, focusing on the ways in which the labor process, and the state, indeed modern history itself, may be derived from the imperatives of accumulation. There is, of course, the Marx for whom nothing human was alien, the utopian who proclaimed that socialism consisted of a "free association of individuals," who worked in the mornings and wrote poetry in the afternoon and evening. I want to concentrate, however, on the problem for which Marxism as a critical science survived: to specify the conditions for the revolutionary transformation of society, specifically, how it is possible that capitalism may be abolished and communism brought into being. My argument is that the split in Marxism since the late nineteenth century devolves around the questions raised by capitalism's transformation during that period and which are still with us.

The empirical issue is the fate of the working class after the organization of powerful trade unions and mass socialist parties, especially in Germany and other advanced capitalist countries. The notions of "advanced," "late," or "monopoly" capitalism were invented by various theorists to account for the delay of the revolutionary process and the configuration of the workers' movement into a powerful instrument of social reform. In the context of a rapidly industrializing late nineteenth century Germany, the introduction of Bismarckism may be considered the decisive turning point in the development of capitalism. For Bismarck not only refused the proposition widely held by political theory that the overthrow of feudalism brings with it an era of free competition and its political form, bourgeois democracy, but also demonstrated that reforms benefitting workers might be compatible with capitalist development. Even though workers, their unions and the socialist parties were obliged to wage determined parliamentary and extraparliamentary struggles for such gains as pensions, health care and shorter hours, as long as capital accumulated more rapidly than the costs of these social "wages" it appeared that such struggles were not necessarily anti-capitalist. On the contrary, the workers' movement grew with capital's expanded reproduction.

So successful were the effects of the state interventions into the economy, particularly its organization of investment as well as regulation of production costs, including a portion of wages, that the first major crisis in socialist theory was framed in relation to the evaluation of these measures. Orthodox Marxism was defined as the doctrine according to which the breakdown of capitalism was an ineluctable feature of the system. Reforms that could be wrested during the expansive phase of the accumulation process would be reduced or taken back in the crisis period. Given the level of political and economic organization attained by the working class, capitalism's downfall became inevitable as it was unable to meet the material needs of the masses.[j] For Rosa Luxemburg, who became the leading theoretician of orthodoxy, history calls out the tasks of revolution to the proletariat, but the forms of crisis and the response of the workers are not determined in advance. Nevertheless, Eduard Bernstein's declaration that the expected crisis may be permanently deferred by the organization of capital and its close integration with the state was to be rejected. Bernstein's explosive thesis, advanced in his *Evolutionary Socialism*, attempted to critique Marxism's theoretical adequacy in terms of what had been accepted doctrine until that time: Marxism was a theory of history according to which socialist revolution was not a moral imperative, but was inevitable as capitalism became increasingly incapable of meeting the elementary needs of the underlying population. Bernstein theorized that reforms were not ephemeral gains confined to the period of expansion, doomed to extinction as the anarchy of capitalist production forced the ruling class to renege on its agreements. If Marxist theory of revolution depended on the concept of periodic and deepening crisis, organized capitalism was an historical refutation of this expectation. For Bernstein, the time had arrived to jettison the theory, but retain socialism as an ethical ideal. The historical relevance of apocalyptic visions of socialism was limited by the very success of working class in winning and institutionalizing its gains. According to Bernstein, socialism should be the doctrine of the workers' movement *as it really exists*, not as its theoreticians would like it to be.

In the debates within German Social Democracy and the Socialist

International at the turn of the century, Bernstein's position was decisively rejected, even though the practices of the socialist parties and trade unions corresponded to his description. For such leaders as Kautsky, Luxemburg, and Lenin there could be no socialism, much less Marxism, without the vision of a revolutionary transformation that arose from the inner workings of capitalism. Although Bernstein's conception of socialism was grounded in his reading of historical experience of advanced capitalist societies, his refusal to make a radical separation of present and future was intolerable to a theory requiring a view of history as a process of revolutionary transformation grounded in the contradictory character of social relations. Bernstein's personal disgrace in the history of socialist thought ought not to obscure the fact that his hubris in asserting that the practice of the workers' movement in reforming capitalism already constituted a new configuration for a future without *revolutionary* consequences, has been the spectre haunting Marxism since the First World War. For contrary to early expectations, the seizure of political power by the Bolsheviks revealed exactly what Lenin had forecast: world capitalism was most vulnerable at its weakest links – the colonial and semi-colonial countries.[k] Socialist revolutions in the West remained a flag signifying a future that was sharply disjoined from the reformist present, but was, in no advanced capitalist country, a practical program for the workers' movement.

In his preface to *Evolutionary Socialism* Bernstein acknowledges that his conclusions were "deviant" in relation to the "Marx-Engels" doctrine by which he had been so deeply influenced. He understood the materialist conception of history to mean that there is historic necessity in the development of the productive life of society and that class war constitutes the motive force of historical change. Today, many of the Social-Democratic parties of Western Europe follow, in the main, Bernstein's refusal of these cardinal points of Marxist theory, but it may be argued that the dividing line between Leninism and social-democracy as regards the application of these issues in advanced countries is the retention by the former of the doctrine of revolution on the basis of historical materialism even in the wake of failed practice. At the same time, there is virtually no practical programmatic difference between socialist and communist parties in the West except on crucial questions of international affairs. Both sides fight for reforms within the prevailing order – but for different reasons.

The issues raised by Bernstein became central problems for

Marxist theory in the interwar period. The problem had already been formulated in Rosa Luxemburg's classic reply to Bernstein; *Reform and Revolution*, published at the turn of the century, taken together with her equally powerful work on the *Mass Strike*, is a clear set of statements of a Marxism that has become the classic alternative to "revisionism." Those who continued to follow Marx's insistence that the laws of motion of capitalism led inevitably to the abolition of private ownership of the means of production, and that the workers' movement would be inexorably drawn to forms of practice that more or less systematically renounced reform *within* capitalism as well as programs to reform capitalism as such, found in Luxemburg an eloquent spokesperson. For those who came after, the problem for Marxism remained to specify the critical trajectory of the processes of capital accumulation, the inner contradictions of the formula for the rate of profit, the spread of capitalism on a world scale and, on the basis of a scientific understanding of these developments, to educate, agitate and organize among the workers for revolutionary action.

Luxemburg's statement of Marxist orthodoxy implies that the political and theoretical orientation of the leadership of the workers' movement, trade unionists and socialists, could temporarily affect the course of revolutionary struggle by means of ideological and political perfidy, but that such movements as the right wing of social democracy could by no means constitute more than temporary detours in history's forward march. If Marxist science had any power at all, it included the ability to *derive* political and social necessity from the immanent laws of capitalist development, which of course included the activity of classes themselves. Although Lenin had held these formulations among the central articles of his Marxism, he also argued that the intervention of theory, strategy and tactical proposals were historically important for determining the outcome of any political practice. Similarly, Gramsci's appropriation of Labriola's formula that Marxism is a *philosophy of praxis* suggested a significant departure from Luxemburg's orthodoxy. The consequences of such positions as were advanced by Lenin and Gramsci were not immediately apparent to those who followed them, much less their critics.

As I shall argue in the last section of this book, Lenin's theory of the party constitutes a theory of mediations between the contradictions at the level of economic infrastructure of society and struggles at the level of the state and ideology. For Lenin, the party congealed the scientific basis for socialist practice and the historical experience of the working class and other oppressed groups. Its character as the leading detachment of the revolution was not inevitable and could be thwarted by incorrect theory within the socialist movement. Failing to form a leading detachment that embodied Marxist science, the revolution no longer became inevitable. Thus Lenin stands at the intersection of orthodox Marxism as defined in opposition to Bernstein's heresy and Bernsteinism itself. If the workers' movement as a material practice shaped the future as much as the mode of production of material life, the element of voluntarism becomes historically significant. Gramsci's focus on the theory of hegemony and its relation to revolutionary process led him to emphasize the importance of winning intellectuals to the workers' movement since he believed that those who possessed the means of cultural production could influence, if not determine, the course of history.[1] Lenin and Gramsci formulated their theoretical approaches in environments in which he prospects for proletarian revolution had been rendered problematic by the ideological offensives of the right, the weakness of the workers' movement, as well as the repressive power of the state. Gramsci's theory of revolution becomes, in part, a theory of education as material praxis under conditions where socialism has weak traditions within the working class and the ideological hegemony of ruling classes is nearly complete. It may be argued that Lukács's theory of mediation – according to which class consciousness is no reflex of material conditions – is an immanent critique of Marxist orthodoxy that refuses culture, and ideology, as elements of the social totality. Thus the *new revisionism* of the post First World War period was not politically akin to the critique of post-Marx Marxism advanced by Bernstein and others, but addressed the same issues – issues which did not appear to most Marxists in advanced capitalist countries as real problems. Indeed, the theories of mediation associated with Lenin's theory of party, Gramsci's theory of hegemony and Lukács's theory of reification, were suspect to those who, following Luxemburg, remained persuaded that the intervention of intellectuals within the workers' movement was inimical to its development. According to the Dutch Communists, Anton Pannakoek, Herman Gorter, Henrietta Roland-Holst and the later Korsch, the self-organization by the workers of councils capable of administering production as well as conducting the class struggle was not only the necessary condition for revolution, but also its sufficient condition. The emphasis on self-organization and self-management led to Lenin's polemic *Left-Wing Communism – An Infantile Disorder*, an invocation to the parties of the Third International to acknowledge the temporary defeat of the revolution and the stabilization of world capitalism. Apart from its political merits, this work constitutes a clear statement of Lenin's position with regard to the necessity of political and ideological intervention by the party in the workers' movement. From the theoretical perspective, it stands as a repudiation of Luxemburgism, according to which the party is principally an educational force but renounces its vanguard role in the workers' movement.

The so-called "Council Communists" were the genuine inheritors of Rosa Luxemburg's orthodoxy, which made little room for a theory of ideology, for the relatively autonomous role for intellectuals and their ideas in history – whether on the side of the workers or their antagonists – or for the pursuit of philosophical and other cultural studies within Marxism. It is ironic that Lenin and the intellectuals of the Third International, including Gramsci, who have mistakenly been called the guardians of *orthodox* Marxism, gathered the threads of Marx's and Engels' keen interest in problems of natural science, literature and art. On the other hand, there is the irony of the libertarianism from which that strain of Marxism that owes its pedigree to the writings of Luxemburg derives its rigid separation of politics from culture. For although Pannakoek was a professional astronomer, Gorter a poet, and Rosa Luxemburg a widely read intellectual whose love of literature was amply revealed in her personal correspondence, these left communists joined Kautsky in the Kantian belief in the wall between reason and judgement.[m] Almost alone among the leading theoretical figures of the Second International who later became Communist, Franz Mehring wrote seriously on cultural questions. Thus, the connection between the voluntarism of Lenin and Gramsci and the concern with questions of ideology and culture is intimate.

Although several commentators have advanced the thesis that theories of mediation are defining characteristics of "Western Marxism," I want to make a different claim: questions of ideology and culture become significant within Marxism in proportion to the *underdevelopment* of the socialist and workers' movement, or at the very least, become significant issues in the wake of its defeat. Such was the case, of course, in the emergence of the Frankfurt School and Walter Benjamin as leading cultural critics, and Wilhelm

Reich's efforts to unite Marx and Freud in the period of fascism's ascendancy in the 1930's. Automatic Marxism, on the contrary, is a theory of the insurgent opposition. The appeal to blind historical forces, never absolute in any significant Marxist thinker, is a tendency associated with the most optimistic period in the history of the socialist and communist movements. At the same time, it has served as solace for those suffering the wounds of diminishing successes. However, as a theoretical proposition, the reliance on the conjunction of material conditions with the self-organization of workers such as developed in the Russian situation or the days after the defeat of the German and Austrian empires, signifies a break in the power of the ruling classes that permits once more the appeal to historical laws. As capital mends its sundered seams and resumes the offensive against the workers' movement both through political repression and the reassertion of ideological hegemony, Marxist theory is obliged both to explain the defeat and to recognize culture as a material praxis. The impulse to praxis corresponds to adverse historical circumstances. It entails the kind of self criticism that ascendant revolutionaries are not prone to engage in, a kind of reflexivity about Marxism itself that becomes dangerous in the context of victories forged on the basis of the suppression of difference.

Yet, I will not rest with making sociological explanations. The issues remain: does Marxism require a psychology as an autonomous moment in the social totality? What is the status of mass-mediated culture in the forging of ruling class hegemony? Are the ideological state apparatuses such as schools forms of *cultural* capital rather than mere reflections of dominant economic forces? What is the relation between those who constitute themselves as the conscious socialist element of the workers' movement and the movement itself?

In the United States, Marxists have been called upon to address all of these questions because we have experienced the palpable failure of socialism to establish substantial roots within the workers' movement or, indeed, any significant sector of American life, except for a handful of intellectuals and some members of oppressed minorities. Nevertheless, American Marxism has been among the most economistic of all in comparison to other advanced capitalist countries where socialism is an important political and ideological force in all sectors of society. This does not mean that no theoretical work on education, mass culture or racism has been done. But despite the imperative to address these social forces, U.S. Marxists have almost universally contented themselves with showing the economic roots of hegemonic ideologies and practices. In this country, the intellectual division of labor runs as follows: intellectual historians provide interesting summaries and commentaries of European work that insists upon the importance of culture, philosophy, and education. On the other side, Marxism has its own technical intelligentsia: those writers who apply "orthodox" Marxist economic models to a wide variety of issues including mass media, the labor movement, economic crisis, war, sexism and racism, showing how ideology is a form of mystification concealing class interests, how the coming crisis will manifest itself, how the workers' struggles will respond to the inevitable breakdown of capitalism.

I must acknowledge that my starting points in these interventions have diverse sources. My political position is closer to those who have insisted over the years that the self-management of society by those who produce material culture, including commodities, is the core of an emancipatory vision. I have learned more from those who popularized and theorized about the workers' councils than those who argued for the concept of the party as the organizing force for social transformation. The historical record of socialism as it really exists in Eastern Europe, Asia and Cuba cannot be ignored in the evaluation of the Leninist legacy. This is not to place responsibility upon Lenin himself, or to refuse to acknowledge that Leninism is a variegated doctrine with parts that remain powerful and persuasive and others which must be cast aside. Nevertheless, the tragic fate of the workers' movements in Eastern Europe attests to the absolute divisibility of self-management from socialism as it has evolved. There is no necessary relation between the abolition of private property in the means of production and social ownership and control.

The last sixty years of really-existing socialism raise sharply the question of historical determination and the status of the materialist conception of history, no less than the well-known detours travelled by the socialist movement in advanced capitalist societies. No American who has worked in the Marxist tradition can fail to grapple with the reality of historical disruptions as a *philosophical* issue. Throughout this book, I will argue for a different materialist interpretation of history from that adapted by really-existing Marxisms of nearly all kinds. Here, I merely wish to affirm that to theorize against doctrines of inevitability and the economic interpretations that are common ground of all Marxisms, is not to rescue Marx from his followers, but to offer a way of looking at the world in which Marx becomes a crucial component, but not the outcome of the inquiry. And, finally, to remind the reader that any American contribution to social theory that does not take seriously American history is an act of bad faith.

Nearly a century after Werner Sombart's attempt to explain the failure of socialism in the United States, we are still obliged to grapple with the specificity of the course of U.S. capitalist development. This is not the same question as the theory of "American exceptionalism," in which U.S. history is distinguished from that of Europe on the basis of our lack of a feudal past. In fact, the feudal past of Europe was inextricably linked to U.S. capitalist development in its immigrant populations as well as its system of laws. The course of capital accumulation in this country was much more compressed compared to Western Europe, except Germany. Certainly it was no more rapid than Japan, which after the turn of the century performed a veritable economic miracle when compared to Britain and France. Yet, the doctrine of exceptionalism is a non-theory because it fails to account for the fact that all capitalist countries have different socialist and labor movements and different rates and types of development.

Our task is no different from the problems faced by social theory in any country. It would be an error to forget that capitalism is a world system in which different modes of production are closely entwined by the international division of labor, and labor migration became a distinguished feature of the entire world system after the sixteenth century precisely because of the unevenness of development between countries. Thus, the specific place occupied by the "new world" in the world system, and the conditions under which it was colonized by Europe, constitute differences that may account for its politics and culture. Nevertheless, there are similar features shared by all capitalisms: the creation of a working class internally divided by sex, skill and often race; the division between intellectual and manual labor, which is not merely a technical division but permeated with political and ideological significance because it is hierarchical; the hegemony of family as a site of social as well as physical reproduction of labor power; the transformation of this hegemony in the wake of the ingression of the state in the interstices of social life.

The United States, however, developed into the major world capitalist power under a series of unique conditions. Principal among these is that this country was, from its inception, the only Western nation in which the capitalist mode of production reproduced itself on the basis of slave labor. The question of race has always been the leading political issue upon which the possibility of working-class solidarity rested. Even the industrial revolution and the concomitant abolition of slavery failed to obliterate racism as a crucial social, ideological, and political issue within the working classes, just as the racial division of labor was retained in a transformed way by new industrial order. Secondly, this country experienced its industrial development in relation to the agricultural crises of Southern and Eastern Europe, in which a working class was formed on the basis of immigration. Thus, the native traditions of the white workers were always subordinate to the racial and ethnic character of the proletarian strata. Finally, the concentrated nature of technological change during the late nineteenth and first decades of the twentieth century linked U.S. capitalist expansion to the electronic, chemical, and communications industries, as well as older middle and low technologies such as steel, textiles, and machinery. Race and ethnic divisions were significant in the formation of the U.S. working classes, and the intense technological tranformations proved beneficial to U.S. growth, while its ample internal natural resources such as food and energy provided the basis for the *rapidity* of expansion.

Between the end of the Civil War and the great depression America was ruled continuously by a succession of Republican administrations which were boldly capitalist and repressive. Contrary to those with the discipline of American political science who never tire in their contention that America is distinguished by its pluralistic politics, the dictatorship of the bourgeoisie in that period was unrivalled in any capitalist country except Germany. We should not be surprised that the Democrats were represented nominally by only two short Cleveland administrations and Woodrow Wilson's eight-year tenure in office that interrupted this virtual Republican political monopoly. Moreover, the Cleveland presidencies were by no means exceptions to the general pattern of the gilded age, when monopolies literally bought their politicians as commodities. Our collective understanding of the processes of primitive accumulation of capital has recently confirmed that authoritarian politics may be the most "effective" means towards development of advanced capitalist institutions and social forms. In this instance, the constitutional form, except for the crucial exclusion of blacks and women, presented itself as eminently democratic, but its substance was by no means consistent with political liberty. While democratic, political reform movements effectively contested business takeovers of local governments after the Civil War, their weight at the national level was insufficient to constitute an effective opposition.

There is much ground for the hypothesis that strong political opposition never has emerged within the United States to challenge the power of capital to determine the central direction of social and economic policy. Rather, a section of the ruling class has, from time to time, disrupted the consensus of big capital both for reasons of economic interest and for broader ideological reasons. The subaltern classes of American society have never acted autonomously without the support of a breakaway section of capital, although the relations of hegemony between the partners have differed according to specific circumstances. The New Deal coalition born after 1936 was a major instance where a section of the ruling class joined with workers, blacks, women and other groups to constitute an alternative *within* the framework of late capitalism. In this coalition, the working class and the trade unions became the core of the new hegemony, which dominated American politics until the mid–1950's. Under these circumstances a mass socialist party could not emerge since its political space was occupied by a party committed to both capitalism and social reform. If modern-day socialism in advanced-capitalist societies is indistinguishable from the politics of contestation *within* the capitalist state, there is no reason to believe that a socialist movement could take root where other parties and classes were prepared to fulfill the immediate program of the underlying classes. This perspective assumes that socialism succeeded in establishing itself as the principal party of reform in various European countries because capital proved unable to sustain a program of systematic social reform without severe repression. To be sure, social reform movements have been relatively weak in the U.S. because of the character of the coalitions that were necessary to bring changes about. The labor movement was the core around which the New Deal developed its political hegemony, but never won the moral and intellectual leadership within the coalition, since the breakaway bourgeois elements had already won the most important intellectuals for their program.

This brief outline of some important features of U.S. history is offered to *illustrate* some of the unfinished tasks for social theory and historical research. Race and ethnicity, the specificity of their relation to the formation of the working class, the character of capital and its political, cultural, and social forms, are all questions that underlie a program for an American intervention into Marxist theory of capitalist development. For us, the laws of motion of capitalism, that is, Marxism as a science of political economy, are necessary but not sufficient bases for comprehending the context within which the text of theory must be forged. In my opinion, Gramsci, the Frankfurt School and modern French critical philosophy and historiography offer important clues to those who wish to comprehend the relation of politics, capital accumulation, culture and ideology within an American context. This is by no means an antinomy to the important questions raised by recent developments in the political economy of capitalist development. We must presuppose this work in our quest for a theory of the historical specificity of American capitalism. But, since our understanding of the cultural, psychological, and political dimension is relatively underdeveloped in this country, since we are, like Lenin's Russia and Gramsci's Italy, bereft of those traditions within the underlying classes that make Marxism and socialism a "natural" discourse, we are obliged to place more weight on the issues that surround theory as an educational praxis. For we are at the stage not only of concrete struggles – both defensively and, on occasion, offensively – but also the struggle for grasping the historical specificity of our own situation. To this end, this book is offered to those who share the aspirations.

NOTES

[a] Mills' *Power Elite* (New York: Oxford University Press, 1956) marks the period of his development when he drew away from the Weberian assumptions of his earlier writing, particularly *White Collar* (New York:

Oxford University Press 1951) and his cultural essays. Although Lynd's collaborative work *Middletown* and his later critiques of the production of knowledge in advanced capitalist societies were not consistent with the orthodoxy in Marxist theory of the period, the importance of the materialist interpretation of social structure in urban communities is evident. In Brady, we can discern the impact of those German refugee intellectuals who came to the U.S. from Nazi Germany in the mid-thirties. His analysis of German fascism is deeply influenced by the work of Franz Neumann, whose *Behemoth* became the standard work on the subject, and represented one variety of Marxist scholarship that managed to gain wide respect.

b Edward Kirkland, *A History of American Economic Life* (New York: Appleton Century, 1939); Charles Beard, *Economic Interpretation of the Constitution of the United States* (New York, 1924).

c See especially Paul Baran and Paul Sweezy, *Monopoly Capital* (New York: Monthly Review Press, 1966); Harry Braverman, *Labor and Monopoly Capital* (New York: Monthly Review Press, 1975).

d The URPE Journal is, perhaps, the most consistently-read new Marxist journal in any academic discipline in the United States. Zeitlin and Petras are among a growing number of social scientists influenced by Marxism who have opened new research into the political economy of Latin America and other underdeveloped countries.

e Fredric Jameson, *Marxism and Form* (Princeton: Princeton University Press, 1971) and other books; Stewart Ewen, *Captains of Consciousness* (New York: McGraw-Hill, 1976).

f Martin Jay, *Dialectical Imagination* (Boston: Little Brown, 1973; Russell Jacoby, *Social Amnesia* (Boston: Beacon Press, 1974); Susan Buck-Morse, *Origins of Negative Dialectics* (New York: Macmillan, 1977); Paul Breines and Andrew Arato, *The Young Georg Lukacs* (New York: Seabury Press, 1978).

g Mark Poster, *Existential Marxism in Postwar France* (Princeton: Princeton University Press, 1975); Ronald Aronson, *Jean-Paul Sartre: Philosophy in the World* (London: New Left Books, 1980).

h Perry Anderson, *Considerations on Western Marxism* (London: New Left Books, 1976), p. 25.

i Maurice Merleau-Ponty, *Adventures of Dialectic* (Evanston: Northwestern University Press, 1973). This text is perhaps one of the most important symptomatic readings of Marxism influenced by the Cold War. Although Merleau-Ponty was by no means on the right in the manner, for instance, of a Raymond Aron (whose conception of Marxism was at once deformed and marred by a lack of intellectual depth), his ultimate defense of *individual liberty* was conditioned by his conception of Communism as among its leading opponents. Thus, Merleau speaks forcefully against Stalinism, particularly against its French form. But he is most eloquent when he accuses Marxism of a priorism in its assessment of the proletariat as historical subject. According to Merleau, this is merely a mask for the statement that the theoretician – i.e. the party – is the true Marxist subject. While there is much truth in this charge when applied to Leninism after Lenin, the question remains whether Leninism *is* Marxism in the twentieth century. See my own contribution to this issue in the second part of the present volume.

j This position can find expression in almost all the works of historical materialism during the Second International. See especially Karl Kautsky, *The Class Struggle*.

k V. I. Lenin, *Imperialism – The Highest Stage of Capitalism*. It should be noted, without hesitation, that Lenin's forecast proved prophetic in the years after the Second World War. The problem was whether political independence, that is, the passing of the old colonialism, signified a fundamental change in the character of the relations between the developed and underdeveloped countries. See my own discussion in Chapter 7.

l Antonio Gramsci, *Prison Notebooks* (New York: International Publishers, 1971). A careful reading of the section on State and Civil Society reveals Gramsci's remarkable contribution to Marxist theory in its most powerful expression. Here Gramsci argues that the discourses of politics, culture, and philosophy are not merely expressions of this or that ideology representing various classes in society, but are *material practices* that configure the chances for social power. His concept is of civil society as the site where fractions of various classes, including the subaltern classes, fight out the struggle for power. Gramsci is the first Marxist after Marx to stress the importance of the ideological dimension of domination. His argument that cultural hegemony is a central feature of the rise of class fractions to power over society, that discursive hegemony signals power, prefigures the work of contemporary writers such as Michel Foucault, Roland Barthes and others.

m Actually, Pannakoek and Korsch were deeply interested in the relation of Marxism and culture. As John Gerber has argued, the early writings of Pannakoek are devoted to explicating a Marxist theory of science on the basis of the scientific materialism of one of Marx's followers, Joseph Deitzgen. Gerber shows that Pannakoek propounded a theory according to which culture – i.e. ideologies, beliefs and art – were formed in the mind as a part of the past's legacy upon consciousness. Thus there was no correspondence between ideas and the material world, no chance of reflection theory. Ideas referred to the past as well as the present. The transformation of the material world produces a revolution in ideas, but they are obliged to contend with "false consciousness" inherited from the past. Korsch's book on Marx is, in a large measure, a work of historical materialist method. His concept of historical specification as the mediation that conditions the social totality is certainly directed against what he regarded as the metaphysical appropriation by Stalinism. Nevertheless, Pannakoek's major work in philosophy is completed before the First World War, even if Korsch remained interested in the scientific issues within Marxism until his death, John Gerber, Introduction, in Serge Bricanier, *Pannakoek and the Councils* (St. Louis, Telos Press, 1978).

1

Prospectus

We live in a time when all the old assumptions about politics and history appear enfeebled. Throughout Western industrial societies, both of the capitalist and state socialist types, the theory and practice of workers, intellectuals, women and ecologists have, in different ways, questioned the adequacy of Marxism as a theory of the past and present and as a guide to the future. In those countries where the Marxist traditions are strongest – Eastern Europe, Germany and the Mediterranean countries – the departure from Marxism takes the forms of return to religion or to the tenets of liberal democracy which Marx criticized a century ago. In proportion as the "really existing socialist" countries proclaim Marxism as official creed, rejection of the doctrine becomes tantamount to the demand for the separation of Church and State. Intellectuals and workers who can no longer accept the recital of old shibboleths masquerading as scientific discoveries turn to the only available alternatives: liberal democracy and Christianity, each of which are supposed to have been surpassed by socialism.

Where strong communist and socialist parties in the West have elevated Marxism to the level of both faith and political doctrine, the tendencies of these parties to abandon the place of opposition and become parties of order has prompted an exploration of socialist practice that holds the political party – as a form of domination – responsible, in part, for the deterioration of Marxism. The critique of party bureaucracy becomes congruent with the belief that Marxism is ossified. Having been relegated to the status of monument, Marxism's postulates are inscribed in stone, but have no importance in the discourse of social theory, in the world where real persons try to solve real problems.

Marxism lives in the West as an opposition theory of society only where it has never succeeded in becoming the official doctrine of parties of the workers' movement. In the United States, and especially in Britain, it has become the theory not of the workers' movement but of avant-garde intellectuals, for whom hegemonic liberal pluralism appears infinitely more arid as a way of seeing and explaining the social world. For us in the United States, this most "advanced" of all major capitalist countries, the pejorative judgement of others that the principle theoretical scaffolding of socialist theory – historical materialism – has been surpassed, appears bewildering. The reason is rather simple: we are just getting to Marxism, just climbing out of the mire of pluralism, just attaining some understanding of Marxism's richness as a mode of understanding and explanation. For those reared in the pluralist traditions of American social science and the nationalism of American politics, Marxism's spread to American universities in the 1960's and 1970's was a refreshing antidote. Its class analysis, its focus on production instead of consumption as the site of economic inequality, and its insistence on understanding culture as a material force seemed to correspond and to inspire the turn towards socialism by thousands of young Americans in these decades. The anti-war movement, the struggle for black freedom, and the rise of rank-and-file opposition in the trade unions – combined with the ever-more-frequent economic recessions in the 1970's – persuaded a generation that Marxism was truly *the* counterhegemonic science of society, rendering all competitors thin and unsatisfying in comparison.

For many years I have been among those who refused to acknowledge the problems within Marxism as more than marginal to its essential truth. As a participant in the labor and "new-left" movements in the 1950's and 1960's, I became an anti-Stalinist, independent Marxist. Having been forced, in the late 1950's, to abandon my orthodox Marxism in the wake of historical events – principally developments in the Soviet Union and Eastern Europe – I became influenced by the Frankfurt School's critique of mass society and by Wilhelm Reich's theory of fascism, which explained fascism's success not principally in terms of a reign of terror against the workers and the people, but as a movement that gripped the masses because it apparently offered a way to meet their need for freedom, which was always tied to questions of sexuality. While Marxism has no critique of everyday life, particularly cultural and sexual relations, I believed these omissions to be subject to amendment. Marxism needed what psychoanalysis had discovered about the individual and the family, it required a theory of consciousness not umbilically tied to the economic infrastructure, and it needed a theory of the relative autonomy of the state. But the historical scaffold was firm, in my view. If dogmatists and sectarians refused to comprehend the specificity of late capitalism, this blindness could not be ascribed to tendencies within historical materialism. The power of orthodoxy could be traced to the recalcitrance of the socialist and communist parties. The May 1968 events in France persuaded me that it was no longer possible to merely point to the aberrant conservatism of the communist parties. A theoretical examination was needed to account for the fact that communists could, under certain conditions, join the forces of order. For there was no doubt that the French Communist Party had collaborated with de Gaulle in ending the general strike and in refusing the mass demands for new social relations. I was obliged to return to the work of Max Weber and Robert Michels, whose theories of bureaucracy seemed to illuminate the situation far better than Lenin's labor aristocracy thesis. Lenin had argued that the perfidy of the leading workers' parties in the First World War could be ascribed to the distribution of imperialist booty among a narrow stratum of the leadership.[1] The thesis of bureaucratic domination, adopted from Weber by the Frankfurt School, provided a structural amendment to historical materialism, which – in its fealty to class analysis – remained wedded to economistic explanations for the triumph of reformism within the workers' organizations.[2]

But in the late 1960's and early 1970's, the fundamental theorem of the working class as the bearer of historical change remained, for me at least, intact. For what other class or stratum possessed the social weight to win the struggle against capital? I suspected, even as the early 1970's revealed a relative quiescence in the workers' and socialist movements, that to abandon the working class was tantamount to giving up the struggle for socialism, or, at best, relegating it to an ethical goal. These tendencies in modern social democracy – to give up class struggle – were, for me, anathema. With Georg Lukács, I argued that the place of the workers as the most exploited class within the structure of capitalist society, combined with their capacity for self-organization, was sufficient reason to remain confident of their historically revolutionary role. The mediations of alienation, reification, and the division between intellectual and manual labor that prevented the workers from achieving class and political consciousness were – once identified and analyzed – subject to human intervention, defining the task of socialist transformation rather than constituting a permanent barrier to revolutionary class consciousness. The English translation of Lukács's *History and Class Consciousness* appeared in 1971, and conjoined with my own work on the American working class. The commodification of everyday life, the colonization of the imagination by mass culture and the theory of socialist and labor bureaucracy seemed sufficient analytic and methodological categories to correct the simplism of the older Marxisms. There appeared no reason to challenge the materialist conception of history itself.

We have been buoyed by the Marxist professions of nearly all revolutionary movements in the Third World in the last thirty years, beginning, of course, with the Cuban revolution. Revolutionary Marxism appears to Americans to be affixed to the banners of all liberation movements today, in contrast to the socialisms of Africa and Asia of a generation ago. When the "new philosophers" in France, Eastern European dissident intellectuals, and erstwhile Marxists in England and America denounce Marxism as the philosophy of the Gulag, we are prone to dismiss these remonstrations as either the ravings of reactionary opponents of the workers' movement, or conservative protests against bureaucratic socialist regimes or parties which have strayed from the principles of revolution and have become obstacles to the achievement of a new society. We are sceptical of those who drift to the view that bourgeois democracy is irreplaceable and that, in the fulcrum of world historical relations, the West is preferable to the East, despite the persistence of exploitation, racism and sexism in the capitalist societies. For most of us Jean-Paul Sartre's judgement that Marxism is *the* theory of capitalism remains as true today as it was twenty years ago, when it trumpeted his attempt to reconstruct historical materialism *by* reinserting the subject into its theoretical calculus.

But it was Luxemburg and Korsch who succeeded in translating the theoretical debate surrounding the economistic tendencies of the Marxism of the Second and Third Internationals into some practical political judgements.[3] Their criticism of the Leninist conception of the party as revolutionary vanguard and their insistence that the workers alone, with only the assistance of the socialist movement, were able to make a revolution, influenced our political position of self-managed socialism. Now the crimes of Stalin remained no longer specific to the 'cult of the personality,' or to a bureaucracy that could be ascribed to special circumstances. Party bureaucracy, economic underdevelopment, and terror may have shed light on the excesses of the Stalin era. But – even if Stalin was more of a jacobin than a communist – Luxemburg's early attack on Leninism took the criticism much further. The American and Western European new left, or which I was a part, now had a weapon with which to oppose the revival of Leninist parties in the wake of the decline of opposition in the 1970's. We came to realize that the party could no more than an educational instrument of the workers themselves, that a socialism without forms of self-management of production and all other aspects of social life degenerated into stalism, and that Stalinism, far from being an aberration, was a logical outcome of Leninism.

Now the stage was set for a searching examination of the history of the working class. The party formation may have been an obstacle to achieving workers' power, but clearly its monopolization of the means of communication and information only partly explained the refusal of workers in Western societies to take hold of their own movement and struggle for social emancipation. Although Lukács and the Frankfurt School had helped us understand that cultural forms were significant constituents of social consciousness – active mediations between economic exploitation and political organization – the conclusion became inescapable that the Western working class, however militantly opposed to capital, was not revolutionary. Amid the welter of factors accounting for the paradox of a powerful labor movement and increasingly conservative or reformist politics among workers and their organizations, the glaring realization that the theoretical basis of Marxism was being called into question by historical reality had finally to be faced. For historical materialism is not only a theory of social structure within the context of historically specific conditions: it is preeminently a theory which explains those conditions in terms of the activity of humans and explains that activity as the result of those conditions. Since historical materialism insists it can explicate both praxis and its conditions with precision, it also offers the prediction that revolutionary struggle will occur under specific circumstances. That is, it not only constitutes the past but also sets forth the conditions for constituting the future. However, unless the conditions – both 'objective' and 'subjective' – for the formation of a revolutionary class capable of leading the struggle for socialism are stated, the entire paradigm of historical change offered by Marxism collapses. For historical materialism claims its superiority to other theories of history by, among other things, transcending the past and showing the "seeds" of the future in the contradictions of the present.

Now I knew that Marxism had become the leading theoretical premise for the best historical writing in many countries. Its insistence on finding the unknown history of the working class and other subaltern formations had altered our conceptions of the past so completely that liberal historians were required to study social movements and economic history to a degree not known previously, when it had been sufficient for liberal history to trace the development of political institutions and "great" personalities, regarding classes and economic relations as little more than "background" for great events. Similarly, anthropology had been deeply influenced by the materialist conception of history as the story of the mode of production of material life. Cultural forms such as religion or rituals and early social organization could no longer be described without investigating the relations of humans to nature and the relations of production within a given society. Economics and sociology were no longer able to ignore Marxism, which, in its academic guise, had been incorporated into mainstream disciplines as "methodology" or transcoded as "political economy" of advanced capitalist societies. The academic recuperation of historical materialism attested to the heuristic importance of materialist conceptions of social and historical structures.

Yet Marxism had climbed to be a theory of revolution – a discourse of social transformation and emancipation – as much as an alternative to bourgeois social theory. Denying its own historicity, Marxism has always to show how its fundamental concepts remain adequate to both past and present. As the 1970's wore on, it became increasingly apparent to me that Marxism had fallen behind the emergence of new social forces, especially the rise of feminism, ecology and religious social movements around the globe. It either clutched to class analysis or "adjusted" to new developments by offering a "new" historical materialism in which the economic infrastructure remained the teleological determinant "in the last instance" of historical developments, and in which other aspects of social structure assumed "relative autonomy."[4]

While the later, structuralist, theory of history provided more sophistication to Marxism, the questions remained. In 1976, three years after the publication of my Lukácsian *False Promises*, I began my own investigation of fundamental theoretical questions of Marxism. The following chapters are both an attempt to push further on the path to understanding our world better and a self-criticism of my own political and theoretical development. It is still an unfinished work; the following chapters open up more questions than I can as yet hope to answer. For a recent attempt to find some solutions, see my *Science as Power: Discourse and Ideology in Modern Society* (Minneapolis and London: University of Minnesota Press and Macmillan, 1988).

NOTES

1. V. I. Lenin, *Imperialism – The Highest Stage of Capitalism* (New York: International Publishers, 1939), p. 107.
2. See especially Herbert Marcuse, *One Dimensional Man* (Boston: Beacon Press, 1964), especially Chapter 2.
3. Rosa Luxemburg, "Organisational Questions of Social Democracy," in Mary Alice Waters (ed.), *Rosa Luxemburg Speaks* (New York: Pathfinder Press, 1970); Karl Korsch, *Revolutionary Theory*, Douglas Kellner, ed. (Austin: University of Texas Press, 1977), Chapters 5 and 6. See also Kellner's introduction to that volume, and the special issue on Korsch in *Telos* (no. 26).
4. "According to the materialist conception of history, the *ultimately* determining element in history is the production and reproduction of real life. More than this neither Marx nor I ever asserted. . . . The economic situation is the basis, but the various elements of the superstructure. . . . the class struggle and its results – also exercize their influence on the course of historical struggles and in many cases preponderate in determining their form." Letter of Frederick Engels to J. Bloch, in Karl Marx and Frederick Engels, *Selected Correspondence* (Moscow: Foreign Languages Publishing House, n.d.).

2
The Necessity of Philosophy

The crisis of Marxism deepens, interest in Marxism explodes in America. A group of French philosophers declares the death of Marxism,[5] a British analytic philosopher of language defends Marx's theory of history, pronouncing it an infant science.[6] At the same time, Andre Gorz, standing somewhere between the two extremes, proclaims that Marxism is at once an indispensible way of looking at the social world but has "lost its prophetic value."[7] Throughout Latin America, radical theologians discover in Marxism an important way to liberate theology from its "other-worldly" predilections, but combining the teachings of the Christian church with the "scientific" teachings of historical materialism.[8] But those reared in the tradition of critical social theory – like Jurgen Habermas, whose Marxist roots were sunk into the eroded soil of post-war German social democracy – have decided that a reconstruction of historical materialism was needed.[9] Such a theory would, according to Habermas, recognize the moral and cognitive dimensions of social transformation where Marxism has refused such recognition; a new kind of historical materialism is necessary to insert a principle of *intersubjectivity* as an objective constituent of the historical process. Habermas seeks a secular ground for moral development and a spiritual ground for secular evolution.

Such is the debate in contemporary theory. Idealists grab for materialist legitimacy, materialists grope for a new terrain in which ethical considerations may be accorded a position of relative autonomy in the processes of historical transformation.

1. At the sociological level, the crisis of Marxism is rather easily explained. Among the underlying reasons for the current disorientation among socialist intellectuals who have adhered to the Marxist theory of history is the palpable failure of the proletariat in the most advanced countries of late capitalism to become the self-conscious agent of revolutionary change. Gorz's claim that Marxism

has no prophetic value refers specifically to the expectation that the working class – as the most exploited class within capitalism – was at the same time its gravedigger. Those whose defection from Marxism is grounded in this historical failure hold that the working class has been hopelessly integrated into advanced capitalism by the development of new structures, such as the interventionist state, mass culture, and technological developments that succeed in mitigating – it not removing – economic crises and their consequences for the working class. In addition, the very strength of trade unions – which have produced agreements with employers that provide regular wage increases, codify working rules, and, in the political sphere, have successfully won benefits such as pensions and health care for all and protections against the economic impact of joblessness and old age – has stabilized capitalism, or at least has served to encapsulate workers' hopes within the capitalist system rather than outside it. To this tendency of recent theory, workers have become part of the system, even if militantly opposed to particular policies and governments.

2. The discovery, made sooner or later by most socialists of all ideological hues, that "socialism as it really exists"[10] is not only seriously flawed in comparison to the implied and explicit visions of its intellectual founders, but that the actual socialist regimes may be *obstacles* for achieving human freedom, rather than its bearers. To the extent that Marxism has promised that the condition for the achievement of a self-managed society is the abolition of private property in the means of material production, "really existing" socialism has served as a reminder that other conditions must be present before equality of access to resources, workers' self-management, and conventional freedoms such as the right to dissent, may be secured.

In this connection, it will not do to argue that self-management can only be effected under conditions of world socialism or, at the minimum, when the material conditions for its existence are assured. This argument enabled many intellectuals and militants of the communist movement to remain staunch supporters of the Soviet Union in the years between the two great world wars. Many of them stayed in line during the difficult early post-war period, when the Soviets successfully overcame the economic effects of the scourge left by Nazi destruction. But the failure of de-Stalinization after 1956 has distanced several generations of intellectuals from the

Soviets until, in the past five years, even most Western communist parties have been forced to remove themselves from the hegemony of the Soviet bloc or risk disintegration. Today, images of the Gulag no longer evoke as much as a flutter of protest among most Western Marxists. (The only important exception in this regard is a trickle of Trotskyists, whose defense of the Soviet Union carefully separates the Soviet Union's record on human rights from its substantial economic achievement, particularly the abolition of private ownership of the means of production.) The work of Rudolph Bahro has solidified the perception that socialism exists as an anti-democratic, bureaucratic, and anti-ecological system that has lost touch with its emancipatory precepts. For self-proclaimed post-Marxists, the truth of historical materialism lies not with the libertarian hope of its founders, but with the crimes of its children. For the "new philosophers" of France and their counterparts in other Western societies, the metaphor of the Gulag defines socialism and has been the determinate fate of historical materialism. After the fact of "really existing" socialism, it became the task of those who were interested in Marxism's burial to show that the logic of Marxism finds its apogee in the labor camps and mental hospitals that sequester the system's opponents.

3. Rising new nationalist movements in the Third World have based themselves upon religious ideas rather than proclaiming some kind of unique socialism. The confusion among Marxists regarding the Islamic revolution is a powerful illustration of the current disarray. Marxists at first hailed the overthrow of the Shah of Iran by a mass movement dominated by leaders of religious persuasion, but – having discovered that they were as anti-socialist as they were anti-imperialist – began to hedge on their enthusiasm, retreating to a class analysis that ascribed the revolution to a "national bourgeoisie" unable to complete the revolution. To this day, they have failed to understand the specificity of Islam as a revolutionary, anti-imperialist (and anti-socialist) force. Here, religion is not merely an ideological prop to a class, but has become the form in which revolutionary society may be consolidated. Similarly, many dissident currents within the Soviet Union and other Eastern European countries have adopted religion as the symbolic expression of their rebellion. In both cases "class analysis" – although necessary to understand the course of political and social movement – is clearly insufficient to yield genuine under-

standing, because it subsumes the moral under economic and class dimensions. The rise of the Catholic and Protestant left defies time-honored images and conceptions of religion among Marxists. Although Marx himself comprehended religion as the sigh of the oppressed, Marxism has focussed almost exclusively on its institutional manifestation, finding – often correctly – that organized religion was allied to established regimes, a faithful retainer of the status quo. In consequence, and with few exceptions, Marxism has been unable to grapple with the new currents within the world's religions without the handy tool of class analysis. Thus, on the whole, Marxism remains uncomprehending of Islam, of new currents in Catholic doctrine and of the partial eclipse of political conservatism among world protestants.

Although violations of human rights in Iran have occurred with depressing regularity since Ayotollah Khomeini consolidated his power in 1980, the spectacular death sentence he issued to Salman Rushdie in winter, 1989 underlines the political seriousness of Islamic fundamentalism as a world religion. We have learned by this event that Islam means to exercize power on a global scale and that religious ideas are not merely superstructural phenomena. That they have been intimately linked with power in the Arab world is not surprising, unless you are accustomed to the usual formulae of materialist orthodoxy. In this connection, it is interesting to note that journalists have observed that the threat came in a period when Khomeini's influence may have been waning in favor of a partial move toward secularization among Iran's ruling elite. Such observations are partial explanations but do not exhaust the issue. Modernists seem completely baffled by the resurgence of theocratic politics because they have accepted the evolutionist proposition according to which secularization is an inevitable victor in the war against superstition, that science and technology constitute a value system antithetical to Deism. Clearly, these hasty modernist conclusions have proven to be seriously flawed. While the tendency away from magic and religion accompanies industrial society, it is precisely because modernity has failed in crucial respects, especially spiritually, that anti-modernisms of the left and right are resurgent even as new modernist conquests are recorded in countries of the semi-periphery and the Eastern bloc.

4. The political and social programs of feminism and the ecology movement have evinced a wide spectrum of responses from

socialist and communist parties and Marxist intellectuals. On the one hand, the Western left announces its support of women's rights, but practically and theoretically engages in subtle or blatant tactics of cooptation where appropriation is impossible. The Marxist left agrees that there should be abortion on demand, equal pay for comparable work, and full equality in the home between husbands and wives. But Marxism cannot unambiguously grant that the oppression of women is transhistorical, rooted in male domination as much as class domination. Furthermore, Marxism has historically hesitated before the demand for a sexual and social revolution to accompany the political changes socialists desire. Theoretically, Marxism seems bound to its conception of the priority of *class* over race, nationally, or sex as both a historical and epistemological category. Practically, the doctrine of the primacy of the proletariat as the basis of socialist transformation and movement prevents a bold alliance with the women's movement. Often the socialist left must be dragged kicking and screaming to support the practical demands of women or, equally often, drags its feet in the wake of religiously motivated objections by workers, or of recalcitrance that stems from male privilege on the job and at home.

There are many within the socialist movement who recognize the social and historical roots of the crisis of historical materialism, but hesitate to trace its elements to its theoretical dimensions. Instead, the crisis in Marxism is understood exclusively within the discourse of political strategy, where specific socialist and communist parties are found to be seriously "opportunist" in their practical and political application of Marxist theory. Or, the crisis is ascribed to a series of misunderstandings by his epigones of Marx's intentions and method. The stress on methodological clarification assumes that Marxism is a science of society and history but – because it is simultaneously an ideology[11] lends itself to misconstructions. Thus Marxist philosophy, like contemporary analytic philosophy of science and language, is obliged to clear away misunderstandings by either linguistic analysis – so as to purify and universalize the discourse of Marxism – or to engage in conceptual clarification – in which the structure of Marx's thought is construed in a way that makes space for historical anomalies.

Nevertheless, Marxist scholarship has arisen in the past two decades to new levels of articulation and sophistication. Beyond unearthing new contributions from Marx and Marxism (notably the rediscovery of the *Grundrisse*, the discovery of the unpublished works of Gramsci, republication of Lukács' early works, and the Korsch revival), a plethora of Marx commentators have made serious efforts to rescue Marxism from the wounds inflicted upon it by history. Most notably, the main burden of this commentary has been concerned with overcoming what is commonly termed "vulgar" Marxism. Here the label "vulgar", although containing strong pejorative connotations, is meant to designate the set of interpretations dominant in the socialist movement, i.e. those advanced by Lenin, Trotsky and Stalin in the interwar period and its immediate aftermath.

The failure of proletarian revolution in the West, the deformations of "really existing" socialism, and the new issues raised by feminism, nationalism and the ecology movements – in short, the rise of cultural movements that appear to circumvent or challenge the traditional economist assumptions of historical Marxism – have given rise to a variety of "schools" of Marxist thought. Until the Second World War, those tendencies which tried to come to grips with theoretical problems (as opposed to resting content with making accusations that their political opponents were guilty of perfidy) evolved what may be called theories of *mediation* to account for the historical anomalies that plagued Marxism after Marx.

THEORIES OF MEDIATION

The concept of mediation is, of course, extremely controversial in contemporary Marxist debates. The concept is derived from Hegel's distinction between *sense certainty* as a moment in the movement of consciousness and the *totality*, i.e. the identical subject-object, where the problem of knowledge which implies their alienation is overcome by a series of historical stages towards self-consciousness. According to Georg Lukács, the active mediation between consciousness and its object is historical praxis, not the activity of thought. But mediations are not one-sided; they are both movements of reification and emancipation from alienated labor. Lukács argued that the totality is not "the mechanical aggregate of individual historical events nor is it a transcendent heuristic principle opposed to the events of history" as the Kantians contended.[12] The totality is a "real historical power," the universal that exists in particular phenomena. Contrary to empiricism –

which holds that only particulars have reality and that concepts of totality, the universal and the like are categories of thought – Lukács insists upon the objectivity of the totality. "It should not be forgotten that immediacy and mediation are themselves aspects of a dialectical process and that every stage of existence (and of the mind that would understand it) has its own immediacy . . . in which when confronted by an immediately given object, we should respond just as immediately or receptively and therefore make no alteration to it, leaving it just as it presents itself." Mediation, according to Lukács, is the process whereby this immediacy gives way to the "*structural principles and the real tendencies of the objects themselves.*"[13]

The proletariats's existence as immediacy presents itself as merely trade unionism, that is, the struggle for its reproduction within the capitalist order. But this existence is not the truth of the class as historical actor, according to Lukács. Through economic and political struggles, the *reified appearances of real relations* are revealed, transforming workers from a plethora of groups engaged in immediate struggles for a living wage into a self-conscious revolutionary class.

Lukács was giving theoretical expression to Lenin's theory of the party, which argued that without the mediation of scientific theory and strategic leadership the working class could not become a revolutionary force. Lenin's concept of the party as a scientifically-guided vanguard of revolutionary intellectuals and advanced workers was the earliest theoretical recognition within the Marxist tradition of the incommensurability of the economic infrastructure and the ideological and political superstructure of capitalist scciety.[14] Contrary to the main body of Second International thought – which understood the party as an educational instrument and representative of workers' immediate interests at the level of the state, but failed to draw the consequences implied by the concept of representation of education for a theory of class formation – Lenin followed a suggestion by Kautsky and pointed to the one-sidedness of the proletariat's immediate existence.[15] Only the totalizing praxis of the party apparatus could rescue the proletariat from the swamp of reform. Alternatively, the prevalent theory of the great German Social Democratic Party held to the view that the workers' own organizations became revolutionary under conditions of capitalist crisis, and that the party was essentially one of its instruments, but by no means its leader.

The orthodoxy of the Second and Third Internationals found its roots in a specific "reading" of Marx and Engels. Put plainly, the "mode of production" of material life is understood as the determinant of the "immense superstructure" of capitalist institutions, including law and the state, education, ideology and religion. This mode of production (consisting of the forces and relations of production) is influenced but not determined, in turn, by institutions to which it has given rise. However, despite Engels' famous caveat – that he and Marx stressed the primacy of economic relations and interests in the context of a determinate set of ideological struggles within the socialist and liberal movements with which both were involved, and which therefore should not be endowed with immutable status as truth – the Marxism of the Second and Third Internationals persisted in taking this metatheory literally: *determining, in every instance,* historical development.

Lenin succeeded in codifying as philosophical precept the one-to-one correspondence of base and superstructure by elevating this relation to an epistemological principle. Lenin applied the "correspondence" theory he "read" in Marx's Preface to the *Contribution to the Critique of Political Economy* to the relation between thought and the external world. In a polemic against Ernst Mach and his Russian followers, Lenin attacked Kant's epistemology, which held that thought constituted the object of knowledge.[16] For Lenin, scientific knowledge was obtained by *reflection* of the actual processes it discovered in nature. Scientific law was an approximation of the external world, but could not reproduce an exact "copy." Its relative truth was limited only by the level of development of the forces of production and scientific knowledge, that is, the degree to which humans acted upon nature in order to meet their needs. As the productive forces achieved greater mastery of nature, our ideas would more accurately correspond to their object, which was independent of the will of humans. Thus, ideas about the external world obtained by means of scientific – i.e. experimental and theoretical – investigation were the "superstructure" determined by the external world as "base." Similarly, the relations of production – the class consisting of the ruling capitalist class and the working class, the two great historical actors within capitalist society – determined the whole realm of ideology. Since in every epoch the ruling ideas of society as a whole are the ideas of the ruling class, political, philosophical, religious and other ideas are typically considered so many aspects of bourgeois ideology. Unless armed with Marxist theory, the working class is subject to these ideas (the immutability of human nature, "you can't fight city hall," the natural superiority of men over women) as much as the rulers in whose interest these ideas are promulgated. Marxism, the science of history and of revolutionary change, is like any science grounded in rigorous methodology, an approximation of the actual movement of history and society. Its dialectical "method" allows it to comprehend the apparently anomalous (i.e. "contradictory") nature of the social world, assuring that its generalizations are reflections of the "real" world.

For the purposes of this analysis, I do not propose to rescue Lenin from the charge of "vulgarity," since this term connotes nothing more than (1) the reflection theory of knowledge and (2) a correspondence theory of truth grounded in the distinction between base and superstructure in which the latter is determined by the former, not only in the *final* instance, but in each of them. As has often been pointed out, such a strict determinism forced Lenin and Stalin to adopt an extreme voluntarism in political strategy. On the one hand, all elements of the superstructure were nothing but reflections of class relations and the degree of human mastery over nature. On the other hand, the *party* and the proletariat – armed with Marxist science that explained with precision the course of political and economic development – could overcome the deficiencies of the historical moment. Thus, despite formal adherence to a rather mechanistic view of historical materialism, Lenin evolved a theory of *mediation* between base and superstructure based on the concept of a *scientific politics*. Whereas bourgeois political theory had consigned the realm of the political to the sphere of "art" or ethics, acknowledging only political economy as social science, Lenin insisted that questions of strategy and tactics belonged to the discourse of science. And, since science was the instrument of human mastery, an overcoming of once-feared natural forces, the transformation of politics from a practical art to one in which scientific reason prevailed multiplied human powers of historical change.

Lenin's recovery of the concept of politics as a science owes much to Machiavellian and Hobbesian notions that the state's rule over civil society must be grounded in more than ethical principles.

Rather, it must be conceived as a rigorous and systematic inquiry. In contrast, the parties of the Second International had understood politics within capitalist society as the art of the possible, critically severed from history, whose movement could be discerned with precision on the basis of the "laws of motion" of capital discovered by Marx. For the Marxists of the Second International, the socialist practice of reform within the framework of the bourgeois state was essential for both the amelioration of the immediate conditions of the working class and for building socialist strength for the ultimate revolutionary conflict. But political strategy was otherwise disjoined from the historical process, and could not be considered a science. Even Rosa Luxemburg believed the party's role to consist principally in "calling out to the masses their tasks." The success of the revolution ultimately rested on the masses, not the party. It was the place of political economy to predict the moment and the circumstances under which the proletariat would be obliged to wage the final struggle for socialism. Thus, for the leaders of most socialist parties prior to the First World War, politics within the bourgeois state remained a necessary, but subordinate, holding action. As early as his pamphlet *What Is To Be Done?* (1902), Lenin suggested that the question of the party could not be confined to its necessary educational function. In fact, in his polemic against spontaneity and its advocates, Lenin's precise argument rested on the significance of elevating political strategy to the level of *military* science. Forces would be deployed on the basis of a conception of the division of labor, i.e. specialization. On the other hand, Lenin calls for the end to fragmentation and the development of a plan of work to overcome it. Instead of leaving revolutionary activity to chance, he asks that the Social Democrats provide a systematic training program for their cadre.

The formation of an "all-Russian newspaper" is seen by Lenin as the core of the program, an institution able to unite all revolutionists in "common work," ending the fragmentation that had prevented the Party from achieving unity of strategy and tactics. Standing at the center of Lenin's program is the elevation of theory to the status of "guide" to revolutionary activity. Instead of yielding to spontaneous trade unionism and the economic struggle of the working class, and running furiously to catch up with it, Lenin proposes to "replace this hodgepodge" with a party able to lead the struggle because its ideology has been transformed into scientific socialist strategy.

Thus, for Lenin, a theoretically based socialist strategy mediates between the spontaneous resistance of the workers against capital and the socialist revolution. The party is the only force able to overcome the wall separating the two. The party is the "advanced" contingent of the workers' movement precisely because it has made scientific theory the basis of its political activity. The specific scientific content of politics consists in situating the question of *organization* at the center of political discourse. Once a sober assessment of the "objective" circumstances that condition political action has been made (the task of political economy), all theoretical questions merge with those of strategy and tactics. It would be an error to underestimate the departure Lenin's theory of politics represents from the main body of Marxist doctrine. Of course, Lenin does not believe that the party can replace either the proletariat or control the actions of the bourgeoisie. But given these boundaries, whose content may be discerned with precision, it is only by putting politics on a new – scientific – basis that socialist victory can be assured.

It is not that politics is somehow separated from the historical conditions within which it functions. Just as the categories of political economy were, for Marx, the foundation upon which a scientific socialist theory was erected, so Lenin wished to construct a *theory* of organization as a part of that foundation. The categories that comprise the theory are grounded in the dialectic between specialization and the totality. Its glue is discipline and centralization of command. These are the same categories as military organization. At the foundation is the understanding that the workers, by their own efforts, will not achieve political revolutionary consciousness. Capitalism – with its division of labor and the fragmentation that confines struggles to particular industries, sectors, and regions – does not, despite its breakdowns, create the conditions for revolution without the intervention of scientific consciousness as an objective historical mediation.

TOWARD "CRISIS IN MARXISM" THEORIES

The contradictions of the socialist movements in the twentieth century were apparent to the generation of Marxist intellectuals who reached their majority in the aftermath of the First World War. In this period world revolution appeared on the agenda of the socialist and workers' movements. The stunning success of the Bolshevik revolution in consolidating its power in Russia at first seemed to prefigure the spread of socialism to the most advanced capitalist countries of Europe, vindicating Lenin's notion of the party as mediator. Indeed, the Hungarian Soviet republic and the German revolution of 1918 were signs that Marxism, too, was destined for vindication as a scientific prophecy. However, world capitalism proved capable of staging a powerful counterattack against the proletariat, not only in the form of counterrevolution, as in Hungary, but also – with the aid of a section of the socialist movement – in Germany as well. Germany became the first in a long succession of capitalist regimes ruled by socialist parties. While the condition of the working classes improved considerably under social-democratic governments, neither the "dream of the whole man" or the self-management of society by the producers appeared closer to realization as a result of social-democratic rule in countries of Europe. Moreover, the reformist, socialist-led governments of the Weimar Republic and other European countries were unable to stave off inflation and economic crisis. With the founding of the Third (Communist) International, the promise of a really revolutionary socialism once again was made, only to degenerate into a Stalinist swamp in the late 1920's.

Before, as now, the working class proved unable to constitute itself as a class capable of social rule where its putative interests became those of society as a whole. Divided by the split in the socialist movement, weakened as much by mass culture as by mass unemployment, the workers were defeated and partially absorbed by fascism, or state capitalist parties. The crisis in Marxism first appeared in the context of the rise of fascism, because of all of the "objective conditions" appeared present for a revival of the revolutionary movement in the wake of capitalism's world economic crisis. For Marxists able to perceive the defeats of the fascist era beyond the categories of strategy and tactics (where leaders of socialist factions accused each other of perfidy, and implicitly suggested that the problems of revolutionary action were confined to issues of policy), the rise of fascism and the concomitant collapse of the workers' movement was a second occasion for examination of Marxism itself.

In the 1920's and 1930's several main left-wing tendencies which openly argued for a "crisis in Marxism" could be discerned. By far the most important theoretically was the work of those who, following some motifs of Lukács's *History and Class Consciousness*, stressed the failure of Marxism to take account of the importance of cultural mediations between the contradictions at the level of the economic base and the concrete consciousness of the proletariat. But where Lukács posited the distinction between actual and putative class consciousness, holding that the latter was an objective consequence of capital's logic of commodity production and the division of intellectual and manual labor, the major tenets of the Frankfurt School of critical theory refused his optimism.

The results of the historical tragedy of the European proletariat led Max Horkheimer and Theodor Adorno to the conclusion that there was no inevitability to revolutionary praxis, if by the term we mean the capacity of the working class to constitute itself through its political activity as a historical subject, one which sees itself not merely fighting for particular interests but for the interest of human emancipation. The Frankfurt School drew the consequences of Lukács' theory of consciousness that Lukács himself was unwilling to face because of his adherence to Lenin's concept of the party. Lukács found an explanation for the defeat of the postwar revolutions in the process of capitalist production, rather than relying exclusively on political explanations emanating from leaders of the labor and socialist movements. For Lukács, the central category showing why the workers failed to carry through the revolution lay in (1) reification, (2) the division of labor, and (3) capitalist rationality. While revolutionary praxis was inevitable because of the misery capital visited upon the workers, the underlying form by which capital ruled was impenetrable by ordinary consciousness without the mediation of theory. Lukács provided rigorous theoretical arguments for Lenin's dicta that trade union activity leads only to trade union – i.e. particularistic – consciousness, and that – owing to the structural incapacity of workers within capitalism to generate revolutionary consciousness on their own – socialist consciousness must be brought to the working class from the outside.

Lukács rendered the famous Marxist theory of the proletariat as the revolutionary subject problematic, but without drawing the logical conclusions from the theory of reification. In the end, he held to the classical Marxist view that the capitalist class, the degree of working-class organization, and socialist leadership were sufficient to produce revolutionary praxis, even as the conditions of the reproduction of capital thwarted such a development. Nevertheless, Marxism now had a theory which lent critical weight to the specificity of culture, understood as a moment in the unfolding of the commodity form. Marx's theory of fetishism, assiduously ignored by the theoreticians of the Second International, was understood as a structural category for explaining the persistence of capitalism in the wake of wars and depressions. Whereas Lenin had relied on the theory of imperialism with his "labor aristocracy" concept to understand the failure of the Second International to make "war on war" in 1914, Lukács argued the heretical proposition that the failure referred partially to the workers themselves because of capital's rationality. Together with the later-discovered Gramscian theory of "hegemony," Lukács's work revived considerations of ideology and culture within Marxist theory. But contrary to previous doctrine – which taught that ideology was merely "false consciousnes," i.e. a body of beliefs and values held merely subjectively – Lukács advanced the heretical idea that ideology, rather than being conceived as an imposition from without, was produced as a moment of the lived experience of capitalism itself.[17] The key cultural and social property of commodity production is the "thingification" of social relations. While capital is a relation between that portion of the working day which labor produces for its own reproduction as labor power and the portion appropriated by the employer(s), this relation cannot become an object of knowledge in the immediate process of production. Following Simmel, whose *Philosophy of Money* already suggests the centrality of reification as a theoretical ground for the production of ideology, Lukács argued that the real object of knowledge, capitalist social relations, could not be known without the aid of *mediation*, i.e. theoretical construction. Like Hegel, Lukács insisted that sense perception could only yield knowledge of appearances, while real relations remained veiled in the objects of the commodity world.

"The historical knowledge of the proletariat begins with knowledge of the present, with the self-knowledge of its own social situation and with the elucidation of its necessity (i.e. its genesis)."[18] But only when the working class abolishes its own particular existence, i.e. is able to see itself as a world-historical actor, can the reified consciousness be overcome. And this requires "self-knowledge" which, in turn, presupposes a break in the process of commodity reproduction. For it is not in the "empirically given" that class consciousness may be constituted, but in the process by which the proletariat constitutes itself independently rather than remaining one of the constituents of capital.

Writing *History and Class Consciousness* in 1919–23, Lukács remained optimistic about the possibility of revolutionary praxis. However, the rise of fascism, the degeneration of the Bolshevik revolution, and the apparent ability of capital to overcome the deepest economic crisis in its three hundred years convinced members of the Frankfurt School that something had transpired to challenge the underlying prophetic value of Marxism. For Adorno, Horkheimer, and Marcuse, it was not, at first, a question of abandoning Marxism. Certainly the absence of an analysis of political economy in the corpus of much critical theory is not meant to be a statement of its insignificance. On the contrary, Marx's categories of value, surplus value, and the rate of profit, with later Marxist analyses of imperialism and monopoly, were taken as the necessary presuppositions of their social theory. But the categories of political economy were no longer able to constitute a sufficient basis for social theory, nor were they adequate to historical explanation. It was not enough to make historically specific the way in which the conditions of capitalist reproduction produced a given level and character of political and social consciousness. Whereas Lukács was persuaded that Marx's *Capital* was not only a critique of political economy but also a theory of consciousness that rendered unnecessary new categories to explain historical events, the critical theory of the Frankfurt School remained unconvinced. For it was one thing to argue that the postwar defeats were but temporary episodes in the long march to human emancipation, where history's forward motion was rechanneled into reform and consolidation; fascism, on the other hand, was a regression the understanding of which could not rest merely on the vicissitudes of commodity production and capital accumulation.

THE PROBLEM OF FASCISM

The theory of fascism offered by both the Communist International and its orthodox Marxist adversaries such as the Trotskyists adhered to a view of fascism as an exceptional development of monopoly capitalism. Capitalism, in its crisis, could no longer tolerate democratic liberties where labor and socialist movements were strong; even the elementary rights of workers and members of the middle class to organize freely in their own immediate interests were untenable. To overcome the crisis, argued the orthodox Marxists, capital required a new form of state power. In Italy and

Germany, the state was no mere watchman over capitalist property, but wielded both the club and the law to enforce the domination of capital. Fascism represented the merger of the giant corporation with the state. The "command" state came into being where capital required assistance from the legitimate authority of government to promote investment on a grand scale. No longer confined to rails and other means of communication, state investment and planning would now direct the very processes of capital accumulation, if necessary. The communists argued that fascism was a "terroristic dictatorship of the bourgeoisie" arising on the base of the disgruntled petty bourgeoise.[19] But its essential class character was not petty bourgeois; it was supported by the biggest financial and industrial capitalists, who now required emergency measures to save the system. Trotsky differed with the communists on historical and strategic questions, but agreed with theoretical explanation for the rise of fascism. The working class was defeated not only by force, but by the splits among its leaders. Had the leadership of the working class been united, Trotsky argued, fascism would have been vanquished. He blamed both the social-democrats and the communists for this division, arguing that the sectarianism of the Communist International and the anti-communism of the socialists were largely responsible for the rise of Hitler to power.[20]

Critical theory offered a different way of seeing the rise of fascism. Fascism was no extraordinary development that contradicted the main drift of advanced capitalism. On the contrary, according to Max Horkheimer, fascism was a *logical* development from monopoly capitalism. The end of the market economy signalled the impossibility of sustaining an effective opposition to the authoritarian state. The burden of Horkheimer's analysis is to link capitalism's evolution, particularly the rise of monopolistic control over the market, to the appearance of fascism. Contrary to the main tendency of Marxist explanation, he insists that the authoritarian state is immanent in capitalist development, and that the modern era has brought the tendency toward state capitalism to fruition.[21] In the process, the state has finally integrated its own opposition – the working class and other exploited strata. Horkheimer argued that working class and its parties are inextricably linked to the state, mediated by bureaucracies which not only administer capital but also dominate the workers' movement through administration. *Administration* has become the critical mediation that throws into question the Marxist faith in historical progress. It is the synchronization of the system with its own putative negation that gives Horkheimer grounds for despair. Like Walter Benjamin,[22] Horkheimer abandons the Marxist doctrine of historical inevitability, because the working class is no longer fated to become the determinate, self-conscious negation of capitalism; rather, it may try to advance its own cause which, in 1940, is still understood by Horkheimer to be inherently democratic, if not necessarily revolutionary. Administration of persons and things is objectified in a large bureaucracy on the basis of principles of scientific rationality. This development is not only the property of state capitalism, but of state socialism as well. The workers are obliged to resist all authoritarian regimes, whether their own unions and parties or the state (in fact they appear to be virtually the same thing in Horkheimer's analysis), but the outcome has been rendered uncertain by the passing of the market economy which, in its own chaos, offered the space for resistance.

Lukács' historicization of Weber's notion of rational calculation as one of the defining features of capitalism constitutes the crucial intellectual foundation for Horkheimer's refusal to follow the Leninist theory of the party (i.e. mediation) which Lukács defended so well. Horkheimer shows that the concept of the party as the midwife of revolution is a metaphor inherited from the French Revolution. For Horkheimer, the party is no less an organ of administration than the state, and its midwifery "degrades the revolution to mere progress." Certainly Robespierre and the Jacobins were agents of "progress" in comparison to the feudal regime that they replaced. By centralizing the means of administration and communication, they succeeded in exercizing a revolutionary dictatorship on behalf of the bourgeoisie. Progress is not the object of the socialist struggle. It is workers' self-management of society, according to Horkheimer. But, the "deduction of the capitalist phases from simple commodity production" has played a trick on Marxism. Marx and his followers expected that the contradictions of capitalism as it moved through its phases would create the conditions under which humans could achieve freedom. Horkheimer points out the irony that alongside this truth another, contradictory, truth has emerged: growing capitalist antagonisms have also produced conditions that lead to unfreedom. "With state capitalism those in power can strengthen their position even more" than in previous phases. The clear implication for Horkheimer is that socialism has become no more than a possibility for the future.

Its essential precondition, an autonomous workers' movement, seemed a more distant shore in 1940 than in the nineteenth century.

The dialectical theory of the Frankfurt School leads to a conclusion neither Lukács nor Karl Korsch was able or willing to confront. Under conditions of total administration, self-managed socialism becomes an ethical ideal rather than an historical inevitability. Despite the distance between this formulation – Eduard Bernstein's – and critical theory, the political convergence is striking.[23] Lukács' explanation for the failure of the revolutionary project relied on the introduction of the theory of *mediations* into Marxism, in the hope that a comprehension of the specificity of culture stemming from the commodity form could lead to workers' self-knowledge. Horkheimer admonishes: reification has not prevented the opposition from emerging in late capitalism. But the conjuncture of the merger of the state and capital with the rise of administration as a social form *par excellence* has rendered difficult if not impossible the task of sustaining systemic opposition.

For critical theory, the advanced capitalist tendency to total administration makes critical thought increasingly difficult as well. According to Horkheimer and Marcuse, critical reason had as its historical precondition a free market economy. The bourgeois revolution arises as a defense of the free market against feudal restrictions. Its demand for the autonomy of civil society in relation to the state finds an echo in the demand for the freedom of reason from the repressive apparatus of the Church. Horkheimer's analysis of the eclipse of reason in late capitalism is grounded in the tendencies of the bourgeois epoch itself.[24] Despite the ideology of freedom, the *practice* of capitalism is embodied not only in the free market of commodity exchange, but in the organization of production. Here, in the development of the productive forces, rationality consists in the subordination of nature to human (i.e. bourgeois) will, and concomitantly the domination of human nature by industrial organization. Time as well as space becomes subject to rational calculation. Just as nature (space) is now subsumed by production and is increasingly perceived as "raw materials" to be transformed by the labor process, so the labor process is rationalized according to the criterion of efficiency (maximum production in the least amount of time). Labor becomes a function of time, and time has no significance apart from its role in production. Thus technical rationality replaces both the spirituality of religion, now assigned to the margins of society, and the bourgeois belief that accorded to reason an autonomy not subject to the encroachments of state or civil society.

The passing of the free market is linked by the Frankfurt School to the domination of nature (science and technologically grounded machinery) and the subordination of the labor process to technique (administration, specialization of tasks). Monopoly capital is only the extension of the processes by which technical rationality replaces the autonomy of critical reason. Reason remains critical because its autonomy is insured by the anarchy of production and exchange. The unification of reason with nature not only produced the domination of nature by rational calculation, but the domination of reason by its instrumentalization. Marcuse and Adorno argued that, under these circumstances, art becomes the only truly subversive form of human activity, because it could not be rendered consistently useful for the domination of nature and humans. Its subversive character was guaranteed by its political and scientific impotence. Even when recruited as ideology, it reminded people of a reason which defied this-worldly rationality. For its rationality was not the same as the labor process, but remained opposed to it.[25]

As capitalism develops, its own contradictions become so acute that it is obliged to abolish its specifically bourgeois presuppositions, especially the free market and the autonomy of thought. Now science becomes subordinate to the requirements of production for profit and is, in a large measure, transformed into technology. Consequently, for critical theory, the emancipatory content of bourgeois science has been subverted by its own logic. While scientifically-based technology may be capable of liberating the masses from back-breaking labor, it does not bring social and spiritual emancipation. For technology has invaded reason itself. Reason is no longer subversive to the given order; it has become the condition of the reproduction of domination, both of nature and consequently of humans, by the prevailing social order. Thus the condition of human emancipation, the autonomy of reason, no longer exists except in the margins of society – as art. Even philosophy has become a servant, insofar as it renounces its metaphysical roots and defines its mission as clearing the path for a science that can dispense with philosophy by showing that all philosophical questions are really issues within language, discourse, or communication.

THE NECESSITY OF PHILOSOPHY

One of the great contributions of the Frankfurt School to our understanding of advanced industrial societies is to show that the cause of human freedom cannot abolish philosophy until social praxis has succeeded in realizing it:

> Philosophy, which once seemed obsolete, lives because the moment to realize it was missed. The summary judgement that it had merely interpreted the world, that resignation in the face of reality had crippled it, in itself becomes a defeatism of reason after the attempt to change the world miscarried. Philosophy offers no place from which theory as such might be concretely convicted of the anachronisms it is suspected of, now as before. . . . Theory cannot prolong the moment its critique depended on. A practice indefinitely delayed is no longer the forum for appeals against self-satisfied speculation, it is mostly the pretext used by executive authorities to choke whatever critical thoughts the practical change would require.[26]

In these opening lines of his *Negative Dialectics*, Theodor Adorno indicts, in one stroke, a Marxism that believes itself free of the *obligation* of speculative – i.e. critical – reason. His argument rests not upon an immanent critique of Marx's powerful eleventh thesis on Feuerbach, but on an historical judgement. The proletariat which, owing to its praxis, abolishes the requirement of metatheory, for a philosophy that extends beyond science (theory), has failed to measure up to the expectations of historical materialism. It retains a practice of opposition to this or that policy or program of the "executive authorities" and of capital itself, but – having refused to situate itself on the terrain of history – the proletariat and its organizations can no longer claim the moral authority with which to refuse an intellectual project that insists upon the critical examination of Marxism and its philosophical presuppositions.

For Adorno, departing (in the double sense) from Horkheimer's earlier hope that oppositional practice would realize philosophy, it was not enough to specify the triumph of total administration, to mourn the end of reason. The concrete totality of which Marx and Lukács had confidently spoken had been betrayed by history. The putative subject of history, the working class, may remain the most exploited class within modern society when measured by the categories of political economy, but its subsumption under the canons of technical rationality blocked self-knowledge. The proletariat discovered in the relatively luxuriant unfreedom of late capitalism a means by which its obligation to history could be avoided. The fundamental issues raised by both enlightenment and socialist thinkers had not been resolved by the ability of capitalism to deliver the goods, or by the workers' movement to achieve a version of the "good life" without revolutionary power. But it was beyond the categories of scientific thought to address issues that had belonged to metaphysics. Adorno's emblem, "philosophy lives," really meant that theory lives, and it was Adorno's task to challenge the fundamental concepts of Marxism in the light of the historical anomalies that befell humanity in the aftermath of the First World War.

The "fundamental concepts" of which I speak include the most cherished categories of dialectical thought, of the capacity of history to settle all questions of morality and of ethics, of the sanctity of materialism as an epistemological stance. Adorno's departure from the Horkheimer of *The Authoritarian State* and from Marcuse's pessimistic *One Dimensional Man* consists in an exegesis on the historical judgement that "philosophy lives because the moment to realize it miscarried." For if historical materialism was no science – in the sense that it could abolish the need for speculation, including its moral dimension, but rested on the results of praxis – then the issue was what went wrong, why did history fail to live up to the prophetic vision? Adorno attempted to show that the very *categories*, the presuppositions from which Marxism springs, were misdirected. Thus it is to his *Negative Dialectics* that I must turn, because it remains the most important attempt within Marxism to provide an immanent critique of the entire scaffolding of historical and dialectical materialism. Where Lukács, Horkheimer, Marcuse and Korsch tried *within* the framework of historical materialism to account for the fragmentation and the refusal of the concrete totality to emerge in the twentieth century, Adorno proposes nothing less than the revival of the concept of philosophy and *its* categories. If this return to the Kantian problematic appears anachronistic to those reared in the Hegelian-Marxist traditions (even the recalcitrant Althusser held to the totality, albeit in a non-Hegelian form), it is only because historical materialism has become *historicist*, because dialectical thought has become formal in the wake of the triumph of technical rationality.

Adorno intends, by returning to a critical examination of philosophical problems, to found a materialist dialectics on new theoretical premises: "The call for the unity of theory and practice has irresistibly degraded theory to the servant's role, removing the very traits it should have brought to the unity."[27] The attempt to revive theoretical studies must begin with the goal of emancipatory practice, but for just that reason it requires an autonomy from all given practices as a provisional stance in order to finally find the basis of an alliance, not a unity, with practice. Adorno's purposes remain critical. In fact, his critique of the fate of the dialectic in both Hegelian and Marxist thought is precisely that "dogmatism and thought taboos" have robbed them of critical content. On the other side, those Marxists like Lenin – whose opposition to dogmatism was uncompromising – were led, nevertheless mistakenly, according to Adorno, to abandon philsophy's insistence that the object was constituted reflexively, and substituted a naive realism in its place. That is, Lenin's refusal of the rituals of epistemology in his *Materialism and Empirio-Criticism* – motivated by suspicion that philosophy served the interests of the *status quo* – disabled Marxism for half a century (save those who insisted on the importance of theory at the price of political isolation). What was taken by Marxism for theory was a dialectics that was little more than a version of formal logic, an Aristotelian logic of *identity*.

Adorno's program goes beyond Lukács and the Frankfurt School, anticipating recent French post-structuralist theory. First, he undertakes a fundamental examination of the Hegelian logic upon which contemporary Marxism rests. Despite the discovery by Hegel and the development by Marx that the logic of contradiction was objectively constituted and not merely a property of thought to be overcome by clearing logical confusions, the materialist presuppositions of this move are, in Adorno's view, undermined by the metaphysics of identity. Only a dialectics that insists on *difference* as the ineluctable feature of objective reality can form the basis of a new critical theory. "Its motion does not tend to the identity in the difference between each object and its concept; instead it is suspicious of all identity. Its logic is one of disintegration of the prepared and objectified form of the concepts which the cognitive subject faces, primarily and directly. The identity of the subject is untruth."[28]

Adorno is constrained, therefore, to oppose two central concepts of the Hegelian dialectic which have been carried over into Marxism. Against Lukács he insists that "totality is to be opposed by convicting it of non-identity with itself." The recuperation of difference by a higher identical synthesis is "a primal form of ideology," for it destroys the negativity that difference implies.[29] We may discern in the passionate defense of negativity an attempt to preserve that which the concept of "negation of negativity" nullifies. Here, the anti-Stalinist as well as anti-bourgeois echoes sound in Adorno's polemic. For socialist states claim to have overcome the contradictory differences that are inevitably a mark of civil society, just as contemporary Marxist and some types of bourgeois ideology argue for the end of the dialectic in the realization of the categories of freedom and equality.[30] Secondly, against the later Hegel and Marxism Adorno refuses positivity, holding to the negative character of the dialectic. The negation of the play of difference is not, itself, to be overcome by historical change, reintegrating it into a new given. Difference is suppressed, not liberated, by its negation in a world marked by the domination of nature and humans. "Objectively, dialectics means to break the compulsion to achieve identity, and to break it by means of the energy stored up in that compulsion and congealed in its objectifications."[31]

For Adorno, the link between the Hegelian dialectic and formal logic consists in the shared goal of *identity*. Contradictions are to be overcome for the dialectic which, only under certain historical circumstances, lead to new contradictions. Adorno wishes to assert difference as a condition of arriving at truth and negativity as the condition of freedom. But this does not imply a return to Kant and British empiricism, only an argument for the persistence of the questions they raised and which remained unresolved by Hegel. Adorno explicitly opposes the *a priori* subject, insisting that it is constituted by history, including natural history. Thus, unlike Lukács – whose *History and Class Consciousness* was, among other things, an argument for a conception of the dialectic in which the subject appears as one of its first terms and the object its other – Adorno argues that "The most enduring result of the Hegelian logic is that the individual is not flatly for himself, he is his otherness and linked with others." Thus, non-identity is not difference *between* two things (subject/object) but exists *within* each. This is, undoubtedly, the tribute modern dialectical thought must pay to Freud, for whom the psychic structure was unified but never identical with itself. Consciousness can never fully subsume itself as its object, since the unconscious remains outside its control. The self is fractured objectively; its unity is achieved as a process of repression and displacement, but its negativity is never overcome.

NON-IDENTITY AND DIFFERENCE

Both bourgeois and socialist theory have been forced to recognize non-identity, but in both cases difference is historicized by being pronounced "fragmentation" or "atomism" by liberal thought, for which harmony of interests and classes remains the goal of theory and practice. The differences within physics between wave and particle theories of matter, the indeterminacy principle discovered by Heinsenberg, Einstein's relativity theory, all are accommodations to the impossibility of arriving at a unified field theory, one in which the "anomaly" of difference for a theory which posits identity may be resolved without challenging the presuppositions of science itself. The invention of probability theory, the attempt to ascribe the contradictions of measurement to "subjective" error, or to incomplete or inadequate instruments, and Niels Bohr's complementarity principle, all show the will to totality in modern science. This example of rationalization of difference is reproduced in social science, for which the goal of prediction and control, presumed to have been achieved by physics and other "natural" sciences, is primary. Social science's preoccupation with the problem of "methodology" is a sign of the importance it attaches to perfecting quantitative procedures (cognitive instruments) that lead to the predetermined goal of prediction and the political imperative for social control. Contemporary social science is unable to accept difference, at least in its qualitative connotation. Its elevation of number to the status of the invariant language of social science and spatial relations to its framework is grounded in the logic of identity, for the historical and the qualitative imply difference. For, as Marx's critique of exchange value shows, only when the qualitative differences between two commodities and their process of production (always a qualitative activity) are abstracted or reduced to a common quantitative denominator can exchange take place. Thus, Adorno's critique of identity is also a critique of modern science as much as are the philosophies of Heidegger and Husserl, which – while purporting to be concerned with the play of difference – actually seek the identical in a new doctrine of being. Similarly, Marxism's adherence to the concept of a totality produced by the identity of the subject – humans – with the object – nature – prevented it from reconciling itself to the differences between the two. "The objectivity of historic life is that of natural history."[32] Praising Marx, Adorno quotes a passage from *Capital* where Marx places the limit upon consciousness, including human praxis. "Even if a society has found its natural law of motion, natural evolutionary processes can be neither skipped nor decreed out of existence."[33] Adorno finds this "social Darwinism" in Marx to be eminently critical, rather than regressive as in Herbert Spencer, because it recognizes the disjunction between human desire and its object, but at the same time understands that nature gives rise to the social process and becomes part of the social process as its "unconscious". Thus Adorno relies on Marx to affirm his critique of Marxist voluntarism which, in the last instance, subsumes nature under history, social processes under conscious activity, otherness under identity.

Adorno's appeal to Marx for support for his dialectic of negativity is also an attack against contemporary Marxism's tendency to ontologize history as the ultimate ground of being: "When history becomes the basic ontological structure of things in being, if not the *qualitas occulta* of being itself, it is mutation as immutability copied from the religion of inescapable nature."[34] Dialectics recognized the "painful antithesis of nature and history." On the contrary, the ideal of the enlightenment and of contemporary Marxism to gloss over this opposition has led to a kind of "crypto-idealism" and, as Horkheimer and Adorno argued in the *Dialectic of the Enlightenment*, not to the realm of freedom but back to human domination. "The moment in which nature and history become commensurable with each other is the moment of passing." This cognition may be seen in Benjamin's *Origins of German Tragedy* for in tragedy history appears as writing and, in turn, is already inscribed with the countenance of nature which, according to Benjamin, "is really present as a ruin." The ruin of nature in "pictographs," its passing into history, is the hideous outcome of a scientifically-based technical rationality, the moment when nature – once hypostatized by religion – is demystified and becomes an object without qualities "for us" (Engels).[35]

THE PROBLEM OF PRAXIS

Marxism's glorification of the domination of nature prefigures a radical historicism for which nature has been relegated to the periphery of the social process and human praxis elevated to the sublime. Thus does contemporary Marxism abolish the limits to human action, which would be the necessary concomitant of a theory of non-identity. Lukács developed his theory of the primacy of praxis in the context of a hegemonic Marxism which, in the zenith of the Second International, was afflicted with "naturalism" and thus became a necessary corrective to mechanistic determinism. His standpoint must be understood as an antimony to Kautsky's appropriation of natural history, in which praxis was merely the inevitable outcome of capitalist crisis. The crucial contribution of Adorno's theory of the negative dialectic is his assertion of the non-identity between nature and history, subject and object (subject as object). But Adorno cannot generate a theory of praxis, claiming that such a project would be premature in the wake of the subsumption of theory by practice in the twentieth century. There is no space for conscious praxis in Adorno's *Negative Dialectics*; this is the result not only of the historical assessment of Marxist voluntarism, but of its assignment of praxis to the theoretical. Adorno's praxis is, in the final sum, theoretical activity. The dialectic of non-identity, the careful argument for negativity as a transhistorical principle, is an argument for critical theory as the only possible praxis in a world in which history has become repressive.

Unlike much of contemporary Marxist theory, which blames Stalinism and the deformations of socialism "as it really exists" on purely historical aberrations or authoritarian dogmatism, Adorno's attempt to resuscitate philosophy simultaneously condemns the foundations of historical materialism. For Adorno, the causal determinism inherent in Marxism is no aberration of Marx's epigones. It is grounded in the outcome of Hegelian philosophy, to which Marx was heir. Historical materialism seeks not only the negation of the *status quo*, but the negation of the *negation*. For Adorno, this is nothing less than a call for the end to critical thought, for the suppression of reason, save that reason which is instrumental to the reproduction of the given: technical reason. The emancipatory goal of socialism is subverted by its own historical logic. As Marxism reads history, contradictions appear as a consequence of class-divided societies. The very principle of historical specification (Korsch)[36] which liberated nineteenth-century social theory from the metaphysics of the absolute spirit has become a fetter on critical theory, preventing it from performing its vital, if autonomous, function in relation to practice: the disintegration of the "prepared and objectified form of the concepts" so that the differences repressed within them may be released. Stalinist theory ascribes to historical determinations the objectivity of contradiction. Even if differences remain under socialism (cf. Mao's concept of non-antagonistic contradictions) these are to be conceived not as inherent in the nature of the social system. Difference is thus rendered harmless by the Marxist theory of socialist society. For if classes in the Marxist sense of the term disappear, the historical basis of contradiction also disintegrates.

Critical theory holds the principle of disintegrative reason as the absolute from which there is no appeal if the hope of human freedom is to be kept alive. Thus, for Adorno, the very practice of human emancipation must promote theory as a permanent feature of its project. The "realization" of philosophy can no longer be entrusted to the proletariat, or to a Marxism whose adherence to the Hegelian dialectic impels it to the liberal ideal of harmony. As Adorno develops his ruminations on the fate of historical materialism and the dialectic, it is clear that he means to understand that the moment is past when reason comes back to itself and eliminates the object as otherness. Thus nature's subordination to man – bourgeois reason's ideal since the enlightenment, with the ability of science to predict and control nature, including human nature – must be abandoned as a misdirected adventure. But immanent to Adorno's position is that there never was such a possibility in any case. The concept that the contradictory motion of history is a return to reason's identity with itself was only an archaic hope that could never be achieved.

Adorno's contribution is to suggest the lines by which the formalism inherent in Hegelian dialectical reason may be broken. More, it offers the germ of an entirely different movement of critical theory. Since it is explicitly a theory in which concepts such as progress must be denied – especially after Auschwitz (Adorno's metaphor for the triumph of unreason as the logical outcome of technical rationality) – there is no question of deriving a new historical subject which might, putatively to be sure, be assigned the role of bearer or personification of the historical process. For this reason, "Dialectics is the self-consciousness of the objective context of delusion; it does not mean to have escaped from that context. Its objective goal is to break out of the context from within."[37] Yet thought may transcend its object by means of a logic which grasps the "coercive character of logic," embracing an absolute which is not identical with itself or coming to rest as a totality.

While it was necessary for Adorno to do battle against the forms of thought which have merged with the object to form a repressive totality of domination, the absence of a philosophy of emancipatory praxis in his work presupposed the priority of theory in the wake of a practice which could do no other than serve the *status quo*. It was not that Adorno privileged the theoretical reconstruction of the dialectic in some abstract hierarchy of human activity in which mental labor was given a reified status. The point of his argument is against the subordination of theory to practice, a view held by those who wished to change the world without confronting the repressive totality in which thought is made an instrument of unfreedom. His project, to free the forms of thought from their instrumental rationalist premises, can only be welcomed – even if the history is thereby rendered disembodied.

It remains for us to find the bearers of a non-identical dialectic. We must begin to draw the implications of the revival of theory for a political praxis that itself remains non-identical with the theoretical underpinnings and the specific content of the historical materialisms of the Second and Third Internationals, but we cannot be satisfied with the theory of mediation offered between the wars as a means to preserve Marxism. At the same time, the project of founding a praxis whose aim is to emancipate humanity from the conditions of social domination but which insists on theoretical grounds, must be considered profoundly Marxist in outlook, if not in doctrine.

ASPECTS OF THEORETICAL CRISIS

It may be useful to review the argument in the previous section before suggesting a new approach towards the reconstruction of historical materialism. The crisis of historical materialism which forms the specific theoretical content of Marxism was *detonated* by social and historical developments, but cannot be confined to them. Certainly, the *refusal* by the proletariat in Western advanced-capitalist countries to enter the historical arena after the First World War as a subject in the Marxist sense could not have helped but produce the conditions leading to a comprehensive theoretical examination of the foundations of historical materialism. Similarly, the inability of the proletariat in "really-existing" socialist countries to form a self-managed society in the wake of the triumph of communist bureaucracies (conjoined, of course, by two world wars) ignited a wave of anti-communism among Western left intellectuals and workers. The rise of religiously-inspired nationalist revolutions in the Middle East, Ireland and Third World countries raised serious questions concerning the Marxist expectation that the national revolution must pass into the socialist revolution. After three decades of nationalist rule in the Middle East and North Africa, new forms of state capitalism – ones not based upon advanced industrial development – may have consolidated a long period of rule. Finally, the rise of feminism and the significance of race in world politics raise serious issues concerning the adequacy of the Marxist penchant for reduction of social antagonisms to their class dimensions. Feminist and black-nationalist theories challenge the very core of Marxist theory of historical periodicity, as well as the historicist assumptions of many tendencies in contemporary historical materialism.

The movement of theory that has been called, erroneously, "Western Marxism" arose after the First World War to explain some of these developments not by means of a "revision" of Marxism, but by returning to Marx himself, by reviving "orthodox" Marxism against its revisions by the leaders of the Second International. The crucial innovation – or, to be more precise, discovery – of the postwar Marxists was the concept of *mediation* between the economic base and the superstructure of capitalist societies. The notion of mediation was drawn from no less an authoritative work in the Marxist literature than *Capital* itself. Lukács' contribution was to discover in the theory of commodity fetishism the source of capital's capacity to gain ideological hegemony over the proletariat. Ideology was seen not as false consciousness but as a moment in the reproduction of capital, a necessary rather than contingent feature of commodity production and class struggle. The unique contribution of the Frankfurt School was prompted by the rise of fascism which called into the question the *capacity* of the working class to transform society. Whereas Lukács adopted the Leninist theory of the party as educator, organizer, and demystifier of the commodity fetish and its consequences, Max Horkheimer and Theodor Adorno refused this solution. Rather, they found in Weber's sociology the notion that capitalism was a way in which the entire social world was subject to rational calculation and thus made relatively immune from fundamental social transformation. For them, the theory of bureaucracy was adequate to understand the role of the party as a purveyor of a new unfreedom, as well as one that could deepen Marx's and Lukács' theories of political and social consciousness. Further, they challenged the view that the domination of nature was a form of emancipation, and the ideas of progress and historical inevitability which pervaded Marxism. In his later years, Adorno attempted to codify these discoveries in a new and fundamental critique of the materialist dialectic, with a view to its reconceptualization. The theory of *Negative Dialectics* asserts the non-identical character of the objective world, the non-overcoming of contradictions, and the importance of the incommensurability of nature and the social world. Marxism remained, according to Adorno, ensconced in the categories of the Hegelian dialectic, in which the overcoming of the negative was the outcome of the contradictory historical process; Adorno insisted to the contrary that the survival of critical reason – the necessary condition for an emancipatory praxis – demanded that theory should not be subordinate to technical rationality. The critique of instrumental reason advanced by the Frankfurt School was at the same time a theory of the principal form of domination characteristic of late capitalist societies. According to Marcuse, the power of late capitalism consisted in the presentation of technology and science as the only acceptable rationality. The material basis of technology and science as *prima facie* evidence that capitalism *is* civilization rests on the integration of the relations of production by the productive forces. Marcuse's critique of technology exposes the ideological content of science by showing its instrumentalization in the service of domination. Thus the burden of the Frankfurt

School's argument is to show that technological rationality is a kind of unreason because it subverts the function of reason in history – human emancipation.

What is startling about this judgement is the degree to which it violates the eighteenth-century idea of progress that linked science and technology with human freedom. Marcuse showed that the subsumption of science and technology under capital resulted in their irrationality from the point of view of the goal of freedom. Whereas virtually all nineteenth-century thought was locked into the presuppositions of social evolutionism – which postulated the relationship between human mastery over nature as the condition of the emancipation of humans *from* nature – Marcuse and others argued that the transformation of nature by means of the *ratio* had deleterious consequences for social relations, and forms of thought as well. Accordingly, until science and technology could be freed from the bonds of instrumental reason, that is, until knowledge was separated from the commodity form in which it was subordinate to and became a kind of cultural capital, it would remain a form of ideology as well.

Despite the appearance of *One Dimensional Man* as late as 1964, the Frankfurt School's theoretical life as a more or less coherent tendency *within* Marxism ends with the Second World War. In his later years, Horkheimer became a more or less unabashed champion of bourgeois liberalism. As we have seen, Adorno's rejection of the Hegelian-Marxist concept of the dialectic placed his work outside traditional historical materialism, although it may not be claimed that he was a post-Marxist in the contemporary sense since he was still grappling with the old categories, with the old problematic of human emancipation.

HABERMAS AND LATER CRITICAL THEORY

Jurgen Habermas finally severed the relation of critical theory to Marxism by undertaking a fundamental reexamination of historical materialism. Habermas, too, departs in the double sense from critical theory's appropriation of Weberian "rational calculation." Where Marcuse, for example, borrowed from Weber in order to enrich the critique of capitalist rationality and, in effect, turned Weber around by showing the subversive possibilities of his thought (just as Marcuse's misreading of Freud pressed the conservative Freud into the service of emancipation), Habermas turns Marcuse around and returns to Weber.

Habermas asks that the critique of technical rationality be abandoned because Marxism's expectation that human emancipation may be achieved through the transformation of social labor controverts the evidence of biological and social evolution. In his criticism of Marcuse's critique of Weber, Habermas calls technical rationality merely the "rational-purposive" action necessary for the reproduction of the human species.[38] Marcuse's call for a new relationship with nature in which "repressive" mastery is replaced by one that is "liberating" is, for Habermas, a false project because it would imply the possibility of a new science and a new technology. Habermas argues that science and technology are forms of human knowledge that are rational because they serve human purposes, however instrumental to these purposes technology is rendered.

According to Habermas, Marcuse has failed to specify how human knowledge may become liberating in the sphere of work, how our relations to nature may be transformed in accordance with the parameters of human survival. Having found that Marcuse lacks an empirical basis for his claim to found an alternative science and technology in which political domination does not circumscribe rationality, Habermas makes a crucial distinction that is to become the foundation of his own reconstruction of social theory, the obliteration of historical materialism. According to Habermas, Marcuse's mistake was to confuse two distinct realms of human action: work and interaction. The Marxist belief that work relations could be transformed according to the canons of emancipatory socialism miscarried because capital had already organized the labor process based upon the elevation of *knowledge* as the principal productive force corresponding to human needs. This development is merely the logical outcome of biological and social evolution that points to the development of "scientific-technical" progress as the realization of human interests as a whole. The labor process was no longer an issue for critical examination. Thus, science and technology cannot be "ideological" if by the term we mean ideas, beliefs and norms which correspond to particular interests, that is, interests not shared by society as a whole.

Work is redefined by Habermas as "rational-purposive action" governed by "technical rules based on empirical knowledge." These rules imply predictions that may be correct or incorrect but, in any case, cannot be verified normatively, that is, are subject only to the rational calculation of alternative technical choices, not political criteria. This type of discourse is context-free, i.e. outside of history focusing on problem-solving in the service of power over nature in order to develop the productive forces. Following Weber, Habermas understands the state as one of the primary forms by which purposive-rational action of this kind is institutionalized. The state thus becomes a neutral instrument, a sub-system along with the economy in the sphere of rational – i.e. non-ideological – domination.

The inclusion of the state in the sphere of work rationality may, at first glance, appear remarkable from the perspective of critical social theory. But on closer examination Habermas is simply being consistent with his first postulate, that any action that belongs in the sphere of the reproduction of the forces of production must be considered technical, i.e. outside the sphere of moral discourse. In modern industrial societies, the state acts as a force of capital accumulation, as an institution intervening in the development of the productive forces. Its planning functions, the system of law that governs contracts, its investments become types of problem-solving. For Habermas, the state is no longer a repressive apparatus, a form of institutionalization of class domination, but primarily a technical apparatus instrumental to the domination of nature. Thus he recreates a conception of the state closer to that of Hegel and Hobbes than to Marx. Emancipatory "politics" must now be confined to the sphere of *interaction* which, for Habermas, remains relatively undeveloped in the wake of the emphasis of industrial societies on perfecting their institutions of purposive-rational action.

In his later work, Habermas is constrained to reintroduce the problematic of social domination into the productive sphere. The essays in *Communication and the Evolution of Society* and *Legitimation Crisis* recognize implicitly that the distinction between work and interaction is not nearly as absolute as was suggested in the earlier Marcuse critique. To the extent that in democratic societies the legitimacy of the state rests on the consent of the underlying population, normative structures remain an aspect of rational-purposive action, at least to the extent that the accumulation functions of the state do not appear to have purely technical criteria. On a broader theoretical level, the essay *Reconstruction of Historical Materialism* tries to maintain the earlier distinction between technical and moral reason, and, at the same time, to establish a more solid foundation for their linkages. Perhaps the dualism of the earlier position appeared increasingly untenable in the wake of historical developments as well as theoretical critique, but it is clear that Habermas began to solve the antinomies of his earlier thought.

Habermas's solution – which owed much to the developmental psychology of Lawrence Kohlberg as well as to recent anthropology – was to assert that historical evolution owes as much to the efficacy of normative and cognitive structures as to structures of instrumental or strategic action. Thus, Habermas not only retains the split between work and interaction and argues for the independent development of the former, but precisely reverses Marx's theory of causality, which accords primacy in the processes of historical change to the changes in the infrastructure. Habermas adduces evidence from empirical sciences to demonstrate his thesis that it is the capacity of a society to generate *learning mechanisms* which accounts for its adaptation to conditions of natural as well as social development. Given the contradictions between productive forces and productive relations in the history of human societies, the ability of a culture to resolve these in the interest of its survival depends on the normative structures it has generated that permit the development of its learning mechanisms, rather than its relations of production, i.e. class relations. Those societies survive which can evolve institutions to codify mutual cooperation rather than competition. Hence, for Habermas *organization* becomes Marxism's missing link between infrastructure and superstructure. Organizational forms are the key linkage between *communicative* action (interaction) and *instrumental*, or productive action. While the rules governing each form of action are different (one depends on domination, the other on equality), it is the forms of interaction, transvalued into organization, which are primary for understanding societal evolution:

> The introduction of new forms of social integration – for example, the replacement of the kinship system with the state – requires knowledge of a moral-practical sort and not technically useful knowledge that can be implemented in rules of instrumental and practical action. It requires not an expansion of our control over external nature but knowledge that can be embodied in structures of interaction – in a word, an extension of the autonomy of society in relation to our own internal nature.[39]

For Habermas, the problem of modern, industrially-developed societies is that the "cognitive potential" of society has neglected moral development, pouring all knowledge into the "socialization of production"; this potential will not lead to evolutionary change until mechanisms of learning are developed that innovate new forms of social integration.

Habermas has not offered, of course, a new kind of historical materialism, but its determinate negation. Only unlike Adorno, for whom the negative as absolute constitutes the fundamental condition for social transformation, Habermas wishes to establish a world of harmonious relations, and not on the ground of a transformation of power relations. First, he regards the sphere of production to be free of internal antagonisms. The class struggle which, implicitly, presupposes hierarchy and scarcity as the basis for domination, exists as a vestige of earlier, exogenous conditions, but it neither constitutes the basis of historical change nor remains a vital element in the course of advanced industrial societies. For Habermas, as long as knowledge is the central productive force, the whole mode of production is subsumed under the categories of progressive rationality. The domination, therefore, is not subject to critical inquiry, and human domination must be strictly separated from social labor.

Second, it must be clear that the whole of Habermas's "reconstruction" rests on his rejection of the Frankfurt School theory of the domination of nature as the basis of human domination. The achievement of social integration – i.e. of social harmony – depends not on realigning our relations with exogenous conditions. Habermas views this relation as the greatest achievement of bourgeois society, and claims it must be preserved by any new social order, since it is the *universal pragmatics* of reason. Social integration remains elusive because we have not succeeded in finding those normative structures upon which we may learn from our current crises. These normative structures must be "sought first on the psychological level," according to Habermas, since he has treated all "system problems" as "disturbances of the reproductive process of a society that is normatively fixed in its identity," and this "identity" is conceived as dysfunctional to its reproduction. Thus, finding a new identity for society is the condition for its survival as a reproductively efficient social system.[40]

Weberian theory has come full circle with Habermas. There is no critique of administration as in the Frankfurt School. The question of organization becomes primary for social reconstruction because this is the link between moral and instrumental action. But despite Habermas's claim to find, in moral categories, the key to systemic change, the objective is system maintenance. And why not? If capitalism has solved the problems of scarcity through its evolution of a system of instrumental/strategic action, i.e. a scientifically-based labor process that "solves" the problem of nature's mastery over society better than any other, then our "problem" is no longer one of accumulation, of mastery over nature, but of the mastery of human social organization. Marx was wrong, according to Habermas, because he located the central problems of human societies in the labor process, assuming their normative structures would follow from social production and were conditioned by it. Once work and interaction have been severed, not only is the critique of the labor process nullified as a proper object of social knowledge, but moral development is, thereby, made possible without a fundamental change in the nature of production relations. Habermas's proposal for theory's task is to devise modes of interaction, including discourse, which can assist *society as a whole* to shift its cognitive resources to problems of ego identity, i.e. to the conditions upon which society defines itself morally and establishes, on the basis of this self-understanding, rules of action. Of course, interaction is not context-free and technical in character, since reflexive thought is the basis of distortion-free communication. That is, every speaker must, in order to communicate perfectly, (1) be aware of the degree to which his discourse is informed by interests and (2) separate the two.[41] Thus Habermas ends up with an argument that wishes to make normative structures universal as rational-purposive action, by transforming the speech situation in accordance with canons of reflexivity. The aim is a rational society, one free of "negativity" (now understood as "disturbances" in the reproduction process of society, rather than contradictions). Socialism is, under this rubric, no longer the determinate negation of capitalism, but becomes a new ego-ideal, the normative structure of cooperation and undistorted communication – in short, the rational discourse needed to achieve new levels of social integration, appropriation and positivization of critical theory.

Like Eduard Bernstein's, Habermas's critique of historical materialism postulates that the working class has succeeded, not failed, insofar as it has attained most if not all of its demands *within* the framework of late capitalism. But the demands of the proletariat are no longer the demands of society as a whole. The new needs created by the success of the forces of production and the institutional framework of late capitalism are moral in nature. According to Habermas they address, for the first time, what is specifically *human* about our species. Our humanity consists not in the fact that we produce our means of subsistence; other primates also are required to engage in social production. Humanity is defined by our capacity for reflexive interaction through the invention of language. It is our requirement that whatever we do contains normative and cognitive structures that distinguish humans – by *learning* as a basis of social reproduction.

Of course, Habermas remains within the framework of Marxism insofar as he asks questions that concern processes of social transformation. His departures begin, however, with a precept shared by Marxist orthodoxy – the progressive character of instrumental reason, the irreversibility of science and technology as it has been developed by capital. But he has not succeeded in overcoming Marcuse's contention that a new science and technology, based upon a different relationship between humans and nature, is necessary for social emancipation. Written in 1968, Habermas's critique of Marcuse's theory of the ideological within contemporary science and technology may have been premature; it predated the emergence of the ecology movement and the environmentally-oriented research of the 1970's, which were based upon a solid body of evidence arguing that the results of the forms of the domination of nature of modern industrial societies were inimical to human survival. From the experimental evidence of such investigators as Barry Commoner and others, the empirical criteria Habermas used to condemn Marcuse's insistence on the necessity of a new science seem, in retrospect, to have been vitiated by others. More importantly, Marcuse's argument appears prophetic in the light of recent history, particularly the nearly incontrovertible evidence of Three Mile Island, an event that has become an emblem of the dangers of nuclear power, and a signal that nuclear power, the apogee of knowledge as a productive force, may not conform to canons of rational-purposive action. Equally important, the hazards to the health and safety of both workers and communities produced by the substances used in the ordinary productive forces such as asbestos, polyvinyl chloride, and other hydro-carbons that are among the foundations of "rational purposive action" have revealed contradiction between humans and nature at the level of the question concerning rationality.

However, the appeal of theory to empirical evidence may be a necessary, if not sufficient, condition for historical argument. More germane is Marx's insistence that humans are part of natural history, and Adorno's amendment that the unity of humans and nature is a contradictory process. On the one hand, as Habermas acknowledges, we are a stage in biological evolution. On the other hand, we are not able to claim that our productive forces are rational insofar as they ignore the autonomy of nature.

This is not an epistemological question, but an historical and structural issue. Habermas has ignored the thesis of the *Dialectic of the Enlightenment* that the domination of nature was grounded not only in the mastery required for the reproduction of the social order and of the species, but in the *fear* of the external environment humans have harbored in their social unconscious. This *fear* was historically allayed, according to Horkheimer and Adorno, by the instrumentalization of nature, its subsumption by a quantitatively-based science and technology. The outcome of the relentless rampage of humans against nature, now conceived as pure alterity, was not only expressed in the production of an idealist philosophy that posited the autonomy of the spirit, but also in the destruction of the autonomy of reason, as a kind of dialectical revenge.

And here is Habermas, invoking the rationality of science and technology, of instrumental reason itself, as the threshold of the new holocaust, one that could easily make Auschwitz an historical dress rehearsal. The brutalization of spirit revealed in the Nazi concentration camp was reproduced by the United States in the napalm bombs and the "strategic hamlet" program in Vietnam, the more or less explicit triage practiced by Western powers against Bangladesh and India, and, more recently, in the mass slaughters in Chile and Argentina. All of these are illustrations that social contradictions extend to the state, that the forces of production are also forces of destruction under the concrete social relations of late capitalism, that irrationality conquers on the foundation of technical reason.

This of course does not obviate the importance of Habermas's insistence upon the specificity of normative structures in the development of the mode of production. Habermas's contribution to critical theory has been to underline the relative autonomy of the normative in human history. But in the final analysis we must reject his attempt to substitute moral and cognitive learning for class struggle. It is not only that his assessment of the degree to which the revolutionary *need* has been overcome by late capitalist organization is wrong. This is an empirical question, the answer to which depends to some extent on how one views the problems of war, ecological disaster, and the persistence of opposition within the labor process and in public life. Habermas could easily reply to the empirical arguments advanced here that these are merely "problems" subject to solution through rational calculation, a contention close to that advanced by Daniel Bell and other American theorists of post-industrial society.[42] American social theory does not posit that capitalism has succeeded in overcoming conflicts, even those based on class, only that these conflicts are subject to technical resolutions.

The major objection to Habermas's reconstruction of historical materialism must rest upon theoretical grounds. The issue is joined by Habermas's contention that science and technology are subject to merely technical criteria because they express a *universal* rationality, that is, their development corresponds to the general interest of society. Although in the later work Habermas attempts to ground his separation of work and interaction within social evolution rather than philosophically, it is evident that he misunderstands the relationship between work and interaction because he has accepted the dubious perspective that labor is nothing but instrumental to the domination of nature and related thereby instrumentally to human subsistence. For Habermas as well as virtually the entire Marxist tradition, work itself is not a need whose relation to the social structure has normative implications. By confining the *normative* to the sphere of interaction and the *cognitive* to the sphere of production, Habermas has reproduced the division between moral and instrumental reason that is inherent in the antinomies of bourgeois thought. His theory is but a mirror of a society in which the division between the spiritual and the material is accepted as part of the natural order. Habermas's theoretical construction accepts the division between intellectual and manual labor. His biologistic orientation towards the domination of nature simultaneously argues that "moral development" is the specifically human in nature but that production is fundamentally continuous with our animal nature.

In this respect, although Habermas's attack against the anthropomorphism of Marxism is warranted and constitutes a major corrective to its theoretical premises, he appears to deny the historical character of the production of needs. That is, even if social labor inheres in previous stages of evolution, it does not follow that work as such may be naturalized. For what has transpired in the late capitalist era is precisely that the satisfaction of human needs *includes* work, and this problematic contains a moral and ethical dimension. Workers no longer confine their demands to a decent wage, job security and "pleasant" working conditions. The moral development of which Habermas speaks has historically extended to the quality of working life. Workers are beginning, by fits and starts, to *need* a working life which is marked by reflexivity and communicative action. Habermas's assignment of work to "purposive-rational" – i.e. instrumental – action corresponds to a version of socialist ethics in which the goal of labor apart from physical spheres is rich in interaction but where the labor process is subject only to "technical" rules. In this world of the work/leisure dichotomy, questions of production are devoid of moral content. Needless to say, such a theory becomes technocratic, reproducing the division between intellectual and manual labor which permeates capitalist production and its culture.

Of course, we are still in the throes of a debate in which the labor process has, for the first time since *Capital*, acquired a specific content for socialist theory and labor research. However, recent Marxist writing has focused exclusively on the degree to which the labor process is subject to the logic of capital, that is, it is still preoccupied with the *modus operandi* of the consequences of rationalization of and by science and the technology of production. Harry Braverman, Andre Gorz, and Serge Bologna, among others, have argued persuasively that the "technical" division of labor is both hierarchical and degrading.[43] The degradation of labor is only acceptable, of course, to those like Habermas, who would insist that this is a price worth paying for material abundance and that satisfactions should be sought elsewhere. On the other hand, if work itself has become a part of the moral as well as the political economy, then its intrinsic character is subject to scrutiny as a system of *communication* action. Further, returning to Habermas's own insistence upon an historical/empirical basis for the construction of social theory, the workers' protests common in all capitalist countries in the 1960's and 1970's were directed not against the traditional issue of wages as much as at questions of control and management. Strikes, sabotage and other means of work disruption amounted to a refusal to work under degraded working conditions, that is, under conditions marked by a rationality that aims at reduction of working time required for the production of the commodity. The purposivity of "scientific" management consists in its attempt to delete from the labor process any activity not directed towards capital accumulation. The rationality of production under these conditions presupposes the primacy of organization over interaction in Habermas's sense of the term. Interaction, which is necessarily reflexive, appears as a "disturbance" within the prevailing system of reproduction. Yet, from the point of view of those who disturb, reflexivity is a need and is objectively contradictory to capital's rationality, just as an ecologically sound environment appears as an "interest" of society as a whole against the particular rationality or logic of capital.

To offer a universal pragmatics without ideological presuppositions is itself a "primal ideology." It is only given to those for whom the achievement of the enlightenment, with its binary oppositions, can be regarded as an historically constituted but ontologically immutable ground. The appeal to social evolution must not be taken as irrefutable scientific evidence for a position which has become problematic, owing to the "action-critique" that refuses to exempt either science and technology or the labor process from the criterion of moral development. But it remains for us to constitute this critique on a theoretical terrain.

NOTES

5. Bernard-Henri Levy, *Barbarism with a Human Face* (New York: Harper and Row, 1978).
6. G. A. Cohen, *Karl Marx's Theory of History: A Defense* (Princeton: Princeton University Press, 1978).
7. Andre Gorz, *Ecology as Politics* (Boston: South End Press, 1980).
8. See especially Juan Luis Segundo, *The Liberation of Theology* (New York: Orbis Books, 1976).
9. Jurgen Habermas, "Reconstruction of Historical Materialism," in *Communication and the Evolution of Society* (Boston: Beacon Press, 1979).

10. The term was coined by Rudolph Bahro, *The Alternative in Eastern Europe* (London: New Left Books, 1978).
11. Louis Althusser, *For Marx* (New York: Vintage Books, 1970), pp. 10–12. Althusser argues that some varieties of Marxism, particularly what he calls Marxist humanism, are ideological because they have failed to constitute the object of social knowledge as society. By naming "man" as the subject/object of history, humanism, according to Althusser, has perpetuated the ideological forms of pre-Marxist – i.e. pre-scientific – discourse because it posits an *a priori* subject that stands outside history. In another place he asserts that politics as a practice is a form of ideology, even those political practices inspired by Marxism.
12. Georg Lukács, *History and Class Consciousness* (London: Merlin Press, 1971), p. 151–2.
13. Ibid., p. 155.
14. V. I. Lenin, "What is to Be Done," in Robert C. Tucker, ed., *The Lenin Anthology* (New York: W.W. Norton and Co., 1975).
15. Ibid., pp. 27–8. Lenin quotes a long passage from Karl Kautsky's comment on the draft program of the Austrian Social-Democratic Party printed in *Neue Zeit*, 1901–2. (XX, no. 3) p. 79. In this remarkable passage Kautsky asserts the fundamental principle that socialism as a scientific discourse arises "side by side" with the class struggle. Although they are both the effects of economic relationships, they are separate.

    "The vehicle of science is not the proletariat but the bourgeois intelligentsia" according to Kautsky. "Thus, socialist consciousness is something introduced into the proletarian class struggle from without and not something that arose within it spontaneously." Lenin adopts this viewpoint without criticism and it becomes the basis of his critique of spontaneity within socialist ranks. Also Althusser's distinction between science and ideology originates in this conception, as does Gramsci's argument that every class seeking social and political power must form intellectuals who articulate the class's claim to moral and intellectual leadership, i.e. *hegemony*, over society as a whole.
16. V. I. Lenin, *Materialism and Empirio-Criticism* (Moscow: Progress Publishers, 1967), especially Chapter Two, Section Four, "Does Objective Truth Exist?".
17. Despite Marxist-structuralism's accusation against Lukács of essentialism, I believe his concepts of hegemony and ideology are close to those of Gramsci and Althusser since all of them insist that ideology is an aspect of the structure of society rather than a property of incorrect ideas or "false consciousness." Lukács' theory of mediation is a statement concerning the reality of appearances, that is, their objective existence. For Lukács, drawing from Marx's theory of fetishism of commodities, the origin of ideology is in the permutations of the commodity form.
18. Lukás, *History and Class Consciousness*, p. 159.
19. Georg Dimitrov, *The United Front Against Fascism*. This was the main report to the 7th Congress of the Communist International, 1935.

20. Leon Trotsky, *What Next?* (New York: Pathfinder Press, 1973).
21. Max Horkheimer, "The Authoritarian State," in *Telos* (15), Spring, 1973.
22. Walter Benjamin, "Theses on the Philosophy of History," in *Illuminations*, Hannah Arendt, ed. (New York: Shocken Books, 1969).
23. Eduard Bernstein, *Evolutionary Socialism* (New York: Shocken Books, 1961).
24. Max Horkheimer, *Eclipse of Reason* (New York: Seabury Press, 1974).
25. See for example Herbert Marcuse, *The Aesthetic Dimension* (Boston: Beacon Press, 1978).
26. Theodor Adorno, *Negative Dialectics* (New York: Seabury Press, 1973), p. 3.
27. Ibid., p. 143.
28. Ibid., p. 145.
29. Ibid., p. 147.
30. One finds this tendency in Mao's essay *On Contradiction*, where the distinction is drawn between antagonistic and non-antagonistic contradictions. The former are a property of capitalist societies while the latter tries to explain the persistence of difference within "really existing" socialist countries on the basis of a category that may not imply political struggle, that is, a struggle for power within society. Similarly, the communist parties of Eastern Europe have, until the Polish events of summer 1980, refused to acknowledge the structural differences between state and party, on the one side, and subaltern social classes on the other.

    Since there could be no antagonism between the party of the working class and the class itself, any struggles between them were viewed as the consequence of outside interference from the capitalist powers whose agents infiltrate the workers' movement. A similar line was taken to explain the Hungarian Revolution of 1956 and the attempt to effect fundamental changes in the relations among party, state and the workers in Czechoslovakia in 1968. Since the workers, by their own efforts, would never oppose the party, strikes, demonstrations and other manifestations of opposition had to be the result of outside influences or the political "backwardness" of the workers.
31. *Negative Dialectics*, p. 159.
32. Ibid., p. 354.
33. Ibid.
34. Ibid., p. 358.
35. Ibid., p. 359.
36. Karl Korsch, *Karl Marx* (New York: Russell and Russell, 1963), Chapter Two.
37. Adorno (*Negative Dialectics*) p. 360.
38. Jurgen Habermas, "Technology and Science as 'Ideology'," in *Towards a Rational Society* (Boston: Beacon Press, 1970).
39. Jurgen Habermas, *Communication and the Evolution of Society*, p. 146.
40. Ibid. See especially the chapters on "Moral Development and Ego Identity" and "The Development of Normative Structures."
41. This is, of course, little more than Weber's project for a value-free

"scientific" sociology. See "Science as a Vocation," in Hans Gerth and C. Wright Mills, eds, *From Max Weber* (New York: Oxford University Press, 1958).

42. Daniel Bell, *The Coming of Post-Industrial Society* (New York: Basic Books, 1973). See also S. M. Lipset, *Political Man* (New York: Anchor Books, 1962).

43. Harry Braverman, *Labor and Monopoly Capital* (New York: Monthly Review Press, 1974), and Andre Gorz (ed.), *Technical Division of Labor* (London: Harvester Press, 1976).

3

Nature and Human Nature in Marxist Theory

The revival of interest in Marxist theory within the United States and Great Britain over the past fifteen years has resulted in the development of Marxist scholarship in virtually every area of the humanities and social sciences. These contributions have been thrust to the center of academic debates on a wide range of issues so that it is no longer possible, even in relatively conservative U.S. universities, to ignore or disparage Marxism as a way of coming to grips with the social world. At the same time, the reawakening of Marxist theory and research has produced anew a series of debates regarding its fundamental tenets, particularly in political economy, the theory of culture and ideology, and historical questions. These debates were particularly vigorous during the 1970's when, in all advanced capitalist countries, the promise for revolutionary action of the previous decade abated. Under these circumstances, it was not surprising that left intellectuals would open the discussion of precisely those issues raised by Marxist theory during the interwar period discussed above.

However, even if the debate has been conducted at a level considerably higher than before – due partially to the successes of Marxist scholarship as well as the new political environment of the postwar era – there is nevertheless a strong tendency to want to preserve the most simple propositions against both the evidence of praxis and of argument. But neo-Marxists who follow Lukács and the Frankfurt School, Gramsci, or Korsch in their efforts to discover the specific features of the contemporary world as a basis for new theory and practice are prone to invoking what Charles Sanders Peirce called the "method of authority" to support their arguments. That is, since Lukács the slogan of every neo, plain or vulgar Marxism has been the "return to Marx" to find a basis for the new orthodoxy. Disregarding Marx's own advice to "let the dead bury the dead," scavengers of Marx-remnants insist upon making theoretical activity a process of archeological excavation.[44] Whether emanating from the appropriation of British philosophy of science; the American penchant to meticulous research, aimed at producing a seamless narrative of Marxist cant; the French talent for *bricolage*, in which theory becomes akin to textile recycling worked up from the garbage cans of social theory; or the German treatment of the "classics" of Marxism as Biblical texts to be "read" (e.g. interpreted according to carefully prepared "first principles"), Marxism has been rendered a patient lying on an operating table whose blood spurts from all pores. The carcass, emptied of its living substance, is inert. Korsch's invocation to a "living Marxism" is violated daily by these surgeons; the principle of historical materialism suggests that Marx be read in order to be forgotten. One imbibes not a doctrine valid for all epochs and eras but *a way of seeing*. For the prophecies have suffered the fate of all historically-surpassed thought. They remain monuments to the power of theory to erect an edifice that structured understanding. But Marx – unlike the great German philosophers whose thought he was eager to realize, or the epigones who clutched on to him for dear life against the cruel lessons of historical events – was unafraid of the unorthodoxy of his thinking. If there is a Marx text for every tendency in contemporary socialist movements (even the same text supports antinomous tendencies), it is because Marx was not a Marxist, but rather a theorist of the genesis and development of capitalism, for whom the study of history, philosophy, natural science and political economy were not ends in themselves but necessary moments in the struggle for human emancipation. My own contribution to historical materialism rests in turn on a different foundation from the preponderant Marxist scholarship. Like those who came before, the point for us is not to repeat history, but to change it: to find those changes in theory needed to comprehend changes in the development of human societies and the evidence that contravenes our expectations.

"We know only of a single science, the science of history. History can be viewed from two sides, can be divided up into the history of nature and the history of mankind. The two sides must not thereby be separated; as long as men exist, the history of nature and the history of men condition each other mutually."[45] Combined with other remarks, Marx was careful to state that the history of human societies was part of natural history. The mutual conditioning of the two is not, however, a synchronous metabolic process. According to Marx, early human societies were conditioned more by nature than they were able to impress their own stamp on the external world. The weight of "natural" conditions of social labor powerfully shaped their ideas about the world and the relations of domination between humans and nature. It is by now Marxist faith to assert the civilizing effects of industrialization on these "primitive" notions of nature as primeval. Marx's invective against rural and craft idiocy were made in the service of combatting romantic protest, like Blake's "Satanic Mills" of industry invading England's fast-disappearing green and pleasant land. Although sympathetic to the impulse behind the fierce criticism of the cruel moral and physical degradation visited upon its victims, the factory laborers, Marx had no doubt that the progressive mastery of nature was the presupposition of human emancipation. The "humanization of nature" took precedence over the "naturalization of man" in the epoch of industrial capitalism, and that was all to the good. In the process of the subsumption of nature under capital, the two-sided approach to nature was forgotten. "Production for production's sake," the "ruthless" development of the productive forces is called by Adorno "the violent domination of nature." Alfred Schmidt, in his able effort to rescue Marx from the charge that he subsumes nature under labor, has argued that labor is nature's form of self-mediation:

> The whole of nature is socially mediated and, inversely, society is mediated through nature as a component of total reality. The hidden nature speculation in Marx characterizes this side of the connection. The different economic formations of society which have succeeded each other historically have been so many modes of nature's self-mediation. Sundered into two parts, man and material to be worked on, nature is always present to itself in this division.[46]

Similarly, Kostas Axelos traces the split between man and nature to the self-alienation of man, who "forgets" that he is part of nature and takes nature as an alien object to be dominated through labor.[47] But Marx's position that the evolution of society is a part of natural history eventually gives way to the view that nature is merely the "raw material" for labor, or, in Marx's more technological mode, a "tool house" that provides labor with "stones for throwing, grinding, pressing, cutting, etc." For Marx then, "The earth itself is an instrument of labor, but its use in this way, in agriculture, presupposes a whole series of other instruments and a comparatively high stage of development of labor power."[48]

Thus Marx holds that nature is congealed in the products of labor; nature's existence outside of human intervention is hidden from human eyes, especially in the capitalist mode of production, when the labor process reaches its penultimate level of the instrumentalization of nature. Schmidt offers a line of argument that criticizes the concept of nature as an "abstract in itself external to man," attributing this notion to the universal mastery of nature by man. For him, Marx holds that the just society would be "a process in which men would neither simply coincide with nature nor be radically distinct from it."[49] Yet this invocation of the historical Marx hardly solves the problem of Marxism's relation to nature. The "abstract in itself external to men" is the precondition for the metaphors – promulgated by Marx himself – that nature is a "tool house" and a "laboratory," an object to be worked up into use-values. This anthropomorphism has found its way into Marxism despite the materialist premise enunciated by Lenin: the view that nature is external to human will, but because we are part of nature, science is able to gain approximate knowledge of it.

Of course, the concept of "nature" is an historical creation; it demarcates humans from the rest of the environment, thereby making possible our domination of it. Its otherness, its character as alien *object*, is the basis of both science and modern romanticism. The "awe and wonder" with which the romantics celebrate a tree was scorned by Marx, who reminded the poets that – contrary to common sense, which regarded it as an aesthetic, natural object – a tree was a product of human labor as much as a natural historical thing.

We cannot remove ourselves from the historical character of nature. Nor is the priority of the solar system, including the priority of earth to human life (and therefore "intelligence") in question. Yet precisely because nature is historical our conception of it must go beyond either the metaphors of raw material or pure abstract otherness. In the former, nature becomes nothing more than "our" thing; in the latter, the abstract in-itself gives rise to romantic idealism, in which the external world becomes ontologized, without history. In the context of this essay, nature must be comprehended as historically prior to human existence, following the materialist tradition. Its subsumption under *techne*, however, is a position that has become unacceptable. Marx's technological metaphors must, in the last analysis, be understood as a statement of the fate of natural history as it is comprehended from the standpoint of its domination by man. Rather, Marxism after Marx has taken this not as a *descriptive* but as a *philosophical* point of departure. The task of an emancipatory theory must be to restore nature in its autonomy, recognizing that nature remains congealed within production, but must be released from it. To the degree that nature obeys its own rhythms, it cannot be subsumed under labor/history. Theory owes to romanticism the view of nature as an aesthetic, not alien, other. The religious aspect of this conception must be admitted, for the result of a thorough-going historical materialism for which nature has become a raw material for labor – repressed within use-values – has been the deformation of social relations.

In this regard Engels, despite his naturalistic bias, must be understood as superior to the Marxist tradition. For he insisted that humans were part of natural history, and that the distinction between *homo sapiens* and the natural kingdom was not to be made into a sharp dichotomy. The anthropological fault in his doctrine of the role of labor in the transition from ape to man has already been corrected by Serge Moscovici, who shows that primates engage in purposive activity and that tool-making is not unique to our species.[50] Nor can his insistence on the morphological analogue between forms of matter be supported without the most severe reductionist assumptions. Nevertheless Engels restored the Greek view of nature as a constant process of coming into being and passing away, and one possessing an immanence that resulted in its instrumentalization. Nature's ontological immanence was denied by Lukács on the grounds that dialectics is itself interaction between humans and nature, though it cannot inhere in the objective world (such a view brings deity through the back door). Of course, Lukács is right, but he is merely the antinomy of Engels in this respect. Lukács' extreme historicism is entirely consistent with the Kantian antinomies that he attacks. The denial of the immanence of the external world as part of the *social* problematic sinks theory and praxis into a rationalist morass, from which the revolt of nature is the only, disastrous, recourse.

Despite his own sensitivity to the two-sideness of the relations of humans to nature, Marx left the natural side undeveloped. Thus it is not surprising that the classical Marxist tradition, with Engels alone excepted, succumbed to the celebration of the instrumentalization of nature. Nature was viewed for the most part as formally – ontologically – independent of human will, but in practice taken account of only as one of the conditions of production subsumed under raw materials as productive force. Thus imprisoned in the lexicon of Marxism, nature loses its autonomy.

The historical reasons for this form of social amnesia are understandable. The concept of "human nature" – given scientific legitimacy by social Darwinism, psychology, mysticism, and more recently sociobiology – has typically been appropriated by the most reactionary social forces to demonstrate the immutability of ahistorical society. Concepts such as "instinctual" human aggression, the eternity of the competitive spirit, and the like have been combatted by socialists and radicals who, in every generation, have been forced to insist on the *historicity* of all social characteristics in order to create the ideological atmosphere for social transformation. But contemporary Marxism has become a kind of historicism in the most fundamental sense: relations of society and nature are not comprehended as intrinsic to the theoretical framework of historical understanding. The historical conditions that necessarily prompted both Marx and Lukács to insist upon the centrality of the social dialectic have been surpassed. The unfortunate consequence of the polemics conducted by Marxism against all forms of nineteenth- and twentieth-century "naturalistic" materialism has been to transvalue the concept of materialism within Marxism into an economic category, to pose the significance of materialism in terms of the struggle against social and historical idealism. Philosophically Marxism, following Lenin, holds to a realist view of the object of human knowledge. That is, human knowledge refers to an object which is independent of thought but which remains subject to human manipulation through both science and technology. On the other hand, some structuralist currents in modern Marxism follow linguistics and argue for the materiality of language and social institutions, in an effort to solve the problem of *representation*, which in much of the Marxist tradition remains extremely sticky. In this view, the institutions of the superstructure – education, media, law and the state, language – are not "reflections" of the economic infrastructure but instances of a *structured* totality, in which the economic is the "structure in dominance."[51] This formulation of Louis Althusser and his followers overcomes the curious tendency in Marxism to ignore what is obvious to anyone who has looked at recent history dispassionately: distinctions between infrastructure and superstructure have broken down in late capitalism. Here the term "materialism" becomes a way to give substance to ideology, avoiding the need for a theory of mediation by arguing against the whole Hegelian scaffolding of Lukácsian Marxism.

Yet nature itself has no materiality within contemporary Marxist thought. Nor does it really enter the social process except as a suppressed, unconscious instance of history. It appears as catastrophe, unexplained accidents, and the raw materials of human intervention. The burden of science and technology since Bacon and Newton has been to make society independent of nature's metabolism by adjusting it to our rhythms, by factoring it to human production, and historical materialism too knows only one science: *history as the dialectic of labor*, a practice which is presumed adequate to subsume nature as well as spirit under production.

ENTER FREUD

Another great contribution to social theory casts a long shadow over this proposition, by showing the *unconscious* as a *structurally* uncontrolled instance of the historical dialectic.[52] To be sure, Marx grasped the existence of a "second" nature – believing it to be constituted within humans as the historical sediment of *habitus*, the meeting ground between the physical organization of human beings which generated needs (our biological structure) and the socially-produced needs that became internalized as "natural". Thus, history took place behind our backs and could not be fully known even by its makers. But even Marx was prone to historicizing this observation. When a self-conscious agent situated within history in a special way undertook the task of transforming society in its interest the unconscious could itself be overcome.

Freud's revolution in human thought was to show that nature refused to be subsumed entirely by civilization. Sexuality, libidinal energy, and the "id" were elements of the psychic structure not fully subject to social domination. Human needs – at least in the early Freud – were defiant of the social order, and were historically constituted and subsumed so that the physical and social reproduction of society remained uninterrupted. Yet Freud postulated sex as a "drive," a linguistic move not fully explained by his alleged naturalistic bias. Rather, "drive" is the signal that nature's autonomy is expressed as a "disturbance," threatening the social order in the same way that weather conditions threaten the bread that sustains life. Sex could not be fully subsumed under procreation, nor could its energy be permanently channeled into social labor. While Freud argued in his later work for the *necessary repression* of sexual drives and the control over the unconscious by the superego (admitting at the same time the serious consequences for individuals), he also made systematic the claim that the social order was equally impaired.[53] The dialectic of sex was seen: a necessary repression in the service of social labor, and the disasters that befell humans in consequence of that repression. The human psyche was inscribed with the historical scars of society's blockade of nature as sexuality.

In *Group Psychology and the Analysis of the Ego*, Freud pointed the way for understanding at a level below the socioeconomic analysis common to the social theory of group "interest." In some instances he found that the repression of libido leads to the displacement of the ego ideal to a "leader of superior strength." Whether the leader is an individual – as in the case of Hitler – or an institution – such as the Church or the Party, Freud reminds us that groups are "led almost exclusively by the unconscious." Since the unconscious seeks the discharge of its store of libidinal (sexual) energy group action is one way of achieving a "love relationship." Let us not be detained by quarrels that groups form for rational purposes such as winning some benefit, making reforms, or revolution. Freud's claim is only that to limit our understanding of group action to its rational dimension is to miss a whole range of phenomena that cannot be explained by means of "rational," conscious, categories. In *Totem and Taboo* as well, Freud wished to make the question of the dammed-up libido an historical phenomenon. The "need" for community that inheres in all group formations has its basis in the protest of the unconscious against social isolation. The natural links between feelings of love and the urge for social cooperation are historically deformed by patriarchy, so that group action is often directed by the need to symbolically "kill the father" as a condition for the bond between the band of brothers. But the father is also an ego ideal. When the group is unable to achieve its liberating mission because of the censorship of the superego (moral norms) or has introjected the domination of the male figure, it turns to another father (God, the father, Father Stalin, the Church). Hence, the social bond is maintained under conditions where the libido remains frustrated. But the ego has retained its object.

Psychoanalytic theory's postulate of the unconscious as an historical actor is a corrective to the historicism of contemporary Marxism in two ways. First (contrary to the prevailing view that nature remains unknowable within history because it has been transfigured by social labor), Freud's insistence upon *the substantiality of human nature* establishes a theory of the constitution of the subject at the conjuncture of nature and history. Second, to Marx's motto, "the first historical act is the production of new needs,"[54] the theory of sexuality adds, "and the repression of old needs." For as Freud points out, social labor proceeds not only on the basis of the forces of production already in existence but (as Marx himself recognized) on the physical organization of human beings. However, physical needs are not identical with the demand for social labor. The need for sexual fulfillment is the permanent opponent of labor, and is only sublimated in *work* and *community* which have the potential for satisfying at least one aspect of libidinal needs. The virtue of the theory of sexuality is that it signals a concrete explanation for the incommensurability of nature and history, but preserves their dialectical relation: contradictions between the two are posited as a part of natural history. At the same time, the end of the dialectic implied by a theory in which the development of social production is held as both the necessary and sufficient condition of human emancipation is overcome. For even the most liberated social order can never produce a merger between the unconscious and conscious existence, as long as social labor remains the condition of the reproduction of human existence.[55]

NATURE AND CLASS STRUGGLE

The theory of the unconscious is a sign that nature obeys laws that are independent of social production and, within societies marked by domination in the double sense, capable of making historical its own needs. The "needs" of non-human nature, according to William Leiss, include homeostasis: "a complex set of feedback loops through which the population of each (living) species is continually adjusted in response to competing populations, seasonal and long-range climatic variations, food resources, and occasional local catastrophes."[56] Leiss shows that human culture is constituted by our ability to technologically manipulate the stages of adaptation to our natural environment, which simultaneously creates new needs and provides a spur to further intervention of humans in nature. Leiss suggests that the disruption in the homeostatic patterns by the ideological and technological domination of nature is dangerous for the survival of the human species. "The chief negative aspect of the process . . . the modification of the normal environmental feedback loops is the difficulty of bringing about a practical realization of the need for the rational management of human demands in relation to the tolerance limits of the biosphere."[57] Although existing ecological science has not determined the limits of nature's tolerance to technological intervention, the evidence does support the argument that such limits exist. Nature, then, is not subject to social will, that is, it is not an object without resistance. Its boundaries must be respected in order for the life of a species to be sustained. Leiss appeals to self-interest for evolving a new approach to our relations with both our own concept of needs and nature. A new rationality with respect to nature is on the historical agenda, but it is a different rationality from that of the ideology of domination governing the management of the relation of society to its exogenous conditions until now.

The problem with "sounding the alarm" on pragmatic grounds is that domination is conditioned, if not entirely determined, by the logic of capital accumulation. The production of needs is constructed both on the terrain of technological innovations that permit their satisfaction and also the redirection of libidinal energy to consumption – a presupposition of contemporary accumulation. Of course, Leiss is aware of this limit to the ability of existing societies to embrace a new rationality that would grant the relative autonomy of nature in relation to technological manipulation. His critique of the neutrality of science and technology, implied by the warnings of ecological disasters based upon this ideology, is an important step in the long process by which society learns to make the self-criticism needed to save itself. However, it is precisely when the concept of historical agency is abandoned that the limits of rationalism are most evident. For what is common to Leiss, Habermas, and others – whose distance from the Marxist tradition is grounded in the loss of its prophetic value, particularly the vision of the proletarian revolution – is that they are constrained also to leave the terrain of political praxis. The concept of a rational society seems, in their proposals, to have no political specificity because "self-interest" is defined so globally that the essential condition of politics – antagonistic interest – disappears. The distinction between Leiss and Habermas is, however, significant. Habermas's rejection of Marcuse's contention – that science and technology are, in part, ideological, since they are socially constituted in the framework of domination – makes it impossible for him to construct a political praxis on the basis of his theory. Instead cognition and norms are accorded autonomy and, consequently, Habermas becomes an opponent of the central theoretical presupposition of historical materialism: history is constituted by class struggles. On the other hand, the logic of Leiss's critique of the domination of nature, and his simultaneous rejection of the Marxist theory of class, suggest that the new bearers of historical change are those who constitute themselves as opponents of capital's incessant effort to subsume nature under the sign of accumulation.

Thus the ecology movement, environmentalism, and those concerned with the proliferation of nuclear weapons are the real revolutionaries of our time, if the implied logic of Leiss's analysis is to be followed. This is also the position of such writers as Andre Gorz and Rudolph Bahro, who contend that the state-socialist societies are, with respect to the question of the domination of nature, merely extensions of advanced industrial societies of the capitalist type, however marked by state ownership and central planning. For these "Marxist" ecologists, one must wave a nostalgic but firm goodbye to a proletariat which can no longer be a universal class within advanced capitalism. Their position is that the sphere of production remains the main problematic of contemporary life. But the object of critical theory is no longer the problem of how to insure that the productive forces are developed to a level that meets the requirement that physical life may be reproduced, without disruption, at a level of material culture that corresponds to the historically-constituted possibilities. The transformation by capital of science and technology as the main productive forces of society has multiplied human productive powers. In the process, however, the domination of humans and nature by capital has also multiplied. The problem for Marx was how to release the full potential of science to meet human needs. Socialism was conceived, in the first place, as that form of social organization adequate for the development of human knowledge and skills that were already in existence but suppressed by capitalist relations of production. However, the failure of the proletariat to transform these relations did not prevent capital from subsuming science, transforming it into technological domination and generating *both* new forces of production and new forces of destruction. To be sure, the forces of production that exist are sufficient, on a national scale, for the material needs of most of capital's subjects, although the relations under which they were developed resulted concomitantly in the impoverishment of the majority of the world's population, and the "spiritual" (and local material) impoverishment of workers in the advanced societies as well. For capital has not succeeded in meeting the new needs created by its own successes as well as the social praxis of the workers themselves. These new needs were neither anticipated by Marxism nor are they solvable by capital.

At one time, Gorz contended that among these needs was the desire for work that was not merely instrumental to consumption, but was a means of satisfaction of the need for self-actualization.[58] Under these circumstances, Gorz argued, the qualitative demands for self-management of the labor process, of living space, and for popular control of the social and economic resources such as air, water and minerals were in themselves potentially revolutionary demands, even if a "living" wage had been achieved for most workers. In the 1960's Gorz maintained that the working class was still at the core of the revolutionary project. Together with Serge Mallet,[59] he insisted that the technical intelligentsia – which had become the main bearer of the forces of production – had now become a new working class. After 1968, when French workers joined students and members of the technical intelligentsia in an uprising that was grounded not on the issues of economic deprivation but on the problems associated with the new need for self-managed society, the revolution was recuperated by the political parties of the left which, by this time, were firmly committed to the parliamentary system of the capitalist state. The final disenchantment was, undoubtedly, the collapse of Eurocommunism after the fiasco of the 1978 French parliamentary elections, where the workers and intellectuals, hopelessly split, were handed a resounding defeat at the polls by the parties of capital.

This is the social and historical circumstance that produced the wave of socialist ecological theory of recent years. The new task is to break the power of capital as administration, capital as science and technology, capital as culture, capital as forces of destruction. For the left ecologists, theory must address the possibility that the working class may stand at the other side of the ecological barricade under certain circumstances. Here the emphasis must remain on *possibility,* for it is not foreordained that anyone else can afford to oppose the ecological movement *on human grounds,* even if its immediate interests are no longer identical with historical tasks. The central new issue is how to manage the forces of production in order to prevent the revolt of nature against its domination by capitalist science and technology. For it is not only that capital as a social relation oppresses society; it now threatens to destroy it.

MARXISM AND SCIENCE

In the next chapter, I will further examine the question of historical agents of transformation. Leaving it aside for the present, there is little doubt that there are practical and theoretical grounds for the call for a new relation between humans and nature. The concept that nature exists "for us" must be abandoned. This is not principally an epistemological question about the existence of nature as prior to and independent of human will, for such a formulation does not lead necessarily to the recognition of the autonomy of nature. On the contrary, the position that admits of nature's priority only in an historical and epistemological sense may not be incongruent with the domination of nature, for it implies no normative stance against such domination. As Horkheimer and Adorno have shown, the materialist distancing of humans from nature may be the necessary condition for social production that takes mastery of nature as its central task.

When society recognizes itself as a part of natural history, but adopts a telos identical with the task of transcending its dependence on nature, it creates a new *science* as its instrument to achieve this objective. The separation of quantity from quality, the discovery of laws of nature that obey the requirement that the object of inquiry be subject to measurement, experimental procedures that require abstraction, the universal system, and regularity, these are the key normative structures that constitute the metaconceptual *a priori* of scientific thinking. They are also prior to observation. Scientific conceptualization is subject to the socially imposed requirement that nature's movements be predicted and controlled, in order to meet human ends, whether these ends are motivated by the fear of the environment, profit, or the reproduction of the species. Historical materialism joins Habermas's argument that these purposes are "rational" and not subject to alteration from the political perspective.

Political ecology does not necessarily accompany its critique of the uses of science and technology with a challenge to their normative and conceptual foundations. In its liberal version it merely argues for a more rational use of such resources as the forces of production have developed in the interest of the preservation of human life. The reason for this omission is that liberal ecology, like much of Marxism, separates the domination of *nature* from *human* domination. This connection is difficult to grasp unless we understand that what is meant by "rational calculation" has become the universal *a priori* of human praxis under capitalism. Just as nature is reduced to its abstract, measurable features, so the labor process, consumption, politics, and public life are subject to administration that assumes specialization of the division of labor to be its major tools. The management of things (nature) and persons occurs within the same conceptual frame: the object is emptied of all qualities that may be "disturbances" in the quest for prediction and control. In science, variables that may distort measurement are eliminated in the experimental process; in production the aim of management is – as Braverman and others have demonstrated – to reduce to the absolute minimum those elements of labor skill, workers' choice and fatigue that may obstruct the process of the production of exchange values, measured in units of abstract time. But our external environment, our psychic structure (the two senses of nature) are concrete material objects that can neither be reduced to their quantitative aspects for the purposes of control, nor exploited instrumentally, without dire consequences for us.

Thus, if modern science is socially produced, and society's influence not only dictates its uses but conditions its conceptual structures, new scientific and technical norms must be discovered if the goal of human emancipation is to inform social and natural scientific theory. One of the elements of this reconstruction is already present in Habermas's own alternative to Marcuse's abstract formulation of the question: the proposal for new modes of interaction, for communication practices that are "emancipatory." Science and technology, whose collective character is already established *within* the framework of capital's priorities, insists on its autonomy *not* from social purposes but from those that *subsume* it under capitalist accumulation. The reflexivity of science – which has already emerged partially, insofar as science has become somewhat suspicious of the technical rationality to which capital and the state subordinate it – would be extended to its mode of inquiry into nature. It would subject the experimental method to critical examination, particularly the processes of abstraction by which the object of knowledge is considered in a one-sided manner.

In this connection Paul Feyerabend has made a significant contribution to the critique of the hegemonic ideology, according to which modern, enlightenment science is regarded as a continuous process of theory formation according to the dictates of reason.[60] Together with Thomas Kuhn,[61] Feyerabend shows that – contrary to the prevailing ideologies of science – new scientific paradigms are not internally related to the old ones. Nor, as Kuhn argues, are they derived from anomalies that appear in the course of normal procedures of the previous paradigm. Even if Kuhn wishes to ground transformations in paradigms of science in the discontinuous – by demonstrating that changes in scientific theories do not correspond to the problems or the structure of the old theories – he still posits a kind of cunning of progressive reason, because he holds that the new paradigm "solves" the problems that the old theories were unable to answer without calling themselves into question.

Feyerabend's demonstration that modern science is not a *superior* explanation for the same phenomena, compared to that offered by, say, Ptolemaic science, led him to the conclusion that in our era the dominant paradigm of natural science is merely different, its dominance derived from social, rather than scientific, sources. Older scientific paradigms were grounded in rigorous experimental procedures, sought quantifiable and falsifiable measures of their validity, and were as comprehensive as those proposed by Copernicus, Galileo and Kepler. Therefore, Feyerabend argues, new scientific paradigms arise from extra-scientific influence. Neither the vicissitudes of the methods of science, nor internal crises such as anomalies arising from the data derived from empirical procedures, account for change. Feyerabend is looking for a theory of *ideological* hegemony, but he is unable to find one because he is still gripped methodologically by the philosophical *a prioris* of the analytic tradition from which he draws sustenance, which demands purely logical critique as the procedure of inquiry. This is not to undervalue such procedures. They are an important corrective to the Marxist penchant for the pure content analysis that reduces all logical problems to those of ideology.

Recently Marxist philosophy has begun to appropriate the work of writers such as Kuhn and Feyerabend who – following Karl Popper and the analytic tradition of science philosophy – have criticized the concepts of progress that underlie traditional scientistic discourse. *The analytic mode of critique is what has become important for some tendencies of contemporary Marxism.* By focusing on the ambiguity of the language of science itself – as well as providing a way to challenge its presuppositions of continuous, "normal" progress as an internally generated discourse – the new philosophy of science, despite its reluctance to push further to a critique of society itself, has opened the way for the self-critique of Marxism as a kind of scientific ideology. Feyerabend has posited that the appearance of new science is linked to the old science by their common object.[62] Beyond a single object of knowledge, he argues scientific theories are only commensurable insofar as the broad categories of evidence and verification remain similar. But he has yet to specify the connection of any scientific paradigm to social structures of specific social needs. His "anarchistic" theory of science advocates the proliferation of scientific theories in a free society and denies the hegemonic status of any of them. Thus, there is a missing term in this philosophy. On the one side Feyerabend demonstrates the arbitrary break between old and new theories (arbitrary in the sense that there is no progression from one to the other arising from their internal constitution). On the other side, he offers a program that calls for a hundred flowers of theories to bloom. But because there is no satisfactory social theory of the dominance of a single paradigm, his program remains an ethical ideal which, however commendable, rests exclusively on the validity of another argument: that hegemony is not rooted in the claim of a paradigm to self-critical reflection by means of falsifiability, since all of them possess such procedures.

The technicization of scientific reason is revealed in the increasing tendency of philosophers and scientists to define its field of knowledge as the solution of problems which Larry Laudan, for example, argues are applicable to the solution of all types of problems.[63] Laudan provides an idea of theory within science that illustrates the degree to which science has become defined by the criteria of technical reason informed by domination:

> If problems are the focal point of scientific thought, theories are its end result. Theories matter, they are cognitively important, insofar as – and only insofar as – they provide adequate solutions for problems. If problems constitute the questions of science, it is theories which constitute the answers. The function of a theory is to resolve ambiguity, to reduce irregularity to uniformity, to show what happens is somehow intelligible and predictable. . .[64]

Thomas Kuhn ascribes changes in the construction of scientific paradigms to the anomalies which appear in the course of scientific investigation and which cannot be explained within the old theoretical matrix. These anomalies are "data" which do not fit in the old structure, which now becomes unable to solve scientific problems by means of available theories. Laudan's critique is that Kuhn ignores the *conceptual* problems in science, confining his explanation for change in science to the nonconformity of the data to the paradigm. Laudan focuses on the conceptual problems – particularly conflicts between competing scientific theories – on the basis of *different models of rationality*, conditions that make theories incompatible because they are otherwise inconsistent with one another, or entail a consequence that renders one or both implausible.

Conceptual problems have a variety of sources, according to Laudan. These sources vary from those which are "normative" – where questions of method such as types of inference are involved – to "world view" issues, to those where scientific theory violates non-scientific beliefs (such as occurs when religious conceptions of creation conflict with biological evolution). Laudan has taken traditional scientific philosophy a step beyond its preoccupation with showing that scientific knowledge is internally generated cumulatively, or with demonstrating that problems in scientific theory are principally empirically-based. He points the way to discussing science as a kind of ideology, insofar as its rationality is based in part on socially-generated conditions.

Laudan has gone further than most Marxist and non-Marxist writers in admitting that scientific progress is not inevitable, even if theory increases the problem-solving effectiveness of science. By stressing that scientific problems are in the realm of normative considerations and cannot be considered entirely ideology-proofed, Laudan has – despite his failure to specify the social context within which scientific theory develops – opened the Pandora's box that might lead to a new conception of science. Nevertheless, he remains on the terrain of the programatic, instrumental view of science as a means to solve problems, as the generalized world view of all social practice.

Theory emerges from its historical context. The conceptual foundations it appropriates are not free of those ideological preconditions established by the society within which science exists. Its problem-solving character insures that the "external" conditions for scientific progress influence its internal structure. But the "problem" orientation as it is defined by philosophers and scientists alike must itself be challenged. Suppose Laudan is right: modern science is about problems and theories are results of this problem-orientation. What follows is a model of rationality in which theory, despite its conceptual presuppositions (which may be grounded in social ideologies such as religion or "scientific" ideologies inherent in procedures of logical inference, is dependent on the conditions for scientific investigation. Capital requires that science be subject to its transformation into technology, that its theories be capable of instrumentalization. If Laudan is right, one would expect to find the imprint of technical reason upon science both with respect to its uses *and* its conceptual presuppositions. Hence, an emancipatory movement requires a *new* science, because it would have to be based on a different rationality for knowledge than that which currently prevails. Among the tenets of this rationality would be the construction of a science on a non-instrumental basis, one in which the problems posed would be recontextualized in terms of different conceptions of social need.

Such was the case with historical materialism, which arose to solve a definite set of problems posed by the consolidation of the bourgeois revolution on the basis of class domination. In Laudan's model, Marxism's theory of historical periodicity – in which the modes of production of material life are the determining instances of social life, and whose categories reduce the apparent chaos of the bourgeois market to order, developing categories of production that make intelligible and predictable capital's evolution – corresponds to science. Adorno and Habermas have attempted, each in different ways, to resolve the crisis of historical materialism at a theoretical level, by altering its conceptual foundations rather than by relying on empirical anomalies. Among the normative foundations of Marxism, the problem-solving character of science and technology is taken for granted. The "problem of science" is how to achieve mastery over a nature rendered alien by a multiplicity of historical forces, including the rise of capital and modern science itself. Marxism applied this problematic to society. The task of theory was to uncover the "laws of motion" of history, especially capitalism, in order to better predict the future and control it through forms of human intervention. Marxism's will to uniformity constitutes its major weakness. Even though Marx himself insisted that the social totality was constituted by multiple determinations, the mode of production (consisting of forces and relations of production) was the infrastructure or the final determination.

It is precisely this conception of scientific law that requires overhaul. To subsume our relations with nature under productive forces may have been an accurate description of the actual movement of the history of dialectic of the labor process, but it is no longer acceptable in the light of the discovery that the "mastery" of nature is not unproblematic. Therefore, production itself becomes problematic, and history can only be made consciously by recognizing nature's "needs." The rational management of society would entail recognition of what Leiss has termed the "limits of satisfaction." The radical historicism proposed by Georg Lukács would be rejected since human history is, among other things, constituted by adaptation to its external conditions. A new critical science of history would render the motto "human history is part of natural history" intrinsic to its normative structures.

The return to philosophy suggested by this formulation means that Engels's statement that "the metaphysical outlook in natural science has become impossible due to the development of the latter" must be rejected.[65] For the question is not the priority of philosophy over science, but the recognition that science is not without philosophical presuppositions.[66] In order to recognize that nature has needs which are not subject to human mastery, a distinction must be made between *nature* as a socially-constructed category and the *external world* which is not. The starting point for a new materialist philosophy of the future is to sharply demarcate a world which is not in principle subject to human mastery and one which is. To conflate the two is to submit to the presupposition of domination of nature, to which we are heir. The *external world* is larger than *nature*; there are even aspects of human nature that are part of the external world and therefore not subsumed by history. Nature, then, is that portion of the external world subject to human action, in order to extract from it the raw materials for the satisfaction of historical needs. But these needs cannot be understood as sovereign. They are conditioned by, and must ultimately be subordinate to, the natural "order," not conceived as a self-contained "object" outside us. The epistemological premises of this conception must be rigorously rejected. However, the antinomy of objectivism and pure historicism is equally untenable. By making the distinction between nature and the external world we define the limits of human action upon nature, for nature itself becomes only that part of the world which can *safely* be subsumed under production.

This does not imply a return to Aristotelian thought, in which the object becomes a "metaphysical" substance not subject to transformation through labor. In principle labor may – to the detriment of human life, including ethical life – dispense with substantiality. Essentialism is indefensible from the historical perspective as well as the perspective of modern science, which has discovered that nothing in nature is immune from human intervention. Nevertheless, the discovery of the limits of human intervention takes place at the moment when the survival of the species is called into question. In addition, as needs are created for a social world without hierarchy and domination, the present configuration of the extension of domination to the entire external world – and through genetic and cultural engineering the world of second nature as well – becomes increasingly intolerable from the point of view of these needs. Thus, philosophy's task is to draw the limit of human intervention into the natural order by making a categorical distinction between nature and the world independent of human will, which we will define as "external."

FEMINISM AND MARXISM

This is another way of posing the challenge made by feminism to Marxist theory. For although Marxist-feminism has recognized the relative autonomy of partriarchy from class structure, it has been unwilling to go further than to admit that the transformation of relations of production would not solve the problems of sexual hierarchy. Yet, there is no linkage within Marxist-feminism between the domination of nature and the oppression of women. To make this connection would be to undertake a fundamental critique of the philosophical anthropology of Marxism, for which the civilizing process is identical with the mastery of nature on the basis of the rationality of scientific and technological progress. The feminist critique of Marxism is fundamentally oriented to the issue of women as the otherness of civilization, the human analogue to the project of the subordination of the external world to human will, except women in this paradigm become "nature" to male humanity.

There are two critiques of this position from a feminist perspective. One, commonly referred to as *cultural feminism*, argues that male domination is rooted in biological difference between men and women. The subjugation of women takes place *transhistorically* by force. Men have captured social power in order to maintain privileges. In effect, the human concomitant of the domination of nature is the domination of women. Women are dominated ideologically as well as physically to the extent that they become convinced that male power is rooted in nature and is therefore just.[67]

Cultural feminism recognizes no historical specificity to women's oppression, and ends up in a non-political separatist stance. In contrast, some kinds of *radical feminists* have typically acknowledged the transhistorical character of women's oppression and joined in the criticism of Marxism's refusal to recognize that the domination of nature is also the domination of women by men; that women come to believe in a sexual division of labor where women exclusively bear and raise children is, in itself, an aspect of oppression. Further, some tendencies in radical feminism oppose the family, and oppose Marxism's refusal to comprehend the degree to which the family is the representative institution of patriarchial society. The concept of patriarchy – where male domination is institutionalized and made an aspect of the "natural order" – becomes, for these feminists, prior to and independent of class as an explanation for human domination.[68] For it is in the relations between men and women that the domination of nature is most clearly revealed. Just as, out of fear, humans dominate nature by the procedure of distancing themselves from abstracting nature's qualitative features, so men dominate women by divesting them of qualities that are not subsumable under family life. When Freud complains that women's needs are incomprehensible by rational investigation, this is a sign that women have become the Kantian unknowable from the point of view of patriarchy. Freud's inability to discern women's wants also reveals a form in which women have become, for men, nature's displacement. Nature refuses to be subsumed under the sign of the production of human needs; women refuse to be subsumed under the sign of the patriarchical family. The revolt of nature and the revolt of women are historically conditioned. Radical feminist theory is not Marxism's antinomy because it does not equate women's oppression with conceptions of biological hierarchy.

Cultural feminism, following the suggestions of some anthropological theory, often argues that matriarchal societies were primal in human history, and that women are naturally superior because of their capacity for nurturance arising from the function of procreation. Those feminists who remain unconvinced of this argument assert, however, that women are not subsumable under class because the institution of patriarchy may be compatible with the socialist movement as it really exists. For even if capital as a social relation is abolished, if ownership of the means of production no longer rests in private hands, it does not follow that women achieve liberation from the patriarchal order as long as the fundamental institutions of male domination – the family and the sexual division of labor – remain.

THE QUESTION OF FAMILY

The question of the family remains ambiguous within Marxist theory, despite Marx's and Engels's well-known opinion that marriage is a form of prostitution. Their critique was, of course, directed against Hegel's attempt to situate the "whole" individual into the family, which he identified as the ethical site of human existence.[69] Marxism has shown that the family is situated within the complex of capitalist social relations, from which it cannot escape, however much it wishes to do so. The marriage act is itself an instance of commodity exchange. The modern bourgeois family embodies a contract between consenting parties, wherein a woman agrees to occupy the man's bed in return for which she gains economic security (of a sort). Of course, the working-class family retains the form of the bourgeois contract, but little of its substance. As often as not in advanced capitalist and "really existing" socialist societies, women are obliged to become wage laborers as well as workers in the home. This double burden exacerbates the injustice of family relation, even from the strictly bourgeois point of view. Further, by consenting to monogamy women must theoretically renounce pure sexual pleasure, as Horkheimer has pointed out.[70] Thus, there is a triple burden on women which no concept of the family as a "haven" can erase. At best, according to Horkheimer, "the family was a place where . . . suffering could be given free expression and the injured individual found a retreat within which he could put up some resistance." But Horkheimer was talking about what he called the "golden age of the bourgeois order" where – despite the fact that all of its members were being reduced to "sub-human status" both within the sphere of the market system and within the family itself – "relationships were not mediated through the market and individual members were not competing with each other."[71]

Horkheimer's dialectic of the bourgeois family remains the most eloquent description within Marxist literature of the way in which the family maintained a two-sided character. However, the use of the pronoun "he" to describe its virtues excludes women not only discursively but also from the lived experience of its ethical/tragic character. Women are "domestic servants" but also wage workers, imprisoned in mores that demand sexual repression as the price of respectability. The capacity of women to legally contest child custody in most countries still depends on their ability to show that they have observed the canon of repressed sexuality. Since Marxism's critique of sexuality has remained its *social* Achilles heel, it has been unable to go beyond the critique of the *bourgeois* family to an understanding of women's oppression in both capitalist and state-socialist societies. This view is contrary to Marcuse's assured statement that the "sexual question" no longer retained its subversive content in the face of repressive desublimation, where sex became a free object of consumption, available to all, because technological rationality destroyed even the vestiges of bourgeois morality.[72] First, Marcuse's optimism/pessimism was situated in the 1960's when a genuine cultural revolution occurred that, to a certain degree, was based upon its rejection of prevailing morality.

His judgement was directed against the tendency of that movement to slide over the recuperative aspects of sexual freedom. Second, the counterattack of the hegemonic forces of social order that rage to this day, has partially succeeded in restraining the impulses of conventional morality, even if the institutions in which they are inscribed have not reasserted themselves unambivalently. Today, in America, the will to marriage and family has once more appeared on the surfaces of public life. At the same time, neither marriage nor the family seems able to stabilize. They are undermined by the fact that cultural transformations have merely gone underground, have become part of what may be termed the "social unconscious."

The crisis of sexual repression rages even as its forms of existence are once more in vogue. While it is still true that many people feel they must marry, or feel they must say they have been married – because marriage is still a sign of desirability, and the need for community has not been fulfilled by either political or social forms – desire cannot be contained by the old institutions. For as is well known, commodity production is no longer an activity that is grounded simply in the old so-called "material" needs of food, clothing and shelter. It now lives on the new needs as well. Commodity production is *desiring production*, since the Pandora's box of the historicity of needs defies even the ecological norm that satisfaction must recognize its limits. Desiring production is the Sherman tank of the social nexus. It destroys the institutions that it has built in order to reproduce itself. It may be shown that this process owes its origins to the logic of capital, for which the moral order is both necessary and an obstacle to expansion. Yet, Jean Baudrillard is right to insist that capital can no longer be taken as the sole – or even the chief – referent of desiring production.[73] Having released sexuality as a need, capital can only seek to displace desire to commodities as a condition of its own existence. But desire is the ontological need that becomes *surplus* in relation to capital (remember Marx's formula that capital is a surplus in relation to *necessary* labor time). Thus desire is the surplus of the surplus, and the social order is condemned to define itself in terms that undermine the normative structures of imposed discipline and repression.

Those who have appointed themselves the guardians of these normative structures argue, in effect, that the bourgeois family is superior to the atomized individual, who has been rendered defenseless by desiring production.[74] So, however tragic is the fate of the beleaguered family, its ethical character is worth saving in the wake of the degradation of narcissism. But writers like Christopher Lasch – who has recently advocated this "solution" to the current malaise – have missed the point. The family can no longer be a site of resistance, as Horkheimer argued more than forty years ago, because it no longer "fosters human relations which are determined by the woman"[75] without at the same time fostering patriarchal authority. For even if the life experience of people continues to reproduce the family, the revolt against authority is a powerful counter-tendency, grounded in the conditions of commodity and desiring production themselves. This revolt has resulted in the refusal of tens of thousands of women to submit to male authority, even if they are constrained by their need for community or the idealized memory of their family as a site of human relations in the wake of universal dehumanization. The "swinging singles" phenomenon, the "me decade" which has become the object of scorn for contemporary conservative and radical critics alike, is not principally the result of an overweaning culture. The mass migration of single women to the cities occurs under conditions where the culture conspires to devalue lasting relationships except within norms that are both archaic and repressive. The nuclear family disintegrates, re-forms, collapses; women find they are forced, often against their will to seek a voice that does not depend on their place within the family. Yet, as feminist theory has persuasively argued, the woman can have no voice in a language which has evolved under conditions of male domination.[76] The community of women is itelf problematic as long as family remains the unexamined norm of everyday life, especially the discourses of desire. Women temporarily consent to marriage and family relations only because they lack alternatives within heterosexual culture. The "community of women," the slogan of a section of lesbian feminism that argues for separatism, is itself shaped by male discourse, which is prepared to make a place for some women within the social order as its legitimate other. The strategy needed to transform the discourse of human relations cannot be addressed within a separatist problematic, because it accepts the *status quo* as a given within which social life may be reconstructed. And since the hegemony of what Gramsci calls "civil society" wishes to present itself as pluralist – making room for all aspects of desire in a shriveled, truncated form as long as they do not challenge the prevailing order – separatism is part of civil society, a mode of stoicism in the Hegelian sense.

SUMMARY ARGUMENTS

With some tendencies in psychoanalysis, radical feminism is concerned with the sexual emancipation of women which consists in freedom from exclusive child-rearing responsibilities, the end of marriage as a legal bond that confers privileges and obligations by women towards men, and, therefore, the demand to choose sexual relations between partners of either sex on a purely voluntary basis. As is well known, this demand was tolerated in the early years of the Bolshevik Revolution and finally suppressed.[77] The socialist movement, because of its radical historicism, which accords to economic priorities a privileged status, has never adopted the program of sexual emancipation. This reluctance is not only characteristic of "really existing" socialist countries, but of nearly all parties and movements that call themselves Marxist. In sum, historical materialism's critique of domination has remained incomplete. Its refusal to make the process of production of material life – and its presupposition, the domination of nature – normatively problematic, has resulted in its neglecting to undertake a critique of everyday life, the core of which is the patriarchal character of sexual relations, in which woman as nature remains subject to man. It is only when the multiplicity of determinations of society becomes a scientific principle for historical materialism that its reconstruction is possible. This process entails a new conception of the monistic view of science and history hitherto intrinsic to all materialism. It is not a question, as Engels proposes, of reducing human history to natural history, rendering the specifically human a reflection or analogue of physical or biological laws.[78] This project is misdirected because natural history is by no means uniform with respect both to space and time, as recent developments in physics and biology demonstrate. The concept of integrative levels does not imply the identity of nature in the sense of uniformity among various forms of the material world, for such a formulation is socially conditioned by the predisposition of the enlightenment towards finding a universal language of nature capable of treating all objects as instances of mathematical regularity. The process of abstraction, then, has this two-sided character. On the one hand, without the abstraction from particulars relations could not be established. The unique features of things would prevent scientific investigation into the commensurabilities between two apparently unlike objects. Indeed, abstraction (which *necessarily* makes some qualities indifferent in the investigative process) is the *sine qua non* of scientific law. Moreover, theoretical work of any kind requires levels of abstraction that enable us to discern and interpret broad classes of phenomena without regard to their differences, or, to be more exact, to understand the limits of difference.

On the other hand, even as Marx argues, the concrete is concrete precisely because it embodies the most general features of nature and history. Processes of abstraction which are the hallmark of modern social and natural science develop in the context of the division between intellectual and manual labor, in which the former is situated at the apex of the social hierarchy. Abstraction is an objective process, not merely a habit of thought. Within capitalist society, its forms are entwined with the entire structure of economy and social organization. As Sohn-Rethel has shown,[79] abstraction implies the indifference of exchange relations to the use-value of the commodity, except as a technical precondition of production and consumption. Labor as a commodity is reduced to merely a quantum of units of time in order to permit its measurement against the labor time of other producers, the type and quality of whose skills are similarly indifferent to the exchange relation. Science is grounded in the same division between abstract and concrete labor. Its methodological presuppositions, its world view and normative structures, have been taken from this division since the Copernican revolution, in which time, motion, force and space became the coordinates of physics. The mode of existence of science is reductionism. It underlies the search for the elementary particles of matter and the unceasing attempt by natural science to construct the entire life world on these foundations. Similarly, in biology, the discovery of DNA as the basic element of life has generated theories in which these forms are conceived as obedient to the laws governing this basic biochemical substance.

While Marxism has always criticized reductionist thought as an instance of that side of abstraction bound up in capitalist degradation as a form of the reproduction of domination, it has failed to come to grips with its own penchant for discovering the mathematic-like equations that mark social processes. Having discovered in the binary structure of the commodity form, particularly the significance of the opposition between abstract and concrete labor for the labor theory of value, Marxism has conflated its own scientific practice with its critique of society. For as Alvin Gouldner has argued,[80] historical materialism's fate as a one-sided science derives from its failure to become reflexive, that is, to comprehend its own historicity. Historical materialism has taken abstraction as a theoretical principle and fallen into the mire of positivism in the bargain. For Marx's discovery of the laws of motion of capitalism in the processes of accumulation has been hypostatized into a productivist bias. Jean Baudrillard[81] and Marshall Sahlins[82] have argued that historical materialism – relying on the concept of the mode of production as the structural form that totalizes historical periods – is ensconced in the ideological presuppositions of nineteenth-century industrialism. For Baudrillard, Marxism's own historicity lies not only in its hypostatization of production, labor and productivity but also in its reading back into history the concept of the mode of production as the motive force of all societies. Baudrillard finds that historical materialism "naturalizes" earlier societies "under the sign of the mode of production."

There is much merit in this critique. First, the concept of the mode of production as the structuring or constituting instance of human societies in the past and present is an instance of Marxism's penchant for uniformity. While production has been the central obsession of bourgeois social development, it becomes implausible with respect to the comprehension of all past societies. Second, even if economics takes command in bourgeois culture, rendering politics, art, communication, and other human activities its adjuncts, Marxism until recently failed to grasp the materiality and autonomy of culture just as historical linguistics remained oblivious to the materiality of the word.

However, Baudrillard and other critics of Marxism's productivism have not posed the central problem. Marxism fears that to abandon the concept of the mode of production as a unifying principle is to lapse into a position in which history no longer retains its lawful character. This concern is not answered adequately by those like Habermas, Sahlins, and Baudrillard, who can point to the metaphysics implied by the "mirror of production" as the reflection of all social life. The problem lies in the will of historical materialism towards *scientificity*, not so much in its dogmatic insistence upon production and labor as romantic *a priori* categories. Indeed, Habermas's argument for the incommensurability of production and interaction proved untenable; he was required to turn to systems theory, the genetic developmentalism of Piaget and Kohlberg, and the functionalism of American sociology to bail himself out of the leaky boat of dualism. Baudrillard has merely substituted a social semiotic for the mode of production, that is, has taken *language and culture* as the leading elements of late capitalism and argued that labor is subsumed under its sign. Nor does the Marxist-structuralist solution, stressing the mode of production as a non-heteronomous system of systems in which history is constituted as a series of conjunctures and the subject itself is conjunctural, offer more than a valuable critique of the orthodox reductionism of both Hegelian and vulgar Marxism. For while Althusser stresses difference as a distinguishing feature of his notion of the structured totality (a unity of objective structures rather than the identity of subject and object), he remains within the problematic of historicism; his theoretical categories – "relative autonomy" of structures within the totality, the non-identity of the real object and the object of knowledge, the difference between the imaginary and the real – address the problem of the formalization of the dialectic as well as the abstractness of concepts of totality, but they have not escaped the humanism against which he argues. For the fundamental presupposition of humanism is not only the postulate of the *a priori* subject. It is also the assertion of the historical as a sphere radically disjoined from nature. Nevertheless, it is in Althusser's own theory of ideology – as the lived experience of the relation to the real of that which is prior to symbolization – that the germ of a theory capable of overcoming historicism is contained. His belief that the unconscious is part of history, as ideology which cannot be overcome by historical change, is a significant advance in social theory because it refuses the rationalism characteristic in most Marxist thought, insisting that humans are constituted by non-commensurable rationalities that are in perpetual conflict.

In its passion to oppose the idealism of those who, following Kant, were unable to find the historical basis for ethics, Marxism denied that its own theory presupposed a system of norms. These norms privilege the most general features of historical development over their specificity. Marxism is profoundly historicist insofar as it occludes nature on the one side and subjectivity on the other. Nature is subsumed under human history, and subjectivity is merely the bearer of historical forces. Herein lie the antinomies of

Marxist thought. On the one hand, theory proceeds on the solid foundation of scientific historical law; on the other, politics and culture remain the sphere of art because historical materialism has no conceptual framework for grasping the relation between the two without recourse to semantically ambiguous terms such as the "relative autonomy of the superstructure" or "putative" class consciousness.

NOTES

44. Karl Marx, *Eighteenth Brumaire of Louis Bonaparte.*
45. Karl Marx and Frederick Engels, *The German Ideology.*
46. Alfred Schmidt, *The Concept of Nature in Marx* (London: New Left Books, 1979), p. 79.
47. Kostas Axelos, *Alienation and Techne in the Thought of Karl Marx* (Austin: University of Texas Press, 1976). This is an important Heideggerian reading of the early writings of Marx that has received too little attention in the Anglo-American Marxist debate precisely because of its philosophical orientation.
48. Karl Marx, *Grundrisse*, quoted in Schmidt, *The Concept of Nature*, op. cit., p. 81.
49. Schmidt, passim.
50. Serge Moscovici, *Society Against Nature* (London: Harvester Press, 1976), pp. 27–30. Habermas relies on this text for the empirical argument that interaction rather than labor distinguishes humans from animals.
51. Louis Althusser and Etienne Balibar, *Reading Capital* (London: New Left Books, 1970). Thus the social formation is no longer, in this conception, viewed as a category of labor, but becomes a system of systems that includes not only our relation to nature and the relations of production but also the entire set of relations that are grouped under the rubric of "superstructure." I would claim that the specificity of the determining instance of the economic infrastructure is lost in the concept of social formation as a totality of relatively autonomous sub-systems.
52. See Sigmund Freud, *Interpretation of Dreams*, Chapter 7; also S. Freud, "The Unconscious," (1915) in Sigmund Freud, *General Psychological Theory*, Phillip Rieff, ed. (New York: Collier Books, 1963). Lacan showed that Freud held the unconscious intelligible by means of decoding: "the unconscious is structured like a language," and that the task of psychoanalysis is to break the code by which it hides itself from understanding through a reading of symptoms as signs of real relations. However, Freud always insisted that to bring the speech of the unconscious to the surface was not the same as controlling it. *In principle*, conscious life can never subsume the unconscious under its processes.

53. Sigmund Freud, *Civilization and its Discontents* (New York: W.W. Norton, 1961).
54. Karl Marx, *German Ideology* (New York: International Publishers).
55. The dream that conscious existence may subsume its other, the unconscious, is a valuable utopian hope, but must remain unrealizable so long as labor – where the domination of nature remains the condition for the reproduction of our species – entails the necessary repression of desire. At the same time, the critique of domination holds out the promise that our collective sphere of conscious existence, its ability to make rational our social relations and relations to the external world, will expand.
56. William Leiss, *The Limits to Satisfaction* (Toronto: University of Toronto Press, 1978), p. 113–14.
57. Ibid., p. 116.
58. Andre Gorz, *Strategy for Labor* (Boston: Beacon Press, 1967).
59. Serge Mallet, *The New Working Class* (Nottingham: Spokesman Books, 1975).
60. Paul Feyerabend, *Against Method* (London: New Left Books, 1975).
61. Thomas Kuhn, *The Structure of Scientific Revolutions* (Chicago: University of Chicago Press, 1962), p. 169.
62. Compare this formulation to Louis Althusser's argument that Marxism becomes a science of society when Marx effects an epistemological break from the Hegelian and humanist assumptions of his own early work. For Althusser, science is constituted in the first instance by its critique of the old science as a form of ideology by means of the positing of a new object of knowledge. If Feyerabend is correct in his claim that the Copernican revolution did not constitute a new object, then it cannot be considered the break from which modern natural science lays claim to have founded a new science of nature in Althusserian terms. Feyerabend tries to show that the old Ptolemaic science fulfills all the conditions of contemporary experimental method as defined by scientific philosophy since Bacon, including a means of falsifying its results. If this is true, Newtonian physics and all that followed achieved hegemony by means other than the truth claims of its scientific paradigm. That is, the difference between modern physics and its predecessors cannot by marked by some methodological *a priori* theory of what constitutes science.
63. Larry Laudan, *Progress and its Problems* (Berkeley: University of California Press, 1978).
64. Ibid., p. 13.
65. Frederick Engels, *Dialectic of Nature* (Moscow: Progress Publishers, n.d.).
66. Although Engels understood that it was not without historical preconditions. He repeats the well-known nineteenth- and twentieth-century position that Copernicus freed science from theology. However, Engels adds: in response to the development of world trade and the emergence of the bourgeoisie as a distinctive social class.
67. Mary Daly, *Gyn-Ecology*; Susan Griffith, *Woman Against Nature*.
68. Shulamith Firestone, *Dialectic of Sex* (New York: Vintage, 1968).

69. G.W.F. Hegel, *Philosophy of Right* (New York: Oxford University Press, 1965).
70. Max Horkheimer, "The Authoritarian State," op. cit.
71. Ibid.
72. Herbert Marcuse, *One Dimensional Man*. This view contrasted sharply with his earlier position in *Eros and Civilization* (1955), that erotic activity was subversive to the prevailing social order since the order rested, in a large measure, on the repression of the pleasure principle. In the early 1960's Marcuse concluded that pleasure could be used by consumer society to insure its own reproduction.
73. For a fuller discussion of the relation between desiring production and commodity production see Gilles Deleuze and Felix Guattari, *Anti-Oedipus* (New York: Viking Press, 1977). The authors try to solve the antinomy between production and culture by positing their mutual relation and antagonism. At the same time they deny the privileged place of one over the other by transcoding sexuality into the Marxist categories of labor. The starting effect of this move is to *remove* desire from its marginal place in both Marxist and liberal discourse, placing it on equal footing with labor.
74. Whence Christopher Lasch's critique of narcissism, in which the heresy of self-love is regarded as socially disintegrative. See Christopher Lasch, *Culture of Narcissism* (New York: Harper and Row, 1979).
75. Max Horkheimer, "The Authoritarian State," op. cit.
76. Luce Irigary, "That Sex which is not One," in *Language, Sexuality and Subversion*, ed. Paul Foss and Meagan Morris (Darlington: Feral Publications, 1978).
77. Alexandra Kollantai, *Writings* (New York: Lawrence Hill, 1976).
78. Frederick Engels, *Dialectics of Nature*, "Introduction."
79. Alfred Sohn-Rethel, *Intellectual and Manual Labor* (London: Macmillan, 1978).
80. Alvin Gouldner, *Dialectic of Technology and Ideology* (New York: Seabury Press, 1976).
81. Jean Baudrillard, *Mirror of Production* (St. Louis: Telos Press, 1975). But Baudrillard has failed to grasp the way in which Marx and Marxism have insisted upon the concept of mode of production in precapitalist societies. For Marx, it was a question of grasping the past as totality and developing a theory of historical periodicity. Historical materialism is a way of making social relations intelligible without resorting to the older notions of world spirit. That is, Marx insisted that history was a process of interaction between conscious and unconscious elements and was grounded in human action without which the reproduction of real life was not possible. To date, no metatheory has succeeded as well as Marxism in grasping human history as a process of constant change. Its value is to have provided a *rational* explanation of historical development. The real objection, then, is not the way in which Marxism's rationality proceeds, as Baudrillard claims. The problem is the constitution of "the rational" in Western theory as such.
82. Marshall Sahlins, *Culture and Practical Reason* (Chicago: University of Chicago Press, 1976).

4

The Question of Class

There can be no historical materialism without a theory of class. Asserting that history is made by human actors, historical materialism explicitly rejects the view which prevailed in nineteenth-century historical writing that ascribed the making of history either to individuals (Roosevelt, Stalin, Napoleon, etc.) or to the objectification of great ideas. In place of these idealist theories, Marx held that it was classes – groups located in a definite relation to the ownership and control of the means of production – whose mutual and antagonistic relations constituted history and social structure. Marx's famous formulation, "history is the history of class struggles," refused to situate social causality outside the power of humans over their own fate. Even Marx's invocation that we cannot make history "as we please" but are constrained by the conditions that we find already in existence cannot obviate the central importance he attached to the capacity of humans to determine their own future.

Vulgar historical materialism after Marx tended to advance the notion that the proletariat – owing to its unique historical situation under capitalism as both the most exploited class and the most oppressed class capable of self-organization – made history. This was seen as a sufficient argument for the thesis of the inevitability of socialism. Given the periodic capitalist economic crises that would deprive the workers of their means of subsistence on an ever-deepening and immiserating scale, the task of the Party was to organize the proletariat to fulfill its historic mission. But, as Adam Przeworski has convincingly shown,[83] the problem of the working class as revolutionary agency consists not only in its historic reluctance to constitute itself as a revolutionary class within advanced capitalism, but also in the very concept of the proletariat as an objective *a priori* class itself.

We begin with Przeworski because he has placed most decisively the question of historical agency in plain view: The trouble with Marxism has been to take the proletariat as a class as an unproblematic category. It has assumed that there is a proletarian class on the basis of an undialectical conception of history. Marxism accepts the proletarian class as among the constituents of capitalism, failing to grasp that as long as capitalism develops, classes are bound to form as the result of struggles (rather than the other way around). The novelty of Przeworski's theory of class lies in his insistence that class formation results from struggles *about* class: only *under certain conditions* do economic, political, and ideological relations make possible such formations.

Przeworski also argues that the relations of production, the location of groups within the labor process, do not "uniquely" determine struggles within capitalist society. The struggles that may lead to class formation are, according to Przeworski,

> structured by the totality of economic, political and ideological relations; and they have an autonomous effect upon the process of class formation. But if the struggles have an autonomous effect upon class formation, then the places in the relations of production . . . can no longer be viewed as objective in the sense of the problematic of "class-in-itself" that is in the sense of determining uniquely what classes will emerge as classes in struggle. What this implies is that classification of positions must be viewed as imminent to the practices that (may) result in class formation.[84]

Przeworski has opened several different questions within the Marxist theory of class. First, he rejects the theory of historical inevitability by showing that classes are not part of the *given* of capitalist society. The formation of classes is seen as an effect of relations which are not located uniquely in the relations of production in the strict sense, although he adopts the Althusserian concept of a structured totality (the mode of production) of autonomous parts. Second, he has redefined the nature of social struggles as discontinuous, determined in the last instance by the stage of capitalist development in which particular groups (widows, intellectuals, clerks, whoever) are prompted to oppose capital's effects upon whatever terrain (economic, political, ideological) struggles are situated. Third, the industrial proletariat is accorded *no* privileged status in class formation, since it, too, is an effect of the course of capitalist development which – because of the development of science, technology and the state sector as leading institutions in late capitalism – may diminish in historical significance.

Przeworski demands that Marxism be true to itself, that it adhere in its class theory to the principle of historical specificity, that it abolish its own *a priorism*. Przeworski has followed the lead of the Althusserian critique of the notion of classes as continuous subjects whose existence and effects are independent of historical change except between modes of production. Historical subjects are *themselves* an effect of struggles about class formation, whose discontinuity is determined by phases of capitalist development which are in turn the outcome of the relatively autonomous economic, political, and ideological relations within the totality of social relations. Although capital tends to proletarianize larger numbers of those engaged in petty commodity production such as farming and trade, independent professions, and craft work, these strata do not necessarily become part of the relations of the reproduction of capital; they do not become *productive* workers. Yet the very process by which they become proletarianized (alienated from the ownership of productive means) leads to struggles on the economic terrain that may have the effect of spurring class formations which are not proletarian in the old sense. Similarly, groups with economic and social interests may choose to engage in struggles by mobilizing within or against political or ideological institutions. For Przeworski, these struggles may effect or may not effect class formation, depending on the specific phase of capitalist development which forms the context in which they occur.

It must by now be evident that the distinction between infrastructure and superstructure – which relies for its validity upon the critical weight of the productive relations and the classificatory concept that class formation is given by conditions of the reproduction of capital *per se* – disappears. The concepts of class formation offered by Lenin and Luckács are also denied: one may no longer propose the party or its ideology as sufficient for transforming an already-formed proletarian class into a conscious historical agent. For Przeworski has asserted that (1) whether classes will form is contingent on the social formation as its determining instance, and (2) when and if they do form, a particular formation may not become a revolutionary class if the political and ideological conditions are not present. The course of social struggles may *not* produce classes that become crucial historical actors in the Marxist sense; if they do, opposition may not be located in "places" occupied by the working class.

An excellent example of this point is provided by the U.S. and British working classes. The British working class has succeeded in organizing itself both on the political and economic terrains as an independent political party, but its ideological orientation remains within, and not oppositional to, the bourgeois order. Self-representation does not signal revolutionary consciousness, because this is not an effect (at least in the recent past) of struggles resulting in the formation of a working class at the political and economic level. Ideological relations are relatively autonomous, even under conditions of crisis in the reproduction of capital. In the United States, the working class has barely succeeded in constituting itself as an independent force for its immediate economic interests, and has not attained the level of political class-formation within capitalism, much less constituting itself as ideological oppositional. Thus Przeworski, following Poulantzas, insists upon the purely conjunctural nature of class formation, abandoning (1) the *a priori* conception of class that relies exclusively on structural criteria such as location within the relations of production, as well as (2) the position of the early Marx that the proletariat is a class "in radical chains." Further, class consciousness is not seen as derived from the place occupied by social actors since, as Gramsci has argued, ideological relations are independent within the social totality.[85]

Przeworski has provided the most radical critique of Marxist orthodoxy in class theory until now, combining a theory of historical specificity with a theory of conjuncture to explain the appearance of classes. At the same time, he holds firmly to the view that historical opposition in this capitalist phase will emerge from those who have been deprived of ownership of the means of production, *but not necessarily those who remain within the productive apparatus*:

> Thus finally we must jettison even the title (proletariat). It is not the proletariat that is being formed into a class; it is a variety of persons some of whom are being separated from the system of production. Processes of forming workers into a class do not take place in a vacuum; rather they are inextricably tied to the totality of processes through which collectivities appear in struggle at particular moments of history. And the outcomes of these processes, while not arbitrary, are not determined uniquely by the structure of social relations. More than one outcome lies within the limits set by those relations.[86]

Przeworski does not go so far as to follow Weber in articulating a theory of class based upon differential market chances for income and goods. The experience of occupational and market-based differentiation "is mediated by the ideological and political practices of the movements engaged in the process of class formation."[87]

Przeworski is concerned to show that those who organize production and those who are indirectly related to the processes of production in late capitalism (state-sector workers, the technical intelligentsia), engage in struggles whose effects may result in class formation as much as the immediate producers. He insists on the social *totality*, and not merely the labor process, as the historical context for class formation. Further, political mobilization of these groups, as well as ideological struggles, are relevant for class formation. The particular combinations that succeed in effecting class formation, the multiplicity of determinations that constitute classes are (in the final analysis) not subject to prediction and control, since historical actors are formed out of complex processes which may be specified (in advance) in their *structural* limits but not their *temporal* course. At any given phase of capitalist development, theory may identify those collectivities that have the best chances to participate in the process of class formation because of their propensity to engage in struggles having what Althusser calls "pertinent effects" on the problematic of class struggles.

Of course, like other structuralist approaches to class, Przeworski's omits the questions of political culture and consciousness, subsuming these issues under the rubric of "ideology". Although he makes an effective critique of the work of those like Eric Olin Wright – for whom "places" within the structure of the production process are sufficient to explain the significance of strata in terms of class and historical change – Przeworski too cannot account for which struggles appear at a certain time and which may lead to class formation.[88] For this kind of determination is of a different order than a meditation on the spatial relations of capitalist social structure. One must have a concrete sense of the historical moment to identify the pertinent ideological, cultural, and political changes that may entail struggles about class.

Since Gorz and Mallet attempted in the 1960's to integrate the historical emergence of the professional and technical strata – the principal bearers of *knowledge*, the central productive place of late capitalism – into a theory of historical change and class formation, many theorists have focused upon this question. George Conrad and Istvan Szeleny,[89] Alvin Gouldner, and Rudolph Bahro, among others, have contributed substantially to comprehending the places of these strata within the class structure of advanced capitalism. But Przeworski is not working exclusively within the Marxist problematic of the links between new forces of production and the relations of production. His conception of the variety of persons who may participate in class formation is potentially broader than the idea that new classes are effects of struggles within the processes of material production. The notion that ideological and political relations as well as the struggles of immediate producers (whether mental or manual workers) are possible bases for class formation opens a new terrain for the theory of historical change. Further, the idea that *more than one outcome* may result from a given set of struggle undermines the concept of historical inevitability, with which Marxism has been obsessed for more than a century.

NEW HISTORICAL ACTORS

I do not mean to devalue the importance of recent developments in the Marxist theories of class. Except for the most dogmatic reader of Marx and the Marxists of the Second and Third Internationals, there is little dispute today that those involved in knowledge production, managers, and workers of all categories in the state sector may be significant new historical actors. The disputes around their role and place within the social structure (whether they are progessive or integrated elements within capitalist hierarchy) are both theoretically and empirically important. If Przeworski's suggestions for seeing these questions are to be followed, one may not resolve the problem of the historical significance of particular groups or strata alone on the basis of their *position* within the social structure but must also render concrete the *political* and *ideological* relations of these strata to the system as a whole. Struggles by members of the technical intelligentsia which result in the formation of labor unions may, under conditions of economic crisis lead to political mobilization in a particular ideological context while other conditions might have different effects on class formation. Such has been the case of American state-sector employees who, in the conjuncture with the struggles for black freedom and against the Vietnam war, became among the most militant and ideologically-advanced segments of the American trade unions. In another instance, technical employees of the French media occupied radio and TV stations, newspapers, and cultural institutions during the May events in 1968. In neither situation was it foreordained that these groups would have either engaged in struggles or that the struggles would take the particular form they did. The reticence of public employees to form unions in the wake of the mass labor upsurges of the 1930's and 1940's was a remarkable non-event in the history of the American working class. To employ Ernst Bloch's term, they experienced the depression and its aftermath in a different "now" than industrial workers.[90] The non-synchrony of their relation to the crisis, compared to other categories of workers, is not explained by different economic conditions between private and public sectors, since the loss of job security and the deterioration of working life was in both cases a widespread effect of the offensive of capital. Here we see the workings of ideological relations on group struggles: even as periodic layoffs, pay cuts, and worsening job conditions were being experienced by public employees, the ideology of "public service" prevented all but a handful of them from joining unions. By the early 1960's this ideology had suffered significant erosion. The *objective* proletarianization of segments of the middle strata and clerical workers, combined with the emergence of their *consciousness* of a new relation of the public sector to the social hierarchy produced unionization. The private sector was enjoying a privileged position in the structure of social relations; public employees formed and joined unions in the millions in the 1960's, coincident with both the entrance of young, black, and women workers into the public work force and the simultaneous erosion of the ideology of public service (even as funds for all kinds of state-sector activities increased dramatically). Having decided to join unions, only one of the options available was to make them militant and relatively progressive within the ideological spectrum of the American labor movement. It may be shown that influences extrinsic to the relations of production within the public sector played an enormous role in configuring this development – for example, the black freedom movement and the feminist movement of the late 1960's, both of which derived their social power from ideological and political relations as much as the economic conditions of discrimination and oppression. For what must be explained in the new militancy of younger public employees in the 1960's and 1970's is their willingness to engage in illegal and normatively ambiguous strikes from the perspective of canons of professional ethics, and their widespread politicization towards relatively "progressive" positions. In this instance, feminism and racial nationalism became decisive forces leading to class formation. These movements, grounded in moral as well as economic presuppositions, derive their appeal from the rhetoric of freedom, not merely the promise of equal opportunity that has become the economic hallmark of liberal struggles. Freedom implies a different way of life, new relations between the sexes at the social, cultural as well as economic levels, and the recognition of the transhistorical status of race and nationality. There is no theoretical space for what E. P. Thompson calls the moral economy of different groups within the reductionist assumptions of class theory. Moral and normative structures that cannot be explained by means of the categories of political economy are either ignored or denounced as diversions from "real" struggles.

CLASS AND CULTURE

Here the concerns of the previous chapter conjoin with questions of class formation. Interests and groups defined as marginal because they have become "disturbances" in the system of social integration are precisely the struggles that may be the *most* significant from the point of view of historical emancipation from social hierarchy and domination. Some recent feminist theory insists that women are a *class* whose formation cannot be subsumed under the Marxist schema of historical periodicity because patriarchy is nearly as old as human history – some insist that male superiority is as old as society – and is the mode of structuration of social relations. This suffers, of course, from an error common to Marxism. Patriarchy predates capitalism, but classes are effects of concrete struggles conducted by groups whose political, social, and ideological relations open the possibility for opposition. The struggle of women for social and political emancipation has assumed a powerful place within contemporary political life, outside the realm of the labor process as well as within it. The heart of the women's movement, transcending particular struggles for equality, is the demand for new sexual relations, or to be more precise for the politicization of the sexual. The simple demand for the self-control of women's bodies asks that the mind/body split at the heart of the domination of nature be healed. When women no longer surrender their bodies to scientific manipulation, to patriarchal normative structures that prescribe a certain relation of biology to culture, the infrastructure of social reproduction is impaired. Feminist struggles have the possibility for contributing to a new configuration of classes within contemporary society because they go beyond the limits of economic self-interest. In Marx's own terms, they are conducted *in*, but not *of*, society. The implied demand of feminism for the abolition of patriarchy – which implies the configuration of what we mean by "Western culture" – could have truly revolutionary effects.

The refusal of contemporary Marxism to extend its critique of capitalism to the critique of Western culture is more than an unfortunate form of amnesia. Nor can historical materialism decide that there is a division of intellectual labor in which Marxism and feminism are two complementary theories. Feminist critiques of patriarchy problematize the entire cultural apparatus upon which Western civilization (and most Eastern civilizations as well) rests. Just as Horkheimer warned that those who would not speak of capitalism should keep silent about fascism, since one was the outgrowth of the other, so one might extend the admonition to a Marxism that refuses the feminist attack against hierarchy.

These are not merely questions about "ideology". A culture is the lived experience of a people sedimented in institutions, practices, habits of everyday existence conditioned by the mode of adaptation to the environment. Cultural forms are necessary for the reproduction of society, for sustaining its division of labor and social hierarchy. Within all class societies, intimate relations are not merely necessary for the reproduction of the species. The family, far from being principally "a haven in the heartless world" (in fact, for many it is no haven at all), is preeminently the site in which the collective laborer is constituted ideologically and socially. The threads holding children to society are those woven into family ties, even if school, mass-mediated culture, religion, and other ideological apparatuses have been recruited to repair the ties that become loosened or broken because of changed economic, political, and ideological relations. Even when the child rebels from the authority of parents, particularly the father, it is through forming a new family that the rebellion is satisfied. The family is usually constructed by marriage or its surrogates; there are very few instances where an alternative form is constructed whose place within the social hierarchy opposes the prevailing order.

Feminism's fundamental attack against the patriarchal culture attests to the weaknesses of family relations in late capitalism. For feminist theory is itself an effect of the erosion of patriarchy and male supremacy in the wake of the massive recruitment of women to the labor force, to higher education and to the cities as unmarried adults. Since the family was deprived of its place as the site of production by the modern factory system, it has been placed in the role of guardian of the private sphere, protecting its members from industrial life. Instead, as Carol Ascher, Ann Oakley, and others have pointed out,[91] it has not remained immune from the machine age. Modern appliances and the application of Taylorism to housework and childbearing are ways in which the logic of capital intrudes on the autonomy of the family. As women have discovered that their integration into wage labor has not freed them from the drudgery of housework, they have increasingly, if discontinuously, rebelled against the sexual division of labor in which their presumed "natural" quality of nurturance is pressed into the service of male privilege.

The work of Dorothy Dinerstein, Nancy Chodorow and other feminist theorists[92] has shown that child-bearing has become the double bind tying women to patriarchal domination and becoming the *sine qua non* for the preservation of the family against the erosion visited upon it by ideological and economic relations. The naturalization of child-rearing is the basis of women's oppression: women denied equality in the economic and political spheres find a determinate place in the social hierarchy, one both subordinate to men and secure because it has acquired moral value.

ENVIRONMENTAL ISSUES

A second critical tendency toward a new opposition includes the environmental, ecology and anti-nuclear movements. These three different strains have responded to the subsumption of science and technology under capital by focusing on its effects. Environmentalists have pointed up the dangers that accumulated industrial pollution pose to human life, particularly the release of chemical substances into the air and water supplies. The broad-scale attack against chemical fertilizers, industrial and nuclear waste and the pollution of working environments has politically mobilized millions of persons in advanced-capitalist and state-socialist societies. Environmental movements have entered the electoral arena and have conducted direct action against the interests of big industrial capital and agricultural business.

Similarly, ecologists have extended the critique of industrial technology beyond its immediate effects upon human health and other forms of life by raising the question of the long-term impact of scientifically- and technologically-based culture. Advanced ecological thinking demands that the concept of life be extended to the biosphere, whose rhythms are autonomous from human intervention and must be obeyed in order to sustain our forms of life. This is a proposal to "humanize" nature as a concrete scientific category. It may be objected that such a projection of the concept of life onto the external world is crude anthropomorphism. The reply is the precise reversal of an historical process by which life and non-life were made into dichotomous categories. Since "nature" as distinct from "the universe" is an historical construct, its relations are historical as well. While the application of the concept of "life" to the world in which DNA is not the core is surely metaphoric, ecological thinking refuses this distinction because its effects have been destructive to the biosphere and to what are called "living things." By insisting upon the existence of a universe that is not subject to the ascription of mere otherness, seen logically as merely "not living" or "not human", ecology proposes to undertake not only a searching critique of the domination of nature, but of science and technology as well. As I have already argued in my discussion of the ideological content of science and technology, the absence of an immanent critique weakens the attempt to control the uses of science according to ecological anti-hierarchical criteria. Nevertheless, those who have been able to make scientific and technological practices subject to public debate have contributed to the formation of a new emancipatory movement.

The movements for realigning our relations of "mastery" to our external physical environment raise another issue. Could late capitalism continue to reproduce itself if such a program were adopted? For the applications of the molecular biology of the gene to modifying the genetic makeup of animals (including humans) is fast becoming a major new frontier for investment. Likewise, nuclear power is the great hope that capital can find a solution to rising energy costs resulting from the exhaustion of supplies of non-renewable fossil fuels. Another strategy, extracting oil from shale and water, would entail intensive exploitation and alteration of existing land and sea reserves. Ocean life might disappear from America's coastal waters, and soil erosion of agricultural land and natural recreation areas would occur.

While it is true that the new "silicon" world of microprocesses does less violence to the external environment, because it is based upon technologies requiring smaller quantities of raw materials – its impact on the structure of work itself has become a major "ecological" issue. The introduction of the silicon chip into major machinery-producing industries replaces older skills, associated with artisanship, with new skills that are essentially derived from managerial and engineering "sciences." Manual labor is reduced both in quantity and in quality; the worker who once enjoyed a modicum of autonomy as a skilled machinist or toolmaker is now subordinated both formally and substantively to scientifically-based technologies. As in oil, chemical, and electronic processes, the gap between the level of autonomy enjoyed by the technical intelligentsia and that of the manual worker increases with the spread of science to production processes. In turn, top management increasingly centralizes decisions in its own hands, permitting managerial control (masked as technical control) to take more power in the workplace from the producers than in the older mechanical era. Capital has now moved a step beyond Taylorism and Fordism. Those regimes of managed industrial processes still depended on immediate productivity for capital accumulation. Under those regimes, economic incentives were introduced to insure that workers produce. But the phenomenon of the "refusal to work" – where the collective laborer, having been deprived of autonomy within the labor process, elects to produce as little as possible within the definite time period and will not work except by coercion or, occasionally, substantial economic benefits tied to output – has made the elimination of labor as the principal source of accumulation a major strategy of capital. The quickening pace of automatic processes in ever-widening sections of industry is a result, in part, of capital's recognition that the workers in late capitalism cannot be trusted, despite a high degree of ideological and political integration, to produce goods that are economically competitive on the world market.

The new processes are increasing the proportion of skilled to unskilled workers and simultaneously resulting in the degradation of skill as such. But the new skills are not those which have been historically linked to trade union, socialist and communist traditions. The old working class, which had participated in mass struggles to form unions of their own choosing, and consequently were capable of responding to political and ideological appeals, has now all but passed into history in the U.S. The technical intelligentsia which participates directly in production has shown little propensity to conduct struggles about class formation in the U.S., although this may be the result of its infancy. The new manual workers within industries that have adopted advanced technical processes such as the chip or continuous flow operations (oil, chemical, electronics, oil machinery) are highly paid, separated from the traditional skills of prior generations, and depoliticized because of the decline of labor traditions and the industrial migration to rural areas and small towns in which political culture has traditionally been conservative.

THE CHARACTER OF LABOR

The third industrial revolution, now underway in the most technologically advanced countries, implies a transformation of the nature of the labor process, but also of the character of labor. The measurement of value by definite quantities of labor time necessary for the production of commodities certainly can no longer be theoretically valid, for a single national capitalism, under conditions where the processes of production at every level of the social division of labor (production of means of production as well as the end product) are marked by the application of advanced science to technology. While it is true at the level of qualitative labor that the model for the automation and cybernation remains those tasks that were once defined by mechanical skills and the technical division of labor, the *necessary labor time* required for the production of commodities such as are controlled by computerization, robotization, and memory chips has been reduced considerably. Although the technical composition of capital is miniaturized as compared with the older images of giant machinery, the quantity of labor required for production can no longer be evaluated in terms of time frames, since *knowledge* has become the main productive force. Under these circumstances the labor theory of value must become problematic. For, among other things, it was constituted by classical political economy as an explanation for price. Marx's contribution to the labor theory was to insist that the internal inconsistency of bourgeois political economy was its refusal of the theory in the determination of the origin and the rate of profit. He argued that the rate of profit is determined by the relationship between the rate of *surplus value* (the proportion of paid to unpaid labor) and the organic composition of capital (the *ratio* of machinery or dead labor to living labor). Marx's logical move was to make the labor theory regulative of all relations of capital, especially the rate of its accumulation.[93] For Marx, the labor theory of value and its permutations become the "unified field theory" for the science of society, overcoming the dualism of a political economy that held to the labor theory on the one hand – to explain price fluctuations mediated by supply and demand – and a cost of production theory – to explain the profit rate Marx claimed to have superseded in classical models – on the other.

At stake in the radical transformation of the relation between intellectual and manual labor inherent in the new technologies, where the former assumes a position of dominance over the latter, is the status of the labor theory. This crisis is not only presented to Marxist theory but to capital as well. As manual labor occupies a smaller role in the total social production (including what has been described as "services"), capital has attempted to assess the productivity of various types of intellectual labor, including that performed in the various departments of commodity production, the state sector, and administration. Its effort to reduce intellectual labor to a quantifiable activity has consistently failed, prompting more capital investment to eliminate those aspects of intellectual labor subject to mechanization. Put plainly, capital has discovered that the Taylorist model can only be applied, in limited ways, to some types of non-productive labor or knowledge production.

LABOR AND WORLD CAPITAL

Samir Amin's implied solution to this problem is to locate the application of the theory of value and surplus value in the Third World.[94] Accordingly, the breakdown of the labor theory in advanced countries does not signal the end of surplus value as a regulative principle, as long as imperialism is able to import surplus value from labor-intensive, extractive, and exploitative manufacturing industries (in the technical sense) in the underdeveloped world. Capital formation, then, takes place in the Third World in great quantities, even if the high organic composition of capital in advanced sectors prevents accumulation on a grand scale. This theoretical adaptation requires the presupposition that capitalism is a *world* system, rather than a series of national systems that happen to function along the same lines. If capitalism is a world system, then the laws of accumulation need not be confined to a single country. The low rate of profit in the U.S., for example, is complemented (or paid for) by rates of profit in the Third World far above the average rate required for the reproduction of capital. Here again is Lenin's theory of imperialism as, among other things, a theory of superprofits.[95] The high organic composition of capital generated by concentration and centralization does reduce the profit rate below the average. But since capitalism is a world system and the law of uneven development applies on this scale as well as within capitalist countries, the labor theory has not lost its explanatory value. In addition, the formation of international cartels and the trustification of industries on a national level keeps the rate of profit artificially high. But the apparent contradiction between high organic composition of capital which drives the profit rate down and the actual profits can only be resolved with reference to the operation of the labor theory as a world-wide principle.

However, problems remain. Lenin ultimately rejected Rosa Luxemburg's argument that the tendency of capital was to accumulate on a world scale, thereby bringing the precapitalist sectors into advanced industrial society. Under these circumstances capital would eventually reach its limit of expansion because its growth depends, in large measure, upon its own universalization. But the universality of capital is also the basis of the breakdown of the capitalist system as a whole. Lenin's "law" of uneven development permanently consigned the underdeveloped world to extracting raw materials for the most advanced countries, who would keep them in thrall by means of the "development of underdevelopment." In any case, the systematic underdevelopment of the least-advanced sectors constituted the weak link upon which national liberation movements arose. Imperialism would collapse, according to Lenin, before it reached its technical boundary of capital accumulation.

History has proven Luxemburg more right than wrong. Imperialism is certainly weakened since the end of the First World War, but it has shown remarkable capacity of adaptation to most nationalist movements, which have achieved political independence but not economic or political autonomy. At the same time, the movement of capital into the Third World has taken on the aspect of technological as well as raw-material development. The new stage of world-capital expansion is precisely in the direction indicated by Luxemburg in the early years of the twentieth century, because the hoped-for world-wide socialist revolution has not yet occurred. The export of high technology industries to the Third World is by no means a dominant feature of capital investment in those areas, but the tendency is becoming stronger. While the labor theory of value may have some explanatory power with respect to industries such as agriculture, mining, and labor-intensive, secondary-sector manufacturing, it can no longer be considered an operative regulatory principle in commodity exchange within advanced countries, and it is increasingly losing its force world-wide.

ABSTRACT EQUIVALENCE IN EXCHANGE

Certainly Marx's appropriation of the labor theory of value from the earlier traditions of political economy in France and England was prompted by his concept that *abstract equivalence* was a necessary condition for commodity exchange. The market required that the concrete determinations of types of labor and use-values descend to that abstract universal property possessed by all commodities, regardless of quality, in order to provide a basis for measurement. Marx understood that abstraction became a universal principle under specific historical conditions, even if its *concept* preceded capitalism. Thus, beyond the philosophic choice of labor-time as the universal of commodity exchange, the larger requirement was *abstract equivalence*. In principle, any measurable property that was, at the same time, common to all commodities could serve as the basis of a value theory. Price cannot fulfill this function because it is determined extrinsically by the conditions of exchange. Nor does it inhere in the use-value of the commodity itself. Marx's theory depends, then, on whether concrete aspects in the production of the commodity can be abstracted to a determinant of the exchange relation.

The problem with the adequacy of labor as a logical category is that its empirical conditions of validity have been undermined by historical changes in the technical composition of capital, and by the fact that the national-democratic revolutions in the Third World did not result in socialist revolution. Nor did the advanced countries take the same road. As the market system survives in both capitalist and state-socialist societies, the results of the scientific and technological revolutions (in which production becomes more and more based upon technocratically-controlled systems of knowledge organization rather than the control of wage labor) make the labor theory of value less and less regulative of exchange relations. This does not mean that labor has "disappeared" as a key aspect of the production process, or that its metaphoric/symbolic significance as the key to production is no longer present. But even if it remains the significant measure of value in abstract, or remains the regulative principle of the large quantity of the world's production that is still based upon time–output relation, the concept of surplus value has been increasingly thrown into question.

Exchange relations are more and more governed by political and economic power. Capital formation has become dependent upon the relative weight of different sectors in the international economic and political system. A provisional formulation of the status of the labor theory of value may be as follows: capitalism has found no abstract principle of exchange equivalency to replace labor time, but in the historical sense, the concept of "simple, abstract labor" no longer corresponds to the character of the labor process in the most advanced technological sectors. At the same time, it can no longer be maintained that industrial development (capital formation in primary and secondary production sectors) will be systematically denied the underdeveloped world. Thus, the central thesis of dependency theories that argue for the "development of underdevelopment" as a systematic imposition from the imperialist powers on the Third World has increasingly limited validity. Under these conditions, capital will require a new abstract quantitative principle to regulate exchange relations, but it will not be labor.

This transformation has the effect of producing a labor force for whom appeals to patriotism, social responsibility or ethical norms of craft are increasingly weakened because of a low level of political mobilization. The consequence of depoliticization has resulted in the emergence of a labor force in broad sections of American industry that is highly volatile and "undisciplined", prone to creating "disturbances" in the system of capital's reproduction without simultaneously being engaged in struggles that may lead to class formation because the normative structures of ideological and political relations necessary for such effects are not present.[96] Thus, we have the apparent paradox of an ideologically integrated labor force that is politically inactive because it has accepted its own privatization, becoming for that reason increasingly immune to ideological appeals. At the same time, since it has been removed from even the mediated relation to nature that marked the craft and mechanical eras, there is no question of work satisfaction. Only the fear of job losses which might result from plant removals, discharge, or economic crisis prevent workers in degraded occupations from engaging more often in spontaneous and militant oppositions within the labor process.

The logic of labor in a period where work has lost its transcendent significance is to seek every opportunity to transform work into play, or more precisely, to make as large a portion of working time unproductive from capital's point of view. The insertion of the erotic into working life violates the cultural norms of capital, which historically demanded the strict separation of eros and civilization, and invented the sphere of "leisure" to accommodate the libidinous drives denied in the labor process. Capital's reply to this unconscious effort to find in labor a way towards satisfaction is no longer confined to economic incentives and coercion. Today there is a rather concerted effort to found a *corporate-led public sphere* within the labor process by introducing the doctrine of workers' participation in aspects of management. Certainly there is no question of workers determining what is to be produced or how much production corresponds to accumulation needs. Thus, it is a wizened public sphere confined to bringing workers into the determination of the means by which commodities will be produced. Workers are encouraged by some corporations to decide their own work schedules, to devise methods of production suited to their wants, including choice of modes of the division of labor within the parameters set by the wall of intellectual *versus* manual spheres. In the craft and mechanical traditions workers initiate production methods by inventing new tools, by finding short cuts not mandated by engineering technologies and recombining processes according to the criterion of making work easier and less boring. Corporate management is now attempting, in many instances, to bring these more-or-less underground measures to the surface, to integrate them by institutional means into a doctrine and practice of worker self-management, in order to overcome the chronic refusal to work. Corporations are motivated largely by productivity requirements that underlay profit margins, but can no longer rely on the older ideological appeals that were based either upon consumption or the work "ethic" that demanded a fair day's work for a fair day's pay. The liberal concept of industrial citizenship replaces the older contract under which workers sold their labor power in return for a wage and left the realm of working conditions to mutual negotiations on the basis of the relations of power.

Naturally, not all segments of capital wish to enter the experiments in the creation of an institutional framework for cooperation between workers and their employers that amounts to a new social contract. Nor are workers and their unions uniform in their approval of these proposals. Many workers rightly suspect that productivity and profit are, after all, the bottom line, and know the limits of self-management are priorities about what is to be produced and how much – priorities set in advance of participation. Yet where the new regime has been introduced, production goes up at first, and workers seem to enjoy their new measure of autonomy. After some time, they have tended to resume their previous antagonistic stance, and the "new social contract" of mutual cooperation between capital and labor erodes, if not completely fails. But there is considerable evidence to suggest that the creation by capital of new forms to undermine labor's cultural logic are historically ambiguous because they create both the conditions for reintegration of the workers into capital's rationality and produce new contradictions that become subversive and may lead to class formation.

In this connection, it is useful to examine in some detail the case of the recent burst of strikes among Polish workers. As in 1970, the Polish government, responding to the international commodity and capital markets of which they are a part, was constrained to raise prices on food and other consumer goods. Workers at Gdansk struck, and the strike spread to other centers. But unlike the strikes in 1970 – where a government agreement not to raise prices was sufficient to induce the workers to return to work – the 1980 strikes led to the formation of a national workers' coordination among various sectors of industry. Workers demanded trade unions that were not directly under Communist Party control, and raised a number of economic demands as well. The government was forced to negotiate directly with the workers' committees, and finally agreed to nearly all demands posed by the strike.

The demand for "free" trade unions was, of course, the most radical of all, because it challenged the ideological presumption that the party and its unions were the true representatives of the workers and that competitors were therefore enemies of the workers' socialist state. While labor disputes are quite common in all countries of "really existing" socialism, they are usually local in nature, fought over particular issues, and do not challenge the party's hegemony. The formation of Polish workers into an oppositional class may not have been achieved by the strike, but it moved the project of class formation a step forward, creating the self-consciousness among Polish workers that they were an autonomous force in society not subsumed under the party or government bureaucracies.

This development may not have been possible except under conditions of ideological and political relations that accorded to the workers privileged status in society within the industrializing phase of state socialism. Unless the regime was prepared to use force to suppress the workers – a possibility that appeared foreclosed by the weakened economic and political position of Poland and the countries of the Eastern bloc – it was precisely the party's ideological adherence to the doctrine of workers' sovereignty in face of its denial in practice that ultimately became the sufficient condition for the democratic breakthrough. The regime's legitimacy rests not only on its ability to deliver the goods, but on its doctrine of workers' power. Thus, the contradiction between its forms of legitimation and the reality of bureaucratic domination within the context of economic crisis created the conditions for new forms of workers' autonomy, and even for the formation of an autonomous working class in Poland.

THE QUESTION OF RACE

> Colonialism is not an external practice of monopoly capitalism. It is an internal practice. Its first victims are not the exploited, oppressed and dismembered nations but the populations living in the metropoles, in the dominant countries.[97]

Andre Gorz's argument is that the theory of imperialism has suffered from its exclusive emphasis upon dividing the world between oppressor and oppressed *nations*, rather than comprehending that capitalism's mode of domination is global. Further, the concept of colonialism as an external phenomenon related only by capital export to advanced-capitalist countries divides the revolutionary movement along *national* rather than *class* lines. By underscoring underdevelopment and oppression *within* national boundaries, Gorz has contributed to the project of a Marxism that insists upon the historical specificity of concepts such as colonialism, class, and revolution. The tendency of large sections of the socialist movement to rely on Lenin's theory of imperialism, which was framed under different historical circumstances, has led to "Third-Worldism," the propensity of radicals to view the Third World as a whole as the modern proletariat while the entire late capitalist world is seen as the new "bourgeoisie."[98]

This formulation of the question of historical agency both displaces the site of social transformation and serves as an explanation for the fate of historical materialism in late capitalist sectors. By classifying subaltern classes, including various strata of workers, as privileged in the context of the capitalist world system, a tendency to write off the Western working classes as impossibly reformist is fairly common among segments of the American radical movement. Following from this judgement, the task of the left is understood to be almost entirely directed to the "anti-imperialist" struggle, an emphasis intended to prevent imperialist aggression rather than focusing on the problem of oppression and exploitation within metropoles themselves. Although in the past decade Marxism has largely moved away from the excesses of this position, it has often adopted its antinomy: for much of the American left, the question of political struggle means the exclusion of any sectors but the industrial working classes. Marxism has not only been unable to theorize the role of the "middle strata" in modern capitalism in a manner appropriate to changes in the relation of knowledge to production or to the question entailed by the advent of consumer society, it has also been unable to theorize the formation of the new underclasses in advanced-capitalist societies. Considerable work has been done by radical economists and sociologists in what has been labelled "dual labor market" theory, or labor segmentation.[99] According to these studies, in the era of oligopolistic capitalism two distinct labor markets tend to form. The first, or primary market, consists of those industries and workers in the most monopolized sectors of manufacturing and services. These are typically more technologically advanced, higher-paying, and, in manufacturing and in the state sector, more unionized. The crucial distinction here is the capacity of a firm or group of firms to achieve dominance in market shares by means of the centralization of capital. Union organization and technological innovation follow from this crucial distinction. Thus, even if cars are produced by medium technology (assembly operations are really part of the lower technological mix because there is a relatively high labor/capital ratio), the ability of three large US firms to dominate the domestic market (and in the early postwar period to dominate many foreign markets as well) meant that workers were paid high wages even when they were unskilled or semi-skilled. The degree of technological advance does not automatically follow from the degree of concentration and centralization, although the potential is greater than in the secondary market because of capital availability.

In the secondary labor market, according to labor market segmentation theory, relatively small, highly competitive firms characterize the field. In the garment trades, for example, the number of large firms is small and even when they are substantial their share of sales and profits in the industry remains restricted to a few percentage points. Technical innovation remains on a relatively low level because of the plentiful cheap labor supplies and the scarcity of capital. Moreover, these firms cannot generate research and development activities designed to increase labor productivity. Finally, they are vulnerable to foreign competition – especially from those areas such as Taiwan, Korea, Puerto Rico and semi-periphery nations such as Spain and Poland – where wages are much lower than in the advanced areas. In the postwar period, the once highly-unionized garment sector has become largely non-union. Migration of plants is not confined to other countries, but in the immediate postwar period occurred principally in moves to underdeveloped regions of the United States such as coal-rich

Pennsylvania, the older textile areas of New England and the agricultural South. The garment, shoe, and textile industries migrated to these areas because of their technological marginality. But the entrance of light manufacturing industries to the South did not change the pattern of *underdevelopment* in that agrarian region. The South remained a source of raw materials for Northern and Western production. Coal is still the major fuel for electricity production, and cotton is a major raw material for textiles. While the depression in the coal mines in the 1950's caused a significant population exodus to the metropoles of the Northeast and Midwest, the migration of garment and shoe plants to the coal regions resulted in the employment of women on a wide scale. Similarly, with the exception of military production and some heavy industry in New England, the states of Maine, Vermont, New Hampshire, most of Rhode Island, and parts of Massachusetts and Connecticut became permanently depressed areas in the 1950's in the wake of textile and shoe migration. Consequently, the labor market segmentation conjoined with the *development* of underdevelopment, with certain regions consigned to permanent poverty in the social division of labor.

In the large cities, the two labor markets are equally operative. The first came to include state-sector workers, since in the 1960's millions entered union ranks and drove up both wages and costs of government. Cutbacks followed in social programs in order to insure accumulation. Attempts by the state were made to increase productivity within this sector by means of computerization and organizational consolidation and centralization.[100] In addition, millions of workers have entered private-sector banking, insurance, and administrative jobs as these functions proliferated with the growing role of US business abroad. The "explosion" in administration after the war not only confirmed empirically the theory of late capitalism offered by Weber and the Frankfurt School, but increasingly followed the internationalization of capital and the concomitant division of labor in which the United States became an exporter of high technologies and less and less a producer of finished products in the intermediate range industries such as steel, rubber, and cars, as well as light consumer goods such as garments and shoes. Retail and wholesale trades constitute the heart of the second labor market in the largest cities since the exodus of competitive light manufacturing industries. In addition, the *clients* of the social part of the state sector – those on welfare, single mothers, the aged, and many young people – are members of this group.[101] Despite the employment of millions of jobless during and after the Second World War, American global expansion failed to prevent the growth of those strata permanently or largely unemployed, because (1) the rate of economic growth was not great enough to absorb the unemployed produced by the previous crisis; (2) the contraction of agricultural employment, especially in the South and Puerto Rico, was too precipitous and massive; and (3) labor-saving technologies further restricted job opportunities, not only in the most advanced production sectors but in many services, especially retailing and administration.

Labor market segmentation theory explains how the distinctions within the working classes become wider owing to the formation of sectors in the American economy that have a differential relation to the international social and technical division of labor. Implicit in the theory is the beginning of a conceptual basis for explaining the formation of *new underclasses*, or a sub-proletariat, within the American social structure whose relations to the traditional working class are becoming increasingly antagonistic. For Marxism the concept of a subproletariat is well-known, but only as a descriptive category for understanding the phenomenon of immigration into the advanced countries of Europe, and as a way of comprehending the differences between production in the advanced countries and the semi-colonial peoples of Latin America, Asia, and Africa. However, by recalling Gorz's notion of internal dual-labor-market formation, one is inescapably drawn to the conclusion that to understand the subproletariat merely as a class "fraction" that assumes common ground with the industrial and state-sector working classes (deprivation of ownership of the means of production) conceals more than it reveals. Consistent with my attempt to interrogate the Marxist theory of class, I reject the aggregation of the underclasses with the working class, since I do hold that a common relation to the ownership and control of the means of production is not a sufficient condition for class formation. Propertylessness does not explain relative locations with respect to social structure, nor with respect to ideological and political relations. Second, by articulating the secondary labor market as a different but coextensive mode of production, in comparison to the monopoly and state sectors which constitute the specifically *late capitalist mode*, we are able to generate a category of difference which articulates such phenomena as racism and sexism more precisely than would be possible if they were conflated. Race and sex are forms of ideological relations, but they are also inscribed in the economic infrastructure and in the state. They are ideological relations intimately linked to and among the bases of contemporary struggles around (1) tax policy, (2) competition between working classes and underclasses for jobs and elements of the social wage (the range of welfare and other state benefits that accrue instead of money wages), and (3) the struggles for access to living space. All of these issues are really signs of different locations within the social structure that can no longer be defined by reference to questions of property alone. Thus racism and sexism are material practices containing ideological and political relations, as well as articulations of relation to the economy. The intra-class rivalry among the subaltern classes of capitalism has marked American history since the Civil War, and it remains a central obstacle to the development of a counterhegemonic bloc that might have offered opposition from the left to the historic bloc formed by the New Deal.[102]

Black, Hispanic, and Asian fractions, together with the white aged, the unemployed and underemployed, large sections of women, and the handicapped, constitute the underclass of American society. The historical development of this underclass is linked to the fate of the relatively technologically-backward competitive sectors, the rapid rise of labor productivity due to the systematic applications of science and technology to the labor process, and the requirement of capital to form a vast industrial reserve army of labor that could be pressed into production in times of rapid expansion. The postwar migration from Asia, Latin America, and the Caribbean was a consequence of the conjunction between the agrarian crises in these regions – caused in part by their transformation into semi-peripheries of advanced capitalism – and the problems encountered by a number of US industries in the face of new challenges from international competitors. Seen in this way, the distinction between the American South after the First World War and other dismembered agricultural regions in this country and similar areas of the Third World, is structurally less important then their mutual antagonism to the metropolitan regions of the advanced countries.

However, the metropoles should not be understood as an undifferentiated economic bloc. The second economy of small-scale manufacturing that arose in the way of the consolidation of monopolies in the metropoles is tied to regional and sectoral underdevelopment. For, especially in recent years, the secondary labor market is recruiting immigrants who are not principally documented workers or the native born, but rather illegal "aliens" brought to this country outside the law by capitalists seeking to compete successfully with imports and with the sectors who control the supply of raw materials. In both manufacturing and retailing, a new "underground" economy employing undocumented workers and other fractions of the underclass competes with those industries enjoying legal status. Consequently, the secondary labor market has become partially subdivided by the intervention of the underground economy. Underground businesses do not pay income and corporate taxes; workers are not enrolled in the social security system or included under the purview of minimum wages or health and industrial safety laws. While this underground segment of the competitive sector is by no means dominant, its growth has been dramatic over the past decade, fueled by millions of Latin American, Caribbean, and Asian workers. Of course, the competitive manufacturing sector is only partially commensurable with the retail and wholesale industries, which typically employ documented workers and operate legally (although informal markets – sort of domestic kasbahs – have proliferated recently in many urban ghettoes and rural slums).

The most important feature of this segregation among different aspects of the society has been the concomitant pattern of housing and social segregation. It is not that whites, blacks and Hispanics are segregated merely because of racial hatred; rather, racial hatred is an effect of the unevenness and segmentation of American capitalist development. At the same time, one may not explain race hatred by means of economic relations alone, since at another level racism is an aspect of the development of pre-capitalist, as well as capitalist modes of production. In earlier and non-dominant cultures, racism takes the form of scapegoating or is linked to a caste structure. These forms are, of course, linked to the economic privileges enjoyed by certain groups at the expense of others, but remain relatively autonomous insofar as ideological relations do not develop synchronously with economic and political relations.[103]

In the United States, the reproduction of the hierarchically-organized fractions of the working class takes place by social stratification on the basis of race, ethnicity, and sex. These fractions are not isomorphic with any of the principal levels of social life because their everyday existence, their culture and ideology, become separated, as much as does their relation to the production and distribution of economic goods and political power. The formation of a culture of resistance among oppressed groups is a mode of adaptation to a hostile social environment. Contrary to liberal hopes that the United States may be able to integrate its oppressed groups into the "mainstream" of social and economic life, many racially oppressed strata perceive their communities as a means of protection against the violence of the larger society.

Of course, this analysis should be not taken as an endorsement of the discrimination in education, housing, and jobs that black and Hispanic underclasses (as well as those in working-class and middle-class locations) have suffered. I am simply insisting that integration was only one – albeit the hegemonic one – of a variety of strategies for liberation among black Americans and other oppressed groups. The conjunction of *enforced* segregations with melting pot theory in the 1950's and 1960's made the liberal solution to problems of black oppression virtually inescapable as the guide to public policy. Most American progressives, including the left, find nationalist ideology virtually unthinkable, because American imperialism relied on the old nationalism of expansion. In addition, we are constrained by our belief that the *mainstream* is the only path to freedom. While the right to enter white-dominated, bourgeois culture ought not to be denied anyone, we must pause before granting this road a privileged place in the struggle for a new society. It is entirely possible that oppressed groups, including sexually as well as radically oppressed groups, may choose a different way. (Hence the strategy of *alliance*, rather than integration, discussed below.)

The liberal attack against segregated housing, schools, and other institutions of ideological and social domination misses the degree to which these institutions function in *behalf* of the various strata of black and Hispanic underclasses and middle strata attached to them. The demand for an end to segregation in various social, political, and economic institutions was advanced with particular force in the 1940's and 1950's by fractions of those racially oppressed minorities who were already members of the more-or-less stable working-class and middle-strata. But for much of the black church, the poor, small shopkeepers, and professionals in ghetto communities, these demands were not acceptable.

The rise of black nationalism since the 1960's (after nearly thirty years of decline) is an expression in part of the inadequacy of integrationist demands among various strata within the black communities. In the recent revival, nationalism has taken two principal forms. The first derives from those remaining faithful to the older Garveyite tradition. In the main this form – *cultural* nationalism – usually takes a separatist position, combined in some instances with a call for the return to Africa or the establishment of economic and political autonomy within the United States. Here a distinction must be made from the older Marxist position that claims that blacks – at least in the states of the Southeast forming the "black belt" – are an oppressed nation and require national self-determination as the only adequate political freedom demand. Cultural nationalism does not envisage the United States as a "nation of nations," but advocates black cultural, political, and economic separation from the United States. Certainly, even those nationalists who do not accept this as a solution to black oppression accept many of the ideological precepts of the cultural nationalists, insofar as they hold to the necessity of separate black political and cultural formations.

The second tendency – usually called *revolutionary* nationalism – regards the development of separate black political and cultural movements as the best guarantee that blacks will not suffer subordination within an alliance with "progressive" whites, including trade unions and political left organizations. Thus, while arguing for the autonomy of blacks and other Third World groups, they advocate eventual blocs with the white exploited and oppressed on the basis of a socialist or radical democratic program. Many individuals and groups who hold this position work with whites but eschew integration, arguing that at least for the present this possibility is largely foreclosed by institutional and ideological racism.

I am not claiming here that black nationalism is *the* ideology of the second economy. However, there can be no doubt that the rise of separatist and autonomist orientations among blacks in the last fifteen years is an attempt to forge a vision of a future that does not remain bound to the assumption that the fortunes of the American nation-state are the horizon within which blacks are obliged to frame their demands.

Today, many important intellectuals in the black freedom movement have adopted nationalist perspectives – often combined with Marxism – at least partially because of the palpable failure of integrationist movements to win significant gains within American society, particularly economic gains. Having succeeded in wresting important concessions in social and political rights, blacks have been obliged to face the reality that economic equality is no closer to realization twenty-five years after the historic Supreme Court decision barring segregation in education. On the contrary, the widening income gap between blacks and whites, the increased terror against black citizens signalled by the rise of the Ku Klux Klan, and the dramatic increases in black joblessness in the late 1970's are just some of the reasons that liberal solutions relying on legislative reforms, the largesse of the Democratic Party and corporations seem more futile than at any time since the Civil War.

But there is a new interest in theoretical work on race as well. Just as feminist theory has found that male supremacy only takes on different forms under capitalism but originates in pre-capitalist societies marked by hierarchy, so the discovery of the work of Oliver Cromwell Cox, W. E. B. Dubois, and others[104] who argue that race is linked prior to capitalism by caste has engendered considerable doubt among large numbers of black intellectuals. Manning Marable has argued, for example, that socialism will not abolish racism, that after the socialist revolution, blacks will require their own institutions of social and political power as well as retain considerable control over economic resources.[105] His call for a system of *dual power* differs, however, from Lenin's conception. For Lenin, dual power signified the need for workers' institutions alongside bourgeois institutions during the revolutionary process, but Lenin envisages no duality in the nature of political power in the post-revolutionary period. Marable insists that the revolution cannot subsume the black oppressed minority under its hegemony, but must recognize the autonomy of blacks to manage their own affairs more or less indefinitely. Marable has clearly refused the Garveyite separatist perspective. At the same time, Garvey's influence is still felt insofar as Marable and others remain convinced that the historical legacy of racism is not obliterated in the intermediate term by the socialization of ownership of the means of production. That is, Marable asserts the relative autonomy of ideological relations, their persistence in a rather long transition period between capitalism and the new society.

In the United States and many other late-capitalist states, the left subordinates the struggle against racism to the struggle against capitalism. Unless these questions are raised simultaneously and accorded equal significance with those of class and sex, the abolition of conditions for the reproduction of capitalist relations of production is beyond realization. As Henri Lefebvre has argued, it is necessary to make a distinction between the reproduction of capital – which depends on the existence of wage laborers of production – and the social structure.[106] The conditions for the reproduction of social relations depend upon the capacity of capital to divide labor along race, sex, and ethnic lines, as well as to impose a series of ideological relations in which alternatives to capitalism become inconceivable. These include the displacement of the struggle against exploitation within the labor process to what Lefebvre calls the "bureaucratic society of controlled consumption", which in turn depends upon the transformation of everyday life from collective forms to those marked by isolation and clashes among subaltern groups.

I have advanced the notion that the underclasses are constituted by definite conditions in the reproduction of capital and in the reproduction of the relations of production. A socialist movement that refuses to recognize the separate existence of such underclasses – rooted in sexual, ethnic and racial hierarchies – will be rendered powerless to assist in the formation of the new bloc needed to affect social transformation. Until now, the experience of "really existing" socialist movements demonstrates that such theoretical and strategic perspectives remain lacking except among a relatively small minority, one prepared to speak of the real differences between the position and the demands of blacks, Hispanics, and whites, women and men, but which has refused to alter the parameters of Marxist theory to make room for these insights. Or, as in the case of Nicos Poulantzas, the best work has been confined to theorizing the existence of class *fractions* for a theory of class or (even more importantly) suggesting changes in socialist education and political strategy to recognize that the demand of various groups cannot be subsumed under the old concepts of "proletarian hegemony," "the dictatorship of the proletariat", or even the demand for the "unity" of the working class on the basis of a resolute struggle against racism and sexism.[107] The trouble with these slogans is that they still remain ensconced within the logic of the two-class model of capitalist society, and implicitly argue that the struggle against capital is sufficient to encompass the demands of the underclasses, ignoring the degree to which certain strata of the working class are situated in places that make them *inherently* antagonistic to the interests of the underclasses. Further, the traditional Marxist position on race – recognizing the "special" nature of racial oppression but refusing to depart from the centrality of "class analysis" for explaining it – also cannot come to grips with the nationalist contention that race questions are not subsumed under the categories of economic difference or ideological relations, but have connotations that strike to the heart of the "deep structure" of societies marked by social hierarchies.

Let me illustrate what I mean by this concept of "deep structure" in social hierarchy. Race has become the sign under which a variety of anxieties experienced by relatively privileged groups are defined. Among these, of course, is the still-unresolved anxiety associated with sexuality that is virtually always linked to political and economic repression.

Racism, like sexism, is rooted in the domination that social and economic hierarchies have attempted to inflict upon nature, including human nature. As I have already argued, "woman" is linked with the uncontrollable in nature. She becomes the "dark side" of universal human nature insofar as she is identified by men with the irrational, emotional, physical, sexual feelings which are displaced as the otherness of socially-constituted "rationality."[108] Race has become one sign under which the male fear of castration emerges. Blacks are invested by whites with the sexual powers and opportunities denied to "thinking," work-disciplined beings. If the repressed male psyche refuses to acknowledge this loss consciously, buried sexuality rebels in the form of white violence against blacks, as has become evident once more in various incidents in the early 1980's. Just as "work" obliges the repression of desire in the service of production and physical reproduction, "blacks" become one of the major repositories of desire; they are held to be shiftless, lazy, and erotic – a constellation of qualities intimately linked by Western imperial ideologies to "irrational" practices. Contrary to the actual situation – where blacks occupy some of the hardest, least-prestigious, and lowest-paid jobs – they are accused of refusing to work in order to indulge their illicit lifestyles. Lacking the elements of that repressive rationality upon which Western civilization is constructed, blacks are mythologized as libido-ridden, mentally and morally incompetent.

Black women occupy a special place in this system of stigmatization. They are labelled temptress, symbolically considered the embodiment of the dark side that links race with sexuality, and are accused of moral promiscuity. They are consequently held responsible for a multitude of sins, ranging from the fiscal crisis of the state brought about by excessive welfare expenses given to loose-living, single, black and Hispanic mothers, to constituting a threat to Christian morality. Their men are memorialized in white-dominated artistic culture as hustlers, pimps, and thieves. (This has been made paradigmatic by *Porgy and Bess*, a theme which periodically reappears on Broadway and in Hollywood.)

These are the conventional stigma attached to all underclasses in history. Race is the transhistorical sign for those assigned to the margins of the social and technical division of labor, rendered powerless by the labor process while believed to be the embodiment of masculinity or sexuality. The distinction between black men and women narrows within this perspective. To the degree that black men are identified with a forbidden sexuality, they are also linked to the nature (woman) within us all that cannot be freed from the bonds of repressive social relations. The powerful effects of sexual jealousy may be expressed as moral condemnation, physical violence, and the tendencies among workers and other subaltern classes to sanction discrimination against oppressed minorities in this society. But there can be no question of subsuming racism under the economic dimension of competition for jobs or access to the benefits of state action such as are provided by the social wage. The element of sexual jealousy entailed by racism cannot be eliminated without a transformation of sexual relations and our collective relation to nature.

I realize that the attempt to link race and sex is controversial in the current debate within both the women's movement and the black freedom movement. I am not, of course, claiming that the nature of women's oppression is identical to that of blacks and others subject to racial oppression. The roots of each is different within the evolution of capitalist societies. Moreover, patriarchy is not identical with the class and caste formations from which racism finds its sources. Nevertheless, the displacement of intra-class rivalries to questions of sexuality and the deep structure that unites these phenomena in the domination of nature cannot be ignored. To claim that racism or sexism can be overcome by means of transformation in the capitalist relations of production forgets that these forms of oppression predate capitalism.

On the other hand, the conflict between movements against

racial oppression and those seeking women's emancipation is comprehensible on a level that is not entirely consonant with the categories of political economy. The historical replacement of the struggle for racial equality by the demands of women within the ranks of the white left at the end of the 1960's engendered considerable resentment in the ranks of the black and Hispanic freedom movements. It was not a problem that had to be posed as oppositional. But the specific history of black, Hispanic and white relations during that period tended to make these exclusions more probable. Recall that the civil rights struggle of the 1950's and early 1960's was compatible with the general orientation of white liberals as well as large segments of the left. When many of the key leaders of the black "left wing" of the civil rights movement began to make the change from integrationist perspectives to cultural or political autonomy (or both), white supporters became confused and resentful. The conjunction of the emerging women's movement among considerable forces on the left with this burgeoning conflict within the old civil rights movement changed many loyalties. Many black and Hispanic men suddenly became part of the problem, rather than being part of the solution. And, in the narrowing arena of what became known euphemistically as "affirmative action," Third World candidates for jobs were pitted against women. Ironically, state and monopoly sector employers were permitted to manipulate these competing demands. Several years in the 1970's were alternately known as "the year of the Woman," "the year of the Hispanic" or "the year of the Black" as oppressed groups competed in the academic, social services, educational and other professional arenas for elusive opportunities in the midst of a long-term economic slide.

AGGREGATION OR ALLIANCE

By making the theoretical connection between the institutional and ideological forms of racism and sexism, and linking these further to the formation of the underclasses and other marginal economic groups, the perspective for the creation of a new historical alliance acquires a degree of cogency not possible by means of simple aggregation. For each struggle, in different ways, challenges the underlying assumptions about social relations that are conditions for and conditioned by the relations of humans to nature. Of course, to try to understand the commensurability of these struggles is not to signify their *identity*. Rivalry among various strata of the working and underclasses arises from their structural differentiation and articulation within social relations. On the other hand, the historical legacy of rivalry must be overcome if a strategy of emancipation is to be forged that recognizes the autonomy and the necessary contradictions for the constituents of a new alliance, but yet insists on an objective basis for their unity against capital.

These ideological relations are imbedded not only in the mentality of the vast majority of white Americans (and increasingly Europeans as well) but are inscribed in a matrix of social institutions linked to the state and to the organizations of the working classes, such as trade unions. Thus racism cannot be expelled by the advent of a society based upon social ownership alone. Nor can the most relentless struggle against racism in state institutions and the labor movement suffice, as important as these struggles will remain. Racism can only be overcome to the extent that the empowerment of all humans results in the recognition that race has become a category under which domination and the fear of human nature express themselves. Its overcoming requires a society comfortable in work that is no longer merely instrumental, in sexuality that is freely expressed (because, as Wilhelm Reich has put it, work economy and sex economy have become democratically self-managed) and in forms of power fashioned among the formerly oppressed themselves.[109] Clearly, the process by which a new society free of domination will emerge is infinitely more complex than the founders of socialism imagined. For even if Marx understood that racism was an ideological partner of the process of primitive capitalist accumulation and that labor in white skin could never be free as long as black workers labored under slave conditions – or, indeed, colonized peoples existed in places like Ireland and India – there has been little understanding among Marxists that the "race" question depends for its solution upon the solutions to questions of sex, hierarchy, and therefore of caste. The colonized resist the production of seriality in various ways. Having been placed outside the normative structures of the dominant society by means of the imposition of otherness as a stigma, the oppressed live in two worlds. Most of them try to enter the prevailing social order as laborers since this is still the dominant means for the reproduction of life. But there is another side: oppressed groups create a culture through religious institutions and through informal neighbourhood groups that appear as extended families to protect them against the violence of the outside world. The ghetto (for Jews, for Arabs in Paris, or for blacks and Hispanics in the U.S.) is never merely the absence of conventional material or moral culture. It is, among other things, a site of new practices at the levels of everyday life and art, both of which maintain and reproduce the bonds of community against the norms imposed from without. Thus, although the underclasses are obliged to know and to observe dominant norms when they work in the commercial and industrial world, there is a definite struggle against the process by which conventional rules and norms are internalized.

The work of British ethnographer Paul Willis is particularly important here. His *Learning to Labour* shows that the process of self-formation of the working class takes place in schools by the refusal of students to succeed. The rebellion against established authority which deprives working class "lads" of opportunities to integrate themselves into bureaucratic and technologically-advanced jobs also prepares them for working-class – i.e. unskilled and semi-skilled manual – labor. It would be dangerous to offer mechanical analogies to the American situation or the condition of underclasses as a whole. The important extrapolation is that prevailing normative structures may be acknowledged by the oppressed, but they are only made part of what Pierre Bourdieu calls the "*habitus*" of ghetto dwellers.[110] Life in ghetto and slum communities evolves and reproduces its own norms through practices that are counter-hegemonic as well as conformist. Among these is the refusal of many strata of the underclasses to regard stealing and even killing as moral crimes so severe that authorities must be notified, or to believe that work is the path to redemption. Further, participation by black and Hispanic youth in schools resembles Willis's description of British working-class formation. For a large proportion of children of the underclasses, schools are perceived as part of the structure of their oppression, institutions that are oriented to persuade them to enter the "mainstream" of labor, consumption, and other aspects of the prevailing normative structures. The refusal to "learn" is often tantamount to the refusal to become part of the labor force, a refusal of the *habitus* appropriate to the prevailing order.

In the United States, underclass children are not thereby prepared for working-class jobs in the most stable monopoly sectors except under specific conditions, such as in Detroit or Chicago in the 1940's and 1950's, where auto companies and others recruited blacks in great numbers. For the most part, rejection of the curriculum offered by schools means condemnation to occupational and economic marginality. But at the same time, it does not follow that the individual student who departs from the group's rejection of the authority of schools will end up in a different place within the social order. Racial oppression is not *principally* the result of a self-imposed alternative morality, but the alternative morality may resist the transformation of the members of the internal colony into a pure labor force within the elements of resistance. As for the few black workers who attain stable working-class jobs, they share both the norms and practices of the workers in the sector within which they work *and* those of the black community, which are often contradictory to the prevailing norms.

Cornel West has demonstrated, for example, that while the form of black theology is consonant with Christian, middle-class morality, its substance is a theology of liberation, one whose doctrine "that God sides with the oppressed and acts in their behalf" subverts the meritocracy that is built into Protestant belief systems. The church institutions of the black and Hispanic communities must resemble those of their white counterparts because of the dual existence lived by most people of racially and ethnically oppressed groups. On the other hand, their *interpretation* of Christian theology tends to decode its subversive, emancipatory content – as theologians West, James Cone, Juan Segundo and others have done.[111]

The violence visited upon colonial peoples abroad and upon racially-oppressed groups at home cannot be explained exclusively by the categories of economic exploitation and political interest. While it is true that the constellation of exploiters, their retainers among the colonizers, and those among the colonized who collaborate in their own oppression, act in accordance with certain imperial interests, there can be no assertion that each act is justified merely by its economic or political outcome. One the one hand, as Sartre points out, the bestialization of the colonized is a means by which an otherness is produced that justifies the reproduction of exploitation. Here the distinction must be made between exploitation as the systemic extraction of profit from the labor of "natives" working at starvation wages and the oppression of the "other" by means of violence. The condition for the reproduction of the exploitation of colonial labor, according to Sartre, depends upon the atomization of the colonized masses, "the dissolution of the old communities, the constant dissolution of any new groups which they attempt to form and the rejection of integration into the colonizing society." "In short," adds Sartre, "it is necessary that the colonized people should be *nothing* except a labor force which can be bought for less and less."[112] This is accomplished in colonial countries by the imposition by an army of unrelenting violence – as in Algeria prior to 1960 and within the metropoles by the police forces – as well as through vast armies of government bureaucrats such as are found in social work, the courts, prison systems and schools. According to Sartre, it is *violence* that constitutes the means of oppression of the colonized as much as scientific theories demonstrating inferiority. Thus the condition for exploitation is the production of seriality – the destruction of communities or group identity that forms a basis for resistance.

On the other hand, since colonialism at home and abroad is an instance of the instability of the metropole – signifying the deterioration of its institutions as well as of its confidence in the capacity of the system to reproduce itself without recourse to violence – one must recognize that racism has become a mode of existence of late capitalism, not an extrinsic feature of our society. That is, it cannot be removed like a coat in summer; it has become a feature of *culture* as well as ideology. By *culture* in this context, I mean something similar to what Sartre called the "practico-inert" – a set of past practices that has been already structured by society as the constituted moment of collective praxis. At the moment when collective praxis has institutionalized itself (in this case, at the moment when racism has become a part of the field of the "given") it acquires *inertia*, "presents itself as the transcendence of individuality, *by a suffered original statute of reifying sociality*."[113] Having been produced, it takes on the aspect of permanence, appears as part of the natural world. Surely, racist assumptions concerning blacks' lack of intelligence, their heightened eroticism, their destructive nature, are shared to some extent by nearly all American whites. These are more than "beliefs"; they are imbedded in the practices of the reproduction of social life, part of the collective

Imaginary, that is, part of the prelinguistic that is only partially integrated into language.

That is why only a new praxis by the colonized as well as the erstwhile colonizers will root out racism from society. The abolition of the internal colony requires the self-constitution of the colonized as subjects. Otherwise the colony will be reestablished as a *socialist* colony. Such a condition exists in the Soviet Union where, despite the long history of nationalized property, castes as well as classes remain. This is not merely a function of the reluctance of the State and Communist Party to come to grips with the "really existing" inequalities, based upon economic power and on the divisions between intellectual and manual labor that are implied by Western technologies. The differences between the Soviet metropoles and the Soviet periphery are to be explained by the existence of internal colonies whose imaginary foundation is the constitution of Asian peoples as otherness, lacking civilization and, therefore, proper objects of the civilizing process. Seventy years after Lenin and Stalin enunciated the importance of the "national question" in the struggle for socialism and denounced "Great Russian chauvinism," these issues remain unresolved. That is why in the United States the resurgence of nationalism is an implicit critique of the class analysis of Marxism. The formation of black political organizations that insist upon an *alliance* with white-dominated left groups, rather than being subsumed under them, is a step toward a self-constitution that has always presented difficulties for Marxism. Marxism has always tolerated these groups as necessary *transitional* movements whose ultimate fate is to recognize the authority of the party. That is why the break of racially-oppressed groups in history from the authority of their masters always takes a violent form, since even the workers' movements and their "representatives" have been unable to grasp the specificity of racial oppression. Sartre has argued that this violence of the colonized is dialectially linked to the violence of the colonizers. Since racism as a praxis involves the production of the oppressed as pure *alterity* in order to routinize the violence upon which exploitation is constructed, Fanon has insisted that "Man is human only to the extent to which he tries to impose his existence on another man in order to be recognized by him."[114] The violence practiced by the slave is not one that has as its object the enslavement of the master, but the master's recognition. Such recognition, according to Fanon, cannot be achieved by means of the voluntary act of the master, but only when the slave *makes* the master recognize him (her). But it is necessary for the (former) master to engage in the act of recognizing the slave as no longer the other – as the object of his subjectivity – if the master wishes to *abolish himself as a master*. Fanon's reading of Hegel comprehends the relationship between the master and slave as displaced to the question of race and refuses its suppression by the categories of class. This implies the absolute necessity of a struggle against racism among subaltern classes, without which their own participation in the subjugation of blacks will reproduce itself as the practico-inert of the collective praxis of the workers' movements.

Among the consequences of this new recognition would be the ability of trade unions, left political formations, and intellectuals to welcome the existence of independent black and women's organizations which would not merely retain separate organizational forms but which would retain their separate political programs as well as social and cultural lives. For without political autonomy, all of the calls for self-determination ring hollow. Even if the left can tolerate cultural separatism among blacks, Hispanics and women, the tradition of Marxism as a master *discourse* of liberation signifies a fundamental *will to dominate*, generating suspicion that the Marxists are merely being strategically and tactically flexible when they agree to certain alliances with those who do not agree with them. As with the questions of sex, ecology, and class, the condition for the liberation of Marxism is its adoption of scientific pluralism, or at the very least recognition that the categories of its dialects are historically specific and have lost their universality.

CULTURE AND EMANCIPATION

My main argument in this discussion of the preconditions for class formation, then, has not been to deny the role immediate producers may play, but rather to dispute the traditional Marxist contention that classes are *a priori* subjects defined by their determinate relation to the ownership of production and their place in the structure of production relations. Second, I have tried to show what it means to be faithful to Marx's epigraph, "as old needs are satisfied, new needs are made." The constitution of women as historical actors and emergence of the ecology movements in Western countries provide – together with those fractions of workers situated in the conjuncture of economic crisis and technological transformation – potential elements for a new oppositional class. To these may be added the struggles of the racial underclasses and the struggles for lesbian and gay freedom. Beyond the demand for equal rights, lesbians and gays have raised sharply the long-repressed questions associated with sexual "socialization," especially the way in which the civilizing process implies the imposition of a heterosexual morality and the displacement and the de-erotization of those moments of desire that are present as one of the possible courses of sexual development in all infants to "friendship," especially male bonding and women's conviviality. Each of the struggles challenges the social, economic, or ideological reproduction of society, either because it makes problematic capital accumulation processes or erodes the legitimacy of those institutions that embody normative structures necessary for social and cultural domination. At the core of these challenges are again questions about nature and human nature, both of which were relegated previously to the margins of political culture, the concerns of "cranks," "intellectuals," and "bohemians." What was once the province of a small *avant-garde* – conservationists, free-love advocates who suggested new forms of sexual relations, and labor intellectuals who advanced workers' self-management as an agitational and educational position – has become contested terrain at both the political and ideological levels. While it cannot be safely argued that these struggles are conducted in a manner informed by revolutionary ideologies (except in a handful of cases), or that capital has been unable to integrate them to a considerable degree, it does not follow that their radical content is thereby vitiated. For example, capitalism and patriarchy cannot yield to the demand for new social relations, for meaningful work which obeys a different logic, and, most important, for new relations to nature.

It may be objected that these are not questions that may be posed practically, that they represent a romantic hope that is unrealizable in the context of the scientific and technological revolution which is the reference for both orthodox Marxists and those, like Habermas, who regard the achievements of technical rationality to be irreversible. In *One Dimensional Man*, Marcuse argued that the debate around alienated labor has been resolved by the immense development of productive forces under capitalism. Although later he was to call for a new science and technology corrresponding to the new need to reconcile humans with nature, Marcuse's earlier proposal was to recognize that the demand for a rich and complex working life could not be met *within the realm of necessity*, but could only be realized in the realm of freedom, that is, in the time allotted by society for activities other than material production. The task of socialism and the workers' movement as a whole became identical with the demand for a shorter work week – the reduction of necessary labor to a few hours daily or a few days in each week. Beyond the sphere of production lay the emancipatory affirmative culture where we would have world enough and time to cultivate our aesthetic talents. Work as leisure would become satisfying because it was not tied to the domination of nature and would be entirely voluntary in this sphere. Technology made possible a future free of scarcity, which for Marcuse had been the basis of industrial discipline, sexual repression, the anti-aesthetic of everyday life, and other forms of domination.

The perspective is already present in Marx:

> the creation of a large quantity of disposable time apart from necessary labor time for society generally and each of its members (i.e. room for the development of the individual's full productive forces, hence those of society also); this creation of not-labor time appears at this stage of capital, as of earlier ones, as not labor time, free time for the few. What capital adds is that it increases the surplus labor time of the mass by all the means of art and science. . . . It is thus despite itself instrumental in creating the means of social disposable time, in order to reduce labor time for the whole society to a diminishing minimum, and thus to free everyone's time for their own development.[115]

Increasingly, the struggle of labor consists in preventing capital from converting the free time generated by science and technology into surplus labor time. Since the grand achievement of capital is its subsumption of science and the creation of technologies that reduce manual labor to a bare minimum in comparison to knowledge as a force of production, there is no point hoping for new forms of work relations. The best course, according to Marcuse, is to use free time differently since this is the true realm of freedom, where the full development of individual powers is possible. There is no doubt that the struggle for work relations that are configured by a conception of autonomy and self-management which restore to the producers control over the labor process – including what shall be produced, by what methods, and how much – is far from realization. At the same time, capital has failed to resolve the crisis of productivity except by means of creating a sphere in which self-management is *simulated* instrumentally in its service. The scientific and technological revolution still requires the support of those who are assigned to manual occupations or technical jobs that are bereft of autonomy. And these groups cannot be motivated by the promise of the unfreedom that pervades the sphere of free time, because this sphere has become permeated by capital's logic as much as the workplace.

I am not making the claim, for the present, that is in the constitution of human nature to wish work that is at once capable of being considered relevant to the central processes of the physical reproduction of society *and* satisfying because it grants to the worker considerable autonomy over the labor process. Such essentialist claims are not consisent with either the view that historical conditions constitute the social and individual needs or my belief in the dialectic between humans and nature. However, a science and technology based upon a rationality that denies work autonomy in the sphere of necessary production is unacceptable in late industrial societies that have not been able to deliver on their promise of erotic satisfactions through consumption, including the displacements of art in spectator entertainment forms. While the immediate producers are no longer the sufficient condition for oppositional class formation, neither can they be *replaced* by struggles that center on questions of sexuality and the environment. Rather, new class formations will develop at the conjuncture of work and interaction, on the basis of a new opposition that wishes to create a new culture, including a new work culture which posits as a goal the abolition of the division between intellectual and manual labor. Therefore, it is not a question of restoring craft traditions that have been permanently replaced. Society will not condone the return of labor-intensive technologies when machines can produce an equally useful and aesthetically pleasing object consistent with ecological and social normative structures. But the convenience and immediate economies of technical processes must be judged against two major criteria that have hitherto been ignored.

The first is still within the realm of political economy. As early as 1951, R. William Kapp asserted that *the costs* of private enterprise were not borne only by the individual firm, but socially as well.[116] Economies in the costs of production for the individual corporation may be expensive for the society, since the tendency of industrialism has been to socialize such costs as education, cleaning pollution, providing water and other overheads which are, nevertheless, essential for production. The mode of analysis suggested by Kapp would transform our ordinary ideas about the benefits that might accrue from given technological innovations. What follows is that some technologies are not economic, since they force the public sector to bear considerable costs in order to support them. These costs would increase taxes and withdraw more from consumption and in-vestment than the labor time saved on production. Given this negative ratio of cost to innovation, labor-intensive technologies might prove more efficient even from the perspective of technical rationality.

But the second type of rationality, work satisfaction, is far more serious a threat to technological change that is inherently labor-saving. As I have tried to show, those spheres of production not amenable to eliminating labor as such have witnessed corporate initiated efforts to modify management rationalities in order to insure technically rational outcomes, i.e. the average rate of profit or higher. The new work culture would evolve normative structures according to a new criterion. These include the right to configure labor time in a manner consistent with gratifications, both with regard to products that are the most socially useful within a range of options consistent with a rationality-determined goal of emancipation from deadening labor, as well as ecologically and sexually unsound work. This rationality would not replace technical reason entirely. The new emancipatory reason becomes the boundary of technical efficiency, a criterion that could be the major element in the calculation of resource allocation, and a crucial presupposition of scientific and technical innovation. Further, the *a priori* of maximum producers' autonomy would play a central role in the development of administrative styles. Such issues as centralized versus decentralized management of production and services would be decided by producers and consumers on the basis of a set of issues which include their pertinent effects on environment, the division of labor (which is really the problem of hierarchy with regard to responsibility and control over the entire work process), individual tasks and the "full development of individuals."

The new demands that have racked late capitalism are only partially separated from its economic crisis. The transhistorical character of the environmental, feminist, and work-related movements consists in their demand for a new *culture*. This is what separates the new needs from movements that are ensconced *within* industrial societies, asking only for distributive justice, or confining themselves to requests for the management of *existing* forces of production by self-managed workers' groups. For if the new needs that have been recognized within late capitalism break through the historicist assumptions of Marxism and are connected to the question of the domination of the two natures, then the movements for ecology, feminism, and new work relations suggest an adaptation of humans to the object world that is incompatible with existing social arrangements. The conjuncture of struggles constituting themselves on the basis of these needs may form a class whose demands cannot be met by hierarchical, patriarchal capitalist society. Science and technology are the central practices of late capitalist culture. To oppose their premises is to refuse the program of a post-industrial society in which free time as well as working life is synchronous with the domination of the external environment and human nature. Just as Marx argued that industrial capital had, against its own intentions, raised the question of the use of the "free time" that had been created by its development of the forces of production, so contemporary capital has itself been forced to raise the issue of its unilateral right to manage production, consumption, and public services. In addition, the "free" exploitation by private interests of nature has become one of the sharpest political struggles of the coming decade, precisely because of the power of the new ecological forces to raise the level of debate to the issue of rationality, and to propose an alternative to the technical rationality of capital. In the nineteenth and early-twentieth-centuries, it was the workers' claim to moral and intellectual leadership, as much as their struggles for economic justice, that constituted the moment of class formation that led to contestation for political and social power in Europe and other capitalist centers. As the century enters its final decades, workers are no longer the bearers of new norms that are capable in themselves of generating a sufficient challenge to capitalist hegemony at the level of ideology and culture.

NOTES

83. Adam Przeworski, "Proletariat into Class: The Process of Class Formation from Karl Kautsky's 'Class Struggle' to Recent Controversies," *Politics and Society* Volume 7, no. 4).

84. Ibid.
85. Antonio Gramsci, *Prison Notebooks* (New York: International Publishers, 1971), especially the chapters on "The Intellectuals" and "State and Civil Society." My interpretation follows the schema developed by Poulantzas, where economic, political, and ideological relations are understood as *relatively* autonomous within a social totality. This formulation clearly owes its derivation to Gramsci's analysis of the role of the intellectuals in contending for moral leadership within a social formation, and to Althusser's insistence upon the materiality and irreducibility of ideology to economic issues. Poulantzas's specific contribution is his theory of the state as the form in which political relations have their specificity. Thus, in this conception, the state is no longer "alienated civil society," but a matrix of ideological and repressive apparatuses which stand in relation of non-synchrony with the economic infrastructure. My differences with the structuralist theory of class and state relate to their notion of the concept of the economic as a *structure-in-dominance*. Since in Althusser's own words the ultimate or "last instance" in which the economic relations purify all the others "never comes", I see no reason, except ideologically, to posit this "law".
86. Przeworski, 'Proletariat into Class', op. cit., p. 399.
87. Ibid., p. 400.
88. Eric Olin Wright, "Class Boundaries in Advanced Capitalist Societies," *New Left Review* (no. 98).
89. George Conrad and Istvan Szeleny, *Intellectuals on the Road to Class Power* (London: Routledge & Kegan Paul, 1978).
90. Ernst Bloch, "Non-Synchronism and Dialectics," *New German Critique* (no. 11).
91. Carol Lopate (Ascher), "Who Knows What Ms Consumer Really Wants," Ann Oakely (ed.), *The Sociology of Housework* (New York: Pantheon Books, 1975).
92. Dorothy Dinerstein, *Mermaid and the Minotaur*; Nancy Chodorow, *Mothering*.
93. Karl Marx, *Capital* (Vol. 3, Part Three, especially Chapter 13).
94. Samir Amin, *Accumulation on a World Scale* (New York: Monthly Review Press, 1977).
95. V. I. Lenin, *Imperialism – the Highest Form of Capitalism*, op. cit.
96. See Stanley Aronowitz, "Labor and the Left in the United States," *Socialist Review* (March–April 1979).
97. Andre Gorz, "Colonialism at Home and Abroad," in *Socialism and Revolution* (New York: Anchor Books, 1970), p. 217. The formulation of the question by Gorz owes a great deal to Jean-Paul Sartre's analysis of the relation of French imperialism to the Algerian liberation movement in the late 1960's.
98. This position is implicit in Samir Amin's work, as well as Paul Baran and Paul Sweezy. See Baran and Sweezy's *Monopoly Capital* (New York: Monthly Review Press, 1966), especially Chapter 11, where the force of world revolution is held responsible for any possible

internal opposition except that of racially–oppressed groups and, peripherally, intellectuals who oppose the policies of imperialism.

99. See especially David Gordon, *Labor Market Segmentation* (Lexington: D. C. Heath, 1974).
100. For a prophetic treatment of the fiscal crisis of the State resulting from the organization of trade unions in the public sector and demands for increased social wage see James O'Connor, *The Fiscal Crisis of the State* (New York: St Martin's Press, 1972).
101. Richard Cloward and Frances Fox Piven, *Regulating the Poor* (New York: Vintage Books, 1971).
102. Richard Thomas, "Industrial Capitalism, Intra Class Racial Conflict and the Formation of Black Working Class Political Culture" in the *Journal of African Afro-American Affairs*, Vol. 3, no. 1, Spring, 1979.
103. Barrington Moore, *Injustice: The Social Bases of Obedience and Revolt* (White Plains, Me.: Sharpe, 1978).
104. Oliver Cromwell Cox, *Caste, Class and Race* (New York: Monthly Review Press, 1964).
105. Manning Marable, "The Third Reconstruction: Black Nationalism and Race Relations After the Revolution," *Social Text* (Vol. 2, no. 1), Spring, 1981.
106. Henri Lefebvre, *The Survival of Capitalism* (New York: St Martin's Press, 1976): "the theory of reproduction (of the social relations) gives us back a reference that is no longer external and partial, but internal and global. Together with the dialectic it provides us with a reconsideration of ideology, the concept of which has fallen into the utmost confusion . . . for lack of a reference. By way of definition: any representation is ideological if it contributes either immediately or 'mediately' to the reproduction of the relations of production. Ideology is, therefore, inseparable from practice."
107. Nicos Poulantzas, *Classes in Contemporary Capitalism* (London: New Left Books, 1975).
108. Among the most important ideological practices which contribute to the reproduction of the relations of production is the mind/body split that is inscribed in the division between intellectual and manual labor, between rational and impulsive "behavior" (usually considered the principal binary of mental life), and the divisions white/black, men/women that correspond to the mind/body dichotomy.
109. Wilhelm Reich, *The Function of the Orgasm* (New York: Touchstone Books, 1973), pp. 12–13.
110. Paul Willis, *Learning to Labour* (Westmead: Saxon House, 1977). Pierre Bourdieu, *Outline of a Theory of Practice* (London: Cambridge University Press, 1977), p. 72: "The structures constitutive of a particular type of environment (e.g. the material conditions of existence characteristic of a class condition) produce *habitus* – systems of durable, transposable *dispositions*, structured structures predisposed to function as structuring structures, that is, as principles of the generation and structuring of practices and representations which can be objectively 'regulated' and 'regular'

without in any way being the product of obedience to rules . . . !" This concept suggests that the reproduction of social relations is structured by practices that are situated within class or group formations and not imposed from above unless they become part of the "structures within which they function." People not only reproduce the relations of production as they are given externally, but constitute alternative or oppositional relations when they have become isolated from the dominant structure. This helps explain the duality of social reproduction and practices that are counter-reproductive within the same logical space.

111. Cornel West, "Black Theology of Liberation as Critique of Capitalist Civilization," mimeo paper, 1980. James Cone, *A Black Theology of Liberation* (Philadelphia: 1970).

112. J. P. Sartre, *Critique of Dialectical Reason* (London: New Left Books, 1973). p. 772.

113. Ibid.

114. Franz Fanon, *Black Skin, White Masks* (New York: Grove Press, 1967), pp. 217–18.

115. Marx., op. cit.

116. R. William Kapp, *Social Costs of Private Enterprise* (New York: Schocken Books, 1975).

5

Forms of Historical Disruption

Historical materialism has always been confronted with the events that have placed one of its central precepts, the unity of history, in severe jeopardy. Marx's scheme – according to which changes in the mode of production may be taken as the markers of different historical periods – operates at a level of abstraction so broad as to render its analytic value doubtful when faced with concrete historical developments. On the one hand, the mode of production is supposed to be constituted by antagonistic but mutually-dependent social classes. On the other hand, all issues such as culture and ideology are understood in their relation to the social totality, to the specific historical period of which they are a part. For Marxism, capitalism is a world system that tends towards uniformity on the basis of the hegemonic weight of commodity relations, and consequently its form of rationality.

Yet, the rise of nationalism and religion as serious world historical forces – ones not always synchronous with the mode of production – has forced Marxism to modify its theory of historical periodicity to fit these developments. Rosa Luxemburg[117] and her progeny of the dependency school of world capitalist development insist that the phenomenon of nationalism is a regressive social force; the logic of capital tended to homogeneity, especially in the relations between the advanced and the undeveloped parts of the globe, and established the conditions for world proletarian solidarity. Since accumulation occurs on an ever-widening sphere and scale, capital was fated to eventually foreclose its own expansion by creating its own competition. The disappearance of the non-capitalist sectors of the world would doom the advanced countries, plunging them into a fateful crisis which only the proletarian revolution – led by the workers in the most advanced sectors – would resolve. While this prognostication has not been without merit in the glare of the historical record, it failed to take account of the degree to which underdevelopment was *produced* by the advanced countries. The economically–backward societies were, according to Andre Gunder Frank and his school, increasingly drawn into the orbit of the advanced countries on the basis of systematic exploitation through unequal exchange. Backwardness was a product of relations of dependency created by the needs of capital in advanced societies. Thus, capitalism was a world system whose nonsynchrony was more apparent than real. Nationalist movements seeking economic, political, and cultural autonomy could not reach their goals because the context of the struggle for national independence eventually forced them into submission. Imperialism bought off the would-be national bourgeoisie, making it a *comprador* class or else forced its subordination through economic and military coercion, even if the shell of political independence was granted. For Luxemburg, only the working class could liberate humanity from the scourge of capitalism and war in both advanced and backward societies, because all of the other classes were in thrall of capital. Socialism could not support the national aspirations of middle classes, since these were the expressions of a dying class or, worse, a class umbilically tied to imperialism. Thus the Marxist theory of the mode of production as the structural coherence of history was preserved.

Lenin's position was quite different on the surface, but its deep structure was similar. While he agreed that the nationalist bourgeoisie was incapable of completing its own revolution of liberation from imperialism, Lenin viewed the nationalist revolution as historically progressive, because of its capacity to politically mobilize the masses of workers and peasants. Nationalism – the revolutionary ideology of a bourgeoisie that seeks to dominate its own market – cannot succeed without the support of the oppressed masses. However, having proposed an anti-imperialist struggle, nationalism is bound to betray its own cause, leaving its worker/peasant allies to lead the anti-imperialist movement in the wake of the bourgeoisie's compromise. Thus, Lenin's law of *uneven development* represents a recognition by one tendency in Marxism that the effects of the external domination by imperialism on the social structure of the underdeveloped society are not synchronous; whereas dependency theory tends to regard uneven exchange between the two as a form of synchronicity leaving no residue of culture, politics, and ideology within an underdeveloped country. In turn, uneven development is a way of explaining the capacity of capital to overcome its economic crisis on the basis of the economic integration and political demobilization of the workers in the advanced countries which are the beneficiaries of capital's export.

Lenin's theory of imperialism has been criticized from a number of perspectives as inadequate to a description of the contemporary world system that developed after the Second World War, even if its analytic powers were considered adequate for explaining the First World War. However, the theory was an attempt from within Marxism to correct the Marxist tendency to devalue the significance of cultural and political struggles that were not consonant with working-class formation. To be sure, Lenin clearly believed his theory more adequate to the explanation of the course of class-consciousness in the advanced countries and class formation in underdeveloped countries. He was not given to granting autonomy to nationalism, but saw it almost exclusively in terms of the problems of working-class economic formation and political mobilization. Similarly, his theory of the peasant revolt subsumed these struggles under working-class political hegemony, and refused to grant them autonomy within the problematic of socialist revolution. Yet he recognized that the peasantry possessed the capacity, in Russia at least, to make demands that were not easily assimilable to the program of the Bolsheviks. Consequently, Lenin's aspiration for a science of politics was constantly buffeted by the nonsynchrony of events. Uneven development became a "law of motion" of capitalism in its imperialist phase, thus preserving the schema of periodicity advanced by Marxism.

One more example of the strains with Marxist concepts of historical time will suffice before advancing the theoretical discussion. During the 1980 workers' strikes in Poland, it became evident that the Catholic Church occupied a place at once tied to the prevailing order and independent of it at the same time. While the Church's role in the strike remained conservative to the extent that it counselled moderation by the strikers, it also intervened on the side of the strikers by pronouncing their demands just. Similarly, more than one revolutionary movement within Latin America and Eastern Europe has turned to the Church for support. The Catholic hierarchy has been split on these requests, caught between its historical role of accommodating the masses to the existing social order and its character as a political institution whose constituencies play a part in the formulation of both ecclesiastical and social policy.

In the modern world no major religion has been able to achieve unification either of doctrine or its political stance. In all underdeveloped countries, religious autonomy from the prevailing social and political structure has become as characteristic as its dependency on their sufferance. At the same time, those regimes whose use of force to achieve social order is limited by the requirement of legitimacy, are progressively more concerned to achieve approval by and cooperation of the Church. Under these circumstances, the Marxist theory according to which the Church is an instrument of class domination, in both the ideological and political sense, has been forced to undergo considerable modification. Even as the Vatican desperately seeks to maintain Catholicism's traditional patriarchal stance with respect to sexual questions (in the wake of a revolt of its own cadre as well as its constituents against these strictures), it has been forced to move leftward on questions of economic and political justice. The nonsynchrony of the Church's own internal composition is matched by its growing frustration in the futile quest for doctrinal unity.

THE NATURE OF TIME

The problem for historical materialism is not confined merely to specific historical judgements such as are indicated by traditional Marxist attitudes towards nationalism and religion. At another level of abstraction – the question of the conception of social time – Marxism is revealed to be seriously flawed; it cannot theoretically integrate the nonsynchronous into its dialectical conception of history. Recall Adorno, who accused Hegel and Marx of having been bemused by their doctrine of historical stages, by the move towards identity theory that tended to imprison difference. The dialectic, for Adorno, becomes a formal system – little more than an extension of formal logic. Contradictions are confined to those that appeal at the level of the internal relations of a given structure in which the teleology of resolution is already implied. But the temporal difference is excluded. Ernst Bloch has attempted to correct this tendency of asserting that

> Not all people exist in the same Now. They do so only externally, by virtue of the fact that they may be seen today. But that does not mean that they are living in the same time with others.
>
> Rather they carry earlier things with them, things which are

intricately involved. One has one's times according to where one stands corporeally, above all in terms of classes. Times older than the present continue to affect older strata . . . [118]

Citing youth and peasantry as types who stand in relation to classes in a nonsynchronous manner, one living in a past, the other in their own future, Bloch argues that the strength of fascism among the masses was gathered because it was able to understand the multilayering of immiserated groups and to manipulate the different nows among them. In contrast, socialism was concerned to flatten the differences, and failed to comprehend the specificity of the struggles of groups for whom time was not only lived in the present, but was bound up equally with pasts and futures. Bloch's distinction between *objective* contradictions – the old synchrony between forces and relations of production in the Marxist problematic – is distinguished from subjective non-synchrony. I wish to extend Bloch's position that we exist in different nows to both *objective* nonsynchrony, as well as a lived experience which itself is *objective.* The multilayering of past, present, and future undermines the old theory of periodicity, which insists on uniform time by reducing differences among social groups, various social structures, and institutions that occupy the same external temporal space. Capitalism is the structure-in-dominance in the historical dialectic of multilayered reality. But this dominance merely signifies that the submerged differences, rooted in temporal nonsynchrony, must refer to the dominant reality as a boundary, not the operative principle of their functioning.

Unevenness, then, is not merely a *spatial* category related to conditions of capital accumulation; it is also a *temporal* category whose effects determine the configuration of politics and social life. For groups whose struggles are rooted in various moments of time, in different political and cultural problematics associated with these moments, the problematic of class may or may not be the effect of their struggles. For Bloch the undecidability of class formation implies that socialist strategy must intervene to insure that a form of integration occurs that is at least anti-fascist, since the historical problematic of Marxism currently omits multilayered reality. In the final accounting, Bloch took Lenin's insight of unevenness a step further. But in 1935 he was still committed to the problematic of working-class formation, or to be more exact, the historical materialist concept of totalizing the non-synchronous.

This was, of course, completely understandable under the circumstances of the imminent triumph of fascism in Europe after Hitler's rise to power. Bloch was trying to convince Marxism to abandon its notion of synchrony in order to forge a united front of the diverse subaltern classes and strata in the struggle against tyranny. For him, it was not merely a question of dealing with the differences between social classes whose formation took place under previous historical conditions and the modern proletariat. He also recognized that, within the structure of late capitalism, immiserated groups such as unemployed youth could not be made simply into proletarians but lived in a different "now" from that of the workers, and were therefore autonomous both in their demands and their needs.

However, we are not only substantially distanced from the context that prompted Bloch to offer a theory of non-synchrony and multilayered reality, but also from his specific formulation of the problem in terms of class formation. For it is not possible for historical materialism to integrate feminism, ecology, nationalism, or religion on the basis of the problematic of working-class formation – which implies the centrality of the contradiction between the productive forces and the productive relations. Each social formation exists in a different now; their temporal reference is not only at variance, but is often mutually antagonistic. The logic of Bloch's theory of the multilayering dialectic undermines the intention to make heteronomous the struggles which contribute to human emancipation.

THE RISE OF RELIGION

For example, the Catholic Church's implacable opposition to abortion and support of patriarchal family relations is tied to the same trans-historical problematic as the feminist movement, but their interests are not reconcilable. They exist at different points on the historical spectrum. The dominant tendency of Catholic theology poses a serious obstacle to feminist aspirations, even as it tolerates national liberation and workers' struggles in Latin America and Eastern Europe. These are contradictory moments in the history of the Church itself, as well as in its relations to various social structures and social movements. Its place in these structures has become ambiguous in proportion to the social power of differing ideological and political relations that affect its internal life. Pope John Paul II knows, as does any prelate, that without its anti-abortion stand and its support of marriage and the family, the Church as a religious institution is seriously undermined, even if it is forced to modify its secular postures. Thus, the Church hierarchy *stands* on its doctrinal grounds against secular liberation, while yielding more and more in relation to social policy to liberation forces struggling against imperialist domination.

In the case of the Iranian/Islamic revolution, these contradictions are magnified to an even greater degree. The conflation of nationalist and religious forces has taken the form of a strong movement towards a theocratic state, where the oppression of women becomes not only a moral invocation to the masses but a matter of secular law. Nationalism in Iran exists in a now where the past and present do not divide religious labor, as in the Catholic Church. The bold step of Islamic nationalism is to make the past dominate the present, integrating the modernist demand for bourgeois economic and political freedom with the ancient requirement that everyday life, including family and sexuality, be subject to the rule of religious-*cum*-secular law. This conjuncture violates the Marxist expectation that nationalism brings in its wake the more-or-less rapid disappearance of the "idyllic relations" of the old order. Incongruously, the Islamic revolutionaries insist they can bring state capitalism to a country within the framework of the old patriarchy that subordinates women by imposing chaste dress codes and sexual behavior, and other social restrictions consistent with male domination. In Iran the revolutionary forces have become the most virulent proponents of both an anti-imperialist struggle and traditions that are fundamentally precapitalist. The Islamic rebellion itself lives in at least two nows; it has virtually no feudal survivals within the economic order, but its social and political orders are situated between the past and the present.

Undoubtedly, an historical-materialist retort to this discussion would remind us that capitalist social relations must maintain their hegemony even if uneven development within nationalist-dominated countries presents temporary anomalies in the social and cultural spheres. According to this view, the mode of production of material life would eventually force a reconciliation of political and social institutions to production relations. But the phenomena of Islamic capitalism, African "socialism," as well as Eastern European socialisms, are reminders that incommensurability marks the relation of the economic infrastructure with ideological, political, and cultural relations. Historically, it may be that the United States and Great Britain were the only capitalist states in which the classical formula of infrastructure determining superstructure even appeared to hold. Of course, even in these instances, the family – which was an inheritance of the patriarchal order that predated capitalism – and the persistence of Catholicism – which owed its birth to the rebellion against Romanism or Judaism, and is a product of ancient society – never corresponded in their ideological relations to the capitalist mode of production, even though the institutions of Church and family made political and cultural accommodations. However, the political and social forces expressed in family and religion are not entirely congruent with the demand of capital to subordinate all ideological apparatuses to its norms. Needless to say, "really existing" socialism has faced the same oppositions to its industrialization of production and secularization of the state. Neither the Marxist nor the bourgeois expectation that the triumph of economy – its replacement of all other ideologies, its elevation to the level of dominant political discourse – has been fully realized. Within the United States, the rise of a new right in the 1970's and 1980's is at once an affirmation of bourgeois norms of free enterprise against the tendency of increased state economic intervention, a defense of patriarchal family relations against the usurpation of its traditions by schools and laws that granted women sexual autonomy, and an affirmation of religious traditions that are anti-rationalistic and, at the same time, highly individualistic. On the one hand, fundamentalist evangelical religions – upon which right-wing politics has attempted to construct a secular analogue – affirm the Protestant notion of *private* experience of salvation, the communication of the individual alone with God, relatively unmediated by ministry. On the other hand, the anti-bourgeois element in this religion consists in its heated defense of Biblical conceptions of evolution and revelatory ideologies that hold to religion as a mystical, emotional experience. Even though the capitalist state has always *tolerated* religion, its displacement to the public sphere is a recurring theme in American history and, in the present revival, takes the form of fundamentalist demands for the modification of public law in accordance with religious precepts.

Thus, the rise of religion as a political force in both undeveloped and advanced industrial countries of the state-socialist and capitalist varieties is not explained as a remnant of the feudal order. Nor is it linked merely to the old agrarian aristocracies, which in the United States had leftovers in the Southern region. The mass-turn to religion and family attests to the fact that the past has a vital life within the present. The secular modernism of bourgeois aesthetics and of industrial society is no better able to comprehend these phenomena than historical materialism, which is in this context just another type of modernity. Religious fervor arises as a rejection of the normative structures of modernity, which view spirituality, intuition, and experience as forms of ideology to be overcome by scientific rationality. Contemporary spiritualism is not only a testament to the failure of scientific materialism and secular humanism to keep religion on the margins of civilized society, but a sign of its "post-modernist" character. For moral culture premeates recent literature as much as it does politics. Just as fascist ideology is at the same time (1) a recuperation of unresolved, transhistorical needs and (2) a type of futurism for which the old aesthetic norms of bourgeois society were archaic and reactionary, so the resurgence of mysticism as the dominant force in the new religions presents itself as a futurist science. It condemns the moral neutrality of science and technology, the refusal of the state to promote spiritual values, and the collectivist proclivities of both Marxism and multinational corporations. What is most remarkable is that persons of all social strata join evangelical religious sects, whereas in the 1920's and 1930's membership in these groups was confined to workers in marginal locations within the political economy, such as in agriculture and in low-paying jobs in the least technologically-advanced sectors.

Marxism has developed a different conceptual model for explaining these developments than has Bloch. Those who insist that modes of production form a unity under which all institutions are subsumed have advanced the Marxist theory of ideology to account for the incommensurabilities of late capitalism. Historical time remains intact in this explanation, but *lived experience* is somehow unable to apprehend the actuality of the social order; it inhabits an imaginary world in which its relation to the real is always problematic. Louis Althusser's heroic efforts to preserve historical materialism found, in the theory of ideology, a way of avoiding the need to come to grips with the problems associated with Marxism's postulate of the infrastructure/superstructure dichotomy.

Althusser argues that struggles, movements, and institutions that stand in a relation of non-correspondence to the infrastructure are "ideological" apparatuses of the state, materializations of the Imaginary (a category borrowed from Jacques Lacan which refers to the intuitive, lived experience of the body . . . lived experiences which overlap, overflow into infinite successions of sensorial, emotional and conceptual jugglings. The Imaginary is situated in the human mind as a Lacanian equivalent of the unconcious, a region in a constant state of flux, unable to enter the Symbolic order except as a representation of trace.). Althusser's notion of ideology is connected to the concept of *lived experience* as a specific relation of non-synchrony to the Real, and to the Symbolic order in a relation of non-identity. This is the most advanced point historical materialism has been able to arrive at in the search for a theory adequate to its object: late capitalist society.

However, as in Bloch, Althusser shares the tendency despite the category of *ideological apparatus* to situate ideology in the *subject*, where time differs from *real* time; but even this distinction connotes the superiority of the latter. Ideology is contrasted with science by the manner in which the object of knowledge is constituted. While the object of scientific knowledge is not the same as the real object, Althusser posits that theory is true to the extent that its conceptual foundations are correct, rather than arguing for the cruder method of empirical falsification. Ideology is ideology because its object is constituted wrongly, even if this relation as lived experience is capable of generating its objective correlate in the form of institutions. The rise of religious movements and the patriarchal family, for example, are no less representations of lived experience than secular politics or the economic infrastructure. But Althusser's Marxism prevents him from dealing with the crisis of temporal incommensurability signalled by the autonomous structures. When he doggedly asserts that the economic structure-in-dominance determines in the last instance the social totality, the genuine advance represented in the theory of ideology is ultimately recuperated for orthodoxy.

The point is to affirm Bloch's insistence on the multilayered and dialectical nature of reality, whether in its "subjective" or "objective" instances. Since Althusser is unwilling to acknowledge the multilayering of social time as past, present and future, he is forced to maintain the separation of subject and object in which only "experience" embodies non-identity. Althusser retains the category of uneven development with which Lenin described the modern world system, and by which revolutions were explained in his concept of the structured totality. The relatively autonomous elements of the totality become identical in the infrastructure of historical time. Thus, Althusser's Marxism is in the last analysis a reductionism, where ideology plays the role that the theory of mediations plays for Hegelian Marxism.

NOTES

117. Rosa Luxemburg, *Accumulation of Capital* (New York: Monthly Review Press, 1968).
118. Ernst Bloch, "Non-Synchronism and Dialectics," op. cit., p. 22.

6

Towards a New Strategy of Liberation

Just as capitalism is the name we affix to the system in which commodity production based upon the domination of nature has become the leading force in world economic life but does not subsume all elements of social, political, and ideological relations, so a new conception of the emancipatory project of which socialism has been the leading proposal must be articulated.

I will begin by returning to Lenin's conception of the party as the unifying force in the struggle for socialism. The revolutionary party was conceived in the Leninist tradition as capable of performing this task because it substituted science for ideology. Since the working class, by its own efforts, could only achieve trade-union consciousness, since it was limited by the social and the technical division of labor and (as Lukács added) by the reification of the social world as a whole, the scientific basis of politics – the socialist imperative of class struggles – must be brought to the working class from the outside. In short, Marxism was seen as the master discourse of class struggle and human emancipation because it provided a systemic, scientific view of past, present, and future.

I have pointed out that the self-liberation of the subordinate classes is the condition of a self-managed socialism. The logic of this position is closely connected to the critique of the party as a bureaucratic apparatus that, because of its *scientific* claims, gains *domination over* the working class, rather than constituting a condition for its liberation. Those who have followed the events of the post Second World War period in both Western and Eastern Europe have observed the evolution of communist and socialist parties from forces of opposition to parties of the prevailing order. The aspiration to control the state by parliamentary or other means is, in the end, a Jacobin goal, not one consistent with an emancipatory socialism. The centralization of command, characteristic of European socialist and communist parties alike, belies their democratic professions.

I do not deny the value of particular struggles supported or led by centralist parties that march under the banner of Marxism, nor the claim that post–1968 socialism in the West has become somewhat multi-tendencied in orientation. But adherence to Marxism as a master discourse prevents these parties from becoming democratic in their internal workings. Marxism serves to rationalize their transformation from revolutionary or oppositional forces situated outside the system of domination to parliamentary groups that represent particular working-class interests within the capitalist state. Thus Marxism covers a multitude of sins, if it can be shown "on a scientific basis" that the historical task of representation is confined at any particular moment to struggles for specific reforms.

In response to a question, a French Communist who teaches social science at a Parisian university remarked: "The Communist Party is not an obstacle to gaining remedies for particular demands of the workers and other strata of French people, but it has become an obstacle to the project of social transformation." Such are the ambiguities of politics in a non-revolutionary period. Even if the socialist movements have gained a degree of moral and intellectual leadership within some capitalist countries, particularly among intellectuals and workers, it does not signify the triumph of specifically emancipatory ideas among key sectors of the population. Today, it means merely that the left has become the most effective, if not reliable, parliamentary and trade-union expression of the workers' conscious interests. And as is well known, even if workers and intellectuals of all kinds tend to vote for the left, it does not restrict their autonomy at the workplace and in the neighborhood. Modern left-parliamentary politics may aggregate desire, but it tends to suppress its extra-parliamentary expressions; these are considered, by the parties of order, to be disruptive of national or class interests. The contemporary task of parliamentary socialism is to make marginal all movements at the base which implicitly or explicitly renounce this mode of aggregation. Thus the left, because of its claim to a master discourse – its "scientific" claims – becomes the most indefatigable enemy of the opposition in those countries where it "represents" the masses within the state.[119]

The time is hardly at hand where emancipatory possibilities are powerful enough to overcome the necessity of parliamentary socialist intervention. Nor does my argument rest on the proposition that the parties of socialism are obstacles at present to the self-emancipation of the proletariat. On the contrary, with important exceptions – notably Poland – the working classes of advanced capitalist societies as well as those in state-socialist countries are heir to a long tradition of compromise with capital, punctuated by frequent though sporadic struggles, some of which exceed the bounds of parliamentary or trade-union action and raise for a brief instant the horizon of freedom.

The direction of my argument is that a master discourse of revolution is not possible. The contradictions of the left may be summarized as the problem of *representation*, both in the philosophical and the political meaning of the term. Lenin and Lukács were aware of this problem in their very constitution of the theory of the party and the theory of reification. The party does not represent the working class as it appears in daily life, for the class is divided by industry, sector, national origin, race, sex, and the like. Trade unions derive from these splits in the class. They are organized by trade, occupation, sector, and – in U.S. history at least – by race. Thus, without the intervention of the parties to pose the question of class, the workers remain serially organized, in Sartre's terms. Their unification depends upon the formation that can weld these disparate parts into a single force against capital as such, rather than against its segments.

Such a formation cannot be of the class. If this were the case, the party would fall victim to all the divisions characteristic of working-class life. The central characteristic of the party is its recruitment of intellectuals and workers who commit themselves to a scientific understanding of the world and agree to guide their own actions according to the imperatives of social analysis. The party brings socialism to the working class as an aim that is not "given" by the circumstances of the daily struggle for workers' demands. Therefore, there is already an incommensurability between the scientific basis upon which the politics of socialism is founded and the "ideological" basis of actual class struggles, or even struggles about class formation. The party does not represent the workers' immediate demands alone; it is the instrument for the realization of their real interest – to transform society in order to emancipate themselves from the bonds of wage labor. But Marxism posits these real interests on the basis of its discovery that the tendency of capitalist development is to proletarianize all strata of workers by reducing all labor to its simple form. Under the conditions that produce the collective laborer, the subject-object of history, a unified proletariat congeals.

The implied judgement of Lenin, Lukács, and Althusser is that, historical tendencies notwithstanding, the proletariat remains both internally divided by nationality and separated from history by the unbridgable gulf created by the domination of the commodity form. The party can only "represent" the proletariat in its multiple immediate interests by suppressing the emancipatory goal which, in effect, remains unrepresentable in the empirical sense. Further, as Robert Michels revealed, after the First World War the party developed as an institution separate from both the immediate and putative interest of the proletarians. It may be argued that the emergence of the party bureaucracy as an element of the social systems of capitalism and state socialism derived from the crisis of representation inherent in Marxism's self-positing as a master discourse of historical change.

The problem of representation inheres in two central features of Marxist theory: (1) its reading of the relationship between the undeniable phenomenon of the degradation of differences based upon labor and the persistence of class fractions, even within its own discourse; and (2) the epistemological assumption of the party as the repository of scientific knowledge which can "reflect" the will of the unified class, even if the class does not "know" it. The second feature has been challenged by the Althusserian school on the basis of its attempt to deny a theory of knowledge as a legitimate aspect of Marxist theory. That is, the concept of representation as it is employed by traditional Marxism presupposes the distinction between knowledge and its object, thereby forgetting that knowledge is both constituted by its object and also constitutes the object itself.

I would argue that the party occupies an ambiguous space. Within the capitalist system (not state socialisms) the left parties, in order to gain political authority within the working class, are obliged to "represent" its interests, at least on the terrain of parliamentary and certain aspects of economic struggle. But the party constitutes the class as a revolutionary subject in its own image of historical necessity. This does not signify that revolution is a Sorelian myth needed to promote the party's self-imposed goals. It means that, through its educational and agitational function, the party may convince a section of workers to become part of Marxism's revolutionary objectives. In other words, there is no question of representation or even of a master discourse that is slated to assume the logical center of historical change.

At the same time, the party is itself constituted by its own discourse as a part of history. Its role tended to be revolutionary so long as it occupied the space of those demands that were not recuperable within the framework of specific capitalist or proto-capitalist societies such as existed in Eastern Europe prior to the two world wars. Among these have been the demands for free trade unions, an independent parliament that possesses real power to legislate reforms, universal suffrage, and the like. However, when capitalist and state-socialist societies emerged as more or less politically stable forms of power in the latter half of this century, the left parties became only *upon occasion* oppositional, when excluded from bourgeois or bureaucratic hegemony. In recent times, especially in Western and Eastern Europe, the historic left parties have become parties of order, the instruments of rule in late-capitalist and state-socialist countries.

Those sections of the Marxist movement that have observed, with horror, the phenomenon of the integration of the party into the state, imagine that they can replace the traditional left as the representatives of the "real" working-class interest. It ought to be clear by now that such an outcome is unlikely and ultimately romantic. For the problems of whether the workers exist as a class in the historical sense or not are insurmountable by means of the old aspirations to hegemony inherent in Leninist political theory. Marxism is no longer the master discourse, the science of society capable of establishing moral and intellectual leadership; it is rooted in old, surpassed assumptions.

TOWARD A NEW POLITICS

What, then, is a politics appropriate to the theoretical propositions advanced in this book? First, *political* forms must be supported by those aspiring to make critical social theory relevant to a praxis that is genuinely oppositional to the prevailing social and political order, as well as challenging the economic hegemony of capital. Theory must comprehend that Marxism's economic *logocentricity* has constituted its major weakness, both theoretically and politically.[120] I do not argue from the premise of either the famous expressive totality of Lukács or the structuralist concept of totality to support this perspective. In both cases, the aim is to overcome differences in order to achieve proletarian identity. Perhaps

Gramsci's theory of the historic bloc is a more adequate formulation of the politics of the present period. Neither those who hold to the *a priori* hegemony of the proletariat – guided by its revolutionary party – or its antinomy, the theory of autonomism – according to which struggles do not aim at even an alliance of various classes and groups in the interest of emancipation – are adequate to the politics of the future. Building from a micropolitics of autonomous oppositional movements, whether derived from production relations or not, a new historic bloc may emerge. It might include any of those forces which, despite their particular oppositions, recognize the task of general emancipation. Surely the character of this bloc would differ in various societies. In some instances, the struggles of peasants for land might constitute in specific periods the cutting edge of historical transformation. In other places, the demand for independent workers' organizations, as in Poland, would lay bare the crisis of representation for the ruling Communist party.

However, in advanced capitalist societies – where the land question has disappeared as a major social issue except in its ecological form,[121] and the autonomy of trade unions is a settled question within the framework of parliamentary democracy – the new historic bloc may be built on new premises. The demand for an end to male supremacy and for the emancipation of sexuality from the thrall imposed upon it by social and material reproduction are crucial elements for the new forces of liberation. Second, there are those movements demanding a new relation between society and external environment, for the restoration of the autonomy of nature, and thus for a strategy of negotiation rather than the domination of nature. Third, those movements demanding the self-management of the workplace and living space, and those challenging the character of science and technologies that perpetuate hierarchy, are part of the new opposition. Finally, there are those who have insisted upon racial, ethnic, and linguistic autonomy within society, a demand that goes beyond the important demand for equality. Even if race has been appropriated by capital as a means to divide its opposition, this historical development does not exhaust the question. Caste oppression, like patriarchy, preceded capitalism *and* outlived it, because socialism does not address the problem of hierarchy so long as it has defined itself exclusively as social ownership of the means of production. In "really existing" socialist countries, the struggle against hierarchy has moved no further than it did under advanced capitalism, even if formal equality based upon race and sex are constitutionally guaranteed. Hierarchy is a property of all societies in which the domination of nature defines the social relations. Since there is absolutely no tradition within "really existing" socialism and socialist movements that challenges hierarchy as a relatively autonomous structure from that of class, socialism has never been able to overcome race and ethnic divisions which are quite distinct, if not completely independent, from exploitation based upon class.

There would be no question of the hegemony of the working class, as traditionally constituted, over the historic bloc, nor of the claim of Marxism to represent more than its own historic perspective. In fact, the new historic bloc would have to become anti-hegemonic as a political and social principle, recognizing the *permanence* of difference, which Marxism believes, at least implicitly, can be overcome by socialist transformation. Thus the struggle for a new society is contemporaneous with the anti-hegemonic movements of liberation, which will remain autonomous both in the course of the struggle and in the process of creating a new society. Under these conditions, Marxism retains its force to the extent that it insists upon the importance of theory taking the point of view of human emancipation, but which does not dogmatically hold to a particular doctrinal canon.

GRAMSCI AND IDEOLOGICAL HEGEMONY

In this context, Gramsci's theory of ideological hegemony, advanced as a central explanation for the persistence of bourgeois rule and conditions for a new form of rule, retains its power. As Norbert Bobbio has shown, Gramsci inverts the Hegelian concept of civil society, and Marx's appropriation of it as the economic infrastructure, by positing the so-called superstructures – particularly ideology and its apparatuses – as the major condition for bourgeois hegemony.[122] Thus, *cultural* questions become the foci for historical change, even if their forms are linked to the reproduction of capital. It is not only that moral and intellectual leadership of the society is a necessary concomitant to political and economic power, but becomes its very condition. Thus the struggle over culture, rather than the struggle for economic advantage, is connected to the problematic of historical change, since under late capitalist conditions economic struggles no longer retain their subversive content.

This is not a statement about the force of economic struggles by subaltern social classes in configuring the course of capitalist or state-socialist development. As I have argued elsewhere in this book,[123] even the most modest wage struggles, or as in Poland the fight for trade unions independent of state/party control, or the fight for racial and sex equality, often force serious transformations in the logic of capital. Yet the process by which these struggles may become part of an emancipatory project requires cultural autonomy as well. For it is this realm which increasingly becomes the terrain of capital's reproduction, not only ideologically but materially as well. The force of the feminist and ecology movements may be said to constitute major forms of economic and political opposition in the U.S. today because they imply a whole new set of relationships that subvert the prevailing social order as well as limiting capital accumulation. But these movements, together with movements for self-management at the workplace and in living spaces for national-cultural autonomy, have developed *against* the master discourse of Marxism, as well as the discourses of male domination, racism, bourgeois science and technology, as well as capitalism. For this reason, there is no possibility that an *alternate* hegemony will correspond to the aspiration of emancipation because that aspiration is counter-hegemonic in nature.

In this connection, the traditional opposition of materialist theory to theology seems no longer tenable. Of course, the Marxist critique of religious *institutions* has lost none of its political validity, to the extent that most of them remain committed to hierarchical social relations of all sorts. But we must take seriously Juan Luis Segundo's objection to Marx's own formulation of the question in his early writings.[124] Segundo argues that, since Marx acknowledged religion to be the *expression of* human suffering and the *protest against* human suffering, the logical grounds for denouncing religious ideas were undercut, even if historical materialism hopes to do away with the necessity of religion by transforming its social basis. If suffering gives rise to religion, then the abolition of suffering should end it. Segundo reminds us that Marx and the Marxists were committed to the abolition of the state, but were prepared to retain its repressive function in the transition period between capitalism and communism. Thus, he argues, the extent to which religion is a form of protest against suffering will not allow for its disappearance in the early stages of socialism. Certainly there is much evidence that sections of the Catholic Church in various parts of Latin America have taken seriously this protest function. According to Segundo, the theoretical basis for Marxist opposition to religion – as distinct from opposition to the Church – is arbitrary, even under socialism.

This point may be extended to a contemporary concept intrinsic to Marxism and other specific theories: that all forms of spiritual explanations for natural and social phenomena can be ascribed to the under developed state of knowledge of the external world, or, in the Marxist amendation, to the underdevelopment of the productive forces. Science, including Marxist theory, provides no space for undecidability or indeterminacy (except as a rational category of science itself), and then transforms the unknowable into a subjective category, showing it to be the result of the experimental method, rather than a property of nature itself.

In the context of the subsumption of science under technology in the two centuries of industrial development, and given the emergence of social science as a functional technique of social control (of which some varieties of Marxism are a part), insisting on the autonomy of the two natures constitutes a type of religious protest. Ecology, feminism, and movements for racial freedom assert the structural impossibility of making nature an aspect of the "kingdom of man." To some, this formulation may appear to be nothing but mysticism. Of course, to insist that the prevailing system of rationality is itself historical; more, to see it as an illusory appropriation of the world by means of its ideology and practices, is to argue that desire is the non-rational in relation to this system. Since Marxism shares with all types of eighteenth and nineteenth-century science a disdain for morality, except that which is suggested by its reading of historical imperatives, it fears desire as an uncontrollable, unpredictable element in the social world. Yet it is here that the new moral science will be born. It is grounded in disparate movements that have not yet formed themselves as historic blocs of equals, but which already have been constituted as a series of anti-hegemonies. The parties of socialism are forced to define themselves in opposition to these movements in many countries; in the U.S., this space is occupied by the capitalist-controlled parties and the liberal and trade-union bureaucracies. The leading impulse of anti-hegemonic, autonomous movements in advanced capitalist societies, as well as those of "really existing" socialisms in Europe, is the *desire for freedom*. Of course, this slogan has already been advanced within the hegemony of the bourgeois enlightenment, but only as the freedom from nature through the development of *techne* and, in social realm, as the concept of individual right. State socialism preserves the first conception but, while historicizing the latter, suppresses it under the notion of the collective right. But Marxism in "really existing" socialist countries does not substitute popular sovereignty for civil liberties. For the science of nature and society are held to be mediations of the popular will because the populace – even the working class – lacks in itself the scientific understanding upon which the foundations of a new society must be laid. The collective *interest* is made coextensive with the concept of will, since will is, in itself, believed to be a purely subjective, reified category.

In contrast, the liberation of desire requires a return to the notion of will, since it does not accept the claims of centrally-organized political parties to *represent* desire. The problem of representation is unsolvable by means of a master discourse. This does not mean that all aspects of Marxism as it has evolved since Marx are historically surpassed. Marxism has become an indispensable moment in the struggle for freedom, the moment when the analysis of the forms of economic and social power that stand in the way of liberation must be made in order to undertake the educational tasks of emancipatory movements. Marxism's insistence upon the principle of historical specificity remains a valuable corrective to theories of social and natural development which, because of their refusal of reflexivity, are taken as divine law by dominant social orders. This critique also applies, of course, to the way Marxism has designated itself as *the* science of social and natural history. It may be shown that this hubris is nothing but the projection of the enlightenment on to the struggle for freedom from the bourgeois order. Thus Marxism has situated itself in the problematics both of liberation *and* domination, despite its claim to be the master critical discourse of the latter. Its program is surfeited with the achievements of late capitalism: the institutions of a centralized state and master planning; the belief in a uniform rationality of science; faith in technology to liberate us from external and our own natures; and the relegation of spirituality to the private sphere.

The new movements of liberation insist that the multiplicity of voices of liberation must remain autonomous, that new rationality consists in the rejection of a science grounded in the imperatives of the domination of nature and of humans. While science and planning are not to be eschewed, the dream of hegemonic power inscribed in apparatuses of a central state must be rejected. Further, the dichotomy of spirit and nature may be healed by the development of a morality which insists that values are not merely arbitrary and connected to specific economic interests, but inhere in the emotional and sexual needs that remain imprisoned by repressive morality. Thus, if religion is the only place where the expression of and protest against emotional suffering (which is grounded in both exploitation and sexual repression) is possible, it will survive the creation of a new society. But alongside established religions that hold to the existence of a deity, a new secular theology is in the making. Like liberation theology in the Catholic and Protestant religions, this secular theology believes that the spirit moves through human liberation and domination.[125] Like liberation theologies, it insists that morality is objective, rooted in unfulfilled needs. Rather than ascribe these needs to transcendent causes, however, it naturalizes them in the biological and historical constitution of human nature. Marx's famous dictum, that mankind never raises problems for which the material conditions for their solution are not already present, applies to the possibility of sexual and emotional freedom as much as it does to the goal of self-management of the economic and social order.

Marxism retains its power as mode of discovery of the ways in which desire is transformed as compulsory sexual and social morality, imposed by ideological institutions of domination as an order from on high. It shows that what ordinary people believed to be properties of human nature are socially and historically *conditioned.* But here is the difference between two understandings of the theory of ideology. According to the old Marxist theory, morality is *determined* by social relations of domination: the category itself is historicized, so that an inference may be made that nature and human nature are merely social productions. This position assumes that ideology (and morality as a form of it) will disappear with the appearance of a rationally organized society. In short, if human suffering is grounded today in economic and political oppression, the advent of socialism is tantamount to the abolition of suffering. This narrow view of human misery has been the bane of Marxism's existence. Suffering will never be abolished; certainly sexual misery will not automatically disappear with a new organization of production relations. Nor is there a necessary relation of priority of the rational management of the economic order over the abolition of male supremacy, the patriarchal order, racial superiority, and sexual misery. As the history of "really existing" socialisms demonstrates, there may be no relation between the two; or, to be more exact, the rational management of the economy may depend on the emergence of a new moral order, including a new science and technology based upon the principles of human liberation, as much as the other way around. Thus, historically considered, social relations determine the *form* which imposed morality takes, but not the fact that morality appears as a controlling force against nature and especially "human" nature. The invocation to sacrifice which was an inherent aspect of scarcity societies is retained under conditions of relative affluence as a form of surplus repression, since the whole category of productivity is linked to the needs of capital in advanced industrial cultures, not the needs of workers.[126] On the contrary, the labor/sexuality opposition retains its full moral force even in these conditions. But the denial of pleasure is not a phenomenon limited by late-capitalist social relations. It extends to "really existing" socialist countries linked inextricably to the world capitalist market which, together with the party and the state, imposes its norms upon recalcitrant populations. Under these conditions it is not surprising that the underlying populations of some Eastern European countries have turned vigorously to religion as the protest against both economic and cultural suffering. The revival of religion in the United States is a testament to the falsity of the proposition that suffering is substantially confined to economic dimensions. It may be argued, then, in the spirit of Gramsci's claim of the primacy of cultural contradictions, that if Marxism is constitutionally incapable of comprehending this feature of all societies in which social rule has taken the form of cultural domination as its premier condition since the material conditions for overcoming scarcity are already present, it will disappear as a force within the movement for emancipation. There is every reason to believe that this may come to pass, despite efforts by some Marxists to undertake substantial renovations in its decaying structure. Thus far, this effort has been confined to a relatively small group of intellectuals, some of whom are affiliated to the parties of socialism. Others are linked to movements of the base which are often in conflict with the parties. But there is not a single instance where a major party of socialism in the Western countries has adopted a critical view of its own theoretical roots, except the German Social Democrats, who honestly realized that, having abandoned the revolutionary *élan* of Marxism, the label had to be cast off. Others retain the discourse of revolution in order to claim the heritage, but are hostile to the development of a creative, living, theoretical debate within their ranks, even if they tolerated the continued affiliation of a few dissident intellectuals.[127] The prospects of a living Marxism are bleak so long as its theorists remain isolated from the practical movement. In the past such isolation resulted in the atrophy of the theoretical corpus: both party intellectuals who remained militants and those who separated from parties became increasingly mechanical and dogmatic. Such was the situation in the period between the failure of the various European revolutions in the early 1920's and the 20th Congress of the Soviet Communist Party in the early 1950's, whose revelations unleashed new vigor in the communist ranks on the basis of anti-Stalinism.

NEW FORCES FOR LIBERATION

Today the creative impulse in social theory comes from outside Marxism. It is lodged in feminism, ecology, theories of new nationalism often linked to racial freedom, and in liberation theologies trying to appropriate the social analysis of Marxism for a new morality based upon secular movements against capitalist oppression. If Marxism can no longer be the master discourse of human emancipation because it cannot break with the bourgeois, rationalist order, it will retain its value as a critique of political economy, the moment of anti-capitalism in the general movement against all forms of domination and hierarchy.

In this connection, it seems to me perfectly clear from a Marxist perspective that autonomous movements whose programs include calls for a decentralized, self-managed economy are by no means immune from the influence of capital's logic. Today, the old model of the concentration and centralization of capital, proposed by Lenin to describe the imperialist stage of capitalism, has undergone substantial modification. Ownership and control is, to be sure, held by a few capitalists on a world scale. The advent of the multinational corporation as a mechanism for the centralization of control investment bears out the Marxist vision of capitalism as a world system. On the other hand, the vision upon which the centrality of the proletariat was based – the concentration of production into fewer units – no longer holds. Precisely because the working classes have organized themselves into trade unions and politicized their interests within the capitalist state, capital's survival depends increasingly on its diffusion into decentralized, small units. The logic of capital forces it to reduce the "organic composition of capital" (the proportion of living labor to machinery) in order to increase the rate of profit. The drive for productivity produced the progressive replacement of labor by machines through technological innovations; labor resisted speed-up and stretch-out and imposed some of its own rhythms upon the labor process in the form of contracts that codified work rules. The resulting migration of capital did not perpetuate the old model of the huge factory in a single space. It produced a new pattern of small units of production, based upon the technologies of miniaturization, which simultaneously reduced (1) the value of means of production; (2) the skills required to operate machinery; and (3) the number of workers in each location of production. Thus the struggles of workers configured the constitution of capital and conditioned its new logic. But the logic of diffusion undermines the subversive character of the autonomous movements, which have posed decentralization as a counter-logic of production. Capital has even appropriated the slogan, if not the substance, of self-management in its worker-participation experiments. These developments confirm Marcuse's thesis that there are no *absolutely* subversive demands under late capitalism.

The dialectical theory of capitalist development – Marxism's major contribution – remains a powerful corrective to hopes that the struggle for freedom can relieve itself of what Gramsci called "pessimism of the mind." Yet the "optimism of the will" that completes Gramsci's motto is expressed by the fact that diffusion of production has not meant a breakdown of centralized control. The demand for a self-managed society on the basis of the formation of an historic bloc that is simultaneously anti-capitalist and anti-hierarchical remains beyond the recuperative powers of the prevailing order, even if no particular form of self-management (such as was obtained by the Polish workers) may have revolutionary consequences.

There can be no doubt, however, that the combined force of these demands leads to fundamental social transformation: those who propose a new cultural logic like the self-control of the body as much as the transfer of power over production, demands for racial autonomy as much as the demand to realign our relation to the external environment. For it is here that the prevailing order must take a stand against reform. All of its forces resist any concessions that cannot be controlled by the state or by capital. The desire for self-management supercedes the institutional benefit.

Here is the element of social movement that remains anathema to all repression. It is based upon the fulfillment of desire. Of course, the fulfillment of desire is limited by the material conditions for its production, but even here the limits are no longer to be established as a system of imposed morality; rather, they must be a conscious recognition of the correspondence between rules governing human relations and our relation to nature, based upon mutual aid and social equality.

At the same time, consistent with the *philosophical* precept of the ineluctability of difference, there can be no vision of homogeneity. But these differences of desire would not constitute the basis for antagonism; they would no longer be the mask for privilege, only different modes of adaptation to society and nature based upon traditions that logically help form communities. A self-managed socialism would imply different visions of the world and different ways to negotiate our relations within the framework of the logics of non-domination.

Marx refused to specify his vision of the future because he believed that it was implicit in his scientific theory of the present and past society. Further, he left it to the future to determine its own destiny, another commitment to self-management. But Marx's future arrived in the guise of state socialism, which was not based on a "free association in which the full development of each was the condition for the full development of all." Free association once more became a hope. Marx's conviction that the "dream of the whole man" proposed by the early nineteenth century utopians would be replaced by scientific prediction was destined to suffer the fate of all theories of inevitability. Socialism is, now as before, a utopian vision rather than a scientifically deduced certainty. But we have taken a second step. *Our* proposals are now rooted in the historical experience of the socialist movement. To this extent, we are still bound up with the Marxist project. The new utopianism is, metaphorically at least, the concrete negation of scientific Marxism insofar as it tries to *preserve* the Marxist moment within a new paradigm of social transformation. Let that, if it will, belong to our desire.

NOTES

119. For a fuller discussion of this question, see Deleuze and Guattari, *Anti-Oedipus*, op. cit.
120. The term logocentricity is borrowed from Jacques Derrida, *Of Grammatology* (Baltimore: Johns Hopkins University Press, 1977). It connotes the process by which Western culture suppresses, in language and discourse, difference (or in Derrida's term "*Différance*") into identities derived from the canon explicated in Aristotle's *Organon*. One recalls Aristotle's three laws of logic, according to which a thing is identical with itself and cannot be its other. Otherness is deferred when it is interpreted as a formal logical contradiction. As I have tried to show in my discussion of Adorno, Hegel failed to resolve the problem of the occlusion of opposition within logical theory by his insistence upon the return to the positive. That is, negativity is conceived in Hegel as a *moment* in the process of the resolution of contradiction into identity. Marxism's adoption of dialectical logic tends to follow the viewpoint of negativity as passing. Adorno and Althusser's more recent efforts have tried to grapple with this problem by asserting that difference is not recuperable under the sign of the totality. The "totality" is a spatial and temporal metaphor connoting a series of relations, the articulation of which depends upon specific conditions. Thus, there can be no *a priori* dominance of one kind of relation over another. Such determinations are contingent. As Fredric Jameson has argued, in his helpful reading of the present manuscript, historical materialism becomes a theory of determination of past relations. That is, it is only retrospectively valid as the decoding of the logic of development from the standpoint of a certain ideologically-grounded paradigm.
121. I do not mean to deny the significance of the developing agricultural crisis in the United States, produced by the conjuncture of soil erosion resulting from one-crop techniques and uncontrolled real-estate development (the effect of realignment of different circuits of capital, privileging industrial and commercial development in rural areas over the older urban centers). However, the solution to the land question in the U.S. and European countries no longer attaches itself to a specific class formation such as the peasantry.

122. Norbert Bobbio, "Gramsci and the Conception of Civil Society," in Chantal Mouffe, ed., *Gramsci and Marxist Theory* (London: Routledge & Kegan Paul, 1979).
123. Chapter 7 in this volume.
124. Juan Luis Segundo, *Liberation of Theology*, op. cit., Chapter 1.
125. Of course, the notion of spirit is used here metaphorically. Spirit should be understood in this context as nothing other than historically-situated desire locating itself as other within the boundaries of a given hegemony, pointing to something new that is not yet capable of being incorporated into the dominant discourse.
126. For the best American discussion of this point see Murray Bookchin, *Post-Scarcity Anarchism* (Berkeley: Ramparts Press, 1971).
127. As in the French and Italian Communist Parties, where many leading Marxist intellectuals have been all but read out of the parties without denying them the right to retain formal membership.

7

The End of Political Economy

INTRODUCTION

The world-wide crisis of capitalism which has been gaining momentum since the early 1970's has simultaneously elevated Marxism to a new status. The collapse of both neo-Marxist and Keynesian certainties that late capitalism possessed an almost infinite capacity to stave off a breakdown led social and economic theory to look once more to "classical" Marxist explanations of the crisis. Within academic circles there is no question that Marxist political economy, although by no means hegemonic, gains new adherents with each passing leading indicator showing a more or less chronic tendency in the western countries towards stagnation if not complete reversal of the almost thirty years of uninterrupted growth in most capitalist nations.

Although there have been other important developments in Marxist theory, particularly new work in the theory of the state, the analysis of the labor process, and a proliferation of criticism of the late capitalist culture, the lively debate underway in political economy remains unmatched in any other sphere.

Apart from the influence exerted by the evidence of the maturing of economic crisis tendencies, some other influences should be noted. Within the general framework of the general rise of Marxist theories and studies, Marx and his followers left more work in this sphere of inquiry than any other. It may be argued that Marx devoted the major part of the last half of his life to the critique of political economy precisely because he came to believe that capitalism subsumed and displaced all of its contradictions in the economic sphere since the problems of culture and politics were the weak links of the capitalist system. Moreover, all bourgeois philosophy and culture gave way in the eighteenth century to political economy which became, in effect, its hegemonic ideology as well as the quintessence of the social praxis of the bourgeoisie. In contradiction to previous modes of production, capitalism placed central reliance on its capacity to produce, circulate, and accumulate capital. Its ideological presuppositions became virtually identical with its everyday practices, consigning the spiritual to the margins. In fact, as Marx was fond of saying, its spirituality was the cash nexus itself. Is it any wonder, then, that of all the human sciences, economics became the most developed in the period of the rise of capital? Since capitalism became imbued with the ideology of science and technology, all human sciences were to be modelled on scientific principles. Political economy strove towards making its discipline approximate the natural sciences with a fervor unparalleled until recently by any other. Philosophy after Kant saw its mission as clearing the underbrush of misunderstandings that arose because of linguistic confusion, but renounced the search for positive knowledge because of its speculative nature. As late as the end of the nineteenth century, sociology and anthropology were still struggling to free themselves from the grip of philosophy. Its founders, Auguste Comte, Emile Durkheim, Georg Simmell, and Max Weber all engaged in the "clearing away" process so as to better establish the discipline on a strictly scientific footing.[128] It has only been in the late twentieth century that these fields have been able to boast of an accumulation of positive knowledge unimpaired by concern for philosophical presuppositions. The replacement of theory by methodology signalled the beginning of the end of self-doubt.

In contrast, economics has remained free of speculative modes of reason for a century. It cast out its philosophical baggage with the emergence of neo-classical theory which arose to dominance in the late nineteenth century. The irony of this conjuncture consists in the fact that capitalism was experiencing its first major convulsions in the 1870's and 1880's. Neo-classicism consists in the suppression of precisely that which Marxism found most fruitful in classical political economy: the labor theory of value. For Stanley Jevons, Alfred Marshall, and the Viennese economists who founded the neo-classical school, casting out value theory was the last blow that science had to deal speculation, for it could not be denied that the concept of value could not be falsified or verified with the rigor of empirical demonstration. Neo-classical theory conflated value with price because it was a theory of appearances, or, to be more exact, it begins by denying the distinction between appearance and real

relations consistent with the leading precepts of positivism. Further, since science can only pose problems for which the means exist for their solutions, value theory was dismissed as a type of eschatology. Of course, the Marxist critique of neo-classicism points out the reason for this judgement at the level of its methodolo-
gical foundation; bourgeois economics has become a theory of market relations. It has no conception of the capitalist system taken as whole in which capital, according to Marx, ciruclates in three modes: money, commodities, and production.[129] It leaves out the sphere of production relations, more specifically the labor process, and abstracts money and commodity circuits from their starting point. Production is subsumed under the category of investment, labor under the wages bill, and means of production under capital goods. This is no mere terminological difference. By excluding the labor process, bourgeois economics can never uncover the origin of profit and, therefore, can never offer a critical theory of the economy. The transformation of political economy into the positive science of economics is a sign of the degree to which economics renounces its own capacity to explain except at the level of appearances. For Marxist critics, neo-classical theory conceals more than it reveals. Its theory of crisis is idiosyncratic, relying ultimately not on structural features of the system, but ascribing economic disruptions to psychological causes: production and employment decline because investors choose to save rather than invest in production because they "believe" that future rates of return will be lower than the rate of interest they may gain on money markets. This belief is based on the "marginal" efficiency or productivity of capital, that is, the return on investment of the least "productive" unit of capital.[130] Marxists argue that the absences in these explanations are those that may be found in the structure of capitalist social relations. Thus, neo-classical theory in the age of permanent capitalist crisis (1914–) becomes not a mode of explanation of the crisis as much as a series of policy proposals to government and advisements to investors as to how to overcome the deleterious effects of a bad investment climate. The assumption behind all types of neo-classical positions, including Keynesian theory, is that the crisis is by no means a chronic feature of the economic system.[131] While there is no agreement on the measures to be taken to "cure" the ailment, the limits of the diagnosis are accepted by all parties. Government intervention may lower the rate of interest on loan capital to stimulate investment: the savers

will discover that productive investment is more profitable. The entrepreneurs will find that cheap loan capital is available. Or, as the anti-Keynesians contend, government should let the market forces work autonomously and remove its regulation and consumption functions as much as possible. This will avoid inflation because government intervention usually costs taxpayers money and withdraws income from consumption. When the government makes up the difference between production and consumption by becoming a consumer, it withdraws income from circulation either by taxes or investable capital from private sources. These moves become self-defeating in the long run. Pure market theorists hold to the view that the government should remain a vigilant bystander, stimulating investment by removing all controls over the market, such as price controls and other regulations that weaken incentives for investment. The Marxist reply is that these monetary manipulations and state-induced stimulants to production, such as arms expenditures and public works, are based on the fallacy of the underconsumptionist theory of crisis, literally an explanation that derives from the ideology of the autonomy of the market. Recent Marxist theory has been constrained to relieve itself of its own underconsumptionist wing in order to find a more adequate theory of the crisis, since bourgeois underconsumptionism seems to have finally reached its limits in both theory and practice.

Despite concrete differences, the new Marxist political economy shares many of the assumptions of its bourgeois counterparts. Among the most important is the classical conception of scientificity. While Marxists try to preserve the critical edge of political economy by insisting on the primacy of production relations for finding the dynamics of capitalist development, it proceeds, having inserted this sphere into economic theory, to found an alternative within the science of economics rather than constituting itself as *counterhegemonic* to economic science as such. For the hegemony of bourgeois economic paradigms are reproduced not only by their *practical* orientation to policy, but also by their adherence to method as defined by eighteenth-century natural science. Among the major premises of this method is the requirement that all relations shall be subject to quantification – since the book of nature, including human nature, is held to be written in the language of mathematics. Thus, the ability to penetrate the nature of the economic process is contingent upon framing questions that may be answered by mathematic calculation.

Second, modern philosophy of science holds that a theory may not introduce multiple causality such that indeterminacy becomes an operative principle. The requirement that theory be reduced to a simple formula which, however, possesses a broad explanatory power is among the hallmarks of modern science. This is the core of what science means by lawfulness.[132] While physics has gone beyond the eighteenth-century conception of cause and effect, it is still constrained to explain anomalies by means of its fundamental core paradigm or risk extinction. Thus, the requirement for a logic of scientific explanation based on the criteria of falsifiability, quantification, formulaic simplicity.[133]

The infrastructure-superstructure formula of Marx's famous *Preface* constitutes the broadest level of his claim to scientific rigor: "The mode of production of material life determines . . . ",'[134] is, at once, a statement about the relation of politics, ideology, and culture to the level of human mastery over nature and the relations or production that arise from it, and a clear invocation of determination of the entire social sphere by conditions of production. Marx's theory of relations of production still meets the criterion of science because it names the moment of determination, a mechanism with which social inquiry can transcode or reduce all social phenomena to economic terms. Recent efforts to introduce a theory of mediations into Marxism, according to which "counteracting causes" may displace or deter the working of the law (in Marx's words, referring to his theory of the falling rate of profit as a law of a "tendency"), do not in any way obviate the determination of the totality, in the last instance, by the economic infrastructure.[135] For every scientific theory that proceeds from the classical formulation of the requirement of paradigmatic simplicity is an identity theory. All mediations must be resolved to the terms of the theoretical core. Multiple determinations are ultimately resolved within the terms of the formula. Even deviations are explained as "probabilities" or possibilities that may be logically inferred from one of the terms of the equations.

Marx's fundamental explanation of capitalist crisis possesses the elegance of a scientific formula. It may be expressed as an algebraic equation which is merely the mathematical form of a set of determinate relations:

$$\frac{s}{C + v} = p'$$

For Marx, this equation constitutes all the necessary terms for explaining as well as defining a crisis. The crisis is *defined* as a systemic disruption of the accumulation of capital, which in turn depends on the ratio of surplus value (s) to the cost of production (c + v) – machinery and raw materials (c) and wages (v) – which is equivalent to the actual rate of profit. When the rate of profit falls below that which is sufficient to pay for capitalists' personal consumption, the amount of capital needed to replenish the existing stock of capital at the current level of production, and a surplus that is available for investment in the expansion of production, capital will cut back the scale of production until the requisite rate of profit is restored, assuming its capacity to raise prices is limited by competition. Or, capital will attempt to merge smaller capitals to create a monopoly, oligopoly, or other arrangements that will reduce or effectively eliminate competition among capitals. In a period where capital has become international, these options are played on a global plane but, according to Marxists who follow the Leninist version, cannot restrict competition on a world scale even if they succeed within the national market.

The falling rate of profit may be retarded or reversed by international trade in commodities or capital export, assuming the rate of return from this source exceeds that of the domestic market. However, competition for international markets often restricts this option for the least favored capitals. In the chapter on the counteracting causes of the falling rate of profit, Marx shows that the tendency of the rate of profit to fall may be attenuated by other means as well. These include cheapening the elements of constant capital by lowering the amount of socially necessary labor time required for the production of machinery or for the extraction of raw materials, increasing the mass of surplus value even if the rate of surplus value to variable capital declines. In this mode, the turnover rate of capital is reduced by increasing the proportion of constant to variable capital by technological development, which reduces the time required to reproduce the laborer and increases the productivity of labor.

Marx's theory of crisis and its counteracting tendencies is the core of his critique of capitalist production. Contrary to the common-sense view that crisis may then sound the death-knell of capitalism, Marx held that crises were the condition of capitalist development. Although deepening periodic crises constitute the material conditions for the Marxist theory of revolutionary change under capitalism, "a crisis is always the starting point of a large amount of new investment . . . ; it constitutes from the point of view of society, more or less of a material basis for the next cycle of turn-over." The "continuous revolution of the instruments of production"[136] prevents the crisis from becoming permanent because capital will turn over its machinery, factories, and other fixed capital before they have worn out. Here the distinction between the technical conditions of capital and its value form is absolutely fundamental to understand. Marx argues that the technical requirements for turning over capital become secondary if not irrelevant to the decision to invest in new fixed capital. Capital will disregard "wear and tear" if the opportunity for investment at a high profit-rate presents itself.

THREE THEORIES

Much of this chapter will concern the various explanations given since Marx for the refusal of world capitalism to disappear. Those who follow the main line of Marx's later work are prone to ascribe the durability of capitalism to the same logic that might produce its eventual breakdown. Just as the tendency of the rate of profit to fall may result in the reversal of the accumulation process, mass unemployment, wage cuts, and, given a sufficient level of organization of the working class, a pre-revolutionary situation, so the same "law" also has been employed to show why the working class has failed to fulfil its historical mission. Marxist theory seems currently preoccupied with the breakdown problem, which is just another way of expressing the crisis of Marxist explanations of the apparent long-term tendency of capitalism to resist its own downfall.

One of the central problems in finding a "unified field theory" of what has been called "late capitalism," "state monopoly capitalism," or "advanced capitalism," is to decide upon the precise logic of capital such that its syllogisms contain a wide enough range of hypotheses that can be verified or falsified either by historical or structural criteria. For the controversies within Marxist crisis theory devolve, at the most fundamental level, upon the issue of the *regulative principle* of capitalist historical development.

I have been able to distinguish three main positions on this question: Lenin's theory of monopoly capitalism, dependency theory, and capital-logic theory. The appearance of divergent theories of capitalist development within the framework of Marxism may be explained with reference to three distinct influences: (a) different conceptions of science, (b) specific political tasks and experiences that conditioned the shifts of emphasis and even the theoretical perspective, and (c) differing assessments of the historical changes within capitalism that displaced the crisis tendencies without suffering breakdown.

Lenin has worked from a conception of capitalist crisis developed by Marx as one of its possibilities: the so-called realization crisis. In this variant, the problem of capital accumulation does not derive from the basic conflict between capital and labor at the point of production, but in the difficulty of finding investment outlets at the average rate of profit. Although many who follow Lenin would agree that the cause "in the last instance" of the realization crisis is the contradiction between capital's expansion and the structure of consumption as it is limited by the nature of exploitation in the process of production, the emphasis falls not on the labor process but on the process of circulation. It might be argued that Marx's own discussion of crises in the second and third volumes of *Capital* confirms this emphasis. Nevertheless, Lenin's theory of imperialism derives from the capacity of capital to displace its crisis tendencies by means of export in the late nineteenth and early twentieth centuries. Further Lenin was constrained to explain the apparent betrayal of socialist principles by the social democrats and a fragment of the working class when they supported their own governments in the pursuit of capitalist interests in the First World War. The theory of imperialism changes the focus of Marxism from an analysis of the revolutionary possibilities within the advanced countries to the underdeveloped countries precisely because of the historical changes introduced by the internationalization of capitalist contradictions in the late nineteenth century.

Dependency theory responds to the failure of Leninism to explain the integration of the underdeveloped countries of the Third World into the capitalist world system after the Second World War. It challenges a crucial point of Marx's theory of history that was retained in the Leninist conception of capitalist development: the theory of stages. By grafting, perhaps unintentionally, structuralism onto Marxism, dependency theory offers an entirely different mode of explanation for capitalist development. In a period when socialists learned that political independence did not necessarily constitute the basis for the creation of a new social system but could be a more efficient version of the old relationships between core and colony, dependency theory offers a systematic way to understand this phenomenon without recourse to purely voluntarist explanations.

The third position, capital-logic, tries to overcome the apparent failure of the Third World revolution in a different way. A theory of late capitalism as a specific historical stage, it incorporates the theory of imperialism into an entirely new paradigm: it is in the logic of accumulation itself, literally at its origins in the labor process, that the whole development of capitalism, including the problem of the proletariat as historical agency or subject, may be understood. Unlike Lenin and dependency theory, which subsume the labor process into the process of circulation of capital, capital-logic remains oriented to production relations, both with respect to its value form and its technical character.

(1) *Lenin's theory of imperialism*. The orthodox view stems principally from Lenin's reading of Marx's third volume of *Capital* and the accumulation chapters of the first volume. For Lenin, the crisis caused by the overproduction of capital (the means of production principally) gives rise to a tremendous concentration and centralization of capital. In order to recover the average rate of profit capital is forced to partially suppress its competitive stage and enter a new one, the monopoly stage. The formation of monopoly capital, whose principal form is finance capital (Hilferding), that is, the merger of bank and industrial capital, increases the power of capital to control its own crises, at least in the short run. By eliminating the weakest capitals within the national market, capital in certain "advanced" countries is able to extend its hegemony over international markets. This process of monopolization intensified after each successive capitalist crisis in the late nineteenth century, so that by the first decade of the twentieth century capitalism on a world scale can no longer be characterized by the intense competition among an infinite number of small capitals. Now the world has been divided among a tiny group of capitalist powers. This does not imply, however, that competition has been relegated to historical memory. On the contrary, competition becomes more fierce on an international plane, leading inevitably to world war and crises on a global level. The logic of capital consists in the replacement of competition on a local basis by its globalization. By bringing the entire world into the capitalist orbit, the monopoly-imperialist

stage marks the last stage of the history of capitalism.[137] It is not, as Rosa Luxemburg argued, that capital reduces its markets overseas because imperialism generates capitalist development in the colonial and other economically backward countries and thus produces a crisis in the home country.[138] Lenin's point is that capitalism generates new markets in the colonial world by bringing into existence a working class and a new bourgeoisie that yearns to control its own internal market. The contradictions within the advanced world, arising from the falling rate of profit or overproduction that results in a "realization" crisis, are attenuated only locally and are displaced to the "weakest" link in the imperialist chain, the underdeveloped countries, which, in the process of striving for economic and political independence from imperialism initiate a new, and from the classical point of view, "improbable" revolutionary wave that ultimately makes the existence of world capitalism problematic.

By emphasizing the immediate results of the falling rate of profit within a competitive context and the growing problems of valorizing capital, Lenin is not going outside the algebraic reasoning of Marx's own breakdown thesis. He finds in the counteracting tendencies to the falling rate of profit the source of further contradictions. That is, the solution to the problems arising from competitive conditions calls into existence new social forms which, because they remain regulated by the laws of value and surplus value cannot constitute genuine solutions for they merely *displace* and *intensify* the contradictions. Lenin's debate within the international socialist movement in the period coinciding with the outbreak of the war was with those who argued that the new monopoly stage ushered in a new era of organized capitalism where the system could, by globalization, succeed in more or less permanently repressing its own breakdown tendencies. This view whose founder was Rudolf Hilferding, is now commonly referred to as *super-imperialism*.[139] We will have need to return to this position. For now, suffice it to remark that in Lenin's theory the national character of capitalism remains, despite its monopoly stage and internationalization. It is precisely because of the contradiction between its national form and international imperative that he insisted upon the law of uneven development to explain why revolutionary activity in the new historical stage would occur first at the weakest link of the imperialist chain, the colonies and "semi-" colonies rather than the core or center.

The First World War seemed to validate Lenin's view of the

historic significance of capital export for sustaining the entire system. Ideologies of racism and xenophobia that appeared to thwart the working classes of the advanced countries, notwithstanding the strength of the socialist movement, were matched by the use of surplus profits derived from imperialist conquest to buy off a layer of the working class, particularly the trade union and socialist leadership. The strategic outcome of this analysis was Lenin's insistence that the new situation meant that the world revolution would not occur in the advanced countries as socialists had assumed. Instead, the spark for revolution would emanate from the "weak links" of imperialism, the defeated countries such as Russia and Germany and the former colonies whose aspiration for independence would threaten imperial markets. The loss of markets, as well as the political initiatives of the least advanced countries would ultimately pull the working class within the imperialist countries towards revolutionary action. After Lenin's death the Stalinist and some elements of Trotskyist movement placed the anti-imperialist struggle at the center of socialist strategy within the leading capitalist countries. The struggle of the working classes in the most advanced countries depended upon the success of the efforts of those in the underdeveloped countries to achieve independence, according to this argument. At times, the thrust of their strategic contention rested on the strength of racist and patriotic ideologies upon the working classes. On the other hand, some Marxist-Leninist theory rested on the formation of the so-called "labor aristocracy," that portion of the working class that benefited from imperialist conquest. After the Second World War, there was a tendency in the theory to claim that the entire working class of the imperialist powers had been corrupted by their share of superprofits derived from the colonies and "semi-colonies," especially with the New Left of the 1960's and some of those who adopted dependency theory.

Leninism constituted nothing less than a new crisis theory. Its emphasis upon the national liberation movements in the least developed sectors of world capitalism was predicated on the thesis that capitalism had become a world system of mutual dependencies. In the wake of the failure of the socialist movement following the First World War to successfully transform the interimperialist rivalry into socialist revolution in the west, Lenin's theory possessed the virtue of simultaneously explaining that event and pointing a new direction for revolutionary struggle.

Now, the first task of the socialist movement around the world was to defend its only victory of the war – the creation of the Soviet Union, the paradigmatic example to demonstrate the veracity of Lenin's position. The Chinese revolution was to become a further proof that socialism could only arise out of the struggle against imperialism in the Third World, even if the aims of the revolution were not socialist in form. It was the leadership of the national bourgeois revolution by the Communists that guaranteed its transformation into a socialist struggle, even if the base of the revolution consisted in the aspiring national capitalist class and the mass of peasants. In effect, Leninism, especially after his death, gave to the poor peasantry the status of a modern proletariat. Although the industrial working classes of the most advanced capitalist countries were clearly proletarians in the classical Marxian sense, the corruption of imperialist booty had infected them. Their redemption now depended on the construction of a world socialist system out of the ruins of imperialism.

Leninism after Lenin is socialism in the period of the defeat of the proletarian revolution. It represents an accommodation to new circumstances; the victory of the capitalist ruling classes made necessary two critical shifts from Marxist practice. The first was away from class struggle in the advanced capitalist countries to the struggle for national liberation in the colonies. Secondly, the postwar stabilization of capitalism evoked a major tactical shift within the advanced countries. From the struggle against capitalist society and its state, which had been the program of the left wing of the Second International, Leninism turned its efforts to achieving reforms within it through participation in parliament and the bourgeois trade unions.[140] For the Communist parties after the defeat of the revolutions following the First World War, revolutionary activity took the form of support for national liberation struggles, the struggle for parliamentary and trade union hegemony, and support for the Soviet Union (and, later, other socialist countries).

The tactical shift to the struggle for reform was especially pronounced during the rise of fascism, even if Marxists believed that fascism was a response to the capitalist crisis. Anti-fascism replaced the direct struggle for socialist power and became the basis of an historical compromise between the communists and the socialists on the one hand, and between the working class and the "democratic bourgeoisie" on the other hand. Class politics were suppressed within the larger struggle for the preservation of democratic freedoms, an emphasis that has never been abandoned since the 1930's by the communist parties in the advanced capitalist countries.

The theory that the crisis of capitalism consisted not only in the tendency towards mass unemployment and the decline of production but also the tendency of imperialist wars proved correct in the twentieth century. But what had been consistently underestimated by the entire socialist movement was the extent to which a degree of stability could be achieved in consequence of the introduction of the intensive regime in the west with its concomitant ideological structures – that is, the systematic introduction of labor-saving technologies, new forms of administration, and mass consumption *within* the advanced capitalist countries.

Marxist theory after Marx tended to emphasize the crisis rather than its counteracting causes. Lenin understood these counteracting measures as forms of displacement as well as attenuation of the crisis. No policies such as capitalist planning or large public expenditures could succeed permanently in reversing the crisis, only retarding and displacing it to another arena. If the export of capital temporarily relieved the realization crisis, it generated rebellion in the colonial world. If state capitalist planning absorbed some of the surplus at home, Lukács provided the argument against the possibility of controlling the crisis in the long run. Lukács granted that the bourgeoisie may "clarify its class interest on every particular issue," but it "will be unable to control its own system of production even in theory"[141] because of the fragmentation of competing interests that is built into the private appropriation of capital. No less than the intra-class competition that is the mark of the working-class movement during its existence prior to the revolution, the intra-class competition within each national capitalism and certainly on a world scale prevented the bourgeoisie from acting according to its collective interest, even if it possessed class consciousness.

Lukács here is echoing Lenin's conception of the inexorability of inter-imperialist rivalry which for him renders inevitable the tendency towards world war in the monopoly, imperialist stage of capitalism. The revolution is the outcome of these wars for the redivision of imperialist spheres. Capitalist rationality is confined to the level of the firm, specific issues, and temporary international agreements such as are made by cartels and over trade and tariffs. According to Lenin, no permanent stability or organized form of capitalism on a world scale is possible. Ultimately, if not through depressions, certainly the drive to wars would expose to the masses, with the help of the communist parties, the inherent irrationality of the system and its incapacity to meet their needs.

As reasonable as Lenin's argument appeared in the wake of the First World War, it is not sufficient to explain the course of events since the defeats of the first socialist revolutions that followed it. Although it is still true, as Lenin and others demonstrated, that the internal powers of the capitalist marketplace were insufficient to realize capital and insure reproduction, the option of imperialism has been shown to be only one of the outlets for surplus capital.

Dependency theory has argued that the export of capital is not always connected with the phenomenon of overproduction. Capital investment, in order to produce raw materials from undeveloped areas may reflect the problems of primitive accumulation or result from the technical incapacity within a particular capitalist nation. For example, Great Britain exported capital in order to facilitate the extraction of raw materials such as cotton and iron long before its monopoly stage. In this case, capital export was a condition of reproduction because the rate of accumulation called forth the demand for an ever rising quantity of raw materials that England could not generate internally. Capital export throughout the eighteenth and nineteenth centuries was associated with western economic development rather than the appearance of a surfeit of capital. This problem was true of nearly the entire continent, which simply did not possess the technical conditions such as natural resources for capital accumulation.

Lenin attempts to circumvent this issue by designating this period of colonial conquest as "mercantilism." Yet, Marx noted that the basic tendency of capital to migrate was related to two factors: the technical issues discussed here and the capitalists' effort to find outlets that yield the average rate of profit. What Lenin argued is the imperative suggested by modern imperialism. In his view, capital export became, in the late nineteenth century, the fundamental condition of its reproduction.

Yet, capital migration is not exclusively a problem of capital export beyond national borders. The historical evidence shows that much of the migration takes place within the advanced countries themselves. The movement of capital from traditional northern industrial centers within the United States to the south and, later, to former agricultural regions in the north is coincident with, not subsequent to, the export of U.S. capital. Similarly, as Andrew Gorz shows, every older European country is marked by capital migration between developed and less developed regions. He calls this process "colonialism at home."

For example, the historical development of Italian capital occurred in the north, leaving Sicily and other southern regions in a semi-feudal condition so that later there was room for capital migration to the south as well as a ready supply of labor for the expansion of Italian capitalism in the north. The importance of underdeveloped regions within national borders does not obviate the significance of outright colonies that provide outlets for capital as well as sources of reserve labor. Lenin noticed the importance of unevenness for capitalist development but restricted its significance to the external colonies.

Which raises a question about the whole corpus of Lenin's theory of imperialism. The Leninist notion of imperialism as "the highest stage of capitalism" includes the concentration and centralization of capital and the development of monopoly within key sectors of the national economies of advanced nations. Yet it points to the phenomenon of capital migration across national borders as the main means by which capitalism in the advanced countries attempts to prevent economic crisis. According to Lenin, "an enormous surplus of capital has arisen in the advanced countries" because "in a few rich countries . . . the accumulation of capital has reached giant proportions"[142] and has no immediate outlets for investment, owing to the restricted character of domestic consumption.

Lenin recognized that the unevenness of capitalist development is most apparent within the advanced countries in the form of the backwardness of agriculture. This backwardness has its roots in the failure of capital to establish both the technical and economic conditions needed for the production of cheap food. Moreover, the plethora of small producers makes this sector's profitability lower than the average rate for the economy as a whole, which prevents significant capital inputs and technical development. In these circumstances where, according to Lenin, investment in agriculture "lags terribly behind industry,"[143] the export of capital becomes the chief means by which concentrated capital within the advanced countries tries to solve its overaccumulation problem. "As long as capitalism remains what it is, surplus capital will be used not for the purpose of raising the standard of living of the masses in a given country, for this would mean a decline of profits for the capitalists, but for the purpose of increasing profits by exporting capital to the backward countries."[144]

Lenin's whole theory of imperialism as a new stage of capitalism rests on the significance he attaches to the consequences of the growth of the monopolies and finance capital for the emergence of an historically new type of accumulation problem for capitalism. Secondly, the claim that "the export of capital acquires pronounced importance"[145] in solving the crises of overproduction and realization must be understood as the material basis for the other phenomena he describes: "the division of the world among the international trusts has begun; and the division of all territories of the globe among the biggest capitalist powers has been completed."[146]

For Lenin, imperialism draws all the world into the capitalist net, and, although it distorts the configuration of economic development among the backward countries, it sets the preconditions for the development of socialism as well. The heart of Lenin's proposals for world socialist strategy, which sharply departed from those of conventional Marxism, rested on his theory of imperialism. If imperialism was the highest stage of capitalism because it rested on the formation of monopolies and was characterized by the need of advanced capitalist countries and the cartels to export capital as a condition of their survival, what followed was the importance of withdrawing the backward countries from the imperialist orbit. Marxist support for movements of national liberation, albeit bourgeois in form, was actually socialist in substance because these weak links of the imperialist chain would serve to heighten the crisis of capital surplus and reveal the system's irrationality to the world's working class and poor peasantry.

The importance of Lenin's theory of imperialism for explaining much of the contemporary doctrine of "Marxism-Leninism" cannot be overestimated. In the first place, it became a fundamental explanatory tool for the failure of the socialist movement to oppose the imperialist war itself and its betrayal of the revolution. The famous notion of the so-called "labor aristocracy" is based on the success of imperialist conquest in bringing back to the advanced countries superprofits extracted from the low wages of colonial labor. The aristocracy shares in these superprofits as the price of its collaboration with the bourgeoisie. This crude sociological doctrine may not stand the weight of analysis or of evidence. For one thing, it completely ignores the strength of ideology over the whole class,not just its leaders. For another, it implies a rather dubious theory of class behavior according to which the underclasses are fated to follow their corrupt leaders. If Lenin had advanced a theory of the corruption of the whole class, its plausibility would have been greater in the light of events. Instead, he insisted upon the purity of the masses in the wake of the moral perfidy of its leadership. Yet, this doctrine became the basis of the Stalinist attack against the social democrats in the late 1920s as "social fascists" and an argument for the turn towards anti-imperialism as a substitute for socialist revolution. Only the weakening of imperialism, according to Stalin's interpretation of Lenin, could break the grip of the labor and socialist leadership over the masses.

Second, the theory of imperialism became a theory of knowledge for many socialists. To a large degree it prevented many socialists from taking a critical look at their own situation beyond the categories suggested by Lenin and Bukharin. (Bukharin's *Imperialism and World Economy*, 1915, was actually the first formulation of the new theory that Lenin reintegrated and expanded in his own book *Imperialism* in 1916). The Marxist critique of exploitation and its critique of bourgeois culture and ideology were subsumed under the ideological categories of imperialism, particularly racism and patriotism. On the other hand, it fostered internationalism to a degree unknown within the socialist movement since Marx. Yet it was an internationalism based on the psychology of guilt and thus was profoundly bourgeois in its content, while revolutionary in form.

Equally important, the theory succeeded in turning the attention of much of the Marxist movement away from problems of alienation, exploitation and class struggle. It is not a question of denying the importance of imperialism as a major feature of capitalist development in the twentieth century. Lenin and Bukharin helped call attention to the problem of surplus capital and of its colonial consequences for the working classes. But the politics of their designation of imperialism as a new stage of capitalism led to results that were to distort the development of the socialist movement for several generations. First, this theory shifted the focus away from the concept of the proletarian revolution to the bourgeois nationalist revolution. It permitted nationalism to drape itself in the flag of socialism and dissolved revolutionary socialism within the ideals of nationalism. Secondly, it led to a redefinition of the revolutionary agency. Since the bourgeois revolution in colonial countries passed into the socialist revolution without the benefit of a modern proletariat, according to Stalin, all that was needed was a revolutionary Marxist-Leninist party to do the job. The party became the surrogate proletariat in theory, while its actual, albeit disguised function was to substitute itself for a national bourgeoisie. The bourgeoisie was, in Lenin's terms, unable to complete even its own revolution. Thirdly, the substance of socialism became confused with nationalization on the one hand, and economic accumulation on the other. Under this rubric a multitude of sins could be covered and legitimated.

By the First World War, most Marxists were aware that the basic problem of late capitalist development was its chronic surplus accumulation of capital. The development of monopolies proved that competition was ill-suited to capitalism in its advancing years. On the one hand, the immense productive forces set in motion by a diminishing proportion of labor in large-scale industry led to a constant problem in terms of maintaining the average rate of profit. On the other hand, the counteracting tendencies, the huge volume of goods and capital generated by social labor, were barely able to keep up with rising costs of production of each unit. Thus, competition was fated to give way to the merging of even the largest of capitals with each other. The displacement of the crisis to an international scale preserved the forms of competition, while raising the absolute necessity of a world system of organized capitalism if the order was to survive.

But a few Marxist theorists allowed that, failing to export capital to less developed regions, there were other means to insure reproduction. Rosa Luxemburg postulated the breakdown of capitalism owing to the disappearance of the middle class at home, and the markets of underdevelopment abroad. Lenin expected that imperialist wars would produce nationalist revolutions at the weakest links and proletarian revolutions in those defeated advanced capitalist countries. Failing wars, depressions would certainly mobilize the working classes in the advanced countries to overthrow the system.

Even as the capitalist system experienced deep-going and apparently inescapable economic crises in the 1920's and 1930's, capital's options were in the process of development that did not depend on the export of capital. In the first place, as we have already seen, Lenin understood the possibility that the development of capitalism in agriculture was a type of productive investment that would not only provide a new outlet for the surplus, but would also yield a fantastic development of food and fibers and make possible cheap food. In turn cheap food would increase the rate of surplus value to the extent that wages could be kept relatively low and would relieve the pressure on the profit rate. At the same time, relative consumption of other commodities could be increased as a means to alleviate the problem of the overproduction of commodities as well as capital.

But Lenin excluded the possibility of a huge increase in capital's application to agriculture. In this respect, history has proven him essentially incorrect both as far as the United States and western Europe are concerned. The growth of capital investment in agricultural production has been phenomenal in the twentieth century. According to Durost and Barton, in the period 1870–1900, the same period Lenin marks as the dawn of the age of modern imperialism (he calls the Spanish-American war a "first" for U.S. imperialism), production per farm worker increased in the U.S. by 50%, and agricultural production rose by 143% due largely to the application of research, machine production, and other technological improvements to farming.[147] With the exception of the period 1920–40, when agricultural exports and productivity slowed considerably, the trend towards increased capital investment in agriculture has been continuous throughout the twentieth century. From 1940 to 1960 the amount of capital invested in farming rose by 2½ times to more than $18 billions, and the rate of increase of investment continued in the following decade, reducing the number of farms and increasing the average size of farm units.

The evidence within American agriculture demonstrates that part of the surplus generated by large-scale industry did migrate to the farm sector within this country. In fact, contrary to Lenin's flat statement that "capitalism being what it is" agricultural production will not in substance be modernized,[148] that is exactly what happened in the U.S. Of course, the provision of cheap food did not solve the problems of capitalism in agriculture. The productivity of this sector ran far ahead of the internal market for agricultural commodities. The restricted character of consumption at home still required that 25% of farm output be exported throughout the entire twentieth century. Beyond exports, the government was required to provide incentives for farmers not to utilize farm land and to retire some of the actual crop every year in order to prevent farm prices from being constantly depressed. In short, American agriculture has experienced the same problems as capitalism as a whole. It constantly generates surpluses that require new markets.

Capital investment that resulted in the mechanization of farming also affected the pattern of the relations of agricultural production. From the predominance of family and other small-scale farms up to the 1880s, the past century has witnessed the almost complete transformation of farm ownership to medium and large corporations. This trend is particularly pronounced in the period since the 1930's and accelerated after the Second World War when the machine replaced hand labor in almost all major branches of that industry. Thus, corporate capital found sustained and profitable investment in the farm sector within the U.S.

After 1900, U.S. capitalism was to find another major outlet for its accumulated capital that did not rely on the exploitation of either foreign markets or raw materials. The American south had remained an underdeveloped part of the country during the steep rise of industrial capitalism after the Civil War. Mainly an agricultural region producing cotton and tobacco, the south suffered the most backward semi-feudal social relations. In this sense, the farm south, until the 1950s, resembled the European pattern. Tenant and share farming lived side by side with a growing corporate sector that did not exercise economic hegemony over the agricultural production of the region until the early 1930's. The south slowly entered a period of intense industrialization in the first twenty years of the new century. New England and middle Atlantic textile, shoe, and lumber mills migrated to the region in search of cheap non-union labor, proximity to raw materials, markets, and low taxes. One of the reasons for the migration from the north was undoubtedly related to the growing militancy of northern workers in the first decades of the twentieth century. The great textile strikes in Lawrence and Paterson and the industrial strikes of steel, garment, and miners in the coal and non-ferrous metals field prompted employers to seek a more docile and inexperienced labor force. The relatively vast labor surpluses generated by the expansion of machine-based farming helped to create the new industrial reserve army in the south that was becoming available for such capital migration.

The trend towards the industrialization of the south was greatly accelerated during the 1920's and again after the Second World War. The surpluses that Lenin believed could only be exported to colonial and semi-colonial countries found ready outlets with the least developed regions of the advanced capitalist countries themselves. In various ways, the partial industrialization of Sicily, Eastern Europe, Scotland, and Germany corresponded to the somewhat more pervasive trend in the United States.[149] The significant feature of the industrialization of the south in terms of the theory of imperialism as enunciated by Lenin does not reside so much in the structure of investment as in the particular content of his claim that the underdeveloped world constitutes the major means for the absorption of capital surpluses.

Gorz has argued for an expanded notion of colonialism in which Lenin's concept of unevenness of development is understood as a phenomenon that encompasses both the "backward" world and the least developed regions within the metropolitan countries. Insofar as the agricultural and the industrialized sectors of the south constitute a part of the advanced capitalist countries, the expanded areas for investment need not be confined to the colonial world, but can be understood in terms of the uneven development of various sections of industrial countries themselves. Although Gorz expands the notion of colonialism in order to keep the old concept intact and show its application beyond external territories, the specific idea that external investment is the only or even the major way for monopoly capitalist countries to survive is undermined.

The expansion of U.S. capitalism within its own borders also has forms of productive investment. As I have pointed out, the major type of productive investment reaching beyond mechanization of manufacturing is the mechanization of agriculture and the total economic development of the underdeveloped internal regions, particularly the southern area extending from the Appalachian mountains to the Gulf coast and east to Florida. In the American south, capital investment expanded over the entire range of possible investment. At the base were the tremendous capital expenditures in the provisions of the infrastructural preconditions for industrial development – railroads and communications systems, education, hospitals and other health facilities, and housing. Beyond these necessary "preconditions" were huge capital investments in establishing the textile, steel, lumber, paperboard, and mining industries of the several regions that comprise the south. In addition, especially after the First World War, the mechanization of southern agriculture linked with the mechanization and modernization of U.S. agriculture as a whole. Agricultural investments were a key form of productive expenditure that absorbed surpluses generated from the huge industrial machine that had been developed in the last third of the nineteenth century.

There are serious problems with the interpretation of the theory of imperialism to mean the exploitation of underdeveloped regions as well. Since the end of the Second World War, the ratio of foreign investment by U.S.-dominated corporations in Europe, Japan, Canada, and other advanced capitalist countries to that in underdeveloped, "Third World" areas has risen steadily. It is still true that nearly half of all U.S. foreign investment is in the key oil industry, and a sizeable amount of other investment is devoted to raw materials extraction in the Third World. Much new export capital has flowed to advanced capitalist countries. U.S.-based corporations have penetrated the British car industry, the French communications/data industry, German chemicals and other leading sectors throughout Europe, Canada, and Japan. Even in Third World countries, a larger proportion of capital is used to develop manufacturing industries that often compete with those within advanced countries. Of course, much of this capital has moved into the production of consumer goods such as autos, electrical equipment such as radios and television in Japan, and textile products. But multinational corporations based in the United States have also built oil refineries and chemical plants in Latin America and the Caribbean. New petrochemical complexes are scheduled for construction in the Middle East and metals refineries are being built in Africa.

To some extent, some foreign investment is already becoming disaccumulative because penetration has taken the form of investments in the cultural apparatuses of Third World countries. Coca Cola bottling plants, purchase of radio stations and newspapers, investment in management systems rather than goods production, export of software rather than hardware, all indicate a growing tendency towards investments in foreign countries whose dual objectives are social domination *and* profits. Imperialism has a distinct cultural aspect and its social role has gone far beyond the task of finding outlets for raw materials investments and productive ways to dispose of surplus capital. The relations of unequal exchange that obtain between the most developed and Third World countries generate a system of dependency that extends to the political sphere as well as the cultural and social. The Leninist expectation that movements for national independence constitute an irreparable blow to imperialism despite the fact that they are often led by disaffected elements of the nascent bourgeoisie has been frustrated by the structural dependency of both the bourgeoisie and the native latifundist classes on the metropolitan powers. Thus, revolution in the Third World does not necessarily sound the death-knell to imperialism if it can retain economic and political hegemony within the framework of political independence. The quick integration of newly-independent African and Middle-Eastern and Asian nations with dollar, franc, and pound areas attests to the durability of the dependent character of international relations since the development of capitalism in the sixteenth century when colonial conquest was not based as such on capital export as it was upon the requirement for raw materials.

Harry Magdoff has attempted to counter such an argument and preserve the integrity of Lenin's theory in the light of the admitted quantitative superiority of investments in services and waste in proportion to capital export. His argument upholding the notion that imperialism is a necessary stage of capitalism rather than a highly profitable policy of the monopolistic groups, hinges on a sort of "key sector" analysis.[150] According to Magdoff, imperialism may not define the range of surplus investments for industry as a whole but it is crucial for those industries that correspond to what Veblen called "the technology of physics and chemistry": steel, electricity, oil-refining, synthetic organic chemicals, internal combustion engines, etc. To protect their assets and maintain their leading positions, the most advanced monopolistic industrial corporations are impelled to seek control over supplies of raw materials and over markets. Thus, for Magdoff the drive for raw materials and markets for goods and capital outlets generate a kind of hegemonic relationship between the giant corporations in the most advanced industries and the state. Answering those critics who point out "the relative smallness of private investment in the underdeveloped world," Magdoff replies that these key sectors have immense "influence on the dynamics of the U.S. economy. Without raw materials extracted from colonial nations the economic growth of the metropolitan nation suffers. In turn, the economic growth of advanced capitalist countries enables them to trade and exchange goods on favorable terms, thus enabling military and economic aid to reactionary regimes to the third world countries, huge foreign investments and the like."[151]

The curiosity of Magdoff's argument is that, on the one hand, he reaffirms the crucial role played by investments in raw materials for maintaining the continuity of the advanced technological sectors within the metropolitan countries, while at the same time playing down the role of imperialism as a critical means by which surplus capital is exported. For Magdoff, the role of imperialism appears to be related to the viability of the most oligopolistic industries rather than capitalist economy as a whole. Granting the relative smallness of capital investment in the Third World compared to the investment in other advanced capitalist nations or even within the country itself does not daunt Magdoff from affirming the old conception of imperialism as "necessity."

Yet the size of internal investment compared to all forms of foreign investment in modern times cannot be dismissed so easily. Investment in raw materials for resources-poor countries such as England and France has always been important for their sustenance. And, especially in the case of European capitalism, this type of investment predates the chronological conception of imperialism as a "new stage." The critical point of Lenin's thesis does hinge on the *export of capital* that arises from the appearance of substantial capital surpluses in the era of concentration and centralization into large corporate units. What seems apparent beyond doubt is that the role of productive and unproductive investment within the advanced capitalist countries is far greater as an economic outlet than that of all types of external investment – both to other advanced and Third World countries. Moreover, the economic, social, and political consequences of unproductive investment that constitutes a disaccumulation rather than a further accumulation of past productive labor may be far greater than, or at least equivalent to, those wrought by foreign investment.

The forms of unproductive investment that constitute the basis for the permanent war economy are certainly closely related to the protection of foreign investment insofar as wars, military aid, and "police actions" are necessary to provide a favourable political climate for the export of capital. There is no intention here to deny the significance of either the export of capital or militarism in the United States. But military expenditure is not determined by imperialist conquest alone. It has become a very important outlet for capital seeking to increase the rate of profit, especially because it is backed by a firm commitment by the state to exempt such investment from the vicissitudes of the market place. And, it may be argued, this use of military spending as disaccumulation is at least as significant as its actual use in relation to wars and other interventions abroad. The economic role of military spending far exceeds spending for actual war purposes in any given war. Its significance in relation to employment, investment, and many other economic indices is not circumscribed by U.S. foreign interests.

Nor would it be correct to interpret this argument as an attempt to minimize the importance of the anti-imperialist struggle. There can be no question of the need to oppose U.S. intervention abroad against the legitimate aspirations of other people. Ideologically, chauvinism, racism, and other doctrines that accompany patriotic efforts have had a strong negative effect on working-class consciousness throughout American history. Partly for this reason, the effort to develop bonds of solidarity with those struggling for national freedom against U.S. domination remains a critical test of a U.S. revolutionary movement.

But these strategic concerns should not be confused with the theoretical position under discussion. For the effect of elevating the theory of imperialism as enunciated by Lenin to the centerpiece in socialist doctrine has been to blind the Socialist movement and those who have been influenced by it to a far more important development – the elevation of the commodity itself to its own ideological justification. Without slighting the role of imperialist ideas among the working class, the large-scale production and consumption of commodities in the forms of waste and services have served to reproduce the system both in the economic and social sense. Quite apart from the significance of internal investments in types of production that actually result in real growth such as farming and new industrialization efforts, the huge expenditures in types of commodities whose only justification is domination have become major industries and justifications to capitalist reproduction.

It is curious that Baran and Sweezy, who together with Magdoff were among the most important theorists of modern imperialism in the Leninist mode, have also noticed the significance of advertising, planned obsolescence within commodities, and the service industries for providing outlets for surplus investments. The problem in their analysis is the relatively slight social weight given to these types of investment and what they represent in terms of the development of capitalism. In their magnum opus *Monopoly Capital*,[152] Sweezy and Baran focus upon the large corporation and militarism and imperialism as critical forces determining the shape of modern capitalism.

Again in Sweezy's essay for a Japanese encyclopedia on modern capitalism, written in 1971, the emphasis is placed almost exclusively on military expenditures and foreign plunder as the key means by which capitalism overcomes its inherent tendency toward crisis and stagnation in its late stages. In the last paragraph of the essay Sweezy makes explicit what remains implicit in most Leninist thinking: "The Vietnam war has already proved that wars of this nature and magnitude cause profound divisions and tensions within the involved developed countries. It seems reasonable to suppose that their continuation and escalation will drive these divisions and tensions to the breaking point. If this should happen the classical Marxian version of socialist revolution in the most developed capitalist countries would finally come into its own."[153]

The logic of the argument rests on the assumption that imperialist conquest, a necessary feature of late capitalism, leads inevitably to wars of national liberation. If such wars are conducted continuously, they generate the preconditions for socialist revolutionary thought and action in the anti-imperialist struggle. Sweezy follows Lenin in the belief that imperialism sustains capitalism both ideologically and economically, and that defeats for imperialism may constitute the real basis for socialist movements within advanced capitalist nations.

The reverse argument is that capitalism rests on the production and reproduction of commodities and the fetishistic form that they take as things, institutions, and ideologies that legitimate its hegemony among the underlying population. Capital needs investment outlets and its most available outlet has been in areas which serve the domination of the working class within the advanced capitalist countries themselves. The use of the power of past labor transformed into capital in the process of production for commodities that secure the affiliation of workers to the prevailing system is sustained by means of commodities themselves. To be sure, capital investment in nonproductive services creates a myriad of problems for the capitalist system as I will show below.

(2) *Dependency theory*. The second logic is that the capitalist system has always existed as a world system because the model for expanded reproduction in the second volume of Marx's *Capital*

leaves no room for a "stages" theory. In Rosa Luxemburg's controversial critique of Marx's expanded reproduction schema, she asserted that the crisis of capitalism consists in the imperialist imperative as a structural feature arising from the chronic disparity between the accumulation process which requires the production of a surplus as the *sine qua non* of its specifically *capitalist* existence and the consequent restriction placed on the producers' consumption of all that they have produced. Drawing from Marx's famous emblem that the greatest barrier to the expansion of capital in production is capital itself, Luxemburg has posited the absolute necessity for capital to break down national borders, to destroy feudal social relations wherever they offer a threat to accumulation, or, in some new theories of accumulation, to utilize pre-capitalist modes of production for the benefit of the centers of capitalist production. Luxemburg advanced a theory that showed that militarism and territorial expansion were concomitants of underconsumption in the center, two means by which capital overcame the barriers of the logic of expanded reproduction. The inevitable breakdown would occur because, in seeking to overcome these barriers, capital is constrained to overcome the backwardness of the rest of the world. But, by universalizing itself, that is, by introducing capitalist relations of production in those areas which were used as markets for surpluses that could not find ways to realize their values within the center, the market for realizing the unbought uninvested surpluses would gradually dry up. The undeveloped world would enter the capitalist world system as a competitor rather than remain a non-capitalist dumping-ground.[154]

Modern dependency theory, while departing from Luxemburg's thesis that the breakdown results from a realization crisis, has drawn considerably on her work. The fundamental position of dependency theory is that the so-called primitive accumulation of capital, which traditional Marxism, including Lenin, places within an historical frame of early capitalism, must be considered a permanent feature of the reproduction of capital. Primitive accumulation of capital takes a particular form in the modern world: the transfer of value from the underdeveloped to the developed sectors of the world system. The search for capital and commodity markets, regardless of national boundaries, becomes not a late capitalist development but a characteristic of the entire history of the capitalist mode of production. The major feature of this world system is *unequal exchange* where the center draws the periphery into the capitalist mode of production – but in a unique form. Thus, the forms of accumulation at the center correspond to a concomitant development of underdeveloped forms in the periphery. But, unlike the Leninist model, the world capitalist system consists in different types of social formations of capitalist relations of production, not "semi-feudal," feudal, or mercantilist forms in contradistinction to "advanced" forms in the west. Imperialism becomes not a stage of capitalism but the mode of existence of the world capitalist system. "Capitalism has become a world system, not just a juxtaposition of national capitalisms" (Amin). In its Marxist versions, dependency theory holds to the view that capitalism at the center is propelled by the falling rate of profit. It argues that the overcoming of this tendency by increasing the mass of surplus value takes place by means of a systematic transfer of value from the periphery. In this version, the working class of the center benefits *as a whole* from unequal exchange, so that the locus of revolutionary activity must be permanently displaced to the periphery. Leading figures in this school, Andre Gunder Frank, Samir Amin, and Cardozo,[155] follow Luxemburg in their contention that the concept of a national bourgeoisie able to raise revolutionary demands against imperialism is not only an empirically erroneous rendering of the past century of Latin American and African history, but was grounded in a false theoretical premise – namely, the view that capitalist "integration" on a world scale is only a recent phenomenon. That is, if one accepts the primitive accumulation of capital as a regular and historically persistent feature of the world system, and takes the logic of expanded reproduction to mean that capital will seek its realization regardless of national boundaries, then the next step is to construct a view of the "Third World" as a type of capitalism in which a national bourgeoisie *never* emerges. A *comprador* bourgeoisie tied hand and foot to the center, benefiting, albeit unequally, from its specialized position within the international division of capitalist labor, is disinclined to join, much less lead, a movement for national liberation. On the contrary, it will oppose such movements by force if necessary. Here is the most eloquent expression of the view that the international class struggle must be reconceptualized in terms of the entire center against that portion of the periphery, e.g. the working classes (even the peasantry must be working class if it produces surplus value for the center) who remain dominated by the multiple threads of dependency relations. For dependency theory in its Marxist manifestation assumes that capital does sweep away all the old idyllic relations that constituted a barrier to the accumulation of capital. Amin refers to the economic process as "primitive accumulation" because it is based on theft, expropriation, and intensification of labor exploitation on the basis of the extraction of absolute surplus value.

By extension world capitalism does not break down as long as relations of domination are maintained between center and periphery because the transfer of masses of surplus value to the crisis-ridden center will counteract the falling rate of profit which is based on surplus value extraction that constantly diminishes the living labor embodied in the commodity. Put another way, the dependent periphery specializes in absolute surplus value extraction where the surplus is gained by low wages in labor-intensive production; this process is reinforced by the most brutal and dictatorial political systems based on military force. The logical conclusion drawn by some dependency theorists is that the next stage in the revolutionary process must be not the socialist revolution among the dependent countries, but its movement for economic modernization based on democratic demands. The Luxemburgist expectation that capitalist expansion to the pre-capitalist sectors would remove markets from the centre is not transformed into a political program. Some Trotskyists argue that the revolution in the Third World must combine the specifically capitalist development, that is, the introduction of the modern factory where surplus value extraction is enlarged mainly by replacing living labor by machinery and methods of work organization that degrade and dequalify labor while reducing the time of its production, with socialist development, i.e. the leadership of modernization processes under the working class. In the latter variation, "bourgeois" demands for equality of economic relations combine with similar political demands for democratic state within the framework of a socialist movement since there is no genuine bourgeoisie to lead the specifically bourgeois struggle within the dependent countries.[156] The Third World "1789" takes place under entirely different conditions and must be quickly merged with the "1917". Thus Trotskyism believed itself vindicated by the early years of the Cuban revolution where these features seemed classically present. Of course, when Cuba, owing to its under-development, appeared to enter into new dependency relations with the Soviet Union, replacing those with the U.S., some earlier optimism had to be tempered.

Among the important implications of a strictly Luxemburgist interpretation of dependency theory is to refute the Stalinist hope that socialism may be built in the one country following a successful communist-led peripheral revolution. Even if the workers or technocratic strata succeed in establishing formal political and economic autonomy from the core, the evidence since the end of the Second World War, when nearly all dependent countries in Asia and Africa gained "independent" status, has been that dependency relations are not overturned. There is scarce evidence that the *combined* part of Trotsky's theory of revolutions in the dependent countries has been able to establish genuine economic independence and thus political autonomy in the real, rather than the formal sense. While progressive technocratic strata and industrial workers or agricultural laborers may join in a successful *coup*, a social revolution in the Third World seems out of the question according to some critics. Dependency theory, in this reading, becomes a renewed argument for the necessity for revolutionary upsurge in the center if the Third World revolutions are to be more than neo-colonial.

(3) *Capital-logic*. In recent years, another position has staked a claim to provide a broader and more adequate explanation of the course of capitalist development than either Leninism or dependency theory. This position, associated with the work of Roman Rosdolsky, Paul Mattick, and more recently Michel Aglietta, has received considerable attention among European Marxists but has only been understood in terms of Harry Braverman's work within the United States.[157] Braverman's *Labor and Monopoly Capital*, which has received considerable attention within the English-speaking world, purports to be a study of the labor process, a supplement to the work of Paul Baran and Paul Sweezy in their *Monopoly Capital*, which may be the most celebrated underconsumptionist attempt to comprehend the late twentieth-century capitalist period. As I have pointed out elsewhere,[158] Braverman's book achieved more than he intended. By locating the character of late capitalism within the imperatives of the labor process rather than its displacements in the relations of exchange or forms of capitalist organization, Braverman aligned himself, perhaps unintentionally, with the "logic of capital" group within Marxism, providing it with a concrete study of immeasurable significance.

Essentially, "capital-logic" theory looks again to the formula for the production of capital, the accumulation process, as the source of the eventual crisis as well as its historical development. Lenin and his epigones sought the origin of monopoly capitalism in capitalist competition, which he believed produced the conditions for the concentration and centralization of capital; in capital-logic theory, on the other hand, the labor process becomes the core of capitalist contradictions, for it is upon the capitalist organization of the production of use values/exchange values that the reproduction of the entire system depends. Capital-logic theory does not base a theory of historical periodicity on relations of unequal exchange (dependency theory), nor on the forms of the organization of capital (Lenin). Aglietta and Christian Palloix, two of the most interesting of the recent theorists of this view, argue that the distinction between early and late capitalism consists *principally* in the difference between the extensive regime and the intensive regime of capitalist production.[159] In the extensive regime, the extraction of surplus value depends on such measures as lengthening the work day since artisans still control the central condition for production, the labor process, but have ceded to the capitalist ownership of some of the means of production (the building, large machinery) and the distribution of commodities.

The extensive regime corresponds to the period of manufacture in Marx's historical schema in Volume 1 of *Capital*. The expansion of capital is limited by the fact that the ownership of capital is separated from the control of the labor process. The class struggle appears in the form of the struggle over the length of the working day and the price of labor power. In the United States, as Habakkuk argued, the price of skilled labor power tended to rise under the extensive regime because its supply was limited by the development of European capital and its own requirements for skilled labor. Shortages could not be overcome by capitalists except by raising the wages of this group to a point where accumulation itself was threatened. Since the U.S. had no feudal traditions, it could not boast a viable idigenous artisan tradition of sufficient scope to meet the needs of manufacture. Thus, from the very beginning in the growth of U.S. capitalism, immigration became a major mechanism for insuring the development of industry.

The emergence of the intensive regime in this schema of American history is closely linked, not with the falling rate of profit as much as the limits imposed on capital's expansion by the control of the labor process by the working class. High wages were intolerable to American capital because in a production system in which labor still played a dominant role (where the organic composition of capital was extremely low),the mass of profit could not be enlarged except by wresting the control of the labor process from the workers. As Braverman shows, Taylorism is a technology specific to the capitalist reorganization of the labor process. Its aim is to separate design from execution, so that the new function of management monopolizes intellectual labor once performed by the artisan. Taylor offers higher wages in return for the surrender of skill, that is, workers' power over production. The question was not resolved by material incentives alone. Nor did capitalism makes its transition from the extensive to the intensive regime peacefully. The intensive regime marks the era where the extraction of surplus value is no longer *mainly* achieved by means of intensification of the pace of production, longer hours for the same pay, or outright wage cutting, although these methods are never abandoned. Now increasing the mass of surplus value may be achieved with an increase in wages, providing the value of the quantity of variable capital (wages) within each unit of production is reduced. The intensive regime corresponds to the period where relative rather than absolute surplus value is the major form of accumulation. The reorganization of the labor process implies the increase of the proportion of constant capital to variable capital, although each side of the cost of production may rise, but not equally. The introduction of new machinery aims as much as new methods or work organization to render the power of crafts over the labor process moot. Labor is integrated by the new regime as merely a factor of production. Large-scale industrialization united ownership with control, insofar as managers, engineers, technicians, and scientists are now subsumed under capital as the operational powers over production, replacing artisan labor whose skills are rendered obsolete in the production of exchange values.

The intensive regime implies more than a change in the labor process. It seems to increase the productive power of capital, which now appears to be the motivating force of production since it mobilizes science and technology as productive forces. It places the accumulation process at the center of world history where earlier the "idyllic relations" of the feudal period hung on within the labor process and thus mediated the full triumph of the new economic and social order.

During the period of transition, the artisans form trade unions whose demands for the shorter work-day and higher wages are not as historically significant as their resolve to defend their control over the labor process by protecting their skills. This demand, known within the vocabulary of the labor movements as concern for the "conditions of work," became the cutting edge of labor militancy during the period following the Civil War in the United States, just as British workers had demanded similar protections in the period 1788–1830 when Britain became the "workshop of the world". Labor struggle consisted in the fight against the degradation of skills, and, in the United States, against the capitalist seizure of the manufactory and its transformation into the capitalist factory. The Homestead Steel strike of 1892 becomes, in this theory, a watershed event marking the introduction of what Marx called the specifically capitalist mode of production, that is, the hegemony of the intensive regime where the exploitation of labor takes place on the basis of the progressive replacement of humans by machines *and* the uniting of ownership and control over the labor process.

The details of the strike are, by now, legendary: Henry Frick, the head of the Carnegie Steel Corporation, provoked a strike by the Amalgamated Association of Iron and Steel workers, a craft union that had been among the strongest in the American labor movement. The issue was whether the corporation, having introduced the Bessemer steelmaking process that destroyed the traditional iron and steelmaking crafts, could demand changes in the labor agreement that would recognize the new reality: the objective base for workers, control over production, had been removed by capital. Wages had to be reduced accordingly and workers' power over production surrendered. The strike was a belated action because the managers had already seized the plant and transformed it. Further, since the 1870s and 1880s the new process which required no special skills by labor called into existence a whole new type of labor force. Similar developments in coal mines, machine manufacture, and consumer goods production (garments, textiles) gave rise to the logical next step: the vast waves of immigration that dramatically increased the American population from 1880 to 1920. Previously the recruitment of Irish and Chinese labor in the 1840s had been related to the provision of the transportation and communications infrastructure for the movement of commodities from the farm to the urban centers. Similarly, the shipbuilding industry and its concomitant, the iron industry, were operated under the extensive regime.

Agriculture and railroad construction, having provided "primitive" capitalist accumulation, still did not require the mass immigrants that came here after the Civil War. The intensive regime replaces manual with intellectual labor as the central force of production, their unity, which is preserved in the old artisan mode of production, having already been sundered. It makes necessary the recruitment of new labor. This new organization of labor processes takes the design function out of the hands of labor and places it under the control of capital. What remains is a labor process that becomes repetitive, segmented, and univalent. Every job in "production" (as distinct from maintenance that still requires substantial elements of the old crafts) may be learned in less than six weeks. The "skill" required is merely speed, which is acquired through practice and becomes internalized by the worker as habit, a characteristic of "second nature".

Palloix distinguishes between *fordism*, the complex of technological and organizational shifts in the labor process that is linked to *mass production*, where parts are interchangeable and labor becomes a part as much as nuts, bolts, and pieces of sheet metal, and *"neo-fordism"*, the phase of the intensive system that is introduced after 1920. Neo-fordism is a new stage of the intensive regime. The overproduction of capital and commodities inherent in the formula for both capital and the rate of profit now calls into being a new counteracting cause – mass consumption, as material practice corresponding to the new labor processes and as ideology. Ford innovated in the labor process in a way that is merely incipient in Taylor, since Taylor basically introduced only the principle of measurement into machine operations. Ford transformed the entire method of fabrication and, through the conveyor belt, literally reduced the worker to a function of the machine. But neo-fordism means that the process of production gives rise to a whole new set of social relations. The state was mobilized to capitalize needed infrastructural development during the periods of primitive accumulation, remaining a watchman of the system of social relations. It now became necessary to deploy the state as a consumer of capital and commodities to supplement private consumption. Beyond this, Aglietta argues that its regulative function becomes a central mechanism for arresting and displacing the crisis tendencies of the system.

Recently, American writers such as Stuart Ewen and David Noble[160] have shown that the first half of this century was marked by the rise of organized capitalism, defined both by the centrality of the planning function and consumption within the capitalist framework. The virtue of Aglietta's model of capitalist development is to provide an explanation of the simultaneity of these innovations. Having discovered *how* to multiply the accumulation process by seizing control of the labor process, capital had to find a solution for the crisis of overproduction that resulted from the intensive regime. The rise of advertising accompanied the development of a mass consumption of autos and appliances. Although the drive towards consumer society was somewhat arrested by the depression, the conveyor belt contained its own logic, as did the section work system in the garment industry, the Bedeux and other wage-incentive programs based on rationalization of production. Mass consumption of the products of the new regime continued throughout the 1930s where the ground was laid for the immense upsurge in consumerism after the war.

At first, capital resisted the kind of government regulation of consumption and investment that was indicated by neo-fordism production. The administration of Herbert Hoover introduced the major forms of government intervention, principally the Reconstruction Finance Corporation and other federal programs designed to simulate investment, but it was not until Roosevelt took office in 1933 that the commitment to intervene became a clearcut question of state policy. In the past forty-five years, state intervention into the economy has widened both in scope and depth. After 1938 the permanent arms economy became a major built-in stabilizer which, together with transfer payments in the form of a social wage, guarantees a market for both capital and commodities at the average rate of profit.

But it was the rise of the CIO in the 1930s that gave the major impetus to the completion of Ford's model of accumulation through control of the labor process. The slow rate of growth of this regime in the 1920s had been, in part, the result of the brutal assault by capital on the new unions that had established a beachhead during the First World War. The decline of real wages, following the weakening of trade unionism, contributed to the depth of the depression in this country in contrast to most of western Europe where the labor movement was able to prevent the full burden of the crisis from being transferred to the workers. It also provided a disincentive for the introduction of new labor processes that dequalified labor and called into existence mass consumption.

The firm victories of the industrial union movement in the 1940s provided the institutional basis both for a rise of real wages and for the institutionalization of the social wage (social security, unemployment insurance, relief, the legalization of the eight-hour day, etc.). As much recent historiography demonstrates, the New Deal was by no means committed to these regulatory forms in its first term of office. Only the mass recruitment of workers into the unions and the struggles of youth, women, blacks, and the unemployed gave the impetus for the enactment of most social legislation during the second New Deal. But, despite capital's resistance, there was no rolling back these gains. On the contrary, transfer payments became a major means to guarantee consumption.

At the same time, the proliferation of the state bureaucracy created a new salariat, a middle strata whose fundamental place within the political economy was to perform the functions of regulation and, as unproductive consumers, to accelerate the pace of effective demand for consumer durables such as houses and automobiles.

The consequences of the success of mass industrial unionism for the accumulation process became, for Aglietta, fundamental for enhancing capital's control over the crisis tendencies of the system. Although collective bargaining made possible a rise in labor costs, both in nominal wages and the social wage (so-called fringe benefits), it also facilitated planning and regulation of investment at the level of the firm. Long-term contracts that insured a fixed labor cost enabled capital to predict its quantity of investment, making the fixed portion of capital investment less risky. Second, as we have already noted, contract unionism provided a stable base of effective demand for consumer durables. Third, consumerism entailed a trade off: workers accepted the trade-union emphasis on monetary benefits and slowly gave up their remaining control of the workplace. The rising level of wages also accelerated the rate of accumulation since capital tries to offset labor militancy or the results of labor shortages under the intensive regime by technological change. But the rising organic composition of capital, which is merely the value form of the progressive replacement of human labor by capital, created new pressures on the profit rate. Aglietta explains the ubiquitous phenomenon of waste production after the war (planned obsolescence, product innovation in the consumer goods industries, that is, the pervasive significance of fashion in virtually all commodities, and so on) in terms of the internal contradictions of the accumulation process. These changes are attributed to the need to lower the turnover rate of capital in order to offset the diminishing rate of profit on investment. In Marxist terms, this becomes a major means to increase the mass of surplus value in the wake of the declining proportion of living labor to dead labor in the production of both the means of production and consumer goods.

Finally, Aglietta argues, the contemporary crisis maturing throughout the capitalist world is chiefly caused by rising workers' resistance to the deterioration of working conditions brought about by the changes in work organization and mechanization. Since the intensive regime does not abolish surplus value extraction by means of increasing labor intensity (speedup, increased pressure for high productivity), the long retreat of the workers in the wake of consumerism in the 1950's was reversed in the next decade. Wildcat strikes, "soldiering on the job," lateness and absenteeism, all contributed to the slowing down of the production of the mass of profit and allowed the inherent tendency for a falling profit rate to realize itself.

Capital-logic theories of historical periodicity have wide explanatory value. Dependency theory and classic imperialist theory tend to fail to explain the changes that produced late capitalist societies; they do not provide an internal explanation, only a general theory of the displacement of capitalist contradictions to the underdeveloped world. The virtue of those critiques of capitalist economies that focus on the labor process is that they can show why apparently anomalous phenomena have appeared since the end of the war, such as the shift of U.S. investment from the Third World to the advanced capitalist nations. Today two-thirds of all foreign investment takes place within the advanced countries where the intensive regime predominates. The limits described by Marx on the production of absolute surplus value, such as the resistance of the working class to longer hours and their struggle for a large portion of the social surplus, and the revolutionary movements that have sprung up in response to imperialist domination, have made underdeveloped countries unstable from an investment perspective. Since late capitalism relies on the state and the labor movement to provide reasonable institutional bases for investment security, when these conditions are jeopardized the pattern of capital export is bound to shift.

It is no accident, then, that America, Germany, and Japan have proved the best areas for long-term capital expansion. In all cases, the working class has, as a whole, been less volatile since the Second World War. In the U.S. and Germany, mass consumption has been elevated to the level of ideology as material practice, so that the traditional barriers offered by craft and labor intensive industries were smashed not only by force but also by the profound changes in mass psychology made possible by the productivity of labor itself. For two generations American workers were persuaded that the condition for their own progress was tied umbilically to the accumulation of capital, an ideological stance abetted by the depth of the American depression, the decentralization of industry which destroyed historical bonds of working-class solidarity, and the rise of mass-mediated culture that progressively replaced the barroom and other traditional centers of working class conviviality. All of these may be explained by shifts in the circuits of capital: for example, the surfeit of investment relative to the average rate of profit on the production circuits produced a shift to public and private services. This in turn created a new mass middle stratum and a clerical/administrative working class whose role in stimulating effective demand, corresponding to the fantastic rise of labor productivity, was extremely important in avoiding a postwar crisis. The middle stratum, almost a pure form of a consumer culture, is but the other side of fordism. Like the workers, this stratum lives on the credit system, introduced in the 1920's on a broad scale to guarantee that the intensive regime could reproduce itself. The transformation of the family into a unit of almost pure consumption corresponds to the predominance assumed by durable goods since the First World War.

Evidence of working-class and middle-strata resistance to the relentless march of capital is explained by capital-logicians in purely physical terms. Workers are pushed to the limit by that side of surplus value extraction that relies on traditional methods characteristic of absolute surplus value. Since there are really no relatively autonomous spaces in this paradigm of capitalist development, even the rise of the worker's movement is linked to capital-logic. If the CIO organized the unskilled and semiskilled working class in the 1930's, it only arose because of the breakdown in the regime, but the labor movement could not achieve independence because the logic of regulation which increasingly governs the accumulation process demands that it be integrated as merely another factor of production. Therefore, only a breakdown of the system, itself a result of the logic of accumulation, can produce an independent working-class movement.

To recapitulate: it must be remembered that most capital-logic theorists, including Ernest Mandel,[161] Braverman, Aglietta, and Mattick consider themselves orthodox Marxists. They do not deny the importance of imperialism, nor would they dispute the Luxemburgist position regarding dependency as a system of unequal exchange. For capital-logicians of various stripes, these structures are significant but ancillary means by which capital attempts to cope with the contradictions of its own expansion. They dispute the view that the export of capital resulting from fierce national competition and the declining profit-rate becomes the center of the capital world system. For them, the sphere of production remains the central dynamic of the entire capitalist system. Unlike Sweezy, Baran, and others, for whom the problem of consumption may be seen as an independent variable in the accumulation process, capital-logic places weight on the overproduction of capital and tries to show that late capitalism is defined by the creation of social forms to (1) increase labor productivity and (2) regulate the relations between production and consumption. With Marx, they argue that the conditions of production generate the conditions of consumption. It is this problematic that produces the whole range of superstructural phenomena including the interventionist state, the arms economy, lowering the turnover rate through planned obsolescence, mass-mediated culture, especially advertising, etc. Where Gramsci and Althusser insist, in different ways, on the centrality of ideological structures as elements of capitalist hegemony, Paul Mattick maintains an almost reflex opposition of "idealism" in any form, that is, a theory that does not see in the formula for capital the *source* of all social contradictions. Capital-logicians object to the attempt to unite Freud and Weber with Marx on the grounds that the categories of "domination" and the "unconscious" are hopelessly confused at best and, worse, mask the class basis of exploitation.[162] For capital-logic, science demands the crucial simplicity that allows for explanation of a broad range of phenomena without recourse to discourses that are antagonistic to the paradigm of accumulation. The three versions of Marxist economic science discussed here are concerned, each in its own way, with the criterion of consistency in order to found the new science. Each has succeeded in dealing with the specificity of late capitalism in various ways. Lenin's theory of imperialism arose during the First

World War to explain the failure of the Second International to respond in a revolutionary way to the war of redivision of the world among capitalist powers. At the same time, he was concerned to understand the war as a means to avoid the inevitable breakdown. Consequently, his theory recognizes both the specificity of ideology on working-class activity and the significance of *organizational* solutions to the crisis, e.g. the formation of monopolies to counteract the deleterious effects of competition upon accumulation. *Dependency theory* must be seen in the wake of the failure of Leninism both in the Soviet Union and in Latin American countries and Africa. The expectation that a national bourgeoisie would emerge with which a proletariat led by the communist party could form a temporary, revolutionary-democratic alliance aborted in nearly all of Latin America and north Africa. The national bourgeoisie remained incipient and, as in China, turned against the working class and peasantry, even before achieving independence from imperialism. Thus did Trotsky draw the lessons of the Chinese experience by arguing for the law of *uneven and combined* development, taking Lenin's view that the underdeveloped world is bound to revolt because of the systematic exploitation of its resources and the deformed pattern of capitalist development that accompanies it. Combined development means that stages may be skipped; the national bourgeoisie must be *represented* by the working class of the exploited nation since its emergence is always doubtful and the bourgeoisie that comes into existence at the margins of imperialism is too closely tied to the conquerors to become consistently oppositional.

With the exception of Lenin himself, whose position was always mediated by practical considerations and would therefore not presume to hold fast formulations that were not subject to immediate alteration with the changed circumstances, the result of most Marxist theory is to focus on the *systematic* coherence of late capitalism, an approach that corresponds at the metatheoretical level to a social physics. But unlike the most recent controversies within natural sciences, the moment of indeterminacy is missing. Marxism, in its logical manifestations, is geared to explanations of the past by means of formal criteria and to predicting the future on the basis of them. Subjectivity is constituted by a definite logic whose external parameters are fixed within a relatively narrow range of probabilities.

SCIENTISM, THE PRINCIPLE OF IDENTITY, AND THE DISAPPEARANCE OF THE SUBJECT

My principal objections to the three versions of Marxist theory that proceed from a view of Marxism as a positive science may be summarized in the following points:

(1) The distinguishing feature of Marxist scientism at the metatheoretical level is that it forgets that Marx's critique of political economy was *both* descriptive and critical. Much of the material in the three volumes of *Capital* consists in penetrating the forms of appearance of capital to show that it is a social relation whose logic attempts to transform itself into a set of objective thing-like relations, so that its power appears to be derived from nature rather than class exploitation. Marx often adopts the discourse of the fetish, that is, the systematic form in which capital, presenting itself as the embodiment of nature, circulates. Labor, science, and technology are subsumed under capital as various sides of its own movement. Thus, Marx himself does not always allow for the capitalist social relations, of which capital is the material form, to shine through. Except in a few sections, the working class appears in *Capital* as a factor of production, its social existence circumscribed by the logic of accumulation. When Althusser argues that capitalism as a social formation is prior to the class struggle and that the classes are constituted by the social formation, history is no longer the history of class struggles, but becomes the unfolding of the capitalist mode of production by means of the dialectic of accumulation; labor thereby becomes subsumed under capital. The transformation of the competitive (extensive) stage into the monopoly (intensive) stage signifies the triumph of capital's claim to the status of natural law. The subject becomes the anachronistic carryover from the feudal mode of production, in which relations of mutual obligations constituted a subject with "rights" as well as duties with the guild and the manorial systems. The aim of capital is to reduce the subject to a moment of its development and, if the consequences of capital-logic are to be rigorously followed, the subject is seen as an historical phenomenon whose quintessential existence may be attributed to the absolute necessity of freeing the bourgeoisie and the serfs from their feudal bonds in order to insure the triumph of the commodity and value forms over all production.

Having conquered production, capital then seeks to dispense with the subject. The corporation replaces the individual entrepreneur as the characteristic capitalist and the mass or collective worker emerges in the stead of the artisan. To the extent that the subject or historical agency may still exist, it is evidence for the law of uneven development, a rearguard phenomenon whose extinction is prevented only by the penetration of capital into industries still marked by small proprietorship or the few functions of the industrial system that require skilled labor. In any case, the class struggle is seen as a reflex of capital's Achilles' heel, the fact that labor is the origin of all surplus value and therefore is the *sine qua non* of accumulation. But the class struggle is also regulated by late capitalism by means of the labor contract that insures its position as skilled labor but makes the wages bill entirely predictable over time.

I believe that the primacy of social formation in all three varieties of capital-logic may be explained by two distinct influences: the first, the failure of the working class in the west to constitute itself as an historical agency for socialist transformation. In effect, Lenin's labor aristocracy thesis is merely the homology to Samir Amin's version of dependency theory and the subsumptionist positions of capital-logicians. They have concluded that the working class in western capitalist countries is no longer capable of self-organization; class struggle becomes a reflex of the onerous conditions imposed by the intensive regime or its breakdown. Whence Trotsky's argument against the Proletarian Culture movement after the Bolshevik revolution, or Marcuse's concept of technological domination. For the varieties of Marxist thought which have accepted, albeit implicitly, that the working class has become an object of late capitalism, capital itself is the only possible subject.

(2) Apart from historical explanation, the working class represents an epistemological problem for Marxism. It may be shown that the socialist and communist parties have, unintentionally perhaps, become instruments for the integration of the working class within late capitalism where trade unionism leaves too much room for indeterminacy. The class-in-itself, a slogan for the political unconsciousness of the working class, may be something else as well. Syndicalism was the political position that argued that the conditions of capitalist exploitation were necessary *and* sufficient for the

impulse towards proletarian revolution. It argued that the cooperative mode of production called into existence by the modern factory united the class in a way impossible under previous modes of production. Moreover, the workers' own organizations could not, and should not, be controlled from the outside by any scientific elite claiming to lead on the basis of its grasp of the science of society.

Marxist antipathy to spontaneity derives as much from its scientism as it does from its reading of the history of the working-class movement. Marx, as much as Lenin, believed that the capitalist organization of production into highly concentrated units was the precondition for socialism. Capitalist science and technology would, effectively, if brought under social control, liberate humans from toil. For Lenin, however, the class was perennially in thrall of capital. Neither trade unionism nor the wildcat movements were sufficient to challenge capital at its roots. The party was to be the general staff of the proletarian revolution, since industrialization had rendered the mass of workers incapable of leading itself. Thus, Marxism explained autonomous movements of the workers not as evidence of their capacity for self-organization but rather as a reflection of capital's internal contradictions. The class struggle is no longer understood as the confrontation of two historical actors, capital and labor, each obeying different, but mutually conditioned logics. The class struggle is recuperated by capital, becomes a condition for the reproduction of capital on a new level, involving both displacement of labor as well as shifts in the location of production.

In order to show the limitations of paradigmatic explanations and thus allow for the undecidability of historical development, to show its jagged side, we must have another starting point – namely, the notion that the working class is self-constituting as much as it is constituted by capital. This viewpoint takes the class struggle seriously and restores the perspective of capital as a social relation in which class is not understood merely as the *location* of a social group within the production process, even a contradictory location, but is understood as the underlying logic of the undecidability of capitalist development. In order for this logic to function as a regulative principle, we must investigate the specific *praxis* of the working class, assuming that the praxis of capital is accumulation through exploitation. And, concomitantly, working-class culture must no longer be regarded as a fragment of the artisan mode of production whose existence as such becomes problematic in the intensive regime.

THE LOGIC OF LABOR AND DISACCUMULATION

By recognizing multiple logics, corresponding to Marx's concept that the capitalist mode of production is a system of *multiple determinations*, we refuse one of the metatheoretical assumptions of recent Marxist theory: that the structuration of the mode of production is tied to the classificatory logic of identity. That which constitutes the specificity of capitalism can no longer be encapsulated in a single set of relations, or relations of relations, that presuppose a conceptual identity at the core. As Marx argued in *The Eighteenth Brumaire*, a class is constituted by its common mode of life, a separate culture that permits it to represent itself politically and not be represented by others. Among the conditions for capitalist production is the formation of a free class of laborers that may sell its labor power for a wage. Capitalism eliminates the feudal system of mutual obligations including the rulers' obligation to provide for the ruled. The working class rallies to the bourgeois revolution under the banner of freedom. The introduction of the modern factory, where the labor process is controlled from the outside, is in structural contradiction to the bourgeois promise of freedom. Although capital, under intense pressure from women, workers, and racial and national minorities retreated at the political level from its interpretation of full citizenship rights to mean that only property-owners may enjoy voting privileges, it can never agree to economic democracy. Even though mass consumption under the intensive regime becomes the major means by which workers are integrated into capitalist accumulation as participants, the contradiction between the authority relations at the workplace and political democracy remains irreconcilable. Despite the bureaucratization of workers' organizations, the depoliticization by the workers' parties of the working class, workers do not merely struggle against capital for physical reasons or because of deprivation, the so-called "immiseration" thesis. The spread of workers' resistance in the 1960's and 1970's that, for Aglietta, bears a direct relation to the crisis of accumulation, is the result of an oppositional cultural logic of the working class and the middle strata, the movements of women and youth that refuse the authoritarian logic of capital accumulation.

The roots of this refusal are to be found in the fact that there never was a bourgeois democracy for the underclasses of capitalist societies. The working class and the marginal groups of society have seriously constrained and transformed public life within capitalist society. Although the "proletarian public sphere" of autonomous discourses has always remained partially suppressed by capitalist hegemony, the bourgeois ideal of freedom, which the bourgeoisie long ago abandoned, remains alive among its social objects. To be sure, mass culture has taken its toll on working-class culture. Nor is working-class culture always historically progressive from a socialist point of view. But, as the recent attack on the social wage demonstrates, the accumulation of state-administered benefits and those won through collective bargaining constitute a barrier to capital accumulation, even though union/industry pension funds have become a key source of investment capital. Thus the condition for stabilizing consumption and regulating capital investment becomes at a certain moment an obstacle that results in the intensification of social struggles and a potential source for destabilizing the entire system.[163]

In recent times, productivity gains in almost every advanced capitalist country and the Soviet Union have slowed considerably. Some of the productivity decline may be attributable to the bottlenecks that have appeared in accelerating the pace of new investment because of the declining rate of profit in many industries due to sharper international competition. But by the testimony of managerial and business circles much of the stagnation is due to the growing restlessness and discontent of workers. *Business Week* reports[164] "more concern with job satisfaction and less with job security" at AT&T. "Bell craftsmen such as installers, repairmen, and maintenance workers complain of too much overtime, thus hurting their family life." But the discontent is not confined to skilled workers. The most widely-reported complaint is that pressure is constantly put on workers and low-level managers to "promote productivity." The company is using a combination of methods of absolute and relative surplus value extraction. That is, workloads are increasing and new labor-saving technology has been introduced as well. The company management has conducted a survey of employees that found "some desire on the part of the people to be involved in the (labor) process and that's true societally. It's another way of saying employees respond less well to authoritarianism than to feeling part of the system." According to a unit of the Company responsible for finding ways to improve employee "satisfaction," workers want more freedom at the workplace from surveillance, pressure of the job, and close monitoring by supervision of lateness and absenteeism. Workers and their union are in open revolt on the "non-traditional" issue of workplace democracy, a demand that may be traced only partially to resentment against being pushed to increase output. Workers are reported to be concerned with the quality of their working life, their product, and the relation between Taylorist management and their everyday conditions.

This is only one among a large number of reported instances of worker resistance against the arbitrariness of management, the degraded conditions of labor generated by the dominance of relative surplus value in the labor process. Nor can the demand for participation and control be attributed to a minority of artisans who experience the fragmentation of their crafts by technological change. The generalization of discontent incipiently brings forth the demand for self-management expressed as the demand for freedom in the workplace.

This example raises the following question: the promise of freedom remains a condition for capital accumulation, but is antagonistic to its actuality. In the period of the intensive regime, neither the degradation of skills nor the rise of neo-fordism has been able to permanently suppress the working-class expectation that democracy will be extended from the political sphere to the labor process. As the bourgeoisie abandons its own political program at the moment when the question of the democratization of the workplace constitutes a serious question for the reproduction of capital, it is forced to bring masses of those historically excluded or marginalized from the labor process into commodity production or distribution. In the past thirty years, the entrance of racial and ethnic minorities and women into the labor force conjoined with the struggle for political freedom among these groups. The fight for civil rights and women's equality became central features of a burst of new militancy at the workplace. Millions of public employees joined unions in the 1960's owing to this conjunction, generating a sharp increase in labour costs in the social sector and simultaneously producing the counteraction by capital which, in the 1970's, began to face the challenge of international competition. Under circumstances of stagnation in the productive sectors, the rise of the state's wages bill provoked a counterattack which is still underway to limit and even reduce the social wage. At the same time, capital has been forced to increase the mass of surplus value by intensification of labor in the old-fashioned ways – speedup, coercion, etc. The simultaneous recomposition of the working class demographically brought a cultural dimension into the class struggle. Younger workers, imbued with the ideology of work satisfaction, simply refused the incentives of durable goods consumption to surrender their claims on the labor process. This refusal does not signify the emergence of a new anti-consumerist ethic among the working class, although this tendency is marked among a segment of the middle strata. The question is whether the trade-offs work any longer and if so, for how long. The growing resistance to degradation and the worsening of working conditions has produced a tendency towards displacing consumer goods industries to the Third World and making "department one" (the capital goods sector) the specialized activity of advanced countries within the world system. A second consequence of the falling rate of profit has been that capital has now moved to cheapen the elements of constant capital as a "counteracting cause." These have included: not waiting for depreciation before replacing machinery, and, most important, introducing technologies that "miniaturize" machine processes. The development of microcomputers, calculators, and numerical controls for machine tools are all examples of the dramatic reduction of the bulk and the value of constant capital. At the same time these processes, now widely employed in electronics, communications, administration, and, increasingly, in machine-tool production and steelmaking, reduce the amount of capital outlays required to produce means of production, reduce the size of variable capital, and thus recover the profit rate, at least temporarily.

Here we can see that the logic of labor mediates and determines the direction of capital's accumulation process. There is no way that capital, by its internal development, can produce the desire for freedom among workers. That desire, which becomes a material force and appears first as a counterhegemonic ideology to that of capital's doctrines of consumerism and authoritarian management, originates in the praxis of self-organization at the workplace and in the neighborhood. The conditions of capitalist production within the intensive regime are entwined with the formation of the collective as distinct from the mass laborer. Collective labor is the mode of existence of the working class owing precisely to the abolition of the artisan mode of production. Informal groups of workers develop their own counter-logic of production, albeit one whose boundaries are determined, in part, by the organization of labor by capital. This is the logic of what several writers have called disaccumulation as opposed to accumulation.

The core of the concept of disaccumulation is that labor becomes increasingly unproductive in late capitalism. Unproductive labor takes many forms: a larger proportion of the labor force is engaged in services, both public and private, that do not result in the production of surplus value. Instead, this form of labor shares the surplus value with capitalists both in the productive sector and the unproductive service sector. Secondly, as James O'Connor has argued, unproductive labor occurs on the shop floor in that part of the working day characterized either by the refusal to work (breaks, soldiering, etc.) or work in which capital's logic has failed to dominate the labor process because workers have invented other routes to spending their productive time in their own interest.[165]

As early as Taylor's experiments, management has been trying to find ways to incorporate the "fatigue" factor into production, to eliminate soldiering on the job, to use material incentives to increase productivity. The labor process is organized, as much as possible, on the basis of minute specialization so that the cooperative character of labor, which Marx believed to be intrinsic to the new production methods, is reduced. Workers counter capital's moves towards isolation and segmentation by subterfuge and by the labor contract. Their logic is bound up with the refusal to work or, to be more exact, with rhythms of labor that remain, despite a century of piecework incentives, oppositional to accumulation. The struggle to institutionalize these oppositional measures takes a variety of forms: coffee or tea breaks, more or less frequent depending on the strength of the workers, wash-up times, before lunch and before the nominal quitting hour; insisting upon safe and healthful working conditions that tend to use capital that could be invested in new equipment and labor. These include uniforms, safety shoes, ventilation, slower materials handling, and production norms that are "loose", permitting bonuses or piece rate standards to be met with less output, longer setting-up allowances that are necessary but ultimately not favorable to physical output, etc.

Among the unforeseen consequence of the intensive regime was the degree to which unionization, while raising the nominal wage, helped capital to discipline the working class by insisting that its logic predominate over the workers' logic of freedom and unwork. The bureaucratization of unions, which removed control of grievance procedures from the shop floor and professionalized class conflict, has now provoked widespread counterstruggles by rank-

and-file movements seeking to restore unions to their control. Democratic unionism is no longer consistent with capital's logic of accumulation since it may disrupt the regulative function of the labor contract or, alternatively, enforce those provisions of the contract that are favorable to shop-level workers' control.

Most of the logic of labor remains underground. In addition to resistance there is counterplanning at the shopfloor. In these instances workers try to organize both the pace and the configuration of production to meet their needs. Parts innovations are introduced against the will of management, production norms are set cooperatively, forcing the employers to threaten shutdowns in order to impose their own standards. Of course, work methods do not impinge on the control that capital still retains of the product design, but workers are prone to establish their own productivity norms and work methods.

Anthony Giddens[166] has argued that the labor contract incorporates both subversive and integrative elements into the labor process. While obliging workers to observe certain work rules established by management, many of its provisions regulate the introduction of new work methods, production norms, and job boundaries according to the will of the workers. His argument is that social theory has, until now, failed to understand the degree to which workers possess considerable "discursive knowledge," that is, conceptual knowledge that is not merely related to their practical skills as workers but represents their collective understanding of the forms of power and of their own social interest. The labor agreement, in his view, inscribes much of that collective knowledge insofar as it circumscribes capital's freedom. The history of capital's struggle to gain control over the workplace may be traced in terms of the evolution of the labor contract as well as the development of labor law.

The development of the American labor movement since 1946 is a story of the partial triumph of neo-fordism in comparison to Great Britain where the stewards system retains considerable autonomy from the union bureaucracy. Stewards have their own organizations within the enterprise, acting outside of the confines of the national agreement, negotiating work norms on the shopfloor. In the United States, the triumph of consumerism may be seen in the elimination of a strong unpaid stewards system and its replacement by full-time officials in return for high nominal wages; the provision of the social wage through the labor contract in the wake of the weakness of the trade unions in the political sphere; the rapid pace of technological change that usurped workers' power in the labor process. But too many commentators, including Mandel and Aglietta, have forgotten the record of the past ten years where union leaders have been pushed or replaced by rank-and-file groups, attesting to the persistence of a work culture that has enough social weight to challenge established patterns of union control.

Mario Tronti has argued[167] that workers determine the direction of the accumulation process by their own trade-union activity. His principal example, the United States, illustrates that political consciousness is not a necessary condition for the logic of labor to assert itself as an element of capitalist development. The essence of Tronti's argument is that the organization of the mass industrial unions in the 1930's was a counter-initiative by workers to a political initiative by capital to organize itself collectively. But labor's organized power, although conditioned by the New Deal, was successful because capital's self-organization was not as developed as that of the workers. The fight for the recognition of unions as bargaining agents not only stabilized labor costs, it limited the power of capital. Capital was obliged to develop in certain ways: it required "capitalism to put its cards on the table" by changing its political instrumentalities, that is, adopting the Keynesian program of state economic intervention. Tronti shows that the restructuring of American capitalism was the result of a partnership between the "most advanced part of the capital (which) extends its hands to the most advanced part of the working class," so that the "one's rights become the other's duties." He goes on to claim: "The tradition of the American working class is the most politicized because the impact of their struggles is the closest to the economic defeat of their adversary: the closest not to the conquest of power to construct in vacuum another society, but to the explosion of wage in order to subalternate capital and capitalists within this very society."[168] He argues that the American working class was able to achieve strength *within* capitalist society in contrast to the southern European working class which came to believe that it had to overturn capitalist society in order to win. Thus, for Tronti, the American class struggle proceeds without ideology save that of the absolute power of organization to effect change. While American labor was thoroughly ensconced in the present, it managed to have a profound impact on the shape of things to come. If American capitalism is a model of neo-fordism which Europe only recently in the 1970's attained, it is largely the product of the period of the organization of the mass unions. The irony of this development, that capital, against its own will, turned its defeat into victory, should not detract from the unexpected and dramatic character of the CIO organizing drive. Similarly, the mass organization of state workers in the 1960's has exacerbated the fiscal crisis of the state beyond the expectations of capitalist planners, posing difficult problems for capital accumulation in a way that would not have had the same importance if the wages bill did not rise as sharply in the public sector. Although the extent of worker resistance to attempted cutbacks in social services has lacked the effectiveness of the organizing phase because of the huge tax burden workers have had to shoulder to maintain the state sector, sectoral strike activity, such as that among teachers, police and fire, and sanitation workers, has posed serious problems for the state's effort to regulate the relation between capital accumulation and the social wage.

The task of cutting back or stabilizing the social sector faced a number of significant obstacles. The first has been the strength of teachers' unionism which, despite a conservative leadership, has refused to go along with wage freeze and layoff programs at the local level. Similarly, "uniformed services" have restricted reductions by militance including "sick outs," slowdowns (often effected in the form of "working to rule"), and strikes. Of course, those parts of the state sector that remained unorganized or poorly unionized have been forced to absorb considerable burdens to compensate for the resistance of the most militant state workers. These include administrative employees, university teachers and staff, and professionals outside education and health.

A second problem, which is but an expression of the extent of workers' self-organization, is the difficulty of establishing productivity norms in the public sector. Millions of dollars have been spent on studies to determine how services may be subjected to rationalization – without success. To be sure, much of social welfare has become automated, particularly the determination of eligibility and benefits amounts. But the state services appear chronically labor-intensive, so that cutting back employees is tantamount to a reduction in the services. Under these circumstances, it becomes difficult for the state to balance its legitimation functions with its accumulation functions. For the provision of many state services such as free public education, sanitation, police protection, and recreation facilities is part of the social wage that has been the condition for the degree to which the public sector may be mobilized into the accumulation process by the deployment of tax funds for investment purposes. Public services reproduce the ideology of the neutrality of the state and partially conceal the extent of its integration by capital.

The recent outpourings of right-wing-inspired efforts to limit property taxes and cut public spending has resonated among sections of the working class, particularly those employed in the private sector, for whom the burden of taxes in the wake of the deterioration of public services has become an outrage. The ability of the right to organize an alliance of workers and the middle strata to reduce the public sector is partially unintended from the point of view of capital. During the battle to pass "Proposition 13," the California measure that founded the tax revolt movement, large business groups at first opposed the drastic cuts in property taxes because of their fear of the social and political turmoil that might result. Clearly large capital preferred technocratic solutions to the need to cut the social wage such as those that have been developed by such private corporations as General Electric and AT&T which count on scientific management combined with coercion to increase productivity. The politicization of the struggle to cut the size of the social sector violated one of the precepts of the intensive regime: namely, that no wage cuts are allowed because of the requirement to maintain mass consumption. Further, the absolute segregation of economics from politics which was part of the social bargain made between capital and labor in the mass upsurge of the 1930's and 1940's, is a vital method of insuring the collaboration of the working class with the national and international policies of the state. Although a right-wing breakaway is by no means as dangerous as one to the left from capital's standpoint, the most important break in the process was the fact that the right chose to move politically from below.

The major philosophical assumption of most Marxist theory remains functionalist, even as its metatheory succeeds in avoiding the positivism of bourgeois social science. This functionalism is most apparent in the theory of the state. Where Marxists have been absolutely clear that the state can no longer be viewed within the perspectives of nineteenth-century competitive capitalism, most theorists of late capitalism accord no relative autonomy to its position within society. The "logic" of Marxist theory tends to reduce the state to its position of pure instrumentalism, just as ideology is viewed as false consciousness. In this connection, the insistence of the Althusserian school that ideology is a material practice only becomes the antinomy of the view that ideology is a system of wrong ideas serving class interests. Like Althusser, the leading theoretician of the Althusserian school on the state, Nicos Poulantzas, regards the trade unions, religion, education, and other institutions as apparatuses of the state which, because they are materialized ideologies, function as effective tools of social domination. While acknowledging the intervention of the state within the capitalist social formation at the economic and ideological planes, the position of the state as a protector of social relations, or as contested area is ignored. In his latest work, *State, Power, Socialism* (1978), Poulantzas makes a significant departure from his earlier *political* position, as expressed, for example, in *Political Power and Social Classes*. However, the fundamental metatheoretical perspective remains identical to the earlier work. That is, although Poulantzas understands the state as a site of class struggle within the framework of capitalist hegemony, he has failed to specify the relative autonomy of labor as a *theoretical* category. As in the earlier work, class formation remains subordinate to the mode of production, which Poulantzas regards as a structured totality.

To the extent that the state has become capitalism's spirituality in the wake of its subsumption under accumulation, it embodies a functional contradiction. On the one hand, it is mobilized by capital to resolve the vicissitudes of accumulation crises. On the other hand, universal suffrage, the movement of the social wage, and the absolute necessity of the ideological premise of the state's neutrality all make necessary its independence. In addition, the state's autonomy must be assured by its regulative function in the manner specified by Aglietta and others. This contradiction, sometimes expressed as that of accumulation and legitimation, following the vocabulary of Weber as well as Marx, constitutes irreconcilable logics and produces the multilayering of social reality. The autonomy of the state within the logic of capital, increasingly demanding its subordination, has been among the central features of the rise of the workers' parties in the last century.

In turn, the institutionalization of the social wage has created conditions where these parties have a growing stake in the bourgeois state, but also defend its autonomy from capital. I do not mean to imply that one may draw the conclusion that workers and their parties may "capture" the bourgeois state by means of a successful struggle for democratic reforms such as those represented by universal public education, social health programs, and nationalization of key industries with workers' participation in decision-making. But only the most mechanical theory can defend the view of the state as entirely subordinate to capital. To do so misses the significance of working class and socialist political struggle since the end of the war, where the underlying logic of the fiscal crisis remains subject to the *class struggle* at the level of political discourse.

The role of the public sector in the accumulation process protects productive capital in two ways. First, it establishes an outlet for past accumulated capital that has been prevented from use in the private industrial sector in such activities as highway construction and arms production; at the same time, public sector employment generates personal income that can be used to stimulate production of commodities without itself creating new commodities that compete with the productive sector. Secondly, it maintains the ideological legitimacy of the capitalist system by providing employment for those who would be otherwise redundant and services that are part of the social wage.

The state transfers a sizeable portion of wages and salaries to corporations in order to sustain high levels of production. In the U.S. these reverse transfer payments (compared to social services) are never used in competition with the same corporations in the production of ordinary commodities such as means of production or consumer goods. For example, the arms industry and much of the construction industry, including machinery-manufacturing, depend on government contracts. The government as consumer constitutes a separate sector of the economy as long as the exchange of goods for money does not compete with the ordinary pattern of production, distribution, and consumption characteristic of the general market. On the one hand, the state as accumulator of capital is employed to make sure that the private sector can absorb its excess capacity of past capital accumulation, and thus realize surplus value in the form of sales. On the other hand, most public services and employment are financed simultaneously out of wages and salaries, thereby not interfering with the accumulation process, and out of capital extended as credit which cannot be absorbed in the productive sectors.

State expenditures designed to assist corporations to valorize overaccumulated surplus value only intensify the problem of overproduction of machinery and raw materials if the commodities produced generate new accumulation. For this reason, arms production is preferred over public facilities such as mass transit. Mass transit facilities add to the real capital of society, while railroad and other transportation facilities remain in overabundance; they also compete with oil and car corporations. These corporations prefer highway construction, which is merely a public expenditure that assists in the expansion of the truck, car, and oil industries. In contrast, arms can be declared obsolete and thus generate the conditions of their reproduction; they have the virtue of rapid turnover compared to rails, which depreciate rather slowly, and constitute a separate market for capital.

From the point of view of the investor and of the overall problem of capital accumulation, the expansion of employment in the public bureaucracies may be more desirable than material goods production, because this type of employment, along with advertising, produces no accumulated capital. This, of course, does not imply that the bureaucracy's growth is attributable solely to economic calculations. The bureaucracy is an attempt to give coherence to the increasingly entropic character of the market and of social life in general. It is a form of pure valorization. The investor derives the rate of profit without the burden of excess capacity. The enlargement of the public bureaucracy is the purest form of capital disaccumulation. Here *disaccumulation* is defined as a form of disposal of the social product that puts a brake on the accumulation process in the productive sectors. It is disposed of in purely wasteful ways from the point of view of accumulation, but assists accumulation by valorizing capital.

This conception does not imply that all public spending is inherently wasteful or useless. The term "waste" is not employed here as a moral category. It is used in relation to the process of capital accumulation, which can only occur in the labor process that produces a surplus that can be transformed into capital. That is, labor produces capital when the value of the commodity is an amount over and above the personal consumption of workers and the consumption of the capitalists, the managers, and other retainers, including landlords. In short, while labor is productive if it produces surplus value, its product may certainly be useful even if no capital is turned out. The worker whose labor involves teaching children how to read and write or tending the sick may be considered useful to society and even to the corporate capitalist order in terms of the need to reproduce labor power. But to the extent that its employment represents a deduction of that portion of the social product that would ordinarily be used for the production of means of production or consumer goods and the employment of productive labor, it is unproductive.

Yet capitalist forms are preserved by disaccumulation. Public investment results in the employment of wage labor, presumably at a rate that does not directly challenge the wage structure of private, industrial sectors. The public sector reproduces a hierarchy of social labor that is fragmented, degraded, and stratified, just like the private corporate sector. The ideology of productivity is retained, even though labor which does not produce value cannot be measured quantitatively.

Since capital, according to Marxist theory, is both a social relation between those who engage in the production of profit and those who appropriate it, and the surplus generated in the process of production, disaccumulation cannot preserve the content of capital. It destroys the content, even as it preserves its forms. Or, to be more precise, disaccumulation is important in the preservation of past accumulation and the destruction of new accumulation. This latter, contradictory function is illustrated most graphically by arms production which is both socially and economically wasteful. Yet even this completely reprehensible form of social production is important for utilizing the excess capacity of raw materials extraction and processing industries. At the same time, arms production results in their overexpansion under wartime circumstances, which, in turn, requires the state to act as a consumer as well as an investor.

Until the beginning of the twentieth century, the imperatives of capital accumulation meant that the expansion of all public services except for infrastructural development such as roads, was considered a hindrance to the interests of the capitalist system. Which does not imply that no disaccumulation took place. The provisions of those social services that insured the social reproduction of the labor force, such as schools, hospitals, and sanitation facilities, were grudgingly undertaken, especially during the early period of overproduction following the Civil War. When the productivity of labor, combined with the increased frequency of the periodic crises, reached a point when children could no longer be employed in factories and workshops without dire social consequences, the public education system was developed to absorb this new surplus labor force. Here the calculus of capital expansion required accommodation with the imperatives of social order, even though the school movement was often justified in terms of the categories of accumulation, such as the need to train a sophisticated labor force that acccepted industrial discipline. At this point, we observe the transformation of accumulation from an economic to an ideological category. To a great extent, the ideology became the way to win the support of the ruling classes for the expansion of an institution, the schools, that had been part of the working-class struggle since the 1820's.

The paradoxical spectacle of the need for the absorption of the surplus labor force in the midst of the most rapid expansion of the United States industrial economy in its history raises a series of complex problems about the impulse underlying immigration. The ordinary explanation for the waves of eastern and southern European immigration that accompanied the end of the Civil War is linked to the industrialization and simultaneous urbanization of the North American continent. Immigrants were required to perform degraded industrial labor, just as the earlier northern European immigration was tied to the period of dominance of craft technology. Yet this explanation, so linear and functional in its harmony with theories of industrialization, cannot account for the retirement of children and large sectors of the female work force from industrial production which was taking place during the same years. If industrialization required huge quantities of unskilled labor, women and children could have been recruited in large numbers to perform it. In addition, the government would not have felt constrained to deport Chinese workers who had successfully built the railroads. A more complex description of the development of industrial capitalism is required if the pitfalls of simplistic explanation are to be avoided and a more suggestive theory of capitalist accumulation offered.

Children were sent to school in part in order to facilitate the full employment of adults; women were periodically sent back to the home when labor surpluses prevented their employment in factories. Overproduction of the means of production is a simultaneous feature of the accumulation process, especially after its "primitive" phase. The primitive accumulation of capital was characteristic of the pre-Civil War period when thousands of miles of railroad tracks were laid, when the carriage and textile industries were transformed from craft or cottage methods to manufacturing, when metal-producing, fabricating, and machine tool industries were constructed. The Civil War provided an enormous impetus to the expansion of these industries, and certainly created the arms industry. But the post-Civil War period was one of tremendous capital expansion. The 1870's were marked by labor turmoil precisely because of the overexpansion of the means of production, as much as the introduction of some technological innovations in the iron and coal industries. It was not until the 1880's that the upward surge in the economy resumed after a prolonged period of depression. Once again the upturn was relatively short lived. The development of technology underwent a qualitative change in the metals and coal industries during this period, which resulted not only in the elimination of many of the old crafts, but the increase in the proportion of machinery to labor. Notwithstanding the expulsion of many women and children from industry, immigrants were never fully employed in coal, steel, and metals fabricating industries. By 1890, the understanding by bankers and industrial capitalists that surplus capital was indeed a structural feature of the economic system manifested itself in the drive towards foreign investment and militarism rather than relying on the internal development of the market alone. This decade also marks the beginning of agricultural mechanization and the growth of corporate farming.

Yet the immigrants kept coming. They were part of both the accumulation and the disaccumulation process. On the one hand, they constituted a part of the working class willing to perform arduous and degraded labor in place of highly-skilled crafts workers whose independence and relative autonomy had become a barrier to the expansion of capital at an acceptable profit rate. On the other hand, they were immediately thrown into the pile of surplus labor along with women and children, and the chronic unemployment of a substantial number of them generated demands for closing the American frontier to Europeans in order to protect domestic native labor or skilled crafts who were displaced. If the growth of public education represented the absorption of children by the state, the development of social welfare can be attributed to the need to support surplus immigrant labor, while holding it as an industrial reserve army needed to keep wages in check during the transition from the extensive to the intensive regime. Historically, then, the expansion of social services is a phenomenon of overaccumulation as much as a demand of the working classes. The ideological function of these services is intimately tied to their economic role, just as the accumulation and disaccumulation processes do not appear after the Civil War as successive stages in the development of U.S. capitalism, but are the reverse side of each other and move in tandem.

In different periods of the history of the U.S., the emphasis of social and corporate policy is towards one or the other framework for economic activity. Since the 1920's the most conscious corporate and state leaders have been aware that the old accumulation ethos requires reexamination. Such eminently serviceable attitudes as parsimony, industrial discipline, entrepreneurship ideologies, and the concept of productive labor as the pinnacle of human activity, have suffered partial eclipse in a culture surfeited by capital and commodities. State intervention and consumerist culture correspond to the exhaustion of the market as the regulator of economic exchange and the completion of the monopolization of the most decisive sectors of the economy. It may also be seen as a response to the portents represented by the Russian and Chinese revolutions that were widely interpreted as signs of the setting of the conventional imperialist sun. The freeing of the psyche from the constraints of ideologies of accumulation became a fundamental condition for the expansion of capital. This contradictory development resulted from the chronic overproduction of capital and the immense productive powers of social labor that periodically generate an economic crisis. That is, the transformation of money into capital and back to money at a new level representing the accumulation of new capital no longer proceed smoothly. Instead, the capital can no longer be valorized at an acceptable rate of profit, unless monopolies succeed in administering prices to a level where the average profit rate for the economy as a whole is realized. This inflationary policy becomes part of the preconditions for a new crisis even as it prevents the crisis from breaking out immediately.

For the past 80 years, the United States has attempted to attenuate the problem of overproduction by types of productive investment such as (1) the export of capital to countries that are sources of raw materials and potential markets for U.S. finished goods, and (2) development of underdeveloped regions within our own country, such as the South, the Pacific Coast, and agricultural regions plagued by overproduction resulting from the mechanization of agriculture. But unproductive outlets have also become increasingly important for the reproduction and realization of capital. These include: state expenditures, waste production in the forms of arms production, and the waste that is imbedded with the so-called productive sectors such as cars, plastic, and appliances. In the case of this hidden waste, disaccumulation takes the form of planned obsolescence and junk commodities that are not intimately bound to the historical level of material culture, but consitute elements of the surplus repression by the social order. Examples of such commodities are cigarettes, alcoholic beverages, many of the so-called leisure industries whose impetus is derived from the sales effort and represents the binding of free time by commodity culture. These industries produce surplus value and material goods that correspond to social needs. They are eminently useful both to the consumer and to those interested in social domination. But they represent a portion of the surplus that cannot find outlets within those sectors that either produce means of subsistence or means of production. They represent both surplus capital and surplus wages. Third, is the advertising industry and those industries involved in the sales effort.

In this context, the meaning of the fiscal crisis of New York, Cleveland, and other large cities recently does not consist in problems of state finance and taxation alone. It is the problem of the relation of accumulation to disaccumulation. The imbalances of the capitalist system between these two types of investment resulted over the past thirty years in an excessive emphasis on unproductive or disaccumulated expenditures. During this period, foreign investment increased substantially in both advanced and underdeveloped regions; the American south was industrialized and agricultural mechanization continued its expansion. In addition some new industries were created, especially the electronic/communications, plastics, and other chemical sectors. These "productive" expenditures increased the size of basic means of production such as plants and machinery and expanded the need for technical and scientific labor since these industries are "knowledge"-based rather than based upon manual skills. At the same time, however, there was a relative deterioration of the means of production in our own country as advanced technologies in some key sectors were exported to Europe and Japan. The rate of economic growth of the U.S. economy slowed considerably, placing U.S. goods at a relative disadvantage on the world market, especially after 1955, when Europe and Japan were rebuilt with the help of U.S. capital. These developments produced serious challenges to the U.S. trade and payments balances. When these conditions became acute in the early years of the 1970's U.S. capitalists were forced to modernize some U.S. industries such as steel and machine tools and seek new raw materials sources to counterbalance the threat of expropriation in some Third World countries or very high prices for oil and precious metals.

The pattern of investment in heavy industry abroad, disaccumulated industries at home, and the overproduction of means of production resulted, however, in a liquidity crisis in the wake of these requirements. In an interview[169] Robert W. Sarnoff, RCA chairman, said, "Between now and 1985, it is estimated that America will need to invest $4.5 trillions in new plant, equipment and housing, nearly three times the expenditure of the past decade." Sarnoff went on to explain the need for this "staggering sum," by specifying requirements of "growing complexity of technology, the pressure of inflation, the challenge of international competition . . . and developing alternative energy sources." Sarnoff attributed a number of economic ills such as low growth rates, the sharp drop in U.S. productivity in 1974, and inflation to the relatively low percentage of investment to gross national product in the U.S. compared to France, Germany, and Japan. The point of the interview was to spur congressional action to undertake debt financing of new, privately organized investment projects, tax incentives to those who undertake major investments, and raising equity capital from financial institutions and stockholders. Sarnoff was pointing to the need to raise capital. The fiscal crisis of the state and the demands upon the tax structure to meet current obligations rather than compete for available capital with the private sector are reflections of the determination of large corporations to raise capital for accumulation rather than permit disaccumulation to drain off valuable dollars.

This is not to say that the U.S. corporations lacked capital resources. But they were tied up in past accumulation, in the machinery and plants that were suffering excess capacity because they were either obsolete or in the wrong industries from the perspective of the international division of labor. Since fixed assets are not easily converted into money and much industrial capacity is unused, capitalists like Sarnoff are facing a long-term shortage of available capital with which to undertake investment programs that meet the new world economic conditions. Except for arms production, which remains an important source of profit for many major corporations, public sector funds had to be cut, wages and salaries had to be taxed for investment purposes, and inflationary prices on energy and goods would raise capital. These had become key industries for the solution of the international monetary and balance of payments problems. Disaccumulation, which for the past half-century had been the major means to preserve the capitalist system both materially and ideologically, had to yield to the priority of capital accumulation – at least for the time being.

Yet even now there can be no question of sustaining the system on the basis of the accumulation function alone. The national budget still amounted to more than $600 billion in 1981–82; local expenditures are being cut but are still huge by comparison to even thirty years ago; the gargantuan advertising industry is growing because the realization problems of late capitalism have become more intense. Substantial cuts in these sectors would exacerbate the tendency towards recession or depression. For neither the ordinary processes of production and consumption, nor the imperialist policies of the state and the corporations have been sufficient to balance the forces of economy. The state as a disaccumulator as well as accumulator remains an imperative of the whole social system. The significance of those activities undertaken by the state to assure that the accumulation process remains uninterrupted by disposing of a great deal of surplus capital, deters the appearance of the crisis as much as it prevents overproduction of capital in the short run. The employment of millions of workers in the public sector generates a large market for consumer goods, and, in turn, stimulates orders for means of production. In the long term, the employment-creating functions of the state cannot prevent overproduction of basic goods. Instead, the overproduction problem is exacerbated because capital expansion anticipates demand.

This phenomenon can be most clearly seen during the 1960's when wartime expenditures by the federal government disguised the chronic overproduction both of means of production and consumer goods. Millions of workers were hired in arms production and public administration closely related to the war effort. In addition, much of the production of large corporations in the steel, electronic, electrical machinery, and many other industries were derived from arms contracts. The income generated by wasteful production succeeded in spurring increased production in the consumer goods sector as well as that part of the basic goods sector that produces means of production for consumer goods industries. Finally, the production of the means of production for other producers of basic goods was also stimulated. Here, we can observe the remarkable instance of heavy output of arms without visible shortages in the consumer goods sector – an occasion that effectively disguised the irrational aspects of the U.S. capitalist order for nearly a decade. The state, then, both helps absorb the surplus capital in disaccumulative ways and spurs the accumulation process itself. During the 1960's, the U.S. economy experienced a tremendous leap in the size of some of its fixed assets. But these increases were concentrated heavily in plant and equipment that had particular applications to weapons systems and were not easily converted to other uses. As Seymour Melman has pointed out, the peculiar characteristics of arms production under advanced technological conditions is their specialization and limited flexibility; they are not necessarily transferable to consumer goods production.

CULTURE AND THE STATE

State capitalism is not a purely economic phenomenon. It has political and cultural aspects as well. The intervention of the state in the economic processes has more than purely economic significance. Since no social system can survive for long without the implicit support of the underlying population, unless it intends to rule by force alone, it must create a mythological and symbolic universe that corresponds to the structure of needs of its constituents. A central contradiction of this universe is that it exceeds the limits of the system's material resources.

In the United States, the largest corporations, including financial corporations, may be said to constitute a definite ruling class in whose interest the state functions. Yet, the general interest of the ruling class cannot be subsumed under the program of any single corporation or financial group. Ruling-class consciousness has advanced since the 1920's to recognize that the state must take central responsibility for coordinating its general interest – not only through a system of laws that rationalize the conflicts among elements of the class, but with a system of administration that mediates the relations between the social and economic needs of the ruling class and those of the underlying population. These mediations must, if the system is to remain legitimate, not be confined to the use of force or its implied use. Nor can the economic activities of the state be limited to the issuance of currency, the regulation of trade, and the provision of those social overheads such as education and health services strictly circumscribed by the requirements of social production.

Since the late nineteenth century, corresponding to the first signs that a substantial social surplus of both capital and labor had become a structural feature of the capitalist order, leading members of the ruling class have urged the enlargement of the functions of the state to encompass a whole range of ideologically-grounded roles that transcend the purely economic or order-keeping functions. The material foundation for these new activities is the task of disposing of the social surplus through its absorption in socially wasteful production, or, alternatively, in useful activities that fail to result in net accumulation of capital. (Note: the concept of net accumulation takes into account that some public sector production such as highways and arms actually accumulates new machinery, buildings, and so on. The task is to dispose of more capital than is accumulated.) But the state cannot remain a mere economic instrument if it is to be capable of legitimating the whole social order. If it is reduced to the functional equivalent of capital, it is perceived as a class-based institutional matrix, simply an alienated form of corporate domination, and its unmasking becomes relatively easy in times of crisis.

The task is to explain the opacity of the state, for it is in the moment of autonomy, rather than the moment of dependence upon corporate capital, that it reveals its sustained power to erect a system of beliefs, myths, and symbols that can be successfully integrated into social consciousness. It may be said that if the state were nothing but the police power of corporate capitalism, systemic delegitimation would be relatively simple during such crises as wars and depressions. But it is precisely because these functions no longer adequately describe it that the state remains crucial in the production of social consciousness.

By providing directly a major chunk of the jobs within American society, the state succeeds in sustaining the mobility myths that were part of the nineteenth-century American ideology. When Frederick Jackson Turner declared, in 1893, the closing of the western frontier, the lovely little wars of American imperialism in the Caribbean were conveniently on hand to provide a new frontier. Although the western frontier as safety valve was always more illusion than reality, it was a symbol of the yearning of those trapped by industrial capitalist society for liberation. Henry Nash Smith has documented the significance of the west in popular culture and its broader importance in terms of providing credibility to the American dream of mobility.[170] Although the myth of westward expansion has been preserved in the mass culture of the twentieth century, and still represents both the nostalgia for genuine authenticity in an increasingly fabricated world and the symbolic reinforcement for mobility aspirations, the ideologies that derived from imperalist conquest succeeded in partially displacing the old images. Racism and patriotism were not invented by imperialism, but they were explicitly industrial rather than wilderness myths. The frontier was continued as a sustaining symbol that promised escape from the claustrophobic factories in the somewhat less confined cities. At the same time, the state was still the crucial vehicle for change. While overseas expansion was tied to the development of capitalism in agriculture, as a cultural phenomenon it signalled the partial abandonment of the notion that the road to authenticity was paved in clods of manure.[171]

It may be argued that the Homestead Act of 1869, according to which the federal government agreed to lease 160 acres of land to those willing to work the land for the purposes of farming, is among the earliest direct indications that the state was prepared to link itself to the economic interests of the common people. The betrayal of this agrarian reform program by a combination of political leaders and large corporations is matched only by the betrayal of black reconstruction during the same years. The myth of free land, which helped to sustain the opacity of the state during a period of its unrivalled complicity with the objectives of industrial capitalists, was partially eclipsed by the panic of 1873. Mass unemployment, always a concomitant of capitalist accumulation, was not compensated for by the alleged beneficent intentions of the Homestead Act. Consequently, the 1870's were years of violent strikes, mass labor organization, and the birth of a native popular socialist consciousness.

The rise of the labor and socialist movements during the last decades of the nineteenth century and the first decade of the twentieth century was due, in a large measure, to the simultaneous maturity of the working class in relation to the growth of industrial production, the degradation of factory labor, and the perceptible decline of popular confidence in the viability of the western frontier as an escape from the conditions of working-class existence.[172] The persistence of frontier myths in popular culture attests to the utopian content of culture as such. Social consciousness is not fashioned of whole cloth. Its conflicting aspects were by no means resolved. Yet, the organizational forms of socialism prospered at exactly the moment when agrarian protest against the power of the railroads, the banks, and the "middlemen" was at its high point. William Appleman Williams is right to show the links between populism and imperialism since the latter promised to relieve farmers of their unsold surpluses.[173] But the lesson of agricultural hardship was not lost on the industrial base of the country and the second great intervention of the state after the Civil War into social and economic life.

In addition the waves of immigration conjoined with the establishment of a new system of universal public education, which during the early years of the new century successfully muted many criticisms of the social order. This is not to minimize the continuation of sharpened class conflict that began in the 1870's. Native-born workers and immigrants who had not accepted the frontier myths joined together in building a substantial socialist and anarchist movement prior to the First World War. Yet, once again the mobility aspirations of a large portion of the population were being satisfied by the expansion of the industrial base of the country and the second great intervention of the state after the Civil War into social and economic life. The First World War, with its successful suppression of the growing unemployment, unused plant capacity, and agricultural surpluses that began to appear after 1910, was able to sustain the momentum of economic growth and lateral job mobility. With the war, America witnessed the first massive disaccumulative economy. War expenditures performed the same role in overpowering instability that was to become the hallmark of late capitalism after the depression.

Thus, depression and the Second World War must be seen within a continuity of an ever-greater reliance by the capital on the state as an ideological as well as economic apparatus that legitimates its domination. The state was viewed more and more during the depression as a "welfare" state, only to give way during the war to the concept of "emergency" state. These two perceptions have been attacked by radical historians as mythological. The so-called "revisionist" New Left historians, like William Appleman Williams, James Weinstein, Martin Sklar, Lloyd Gardner, Ronald Rodosh, and others, ably punctured both the myths of mobility and of welfare that liberal historians from Turner to Arthur Schlesinger had promulgated during the previous half-century or more. They demonstrated clearly that the state served specific social and economic interests of the corporations and only provided benefits to workers and others hit hard by the vicissitudes of economic life in order to preserve social order and prevent social disruption. Similarly, a body of literature was produced in the 1960's showing that anti-communism after the Second World War was a legitimating ideology that thinly veiled the need of the corporate capitalists to foster a permanent arms economy and undermine the strength of the industrial labor movement. The cold war may not have been regulated exclusively to the economic intervention of the state. Gar Alpervitz, D. F. Fleming, and Gabriel Kolko[174] are convincing in their argument that the threat of communism to U.S. security has been largely ideological rather than a reflection of military threats from the Soviet Union and China.

Yet the simple task of unmasking does not exhaust the problems of the relation of the state as capitalist to social consciousness. In fact, it hardly addressed the issue at all. Transparency does not occur by means of sheer exposure. The disaccumulative functions of the state, as much as its role as capital accumulator, are the structural equivalent of the agrarian myths. Just as the Homestead Act promised land for the poor and downtrodden who had been ground down by industrial capitalism, so the state promises that the alienation and economic uncertainty associated with capitalist production and its marketplace will be attenuated.

State-generated employment and personal income have become a crucial mechanism for "consumer society." At its most elementary level, the social security system, aid to dependent children, and other programs that separate work from income, at least in consciousness, produce a continuous flow of consumers who are not related to production, except by their exclusion. To be sure, the income derived from welfare is never sufficient to assure an adequate living standard. But its ideological significance is to provide a mass base for consumerism at its purest level and to argue for the humanitarian role of the state.

It may be argued that much state employment and much of the arms production contains a version of this ideology of consumerism. Most public workers are aware of the tenuousness of the concept of productivity when applied to the actual performance of their jobs. Time wasted is a source of considerable guilt and ambivalence on public jobs. The "cost plus" basis of arms production also produced such feelings. Under these circumstances a kind of separation between labor and wages does exist and remains both a source of pride and anxiety for workers. The state is perceived as sucker and as "big daddy" to the extent that workers understand that they are not performing productive labor in consideration of their wages and salaries.

Many workers in the public sector and publicly-related jobs see themselves as largely engaged in consumer activities. With more than 30 million persons on welfare or receiving retirement benefits and another 16 million in public employment, the appearance of the consumer as the other side of disaccumulation may be observed since the depression. Unproductive existence becomes a self-legitimating lifestyle that results from the new importance of the government as employer. The opacity of the state to social consciousness has this powerful aspect: social existence and social consciousness are both transformed. Beyond employment, the state provides part of the material basis for a whole new way of living, a new relationship to politics and culture.

It would be an error to regard imperialism and its concomitant ideologies of racism and xenophobia as the sole or even the major means by which the sense of psychic and social mobility was maintained after the closing of the agrarian frontier. Consumerism, arising on the wave of the appearance of a huge volume of surplus capital in the 1920's, provided an immense way within which those drawn into an alienated, insecure existence could find psychic space, the virtues of hard work and the repression of erotic needs. Mass culture penetrated the unconscious and legitimated its demands, but in a deformed manner. The rise of a psychology based on the rightness of the pleasurable needs of individuals, far from sustaining the potentially subversive character of the unconscious, gave to the upwardly mobile members of the public sector labor force, the professionals, and those engaged in the administration of things as well as persons, a new sense of significance. U.S. capitalism in its disaccumulative period (1920–70) was largely permissive, capable of sustaining liberal democratic ideology, while blessed with a unique political and economic hegemony within the capitalist world.

For industrial workers who had experienced generations of degradation, from agriculture and craft labor, the surfeit of consumer goods and services engendered a fairly complex process of "forgetting." The social amnesia that has penetrated working-class consciousness consists first in the repression of the memories of everyday labor – even as it is in process, but especially after the shift is over. Buying and eating become the wages of alienated labor, the means by which the hunger for recognition, satisfying work and play, and decent human relationships, are spuriously satiated. Secondly, consumer goods, especially those associated with estranged leisure, become confused with the self. They are objectified satisfactions. Workers can only perceive meaning in those activities that have been designated as autonomous, even if they are invaded by the instrumentalities of consumer culture. It is the love of things rather than persons that fills the void created by the suppression of the memories of degraded labor.

Not even the depression placed dampers on the twofold rise of a mass consumer culture and the internationalization of U.S. capital. The dual frontier created the sufficient conditions for generating mass hope for freedom within the bourgeois order. Nor could the blatant antinomy of a highly centralized state and the increasing stratification of a degraded labor force give pause to those who celebrated the American century. The contradiction between the ideal of equality and the doctrine of equality of opportunity failed to deter the mass of working-class Americans from seeking their place in the American sun.

If the state provided the largest body of consumers whose relation to production becomes distant and perceptibly obscure, the corporate form of capitalism generates its own disaccumulative industries. The advertising industry, whose sole economic function is to assist in the process of realization, that is, the transformation of commodities into money and into capital, absorbs nearly 2% of the gross national product, and is equal to about two-thirds of annual investment. The relation of advertising to investment indicates the depth of the permanent realization crisis. It is the ad industry that has been the specific repository of the ideology of consumerism. The ad industry and the closely-related industries of mass communication, such as television and popular magazines and newspapers, constitute the apparatus of the cultural domination of capital, while the state constitutes its apparatus of economic and ideological hegemony.

The central importance of the institutions of cultural domination consists in their singular capacity to address the spiritual needs of the masses just as the state appears to address their material needs in the wake of the failure of the market system. The public sector and the cultural apparatus constitute the main legitimating institutions of capitalism in a period when the degree of integration of the state with the large corporations becomes a characteristic feature of political and economic life. The ideology of public service intersects with the spiritual side of the commodities purveyed by advertising and the mass media through which the sales effort takes place.

The power of advertising over social consciousness is connected to the link between commodities and the unmet needs of most people for satisfying work, sexual gratification, and other elements of eros. To be sure, commodities are never sufficient to allay the hunger that remains after the deprivations of everyday life. Much of radical cultural criticism has been directed to the necessary task of unmasking the false promises inherent in consumer culture. Unmasking is a necessary, but insufficient condition of the analysis, however. With few exceptions, notably Theodor Adorno, few critics have understood how it is possible for mass culture, particularly consumerism, to attain a strong grip on social consciousness despite the frequency of economic crises, sharpening of workers' struggles over production and consumption, and the development of a fairly widespread cynicism about the honesty of those in power.

The power of mass culture resides not only in the degradation and commodification of human needs, but in its capacity to express and produce those needs. The images of mass culture may be the only sphere within daily existence that points beyond the mundane towards the erotic and utopian. Mass culture cannot be understood simply as a degraded form of cultural life. For it is its utopian element that gives it power. Thus the state becomes the concrete image of the parent, who in everyday life has disappeared among many people in relation to the all-embracing mythological role of parental nurturing, and mass culture becomes the love substitute for the fulfillment of erotic needs through consumption. That these blandishments actually construct a new prisonhouse can hardly be denied. But the persistence of their hegemony over social consciousness can only be explained by their promise of happiness and peace, the return to the mythic nirvana.

CONCLUSION

Even if capital-logic is an adequate explanation of the *origin* of the ubiquity of cultural domination in general and mass culture in particular, it cannot account for their autonomy. For having been produced as an aspect of capital's new conditions of reproduction, mass culture reproduces itself on the basis of its own logic, whose economic dimension, while not insignificant, cannot encapsulate its influence, which exceeds its intended function. Mass culture, as the penultimate substitute for community, conceals that fundamental social impulse, but its spurious gratifications reveal it as well. Frederic Jameson's contention[175] that mass culture contains a utopian element signifies the irrepressibility of desire even by the powerful culture industry. Capital-logic can account for the requirement that capital penetrates cultural life by mechanization, transforming art into entertainment, and expanding mass communications on a global scale. But it fails to account for the counterlogic of reception that calls into existence *partially* realized elements of an oppositional culture within the framework of mass culture. If the counterlogic is not theorized as utopia, the proletarian public sphere, popular culture that is rooted in everyday resistance, and the possibilities for transcending capital itself are theoretically foreclosed.

I have traced this question already to its metatheoretical assumptions of scientific method as much as the historical circumstances that have produced the profound pessimism of Marxist political economy. My argument may be expressed in one final principle: the counterlogic of the erotic, play, and the constituting subject may not be reduced either to the mode of production of material life or the mode of social reproduction (family, school, or religion in their capacity as ideological apparatuses of the state). Political economy ends when theory seeks to specify the conditions of transformation. Marxism as critique consists in showing that the science of political economy is descriptive of the commodity fetish. The apogee of critical science resides in specifying the non-subsumable.

This, of course, is the principle of hope of which Ernst Bloch speaks. It is not that some uninterested "instinct" exists that remains prior to or independent of the capitalist logic, and constitutes a subversive side of social relations. Capital is constantly conflating desire and need in order to insure the conditions of its own reproduction. The counterlogic is to maintain their separation, to define desire as that which goes beyond need and is unrecuperable by the prevailing structure. This is the basis for the subversive content of sexuality in those groups that have been forced or place themselves on the margins of social life, and the communities that are established informally by working people on the shopfloor and in the neighborhoods whose existence limits the accumulation process.

None of these forms speaks to the political discourse that must complement discursive knowledged at the cultural level. For the evidence of "black speech," specifically working-class codes that are outside the discourse of mass culture, and the molecular politics that social groups undertake to fight the logic of capital at the level of ecological concerns, prison reform, etc., are, by themselves, not adequate to global structures whose discursive mode is to subvert the autonomy of the margins and the underclasses. Baudrillard had described the political economy of the sign to show how these forms of resistance are made part of the public sphere of commodity circulation. Today's oppositional culture becomes tomorrow's fashion. What I am saying is that the dialectic of accumulation consists in its reliance on the conditions that produce its own limits. The study of the counterlogics to capital is long overdue. For it is here that the crisis will be discovered, not in the operation of "objective" laws.

Of course, the crucial argument of this discussion is that the class struggle is not exclusively a function of capital's logic of accumulation, for if this were so the theories of working-class integration that emanate from both neo-Marxism and from neo-Weberian sociologists of mass society would have long ago laid to rest fears of capitalist crisis. But it is precisely because capital, having created a class of free wage laborers, is unable to prevent the praxis that arises from this freedom that crisis conditions are produced. While it would be folly to deny that the discursive knowledge of the underlying populations remains limited by the conditions of the reproduction of capital, it is also wrong to fail to recognize that the working class does not merely represent a side of capital, but succeeds, however partially, in representing itself or forcing those who represent it to obey a counterlogic. Worker resistance to accepting sacrifices to enable American capital to regain its international position has created serious problems for the profit rate, forcing shifts of investment away from older industrial centers to areas where labor has no tradition of independence. These moves by capital produce new wage laborers who, at first, are grateful for the chance to enter capital circuits. But the honeymoon is short-lived, and union organization, "independent" truckers' strikes, and other undecidable phenomena create new limits on capital's expansion.

The dissemination of information that has accompanied capital's ingression into mass communications (a result of the internal imperative for expansion into new spheres of activity as well as new markets) has contributed to that discursive knowledge against which capital incessantly struggles by its ideological offensives. Like the labor contract which strengthens workers' power while restricting it to the straitjacket of institutionalized class conflict, mass culture brings the news of workers' resistance while tying workers closer to commodity fetishism. The controversy between those who are ensconced in the structural logic of the capitalist mode of production and those who insist on the unpredictable consequences of working-class praxis for capital's configuration reproduces, at a concrete level, the traditional dispute concerning positivism and critical theory in the human sciences. In this dispute, the positivists insist upon the lawfulness of social phenomena by requiring that the criteria of prediction, verification, and formal structure be applied to historical development. Critical theory replies that the intervention of acting subjects, even if constituted by the social formation rather than being considered *a priori* and unconditioned by social laws, actually mediates the operations of laws of social development, rendering them no more than tendencies.

My position, closer to the concept of a critical science, recognizes, however, that the "law of tendency" is a necessary requirement for social theory if it is to avoid the assumptions of a purely voluntarist sensibility. Moreover, structural thinking, a trait shared both by Lukács and critical theory on the one hand, and by those of the Althusserian school on the other, is an important antidote to pure historicism. In our era, structuralism and historicism have become the antinomies of Marxist thought. For those who take the class struggle as the motive force of human history and refuse the immanence that characterizes much of contemporary structuralist thought, the problem is to construct a critical science whose "last instance" is the concrete, the historical specificity of social praxis while, at the same time, making the rigorous distinction between praxis as the constituting moment of history and the way in which history as already constituted takes on the appearance of the social formation's impenetrable facticity. Thus, there is a *positive* moment in all critical theory, a descriptive moment when the unfolding of capital's forms of appearance appears to possess the weight of natural law. The critical moment consists in the activity of showing how these forms are produced by classes and masses. The task is to integrate the descriptive into the critical, making the return to the concrete the dominant movement of social theory.

NOTES

128. See particularly, Max Weber, *Theory of Social and Economic Organization*, ed. Talcott Parsons (New York: Free Press, 1947), especially "The Fundamental Concepts of Sociology," pp. 87–156; and Emile Durkheim, *Sociology and Philosophy* (New York: Free Press, 1974).
129. Karl Marx, *Capital*, Volume 2 (Chicago: Charles Kerr Co., 1909), pp. 56–7.
130. John Maynard Keynes, *General Theory of Employment, Interest and Money* (New York: Macmillan, 1970).
131. Although Keynes' breakthrough in neo-classical theory consisted in his acknowledgement that economic equilibrium may be achieved at a level below full employment, this by no means constitutes a crisis theory. He believed that government action to stimulate investment, employment, and economic growth could, over a rather long term, arrest crisis tendencies even if it produced inflation.
132. Thomas Kuhn, *Structure of Scientific Revolutions* (Chicago: University of Chicago Press, 1962, 1969).
133. Karl Popper, *Logic of Scientific Discovery* (New York: Science Editions, 1961).
134. Marx, Preface to the *Contribution to the Critique of Political Economy*.
135. Marx. *Capital*, Volume 3, Part 3.
136. *Capital*, Volume 2, p. 211.
137. V. I. Lenin, *Imperialism – The Highest Stage of Capitalism*, in *Selected Works*, Vol. 5 (New York: International Publishers, 1946).
138. Rosa Luxemburg, *The Accumulation of Capital* (New York: Monthly Review Press, 1964).
139. See Rudolph Hilferding, *Finanzkapital* (1909); and more recently, Michael Hudson, *Super-Imperialism* (1973), and Michael Barratt-Brown, *After Imperialism* (1964).
140. See Lenin's *Left Wing Communism: An Infantile Disorder* (1920), and Stanley Aronowitz, "Left-Wing Communism: The reply to Lenin," in *The Unknown Dimension*, ed. Dick Howard and Karl Klare (New York: Basic Books, 1972).
141. Georg Lukács, *History and Class Consciousness* (London: Merlin Press, 1971), p. 66.
142. Lenin, *Collected Works*, Vol. 22, p. 241.
143. Ibid.
144. Ibid.
145. Ibid., p. 267.
146. Ibid.
147. Durost and Barton, *Farming and Markets for Farm Goods* (Washington: Committee for Economic Development, no. 15, 1960), p

148. Lenin, op. cit., p. 242.
149. Andre Gorz, "Colonialism at Home and Abroad," in *Socialism and Revolution* (New York: Anchor Books, 1970).
150. Harry Magdoff, *The Age of Imperialism* (New York: Monthly Review Press, 1964).
151. "Reply to Critics," *Social Policy*, 1:2 (Sept.–Oct., 1970).
152. Paul Baran and Paul Sweezy, *Monopoly Capital* (New York: Monthly Review Press, 1964).
153. Paul Sweezy, "Modern Capitalism," in *Modern Capitalism and Other Essays*, p. 14.
154. Rosa Luxemburg, *The Accumulation of Capital*, pp. 416–17. "The general result of the struggle between capitalism and simple commodity production is this: after substituting commodity economy for natural economy, capital takes the place of simple commodity economy. Noncapitalist organizations provide a fertile soil for capitalism; more strictly: capital feeds on the ruins of such organizations, and although this noncapitalist milieu is indispensable for accumulation, the latter proceeds at the cost of this medium by eating it up. Historically, the accumulation of capital is a kind of metabolism between capitalist economy and those precapitalist methods of production without which it cannot go on and which, in this light, it corrodes and assimilates. . . . Only the continuous and progressive disintegration of noncapitalist organizations makes accumulation of capital possible." But, according to Luxemburg, when the noncapitalist organizations are finally "eaten up" and replaced by capitalist economy, the process of accumulation must "come to a stop"; for capital, the standstill of accumulation means the development of the productive forces is arrested, and the collapse of capitalism follows inevitably."
155. Andre Gunder Frank, *Capitalism and Underdevelopment in Latin America* (New York: Monthly Review Press, 1967); Samir Amin, *Accumulation on a World Scale* (New York: Monthly Review Press, 1974); F. H. Cardoso and Enzo Faletto, *Dependencia y Desarrollo En America Latino* (Mexico City: Siglo Veintiuno Editores, 1977).
156. Trotsky's main statement of the Law of Uneven and Combined Development in his monumental *History of the Russian Revolution*, Vol. 1, pp. 4–6 and 13–14, where, in his analysis of the strange turn of events that was the Russian Revolution he provided an account of how the Bolsheviks could, with scientific impunity, advance the thesis that stages of capitalist development might be skipped in a backward country. Gunder Frank follows loosely this line of reasoning in his final chapter of *Capitalism and Underdevelopment in Latin America*.
157. Roman Rosdolsky, *Making of Marx's "Capital"* (London: Pluto Press, 1977); Paul Mattick, *Marx and Keynes* (Boston: Porter Seargant, 1969); Michel Aglietta, *A Theory of Capitalist Regulation: The U.S. Experience*, trans. David Fernbach (London: New Left Books, 1979). I am using the term "capital-logic" in a somewhat broader sense than it is normally employed. The "school" refers to such economists as J.

Hirsch, Paul Mattick and others who derive their entire social theory from the Marxian economic formulas. The work of Ernest Mandel and Michel Aglietta appears to be more broadly based, but my contention is that their position is commensurable with that of the capital-logicians.

158. See Stanley Aronowitz, "Marx, Braverman and the Logic of Capital," *Insurgent Sociologist* (Winter 1979); Harry Braverman, *Labor and Monopoly Capital* (New York: Monthly Review Press, 1974).

159. Christian Palloix, "The Labor Process: From Fordism to Neo-Fordism," in *The Labor Process and Class Strategies*, CSE Pamphlet no. 1 (London, 1976).

160. Stuart Ewen, *Captains of Consciousness* (New York: McGraw-Hill, 1976), and David Noble, *America by Design* (New York: Pantheon Books, 1977).

161. Ernest Mandel, *Late Capitalism* (London: New Left Books, 1975). In this book, perhaps the most elaborate effort from the perspective of capital-logic to take account of the recent history of world capitalism, Mandel directly confronts the explanations offered by dependency theory while attempting to integrate the work of Amin, Frank and Emmanuel within a more or less classical Marxist position based on the categories of value and surplus value rather than exchange relations. Mandel works within the parameters of Marxist theory to refute both underconsumptionist and dependency notions.

162. Paul Mattick, "Les limites de l'intégration: l'homme unidimensionnel dans la société de classe," in *Intégration Capitaliste et Rupture Ouvrière* (Paris: EDI, 1972).

163. The best discussion of the political consequences of the social wage is James O'Connor, *Fiscal Crisis of the State* (New York: St. Martin's Press, 1971).

164. *Business Week*, 16 June 1979.

165. See James O'Connor, "Productive and Unproductive Labor," *Politics and Society*, 5:3, for a discussion of this point in greater detail. The idea of disaccumulation was first advanced in this country by Martin Sklar in an article in *Radical America* (1969).

166. Anthony Giddens, *Central Problems in Social Theory* (Berkeley: University of California Press, 1979).

167. Mario Tronti, "Workers and Capital" in *The Labor Process and Class Strategies*, op. cit.

168. Ibid., pp. 116–17.

169. *New York Post*, 1 July 1975.

170. Henry Nash Smith, *Virgin Land* (New York: 1943).

171. It is interesting to note the persistent popularity of the western genre in literature and films during the rise of U.S. imperialism. It may be argued that this genre became a metaphor for U.S. imperial expansion within a cultural context where imperialism had become disreputable.

172. The growth of the Socialist Party and the IWW consisted in an alliance between degraded native-born skilled workers and por-

tions of the new immigrants from southern and eastern Europe who found in the rapacious character of capitalist development with the U.S. reasons for joining radical movements. At the same time, the failure of American radicalism may be ascribed, in part, to the viability of the Democratic political machines that sprung alive after the Civil War in major northern cities. These machines, non-ideological as they were, did place the state at the service of sections of the working class and gave these workers a political voice.

173. See William Appleman Williams, *Contour of American History* (Chicago: Quadrangle Press, 1961).

174. Gar Alpervitz, *Atomic Diplomacy* (New York, 1962); D. F. Fleming, *Origins of the Cold War* (Boston, 1960); and Gabriel Kolko, *The Roots of U.S. Foreign Policy* (New York, 1964).

175. Fredric Jameson, "Reification and Utopia in Mass Culture," *Social Text*, no. 1 (Winter 1979), pp. 130–48.

8

Marxism and Democracy

INTRODUCTION

Some of the more significant contributions to social theory in the sixties and seventies were made by Marxists who endeavored to "bring the state back in" to considerations of both the nature of the structure of social relations and to prospects for historical transformation. Following the large divisions of this period between structuralism, critical theory and "plain" Marxism (the approach according to which the economic infrastructure determined, in rough correspondence, the crucial institutions of the superstructure), the precise location of the state in social relations, its effectivity and its vulnerability to protest and reform were the crucial issues in dispute. Notwithstanding these differences, Marxist theory remained largely immune to some of the major debates that had animated the socialist and working-class movements of the nineteenth century, especially the question of democracy. No doubt this glaring omission can be ascribed in a significant measure to the certainties of the post-Bolshevik left which lingered throughout the postwar period, at least until the collapse of "Eurocommunism" in the late seventies. For social democrats the body of liberal democracy was to be incorporated into the new socialist societies. In fact, the predominant social-democratic critique of capitalist politics was not substantive but, rather its failure to extend to the economic sphere. The political limitation of democracy under capitalism was not imbedded in its institutions. Effectively, therefore, democracy was identical with the definition of socialism, but made more global.

On the other side, those who followed Marx's and Engel's critique of "bourgeois" democracy (of which more below), agreed that the working-class movement needed the liberal state for the sole purpose of organizing to overturn and replace it – without civil liberties, not only the right to strike but also to "use" the state to ameliorate working conditions such as health and safety regulations, abolition of child and sweated labor, and a measure of social security. But, in the main, the left followed the Leninist critique of the capitalist state as a stacked deck. Therefore, liberal democracy could never be conceived as a goal of working-class political struggle, but only as a means to another end, the abolition of the state and politics as such.

The breakup of communist ideology in the seventies has led to the revival of discourses of left republicanism, citizenship, and liberal versions of parliamentary democracy according to which representatives, accountable to their constituencies, are to supplement, but not replace, party politics. In effect, the left, including many Marxists and those influenced by Marxism have made a startling rediscovery of liberal political theory. Norberto Bobbio,[176] Adam Przeworski,[177] Ernesto Laclau and Chantal Mouffe[178] have, in somewhat different ways, gone so far as to displace the social in favor of a conception of human relations in the model of politics, a return to both Greek and early bourgeois conceptions of society.

The present essay is an examination of this turn in the light of the history of the Marxist discourse on democracy. As will become evident, I defend a conception of democracy which, deriving from Hegel and Marx as well as some tendencies in anarchism, argues that democratic society can be constituted only by understanding citizenship as self-management in economic, social and cultural aspects. In this framework, the idea of participation by producers and consumers of goods (whether of the means of subsistence, services or formal knowledge) in the decisions that affect their lives, can constitute democracy. In this conception, socialist democracy consists in a "free association" of individuals each of whom is expected to participate fully in the decisions affecting the collective. Obviously, the republican virtue is to insist upon rules which ensure equality, and the observance of which sanctions participation. Among these none stands higher on the ethical scale than the creation of a public sphere of dialogue and debate among members, a substantive intervention that, hopefully, limits the degree to which crucial decisions are made by elites and undermines the side of the meaning of "consent" that signifies passive approbation by means of formal procedures.

Clearly, this program would entail considerable transformations – in institutions of representation, the availability of knowledge, channels of communication, length of the working day, patterns of childcare which prohibit women from participation in the public sphere, the scale of production and distribution of goods and services, and governance. Broadly speaking, it would require a radically different conception of what we mean by and expect from "state" power because it would reverse the substantive elements of sovereignty by making all crucial public decisions subject to review and amendment by the people.

Some of the discussion around these issues, especially by Bobbio, focuses on the question concerning representation or, more precisely, on ways of expressing popular will. As I will describe it below, one of the core arguments against radical democracy turns out to rely on the notion of "complexity" in modern societies. Critics of radical democracy presuppose this complexity in their proposal to support strengthening liberal democracy as a socialist end. In this essay I offer the argument that among the errors of nearly all previous Marxist and social thought has been its failure to entertain, seriously (except polemically) the anarchist objection to both the nation-state and large-scale, centralized economic and political subdivisions. Just as the idea of self-managed socialism was developed most fully in the anarchist tradition, particularly by Pierre-Joseph Proudhon, Gustav Landauer and, in a more Marxist vein by council communism, so the critique of the authoritarian features of even the most liberal state fell to the anarchists because Marxism had failed to recognize the relative autonomy of the state, politics and bureaucracies from their economic infrastructure, even in the wake of Engels' warnings against economic determinism. Marxism excoriated the capitalist state for its role as defenders of bourgeois relations of production. But it was not until Louis Althusser and Nicos Poulantzas[179] derived the relative autonomy of the state from their anti-Hegelian critique of the base–superstructure model that a major Marxist tendency made an opening for state theory, and more particularly for a theory of politics. For even if the critical theory of the Frankfurt School had adopted Weber's understanding of the growing sovereignty of the state bureaucracy, the crucial link between the state and monopoly capital formed the foundation of their modern conception of the state. (Here Franz Neumann and Otto Kirscheimer may be considered partial exceptions especially in their work on fascism.) Ironically, the import of Althusser's work has been to provide a new Marxist appreciation of the possibilities of working-class intervention into the capitalist state, an insight brought home most forcefully in Poulantzas's last book, *State, Power, Socialism,* where both the ideal of proletarian dictatorship in the transition to socialism is renounced as well as the classical

Marxist instrumental state theory. Henceforth, the state is to become an arena, perhaps the arena for proletarian class struggle.

My essay appears at the precise moment when the full implications of Althusserian theory for a post-Marxist discourse on democracy are becoming more evident. I share much of the structuralist critique of automatic Marxism, but not the political conclusions derived from this critique. Rather, I hold that the relative autonomy of the state signifies that the struggle against exploitation in production relations and domination in the political sphere are inseparable elements in a discourse of emancipation.

1

> With respect to the proletariat the republic differs from the monarchy only in that it is a ready-for-use political form for the future rule of the proletariat. You are at an advantage compared with us in already having it; we for our part shall have to spend twenty-four hours to make it. But a republic, like every other form of government, is determined by its content. So long as it is a form of bourgeois democracy it is hostile to us as any monarchy (except for the forms of hostility). It is therefore a wholly baseless illusion to regard it as essentially socialist in form or to entrust socialist tasks to it while it is dominated by the bourgeoisie. We shall be able to wrest concessions from it but never to put it in charge of the execution of what is our own concern, even if we should be able to control it by a minority strong enough to change into a majority overnight.
>
> Engels to Lafargue, 6 March 1894

> The proletariat too needs democratic forms for the seizure of political power but to it they are, like all political forms, mere means. But if today democracy is wanted as an end one must seek support in the peasantry and petty bourgeoisie, i.e. in classes that are in process of dissolution and reactionary in relation to the proletariat as soon as they try to maintain themselves artificially. Furthermore, it must not be forgotten that precisely the democratic republic is the logical form of bourgeois rule . . . . And yet the democratic republic always remains the last form of bourgeois rule, that in which it goes to pieces.[180]
>
> Engels to Bernstein

For Marx and Engels the republic is a specifically bourgeois democratic form capable of yielding to organized working-class demands for reforms, but incapable of making room for a proletarian takeover within the framework of parliamentary representation. In any case, democracy cannot be an end, only a means of working-class action: it is hard to envision the development of powerful trade unions and workers' parties under repressive conditions. The working class and its organs of struggle must enjoy rights: so to speak, to publish their press, to assemble freely. Yet, for Marx and Engels, the movements cannot nourish the illusion that emancipation (socialism and beyond) may be brought about by controlling the bourgeois state, even if workers' representatives enjoy majorities in legislative bodies.

Despite these warnings, social-democratic parties persisted in holding the view that bourgeois democratic forms were adequate, given a high level of working-class mobilization, to the achievement of substantial, i.e. structural reforms. These views were held particularly by Bernstein and his followers through the period leading up to the First World War and beyond. Even the intellectual defeats suffered by the revisionists at turn-of-the-century German Social-Democratic congresses at the hands of revolutionary Marxist critics such as Karl Kautsky and Rosa Luxemburg, did not prevent the spread of the argument, more vital in the late twentieth century than when it was first articulated, that the achievement of democratic rights and universal suffrage encompassing the working class and other hitherto deprived strata, constituted a permanent gain which would not be replaced by new forms of rule. The working class and its organizations, particularly its political parties which represented it in parliaments, could under the new circumstances of suffrage, which eventually included women, reform the bourgeois state to near death. Nor could these be regarded as mere "concessions" as Engels was prone to do. The structure of rule could be affected as well by such major reforms as are embodied in the broad rubric of the welfare state, the provisions of which amounted to a significantly different social order. In substance, the quality of life could be permanently altered for the working class, provided it remained class-conscious and politically vigilant.

Of course, these gains and the ideology that accompanied them depended, at their root, upon the given nation having attained a relatively high level of development of productive forces. Equally important, capitalism itself had to have become organized so that the allocation of surplus value between capital and labor was now regulated by the state, corresponding to the growing power of the working-class parties. In turn, this power reflected the spread of trade-unionism and cooperatives, the flowering of socialist culture and therefore the necessity, from capital's standpoint, to forge new terms of political compromise in which consent replaced coercion as the key basis of social rule.

In effect, Bernstein, the recipient of Engels's "lecture" on bourgeois democracy, separated the concept of democracy from the pejorative prefix under conditions where the working class had successfully taken the offensive against capital. He insisted that political action (as opposed to industrial action) did not merely wring concessions but changed the nature of the state and these reflected, not merely a growing alliance with the petty bourgeoisie or even the peasantry, but, more importantly, a new level of proletarian power – the power to control, or at least participate in, determining the destiny of society as a whole. For it was not only the direction of state expenditures that were transformed by agitation and legislation but the configuration of the capitalist system itself, an outcome entirely unexpected by the founders of scientific socialism.[181]

Underlying Bernstein's evolutionary perspective was his judgement that capitalism had stabilized economically, that cartel and monopoly development signified increased rationalization (taken as a neutral, universal category). In effect, having solved the problem of the anarchy of production, advanced capitalism was prepared, in the new situation, to accommodate to working-class demands, even to democratically alter the state form in its own interest. For among the vital presuppositions of organized capitalism, none stood higher than stable industrial and labor relations. Therefore, a new industrial order, marked by workers' participation, through enlightened representatives, in some key decisions of the enterprise as well as the system as a whole, was thoroughly consistent with the idea that uncertainty had to be removed from the economic and hence the political equation. It is important to separate this program from the charge that it signified a surrender of class struggle or socialist ideology. Despite his departure from the orthodox Marxist doctrine that only proletarian revolution could bring social emancipation, Bernstein attributed the new state of affairs to class action. The slogan that the "movement is everything, the goal is nothing" reinforces this idea; for Bernstein there is no question of a permanent arrangement whereby the social-democrats would lay down their "arms", only the need to jettison the dogmatic doctrine according to which only the seizure of power by force could bring into being a new social order.

In practice, even Bernstein's opponents were obliged to work for reforms, especially those which extended democratic rights and the amelioration through legislation of working and living conditions. The chief difference became one of interpretation. For Rosa Luxemburg, these gains were at best temporary; the inevitable economic collapse resulting from chronic underconsumption at home and the closing of the frontiers for capital investment abroad would force the bourgeoisie to seek attenuation of the falling profit rate by cancelling or reducing major welfare-state provisions and cutting wages. These measures would exacerbate workers' resistance, which would likely be met by the now-covert, now-overt state coercion against the movement and its representatives. This resistance, combined with the inherent limits to world capital accumulation would lead to complete collapse of the system.[182]

The debate within German social democracy was reproduced, with appropriate national variations, in all major capitalist countries. Everywhere socialists were perplexed by the distance between classical Marxist crisis theory and the apparent development of an organized capitalism on a world scale. Under these circumstances, victories by the workers' movement in extending social benefits, the level of trade-union organization and the parliamentary strength of the socialist and labor parties produced a definite tendency within the left toward reformism, a tendency that seemed to merge with left support for national as well as class politics.

Germany's entrance into the First World War found the socialist movement divided: a majority of the SPD representatives supported the government's request for war credits and even some revolutionaries such as Kautsky refused to wage "war against war" on behalf of the working class. This experience was reproduced in other democratic countries, where thousands of socialists who actively opposed the war were jailed by their own governments, regardless of the existence of constitutional or legislatively-induced bourgeois freedoms won in the previous decades. Luxemburg herself languished in jail for much of the war, the Liberal Democrat Woodrow Wilson sanctioned the imprisonment of Eugene Debs, the leading American socialist, and hundreds of others were either jailed or deported. These experiences, combined with the deteriorating economic conditions after the war in Germany, the Austro-Hungarian Empire and Russia led to revolutionary upsurge in several major European countries in 1917–19, uprisings that renounced, for the most part, the Bernsteinian arguments of the prior two decades. As Lenin disbanded the Constituent Assembly in Russia, a signpost of the democratic revolution of February 1917, the characterizations of Marx and Engels, that republican democracy was, after all, inextricably linked to bourgeois rule, was revived and became the basis of the political ideology of Leninism. To the main features of democratic freedoms, including parliamentary rule, Lenin posed the alternative of proletarian democracy, a concept drawn from his reading of Marx's *Critique* of the Gotha Program, the practical examples of the Paris Commune and of the creation of workers' councils during the 1905 Russian revolution, which Lenin as well as Luxemburg understood as forms of dual power to that of the monarchy and its Duma. Recall the Duma was a representative body that lacked even the power of a proper bourgeois parliament. In contrast, the soviets were meant to exercize sovereign power over state decisions; they were to be both legislative and administrative bodies which, according to Lenin amounted to a parallel state to that of the monarchy. During the height of the 1905 revolution Lenin theorized that a state of dual power existed because the monarchy was unable to assert its hegemony, which, for Lenin meant a monopoly over the means of violence. The soviets were powerful to the extent that they had obtained the arms necessary to make their "state" organs effective.

The fundamental difference between bourgeois and proletarian democracy has often been portrayed in the phrase "dictatorship of the proletariat". For Marx, this concept signified a transformation in the content as well as the state form in the transition between capitalism and socialism. Since democracy under capitalism was always a form of bourgeois rule, the cards were inevitably stacked against the workers, especially if they managed to achieve a level of representation in legislative bodies approaching a majority or, in the alternative, were able to project their own minority government with the support of parties of other subordinate strata. Engels's judgement that such a republic was already "too dangerous" suggests that we could expect the bourgeoisie to mount a counteroffensive as soon as the left parties attempted to intervene in the process of capital accumulation and alter patterns of distribution of the social surplus through legislation, or the trade unions engage in mass strikes to lower working-hours or achieve more far-reaching political reforms. Engels's rather linear scenario was only indirectly fulfilled in the wake of the collapse of the Weimar Republic, but there is enough prescience in the evaluation of the limits of representative democracy to explain the persistence of revolutionary scepticism regarding the strategic value of this form for the working class well into the later decade of this century.

However, the experience of the early years of the Bolshevik revolution appeared to validate Engels's judgement that the bourgeoisie, both internal and international, would not stand by and permit the new Soviet state to survive without making counter-revolutionary moves to overthrow the new regime. Recall that the new regime immediately faced armed opposition from representatives of the old order, recalcitrant peasants who were organized by both the right and the anarchists into militia that opposed the Red Army (although the Maknovist movement of anarchist peasants attempted to come to agreements with Trotsky and Lenin and were treated cynically by the Bolsheviks).[183] In 1920 twenty-one foreign armies invaded Russia, hoping to topple the regime. These experiences, as much as the Leninist reading of Marx's late writings on the transition from capitalism to socialism convinced the Bolsheviks that the remnants of the liberal state should not be revived in the wake of capitalist encirclement. In any case, according to this argument, representative democracy was inherently a middle-class demand and had never really enjoyed a mass base in Russia. Beneath the Menshevik (social-democratic) judgement that a prolonged period of parliamentary democracy was necessary in a regime of capitalist social relations, were two elements of second international Marxism: from Marx (the famous preface to the *Contribution to the Critique of Political Economy*) came the proposition that no social order ever disappears before all the forces of production within it have been fully developed. Russia, a relatively industrially-backward society, was simply unprepared to accommodate socialist production relations. And there was the by-now canonical view, adapted from Bernstein's, that socialism inherits the main elements of bourgeois freedoms and does not abolish them, particularly representative democracy and civil liberties. These articles of prewar socialist faith were rudely dismissed by Lenin in the wake of the civil war that broke out soon after the Bolshevik seizure of power.

It is important to note that the left criticism of bourgeois democracy paralleled the right-wing criticism of such theorists as Carl Schmitt, who argued that the bourgeoisie was incapable of preserving social order, because of its essentially apolitical stand. Among Schmitt's most powerful arguments is the disappearance of genuine debate concerning public issues in parliamentary regimes. Schmitt derides the liberal claim that these regimes make vital political decisions "through representative institutions, through public discussion, that is, reason".

> The reality of parliamentary and party political life and public convictions are today far removed from such beliefs. Great political and economic decisions on which the fate of mankind rests no longer result today (if they ever did) from balancing opinions in public debate and counterdebate. Such decisions are no longer the outcome of parliamentary debate . . . the whole system of freedom of speech, assembly, and the press, of public meetings, parliamentary immunities and privileges, is losing its rationale. Small and exclusive committees of parties or of party coalitions make their decisions behind closed doors and what representatives of big capitalist interest groups agree to in the smallest committees is more important for the fate of millions of people, perhaps, than any political decision. (CPD p. 49–50)[184]

This from one of the most articulate theorists of the coming anti-democratic German state. As Ellen Kennedy has argued, Schmitt's crucial distinction between "true" democracy, where there is an identity of the rulers and the ruled, and representative democracy, where this principle is compromised, was initially influential on such left-wing political theorists as Franz Neumann and particularly Otto Kirscheimer.[185] Both were students of Schmitt around 1930 when left and right critiques of democracy dominated the intellectual space of Weimar politics. For both tendencies the legitimation of representative democracy was undermined by the growing tendency toward secret government so long as there was no substantive agreement on a set of values from which policies could be fashioned. Owing to the absence of consensus, secret government was bound to replace open, public debate because these societies, in which representative democracy existed, were fatally heterogeneous with respect to social interests, a situation which prevented the emergence of a public sphere of political discourse in which reason rather than violence could prevail. For Schmitt violence was the inevitable consequence of social fissures, themselves exacerbated by neutrality of the liberal state while the social order is torn apart under it.

Underlying these judgements is a critique of the dominance, in political theory, of formal rationality (constitutionalism) and instrumental rationality (pluralism). What united left and right in this respect was the search for a new foundation for substantive reason, a category abandoned with the ascendancy of the scientific world-view that has won ideological hegemony in the bourgeois social and political order. What Norbert Bobbio is, approvingly, to call the "rules of the game", is an explicit abandonment of the search for consensual values upon which to base social decisions except the acceptance by all parties of a procedural definition of democracy.[186] According to this conception, unilateral methods for resolving political differences are renounced, especially the use of violence. What marks the idea of proletarian democracy as an alternative to both the liberal state and parliamentary forms of decision-making is its claim to have grounded political theory in a consensus in which the universal interest has replaced the unprincipled compromises that recognize the ineluctability of difference as the basis for politics which is really the cornerstone of liberal theory. There are, of course, several varieties of liberalism, the leading versions of which are individualism, really an adaptation of Lockean and Smithian conceptions and the interest-group theories of American political science. In neither case does the concept of universality occupy a significant theoretical space. Therefore, the logical necessity of proceduralist views of social rule.

The new form of post-revolutionary workers' democracy, the soviet or workers' council, was understood as nearly identical to the concept of the transitional state, replacing the bourgeois state by representatives of workers' parties which, however, supported the revolution and the necessity of its defense by force against internal and external enemies but might disagree on such questions as economic strategy, social policy, and so on. Since the soviet was not merely a legislative body but an organ of administration as well, it would thwart, at least in concept, the emergence of a new bureaucratic class whose existence could undermine workers' power in the name of efficiency and expertise. Additionally, Lenin and Leon Trotsky feared that this new "socialist" bureaucratic class would administer in its own interest.[187] Similarly, the role of the manager in enterprises was placed in contention by the revolutionary left, which argued that workers' councils should legislate and administer the labor process, distribution, and other ordinary industrial functions. As is well known, Lenin rejected these arguments on practical grounds: the urgent necessity to rapidly develop the productive forces needed to solve the twin military and economic crises made the demand for workers' control a luxury in enterprises as much as in the state. For others the soviets would not, necessarily, replace the representative character of legislative assemblies. The left proponents of retaining elements of representative democracy remained persuaded that developed industrial society was simply too complex for direct democracy – that is, fulfilling legislative and administrative functions in the manner of the Athenian *polis*. Lenin's own optimism on the eve of the October Revolution that a system of direct democracy was possible during the transition, expressed in his pamphlet *State and Revolution*, was rapidly dissipated in the wake of the civil war and the foreign invasion of 1921, events that were to permanently alter the content of the revolutionary dictatorship in the lexicon of Soviet Marxism. Henceforth, demands for direct proletarian democracy were labelled "ultra-left" or ultra-democratic, which endangered the revolution. A minority has always disagreed, insisting that even if representatives are needed for "higher" functions the base of the entire system should consist of popular assemblies that would really run shop-level and neighborhood affairs and can send delegates to higher bodies recallable at any time if they failed to reflect the will of shopfloor and neighborhood groups (not merely represent them in the larger sense). This system would suggest a radical redefinition of socialist democracy which sharply diverges both in composition as well as intention from its bourgeois form. The minority view was articulated best by the group of council communists which in the early years after the war had considerable influence in both the Dutch and German communist movements. The names of the key figures – Karl Korsch, Anton Pannakoek, Herman Gorter and Henrietta Roland-Holst – suffered eclipse until the 1960s, largely because their views, paralleling those of Rosa Luxemburg and the "workers' opposition" in the Soviet Union, were discredited by the apparent success of the Bolshevik Revolution and particularly the prestige of Lenin.[188] Lenin's pamphlet, *Left-Wing Communism: an Infantile Disorder* (1920) was directed to both attacking their petition on workers' democracy and establishing a new line for the world communist movement which, recognizing that world capitalism had achieved "temporary" stabilization (again) after the initial revolutionary upsurge of the immediate postwar years, counselled moderation, especially toward bourgeois democratic governments and those socialist parties that adhered to parliamentary struggle as the substance of working-class and socialist action. Lenin's critique of left-wing communism may be seen as a repudiation of his own utopian State and Revolution; *Left-Wing Communism*'s wide dissemination made Communist short-term strategy virtually identical with that of its arch-rival, social democracy. (Of course, the new policy of the United Front with social democratic workers and parties was understood as a temporary expedient dictated by contemporary conditions. However, with the exception of the shortlived "third period" sectarianism (1928–34) it turned out to be the dominant Communist perspective of the twentieth century, in part, because although stabilized capitalism proved a temporary phenomenon, the development of fascism reaffirmed the United Front policy, but on different grounds.)

For virtually half a century, the Communists and other elements of the revolutionary Marxist left (Trotskyists, left social democrats, Maoists and "democratic" Leninists of various stripes) held fast to the dual perspectives of Leninism: the need for a non-sectarian united front against the right whose common basis is the defense of bourgeois democracy, especially civil liberties and representative government; at the same time, this tendency, which has encompassed the overwhelming majority of Marxist parties and intellectuals influenced by Leninism and the Bolshevik Revolution, retained the idea of the proletarian dictatorship as the model of post-revolutionary transition. For the Communists, the degree of democracy consistent with the transition was determined by the reality of capitalist encirclement. Accordingly, ultra-democratic demands could only weaken the revolution, especially workers' control at the factory level and multi-party political democracy in councils and parliaments. Therefore, the Soviet model, although increasingly criticized, after Stalin's death, for its harsh repression of dissent, was viewed by the CP and its periphery as a more or less adequate representation of the degree to which democracy could be implemented by a socialist state in a world dominated by aggressive capitalist powers on the hand, and the relative underdevelopment of productive forces in socialist societies. Although critical of the failure of the Soviet Communists to address the problems of inner party democracy in a Leninist spirit, namely, to guarantee the right to (socialist) dissent, especially the right of workers to strike and the right of political dissenters to form factions and publish independently of official party organs, mainstream Trotskyism and other independent Leninist lefts have defended the achievement of the Soviet Union, Cuba and China, especially the abolition of private property in the decisive means of production. Thus did the bulk of revolutionary Marxism until about 1970 maintain the classic duality between reform and revolution. One judges the post-revolutionary regime differently from those enclosed within the capitalist orbit and ascribes the shortcomings of socialism with respect to its democratic institutions to the hegemony of global imperialism. Gone, for all intents and purposes, was the earlier quest for substantive democracy, since the possibility of ideological and material homogeneity had been, for the time being at least, foreclosed. Nor were the Leninists prepared to accept the main propositions of procedural democracy proposed by social-democrats.

Under this regime, most Marxists evaluate bourgeois democracy by separate criteria from those that might be applied to countries such as the Soviet Union. Bourgeois countries were evaluated by this section of the left by the degree to which the working class and other popular movements enjoy the ability to organize on the shopfloor and in the legislatures for the amelioration of their working and living conditions. For example, American Communists and Trotskyists placed considerable emphasis upon civil liberties and civil rights and were, until very recently, leading defenders of these freedoms. But, since Marxists expected little, if any, popular control over the workplace and the state so long as capitalist social relations prevail, demands such as workers' self-management of the labor process without altering ownership of the means of production by capital were regarded as contemporary examples of ultra-leftism or utopianism, judgements that reflected the ideological dualism of Marxist perspectives on democracy. In sum for the revolutionary left, except for the New Left of the 1960's, socialism was the absolute condition for true democratic initiatives at the point of production as well as in other sectors of social relations; under capitalism the job of the workers' movements is to battle for concessions, even far-reaching reforms that institutionalize these concessions as "rights" which accompany the formation of a sector of the state bureaucracy to enforce them. Simultaneously, the ever-present danger of right-wing attacks upon basic bourgeois liberties forces the left to devote considerable energies to protecting them. As for the rights of minorities, particularly blacks and immigrants, some Marxists have theorized that the struggle against discrimination in employment, housing and civil liberties, represents a crucial blow against capital's effort to maintain a large industrial reserve army by the method of exclusion of large sections of the labor force from any but the most menial employment. To fight against discrimination in employment, housing and education is to fight for working-class unity, because its success tends to remove the differences in the technical division of labor between blacks and whites which, in the orthodox view, is the material basis of ideological racism.

The separation of present and future by the revolutionary left is undoubtedly influenced by the realities of the social and political environments of leading western democracies. With crucial caveats, to be discussed below, workers' movements have succeeded beyond the expectations of revolutionary Marxists in winning substantial gains through the capitalist state, an achievement that seems to validate Bernstein's judgement that an apocalyptic future is decisively foreclosed by the capacity of capital to learn how to attenuate its own contradictions, to which Keynes has added a crucial verification in his widely-accepted political economy of state intervention into investment and consumption.[189] It is important at this point to note that many socialist theorists nourished in the post-Second World War European environment, particularly Jurgen Habermas, Wolfgang Abendroth and Claus Offe, among others, interpreted the rise of the welfare state as a substantive historical achievement in the direction of "redeeming the promise of representative democracy" by establishing a new consensus regarding social equality. As this view has evolved, socialism has been redefined as "more equality" which may or may not entail the social ownership of the means of production, a demand now relegated to a conjunctural outcome of the resistance of big capital to structural reforms that aim at substantial redistributive justice. The welfare state is understood by Habermas and Offe as a two-headed phenomenon: on one side, it would not have come about without the powerful workers' movement that imposed such measures as income guarantees during unemployment on an unwilling capitalist class; on the other, the welfare state legitimates the liberal state and blunts the chance that a new form of social rule will replace it. In any case, the great compromise struck between labor and capital after the war in nearly all western countries restructured both accumulation and the terms upon which the underlying population were prepared to grant consent to the state. Capital was now obliged to take into account the relatively fixed transfer payments bill when considering options for investment unless it could persuade voters, particularly workers, of a different form of legitimation.

After the Second World War, capital demanded of trade unions, socialist and labor parties that they consent to the Atlantic Alliance's international aims. The majority of movements under social-democratic leadership responded by demanding substantial concessions in the provision of transfer payments whether they succeeded as in Britain in winning parliamentary majorities or not. The welfare state became the price exacted by the labor movement for the new postwar corporativism.

Communist opposition was confined, almost entirely, to questions of international relations since their own conception of socialist organization and mobilization tended to support a commitment to enlarged state intervention, especially in Europe, where substantial arms expenditures were not assumed by the leading governments during most of the postwar period. Given the weakness of the insurgent right during the first two decades after the Second World War, democracy as such remained off the political agenda, giving way to debates concerning the pace and direction of state intervention. Most of the left remained unconcerned about the problems of the formation of a sovereign state bureaucracy that accompanied the growth of the economic and legitimation functions of the state. After all, with the exception of Trotsky's writings, particularly his neglected critique of early signs of bureaucratism in the Soviet Union, *The New Course*, neither Communists nor social-democrats had confronted this question at a theoretical level, reproducing the relative neglect of explicit treatments in the works of Marx and Lenin and the key theorists of the Socialist International, Kautsky, Bernstein and Luxemburg, although the Austro-Marxists seemed keenly aware of the problem in the first decades of the twentieth century.

Nor did the profound threats to democracy in metropolitan countries posed by imperialist intervention in the Third World produce a serious postwar debate. Even the rise of national liberation movements in the colonial world did not initially disturb left complacency. The western left became, at the same time, a national left, one almost wants to say "nationalist", a position which rendered both major wings, communist and socialist, relatively indifferent when not outright supportive of their own governments' foreign policy. With the exception of a non-Communist extreme left and small pacifist movements, both communists and social democrats remained aloof until the U.S. intervention in Vietnam, principally because (with the notable exception of the east-west divide) the left ignored or gave little more than lip service to the north/south cleavage. For example, French socialists actually supported the French colonial policy in southeast Asia and may be held partially culpable in the notorious war-aims of the French government against liberation movements in the region. Similarly it was not until the Algerian war in 1960 that the Communists finally actively opposed the position of their own government. While ritualistically critical of French colonial policies, the Communists had to be forced from the extreme left to take direct action. As for the powerful British Labour party which formed three postwar governments, the Irish question was treated as all former, and subsequent governments had: Catholic demands for Irish unity were rejected and the virtual occupation of the country by British troops has been a continuous feature of the Irish policy, whether under Labour or Conservative rule.

2

It was the rise of the New Left in Europe and the United States that revived political and theoretical interest on the left concerning questions of democracy. The core of the New Left critique of bourgeois democracy consisted in the claim that representative government was a shell; far from being delegates of groups of people, whether geographically or institutionally based, representatives increasingly responded to the discipline of their own parties which, like the trade union and corporate bureaucracies which constitute their fundamental organizational base, have come to represent a constellation of autonomous interests. The party-leaders are obliged to factor in the concrete grievances of the underlying population, but subsume them under the historical compromise between the labor bureaucracy and capital which forms the core of the capitalist state. Far from being an unambiguous benefit to ordinary people, interventionist economic and social state policies have centralized power in fewer hands. Trotsky and Weber had, in different ways, called attention to the dangers for popular democracy represented by the emergence of a relatively powerful bureaucracy in societies in which the state and industrial development were intimately linked, but socialists and communists were fairly supportive of this development. The New Left claimed that the reason for the lack of concern with bureaucracy was inherent in the transformation of the official left into a self-interested organizational colossus itself which is bound by innumerable ties to the established order.

Although in both the United States and Western Europe the New Left emerges around opposition to the efforts of capitalist states to retain colonial empires, its roots are as much in the struggle to redefine categories such as democracy and freedom and to reconstruct them. In the United States, the generation born just before the war which reached adulthood between the late fifties and the mid-sixties rejected both the middle-class suburban culture into which they were inducted and the "ideological state apparatuses", particularly schools, which purported to prepare them for citizenship but merely delivered them to the economic order as workers and professionals. This generation also perceived representative democracy as a shell, a series of institutions marked more by its exclusions than inclusions. In the United States this perception was buttressed by the emerging civil rights movement of the mid-fifties which called the disenfranchisement of blacks to the attention of white America, most particularly the Montgomery Bus boycott of 1955 and the school integration struggles of the late fifties.

Under the mostly indirect influence of the mass society critics Herbert Marcuse and especially C. Wright Mills, the student movement begins to challenge the equivalence of representation with democracy by arguing that the military/industrial complex, Big Labor and the welfare bureaucracies really run the country, subordinating congress to the rank of junior partner of an economic and social monolith. To this oligarchy, the American New Left counterposed the concept of participatory democracy which invokes images of the New England town meeting and other forms of direct decision-making.[190] Of course, few advocates of participatory democracy would surrender the struggle for full voting rights for minorities in representation elections or would derogate the importance of electing genuine peoples' representatives to legislatures and congress. It was never a question of either/or, but clearly the movement's emphasis was always on the creation of new ways to enlarge direct popular control over key social institutions – schools, health facilities, workplaces and the Black Panthers raised, in the late sixties, the "impossible" demand for community control over the police.

These initiatives went beyond ideological debate or slogans at demonstrations at the height of the civil rights movement's strength, the late sixties. In many local communities, legislatures and executive authorities felt compelled to support, with varying degrees of seriousness, new arrangements that took direct account of popular voices and positions; in 1968, the New York City Board of Education surrendered some of its powers to newly-constituted local school boards; hospitals established community advisory boards which had influence, but not real power over administration decisions regarding community access to health care. Civilian boards were established to monitor police behavior and community planning boards, which had been fairly weak previously, gained a genuine voice over urban renewal decisions. Under federal anti-poverty guidelines, the poor had to be represented on boards charged with determining how funds were to be spent at the local level.

Of course, none of these innovations was unambiguously a form of popular power; all of them operated under severe constraints, reflecting the still-dominant position of bureaucracies and legislatures which had agreed to share authority only under severe duress. Few of the new avenues of participation were substantively routinized; on the contrary, when the demonstrations died down and the riots were finally contained in the 1970's, these incipient inroads either disappeared or were reduced to ritualized performances of citizens' participation. Since the major political parties never genuinely supported either in principle or practice the formation of participatory democratic institutions which did not resemble direct democracy, but broadened the base of representation to quasi-legislative bodies, only the militancy of the movements sustained them. And these movements were not themselves secure enough to withstand the inevitable counter-attack which came almost with the direct action phase.

It was not difficult for New Left critics of American democracy to invoke the past as a guide to the future. The fifties were seen as eminently undemocratic, even in representative terms. Millions of southern blacks were literally deprived, by state repression and unofficial terrorism, of citizenship despite constitutional guarantees of voting rights to all qualified citizens; youth under 21 could not vote while, at the same time, subjected to an almost continuous postwar draft, political dissent was ruthlessly supressed and higher education, far from conforming to the ideal of free, self-directed inquiry, was increasingly regimented by academic administration that had drawn closer to the goals of the corporations and their state allies. Perhaps more important, the concept of the Atlantic Alliance, the cornerstone of the international policy of western capitalist countries, was removed from the agenda of political debate by bipartisanship, an agreement between the Democrats and Republicans to leave such matters to the executive branch of government. In this connection the one important instance of debate about international issues prior to the sixties occurred in 1956 when the Democratic presidential candidate challenged the Eisenhower administration's opposition to welfare state expansion. The Republicans regarded the relationship between defense spending and social benefits a zero-sum game. According to this doctrine, even the vigorous economy could not provide both. Adlai Stevenson argued that we could have "guns and butter" and the Republican opposition to expanded welfare masked as a problem of budgets, was really ideologically motivated. On the other hand, allusions to Jeffersonian democracy (absent its regrettable dependence on slavery) provided an ideological basis for asserting an alternative. American New Left theorists such as Tom Hayden[191] grasped the issue as a struggle for power to control the conditions of social life conceived in personal terms. The American New Left did not renounce the individualism characteristic of American ideology; it asserted boldly that the aim of democratic renovation was to empower individuals to take control over the decisions that affected their lives. For the New Left, the field of battle was to be found, in the main, at the local level, where public bodies regulated electrical rates, decided how many units of public housing might be constructed, who should teach the children of people of color and the poor, how often garbage would be collected or whether a street light was to be installed. Some of these decisions bear on which party is elected to public office but New Left activists and theorists argued that empowerment was best achieved by direct action since the candidates presented by the leading political parties may be elected by, but rarely took direction from, their constituency.[192] The relationship between the electors and their representatives was mediated by the directing force of national and international capitalist economic power, the domination by bureaucracies inured from public responsibility, which often neutralized the political weight of elected representatives. This state of affairs rendered the claim to genuine democracy under the current setup suspect. The critique of bureaucracy was no less powerful in New Left theory. The doctrine of corporate liberalism asserted among other things that the individual could be reconciled with a corporate-dominated polity, provided a series of institutional arrangements were developed which cushioned the effects of rapid, large-scale changes in the economy, in social and political life. These arrangements always entail, for this doctrine, a compromise among leaders and administrators of large-scale organizations to insure that private associations control public life, but succeed in winning the approbation of the masses. The private control over public authority consequently excludes anything resembling Lockean and Jeffersonian conceptions of democracy. On the contrary, cold war liberal doctrine asserts the priority of the national security state over everyday life while preserving the doctrine of particularism that is generally confused with individuality. Group interests may be served by state policy to the extent that they become powerful through direct or legislative pressure, but there is no question of sharing power broadly.

The new lefts of Western Europe were products of the powerful communist and social democratic movements of the previous century, but especially of the postwar era even as they broke in certain respects from them. Socialist rather than populist orientation meant that the language of the movements of students and intellectuals was imbedded in Marxist theory, working-class concerns, north/south struggles, and later in problems of immigration and sexuality which they joined with the questions associated with class formation.[193] It did not take much to persuade this generation in Italy that the state and its representative institutions were little more than a caricature of genuine democracy. Political parties offered various and often conflicting programs for society, but the real levers of power seemed to many Italians to be pulled elsewhere, by the Agniellis, the owners of Fiat, for example. Similarly, after an extended period after the war during which political power was barely exercized by the government, but seemed to be lodged in the American State Department, international investors and NATO, the French in a nationalist outburst elected de Gaulle to rule the country in a kind of democratic despotism that lasted from the mid-fifties until the May events of 1968 sent his government reeling.

As is well known, the French May and the Italian "hot autumn" the following year marked the high point of the influence and power of the New Left, just as the pinnacle of anti-war protest occurred during these years in the United States. These explosive movements were directed against the perceived charade of parliamentary and republican democracy as much as against the increasing centralization of all political decisions in autonomous bureaucracies of the political parties as well as state and corporate institutions. On questions that were settled during the immediate postwar period by large-scale institutional compromises, such as those bearing on foreign affairs, parliaments and mainstream political parties remained intransigent to popular pressure. Equally obdurate were the bureaucracies which controlled public services such as housing, health care and education. The New Left's demand for a radical restructuring of these services to allow a large measure of popular participation in administration were usually brusquely rejected as a violation of the principle of delegation of powers to professional experts when bureaucrats did not claim that such arrangements would be grossly inefficient. The Italian workers' movement raised sharply the issue of worker's control over production, an issue far removed from parliamentary action. When employers in the north, especially Fiat, flatly refused to subject the conditions of labor to workers' self-management but insisted that the responsibility of the unions ceased at the cusp of managerial prerogatives to direct the workforce according to criteria of efficiency, a series of wildcat strikes broke out, demanding radically different industrial relations. These struggles found both Communist and Socialist leaders unprepared. When they were not denouncing the wildcat strikes as irresponsible, provoked by the far left, or potentially destructive to the survival of the labor movement itself, they were running furiously to head the movement in order, according to extra-parliamentary critics, to head it off.[194]

In sum, the New Left attack was directed equally to parliamentary and administrative institutions of the bourgeois state and the giant monopolistic corporations. As in an earlier sectarian period in the history of the Third Communist International, social-democracy (or, in the United States, the Democratic party) shared considerable blame for the late-twentieth-century phenomenon of mass alienation in the wake of unprecedented mass political rights. The neo-Marxist critique of bourgeois democracy was directed as much to the so-called welfare state as it was to parliament, as much against trade unions which, because of their corporativism, refused to lead the battle for shopfloor workers' control, for new measures to ensure the workers power over investment, as it was against the owners of large enterprises.

And, of course, the explosive student opposition to the Vietnam war capped a worldwide break with the *de facto* détente between the mass electoral left and its own capitalist states on global issues. The term "explosive" expresses my conviction that the anti-war and anti-colonialist movement in the most industrially developed societies challenged one of the crucial pillars of class compromise, the linchpin of the drift to parliamentary democratic ends among left parties after the war. Of course, anti-war struggles can be linked to specific features of government policy, notably the draft which, in the United States, has been employed selectively throughout its history. But youth objections to the draft are, in turn, related to the larger issue of disaffection, the loosening of patriotic, nationalistic fervor which was effective in recruiting millions of soldiers in the two world wars and during the Korean war. Although the draft was instituted in order to meet troop requirements, no mass opposition appeared in these instances. In contrast, the Vietnam war proved immensely unpopular after 1965 when President Johnson dramatically increased US troop commitments to support the South Vietnam government forces. Clearly, among the generation of 1940–50 at least, something had changed in the conditions of consent. American society was experiencing considerable difficulty reproducing consent even as the economy was ostensibly in a boom phase. The national administration responded to what became a consent crisis by alternate tactics of repression and concessions. Draft-evaders were prosecuted and jailed, deserters condemned, battlefield indiscipline was severely punished. But congress also reduced the voting age to 18 and similar state laws were enacted to reduce the minimum drinking age. Funds for education were made available to Vietnam-era veterans as an incentive to youth to give approbation to US war aims and, of primary importance the American welfare state was dramatically expanded beyond its New

Deal borders, particularly in elementary and secondary education for the poor, income payments, and special compensatory programs for racial and ethnic minorities.

After insisting on universal draft, the administration finally capitulated to student demonstrations by granting mass exemptions to active students, permitting exemptions for those who agreed to teach in elementary and secondary schools, and other concessions for workers engaged in work strategically linked to military production. In retrospect, the movement committed a grievous error by separating its own middle-class base from the sons and daughters of workers and farmers who had no means to claim exemptions and who were, on the whole, not inclined to take the route of dissent even as later developments revealed the degree to which the war was unpopular among American combat troops.

Clearly, the global New Left attributed its relative successes to having adopted an extra-parliamentary strategy, to its liberation from reliance on legal methods of attaining its objectives. Moreover, the mass strikes in France and Italy, the university occupations in Britain, Germany and the United States over issues of both university complicity in war-related research, of academic freedom and institutional governance, and the huge anti-war demonstrations in all countries, even those of the south such as Mexico and Argentina, contested the liberal and social democratic claim that the extra-parliamentary opposition represented a small fragment of the broad population. The New Left theorized the sometimes heady events in two ways. The more orthodox Marxists of the extreme left detected a huge breakaway among the industrial working class which established its partial hegemony over factions of the (new) petty bourgeoisie of students and technical intelligentsia. Another (minority) theoretical tendency argued that new social movements were in the process of coming into existence, composed largely of members of a new stratum of increasingly educated and qualified workers who, owing to the fact that modern industry was now largely knowledge-based, faced the contradiction between their proletarianization and their capacity for self-management of the labor process. Mass estrangement from the prevailing social and political compromises was situated in new, emerging strata which constituted a kind of vanguard of a different kind of class struggle. This theoretical tendency, unlike its orthodox counterpart, placed the cultural revolution on a plane with the proletarian revolution, insisting that questions of race and sex, intimately linked to class, occupied a crucial space in late capitalist society. For the "new working class" theorists, the problem of domination was a central issue, even if it did not displace the question of exploitation. The issue of workers' control, made difficult by the progressive dequalification of manual workers in the first industrializing era, was now thrust to center stage in the period during which knowledge had become the chief productive force. According to neo-Marxist theory, the new workforce remains in the thrall of capital. Despite its relative wage privileges, its position of subordination amounts to a degradation of the quality of working life.

Andre Gorz and others in Italy and Germany argued that, in a period of capitalist rationalization of quantitative crisis-tendencies in the system, the qualitative issues occupied central importance in the struggle for emancipation. Legislatures and bureaucracies of various sorts have demonstrated their capacity to accommodate to quantitative grievances, but cannot yield in any permanent way to the new demands, precisely because these challenge capitalist ideological hegemony and, equally important, power relations in the key institutions of the state and in the enterprises. Gorz's theory, borrowed heavily from the work of Italian and German neo-Marxism, particularly that of Mario Tronti, Rudi Dutschke and older work of the council communists, provided a theoretical as well as historical basis for the extra-parliamentary departure from the half-century of parliamentary strategy of the mainstream left. No sooner had these positions been staked out than the New Left began to unravel in all advanced capitalist societies through a series of developments that provided the basis for a new state offensive against the extreme left.[195]

Another tendency, identified with later Tronti, Antonio Negri and the Italian seventies movement Proletarian Democracy took the argument another step: late capitalism had decisively destroyed even the vestiges of meaningful work. The program of self-management assumed that work could still be invested with significance.[196] Contemporary technological developments had foreclosed these possibilities. The latent tendency of the workers' movement was the refusal to work. The refusal to work had become not merely a demand to be presented to executive or legislative authorities, but was inherent in the workers' practices on the shopfloor – taking informal rest periods, blue Mondays and absent Fridays, sabotage on the line, job actions of short duration that disrupted production, and so forth. While the working class might appeal through their unions and parliamentary representatives for shorter work weeks or more rest periods, their self-organization in small groups, their extra-parliamentary radicalism, often devoid of explicit ideological premises, was the heart of the new class struggle. As usual a close student of latest Italian theoretical and political developmesnts on the far left, Gorz followed suit by positing the identity of industrial labor with a prison, a metaphoric turn of phrase which legitimated the refusal to work as a key element of the workers' struggle.

These developments were influenced, beyond doubt, by the defeat of the revolutionary goals of the May events, particularly abetted by the ability of Communist parties in France and Italy to head off the movement by alternate tactics of denunciation, cooptation and, in the case of France, open collaboration with government forces to break the general strike. In the course of advocating new elections, a substantial wage increase and an end to the strikes, the Communists experienced a sudden conversion to workers' control, a demand they previously condemned as utopian. Similarly, the PCI, motivated by dissident currents within the party as well as a breakdown in its trade union base, temporarily turned to the left, even as its early response to an insurgent feminist movement that was attaining mass proportions was initially hostile owing to its efforts to cement a neutrality pact with the Catholic Church hierarchy which was directly under attack for its abortion and divorce stands by the feminists. During this period, the PCI lost considerable ground among intellectuals and militants in all sectors of Italian society, but regained as the seventies proved inhospitable to New Left ideology.

As the new movements ebbed, a recalcitrant tendency emerged on the extreme left, stemming from profound frustration at the unwillingness of the official left to depart from its denunciations of the militants and its simultaneous efforts to coopt the movements and their own left. The extra-parliamentary movements were treated by established agencies, especially the media, as outlaws which prompted many who had participated in direct action of a peaceful variety to become actual outlaws, to engage in activities that called attention to the kabuki dance between the official left and the capitalist state that effectively thwarted the attempts of the people to break the rules of the game without facing dire consequences. For it had become clear to some in the New Left that parliamentary regimes were more than merely inadequate for the project of socialist transformation; when the "base" chose to sidestep the usual channels of protest and petition, they were met by the full force of the combined powers of capital and their own judases, the official left. Parliamentary institutions were no longer democratic; they formed a barrier to genuine change, just as Engels had forecast.

Of course the emergence of the Red Brigades in Italy, the Red Army faction in Germany, the Weather Underground in the United States did not signify a unified political tendency; programatically and politically these groups harbored major differences. But they shared a single vision: the revolution was a break with the past, a new cultural and social equality in which privilege was abandoned in favor of arrangements that had to recognize the priority of Third World needs in the allocation of world resources, the uncompromising end of old cultural forms of sexual and family relationships. Influenced by the spate of peasant revolutions in China, Cuba and especially Vietnam, these groups demanded that the left resurrect violence as an instrument of political and social change. Thousands of those reared in the New Left were, for a brief historical moment, attracted by what was described as a kind of nihilistic, anarchist tendency in Marxism which, at once, was driven by the anarchist critique of the established left and the doctrine of third worldism, or, alternatively proletarian internationalism.

Now, there is no doubt that this "movement" was animated by contradictory ideas and sentiments as well as an unrealistic evaluation of the contemporary political situation both within their own countries and in the capitalist world. For one thing, the economic and cultural crises of the early seventies signified radicalization but not a specifically political break with the liberal state. Although millions of workers, students and professionals had come to question the degree to which representative institutions remained a vehicle through which their grievances could be resolved, there was no consensus on alternative forms of social and political rule nor were the radicalized prepared to create new political vehicles. Under these circumstances, it was relatively easy for the state and the parties to recoup their losses of the 1968 period. By the mid-seventies, voters, in Europe at least, were turning up at the polls in undiminished numbers compared to the historical data. The considerable fractions of the adult population which were opting out of public life in the United States and western Europe had failed to manifest a strong tendency toward an alternate politics. Instead, as Jean Baudrillard has commented, the seventies are marked by the rise of anti-politics, a mood of pure refusal that has no articulated form except in a widespread cynicism, especially among the young, concerning electorism as such.[197] The issuebabble of established forces, entreaties from official sources to stimulate voter turnout have fallen on increasingly deaf ears. Of course, of all advanced countries, this tendency is most apparent in the United States which has a long history of electoral non-participation. But, it is also a growing trend in France which experienced a 34% abstention rate in the 1988 legislative elections, compared to slightly less than 50% in the US presidential election during the same year. Since the left parties typically capture the votes of poorer and younger sections of the population (and this is where abstention is heaviest), it may be inferred that staying away from the polls is one way potential dissident voters show their distrust of those parties to which they would ordinarily gravitate and, more globally, of the parliamentary democratic system as such.

The growing crisis of citizenship is clearly one of the major political tendencies in advanced capitalist countries, which is not properly described as apathy. Except for a brief period in the early seventies when some established institutions in the major countries of the west were moved to accommodate the new militancy, the last fifteen years are marked by a definite hardening of battle-lines between official agents and the underlying population which, of course, did not support the "terrorists" who had misread their mood. If the crisis of citizenship is predominantly a cultural crisis then what marks this period most is the narrowing of the electorate which, implicity includes only those whose political perception is that voting as an activity is in their interest. To be sure, the constituency for parliamentary democracy includes diverse social movements as well as the older business, professional, agricultural and trade union interests. The Green parties in Germany, Belgium, Sweden and Italy contest parliamentary and local elections. The Greens have won small but significant victories and, equally importantly, have constituted a permanent electoral and extra-electoral constituency. After considerable debate in the late seventies, their electoral participation signifies a strategic decision to wring concessions on ecological and feminist concerns precisely because extra-parliamentary struggle, although necessary, remains insufficient in the wake of the urgency of issues. That a Swedish social-democratic government announced in 1988 its decision to implement the popular referendum that supported closing the nuclear energy plants of that country attests to the possibility of winning substantial victories at the ballot box, even if not strictly by parliamentary means. Similarly, Italian feminists secured abortion rights and the right to divorce by referendum. In the 1988 US elections California voters supported a 20% reduction in auto insurance rates by similar means, a victory against the private insurance companies which was quickly subjected to judicial review as to the constitutionality of the measure.

Although employing the electoral system, these popular victories were not secured through representative institutions, chiefly because the movements perceived these institutions no longer amenable to structural reforms, especially those that propose to intervene from the base in determining accumulation priorities and on social rights. In this respect, it is noteworthy that abortion rights in the United States were won by a decision of the United States Supreme Court rather than by Congress, which had blocked action on proposed legislation and undoubtedly would have continued to stonewall these freedoms indefinitely. In this connection, it is valuable to remember that the first major civil rights victory for blacks was obtained as a result of another Supreme Court decision, Brown *vs* Board of Education (1954), fully a decade prior to congressional approval of a comprehensive civil rights law, a measure enacted in the midst of massive civil disobedience by a rejuvenated civil rights movement, ghetto riots and a stepped-up US military intervention in southeast Asia. At the time of writing, gay rights await both court and legislative sanctions which, in the increasingly conservative social environment of the country are not likely to be forthcoming in the near future.

At the same time, the United States Congress, despite a Democratic majority, passed, in the waning days of its 1988 session two pieces of legislation that augur badly for the premise that representative democracy has popular roots in the country. The most egregious, a new drug law, will impose heavy penalties for drug abuse by individuals; the second, euphemistically labelled welfare "reform", removes income rights for physically able-bodied individuals receiving transfer payments if they refuse work. Of course, there is considerable sentiment for such measures among voters who are, after all, largely recruited from the upper reaches of the society and the most stable sections of the working class; those most saliently affected by these measures are largely unrepresented, even tendentially, in Congress and state legislatures. Nevertheless, the character of the legislation signifies a major shift in the direction of this crucial institution of representative government in the United States. The welfare reform is particularly onerous for single mothers, blacks and youth. It opens the possibility for flagrant violations in labor standards, further weakening trade unions. The drug bill is a historical reversal of the traditional right to privacy, by making use of regulated substances subject to civil penalties (previously it was relegated to the status of misdemeanor which carries much lighter penalties but were honored more for the fact that they were ignored by law enforcement agencies).

Apart from constitutional guarantees for both individual freedoms and local governmental forms, Britain, under conservative rule, has exhibited the dark side of parliamentary representative government and evidence that majority rule is not necessarily democratic: the government's shameful treatment of the Catholic minority in Northern Ireland; its flagrant violation of the spirit, if not the letter, of democratic process by dissolving the left-led Greater London Council and recent measures to restrict civil liberties on national security grounds have revealed the limitation of popular reliance on representative institutions to guarantee liberty. The Greater London Council was premised on the notion of democracy as participatory; its aim was to involve large numbers of people in directing local government through decision-making in the governance of a wide variety of neighborhood and city-wide planning and welfare institutions. The Conservative national government understood well the implications of this experiment: its hegemony was threatened by a radicalized local government which claimed considerable autonomy. The only recourse, to dissolve the entire arrangement, was entirely within its powers, but was profoundly authoritarian.

For those experiencing the relative impotence of parliamentary institutions to resist the initiatives of executive authorities against fundamental "bourgeois" freedoms masked in the language of retributive justice and legal legitimacy, the current revival of the defense of representative democratic institutions within socialist and Marxist debates may, at first, appear puzzling. After all, we who live in these societies in which bourgeois democracy has reached its zenith, at least in comparison not only to Third World societies, but to most of the countries of continental Europe and the

Eastern bloc as well, have become acutely aware of the limits of legislative institutions, especially in the glare focused by heavy corporate intervention in political campaigns to the point where even liberal observers have raised questions about whether the procedural processes such as elections provide voters with meaningful choices. In the 1988 elections, 98% of members of the United States House of Representatives were re-elected, in part, because substantial contributions to both political parties were made by corporate-funded political action committees. The differences between the presidential candidates were limited to social issues, at once a tribute to the permanent influence of cultural radicalism and the virtual consensus between competing elites on economic and foreign policy issues. I will reserve a discussion of the reasons for this appalling state of affairs for the last section of this essay.

Since the demise of the New Left in the early seventies and the relative decline of the social movements such as feminism and ecology in the eighties (relative to the strong position each occupied in some major countries through the seventies), especially in the US, Britain and southern Europe, social-democratic political theory has breathed new life. In the last fifteen years the concept of representative, parliamentary democracy is argued by Norberto Bobbio, recently a socialist senator in the Italian parliament and academic political theorists such as Adam Przeworski, whose Marxist perspectives are influenced by the historical experience of social democracy. To these must be added the recently-articulated idea of the ineluctable link between democracy and markets asserted by Alec Nove and Charles Lindbloom, among others. In short, we are in the midst of a new theoretical defense of Bernsteinism. And the audience for this position is by no means confined to the advanced capitalist countries where extra-parliamentary radicalism seems to have passed into history, except among small groups of Green activists. It has achieved popularity in some Third World societies, especially Chile and Brazil where many Marxists and socialists regard parliamentary democracy as an achievement devoutly to be wished and remains to be won.

Since Bobbio's influence in the current debate is fairly widespread, I will examine his claims with special care. For, not only in the clarity of his arguments, but also in his political trajectory, it is easy to see why many once in the revolutionary extra-parliamentary left now look to his work. His works are widely read in parts of Latin America as well as the United States and Western

Europe because they present, in an uncompromising way, not only an argument for the priority of democracy over socialism, but for the liberal state not as a convenience, from the point of view of the left, but a permanent legacy. He makes absolutely no apology for advocating representative democracy as an end of socialist political struggle rather than a means, and defends the actual historical choices of social democratic movements to take the parliamentary road as the best chance of the workers and other popular movements to attain their needs.

Bobbio writes in the shadow of European history where left-wing critiques of parliamentary democracy preceded the rise of fascism which came to power in the name of national unity and, counterposed a racist and nationalist spirit for liberal pluralism. In contrast to those who defend parliamentary, representative democracy from the point of view of social liberalism or conservative anti-left doctrines, his is a socialist defense of representative institutions and a vigorous attack on the practical viability of their left-wing alternatives. What renders his arguments particularly persuasive is that he recognizes both the historical and structural weaknesses of the democratic claims of parliamentary government. This strategy can disarm opponents whose assault easily demolishes liberal arguments on the contemporary evidence of increasing authoritarian practices in western democracies, if not historical failures. We know that even the most secure democracies are prone to suspend civil liberties on national emergency grounds, that their commitment to freedom ends at the water's edge and that they ascribe many of the blatantly undemocratic practices of parliamentary states to conjunctural deformities rather than being inherent in some features of the system.

Bobbio begins by defining democracy as a "set of rules (primary or basic) which establish who is authorized to take collective decisions and which procedures are to be applied". Of course, these collectivities are more democratic the more inclusive the "who" is, and the closer their procedures correspond to the idea of majority rule. And Bobbio is a strong proponent of constitutional norms that "are not rules of the game as such: they are preliminary rules which allow the game to take place".[198] His distinction between the liberal and democratic state consists in this: "liberalism provides those liberties necessary for the proper exercize of democratic power, democracy guarantees the existence and persistence of fundamental liberties". For Bobbio, "the real society underlying democratic government is pluralist". (28) This pluralism is inevitably a plural ism of elites who are in "competition with each other for votes of the public". This idea, borrowed freely from Max Weber and Joseph Schumpeter,[199] is offered in the spirit of a realistic assessment of the chances for anything approaching grassroots control over political decisions. With many others, Bobbio's pessimism is rooted in a history that leads to the judgement that we must settle for the possible: better to have a plurality of elites competing for the popular mandate than a single elite whose intrusion into every aspect of the social world chokes individual and collective autonomy. In any case, as we shall see, for this school of thought, the liberal state becomes the best chance for avoiding authoritarian rule.

Bobbio advances several basic arguments for taking representative democracy as a foundation for democracy as such: it is the only form of democracy which actually exists, its obverse, direct democracy, is impractical in increasingly complex societies which render the revival of the Athenian *polis* a pipedream; democracy in the workplace and other social institutions outside the state is merely the extension of political to social democracy; the demand for participation is satisfied by voting, an activity which implies that the subject is exercizing decision-making powers through the delegation of authority. For compared to those societies in which such delegation, whether parliamentary or presidential, is not regularly granted, the vote is vastly superior.

Beneath these assertions is Bobbio's fundamental political philosophy. Society consists of groups rather than individuals, each of which has interests. These groups, organized as constellations, form political parties which, however constituted as elites, can win political power by drawing on the interests of the groups to which they are ultimately responsible. That government governs best which governs openly, a statement not of fact, but of value. Decisions openly arrived at are the only assurance that the representative procedures are valid as democratic indicators. In the context of most advanced capitalist democracies, open government appears as normative rather than corresponding to actual practice. While the minimal definition described above of democracy surely exists in many states, two crucial components of its maximum definition are missing: citizens join political parties and other voluntary associations in smaller numbers in proportion as the separation between public and private widens. While the intervention of the state in the economy, social life and personal affairs has been enlarged in the past half-century, popular perception is that the state is increasingly dominated by powerful elites over which they have little control. We now confront a pervasive phenomenon in western countries of anti-politics; the power of corporate and bureaucratic elites has resulted in a studied, deliberate retreat of large sections of the population into private life, even when they vote. In contrast, for radical democrats the act of voting is a process of aggregation rather than participation. While an element of decision-making is entailed by this activity, there is a much more important element of ritual, something like singing "The Star-Spangled Banner" or "God Save the Queen" which, for many, are songs without words, sung in public to avoid embarrassment. Ritual behavior is not an insignificant aspect of voting, especially in those democracies where voting takes place on Sunday, a day when large numbers of people view the polling place as a social site. US voting shows a similar dynamic, but only in small towns and the shrinking number of tightly-knit neighborhoods of large and middle-sized cities where identity is still forged by ethnicity, occupation or club membership. But, for the anonymous working and underclasses living in areas where the architecture, urban sprawl and the consequent absence of a sense of place is reinforced by frequent job-changes and changes in living arrangements, voting is, increasingly, a purely individual and not a group activity; lacking real differences between the parties, people in these situations turn their backs on voting (it does not matter that logical argument can demonstrate, if not "prove" that electing Democrats would benefit the poor and the workers at least in comparison to electing the Republicans: for many, the price of granting legitimacy to the elites is simply too high).

I realize these observations may be taken as deliberate provocations, for many voters do take their franchise seriously. However, if we allow that the practical unfolding of late capitalist democracies are identified with consensual rather than conflictual relations among leading political parties, for example, that the traditional opposition in Italy, the Communists, were capable during the seventies of announcing a policy of historic compromise with the bourgeois parties in order to achieve a stable government (a measure that we understood to be in the working-class interest), then reported cynicism concerning the real choices involved in the act of voting should be taken as an index of the legitimation crisis of contemporary capitalist democracies. For even as Bobbio enters his fervent defense of representative institutions, he is obliged to acknowledge the existence of invisible government, of powerful and increasingly intractable elites which are not responsive to the sovereign claims of the electorate and, in the Italian context, of the prevalence of corruption in public life. At the same time, he has ontologized representativeness as democracy itself, which obliges him to systematically deny the viability of direct democracy. Moreover, he fails to address the large areas of state policy that have effectively been removed from parliamentary debate: the important decisions made by central governments regarding science and technological investments; the most general direction of foreign relations; the question of immigration (where differences between Socialists/Democrats and their conservative opponents vary with only the severity of restriction and punishment); and broad areas of tax policy which are debates conducted among elites but rarely shared with the broad electorate. The questions are indeed complex. Do the parties really discuss these issues in an informed and detailed manner? Are the parliamentary committees charged with considering relevant legislation fully apprised of the issues, much less have access to relevant information? Or are these matters assigned to the scientific, foreign affairs, defense or whatever establishments whose apposite relations are to large corporations not to the voting public? Moreover, as the fate of the dollar in international markets attests, the task of government policy is to achieve closer and more symbiotic links with financial interests; the executives communicate to each other concerning such issues as budget deficits, loans to debtor nations, but also the fundamental direction of foreign policy beyond economic issues.

The point is that the last two decades are marked, in both Anglo-American and continental instances, by the more or less open acknowledgement by executive authorities of the existence of a massive invisible government on an international plane. In the United States this has produced much tension between the President and Congress who disagree on the extent to which the executive branch may take autonomous action. While Congress passes many laws and resolutions restricting the authority of the executive to legislate by means of the "executive order", not only in matters of ethics but also foreign military intervention, the administration shows few signs of honoring such restrictions as representative bodies may impose. This executive "lawlessness" is rationalized by the emerging doctrine of the National Security State according to which the President reserves the right to restrict domestic freedoms, especially press access and expression, and the constitutional requirement for seeking the advice and consent of congress for its actions, when a state of emergency or other extraordinary situations arise. In short, in all countries representative parliamentary institutions have powers limited to those matters deemed beyond the purview of the security state, a purview whose tentacles have expanded enormously since the war.

In his critique of alternative proposals to representative democracy, Bobbio enters what is perhaps his most telling set of arguments. Two of the most powerful analytic arguments advanced for alternatives are that these societies in which democratic governments prevail are marked by powerful bureaucratic domination and alongside this phenomenon we can observe the development of a cultural industry, one of whose sectors is a political industry that manipulates votes through propaganda and through images which massify the electorate rather than providing the space in which interests can be adequately represented. Bobbio agrees that these are dangerous tendencies in late capitalist societies but insists that the enlargement of state intervention is driven by the emergence of new demands by an enfranchized electorate that demands such functions be assumed. Therefore, bureaucracy is a welcome feature of democratization. Second, the politics industry is an eluctable feature of a society which requires the "organization of a consensus" as a precondition of political rule:

> Let us be quite clear on this, no full scale democracy without some sort of political industry. It would be nonsensical and, what is more, unrealistic, at least at the present stage of social and intellectual development in our culture to postulate that a society could exist in which all adults have the right to influence directly or indirectly the way political decisions are made, and who must be taken into account by those in power to a greater or lesser extent (but in any case to a greater extent than in oligarchic societies, where the vast majority of subjects remain politically irrelevant). All societies require the use of techniques for the organization of consensus, though in varying degrees of intensity and intrusiveness.[200]

While acknowledging that mass demonstrations are necessary for the purposes of influencing public opinion and are, under certain circumstances, "civic duty" Bobbio argues that "their effectiveness is short-lived, because once the crowd has dispersed, the excitement that has been whipped up rapidly melts away, and with it also the will to act (without which there is no politics for politics is not only feeling or opinion, but action.)". These lines are quite revealing. Rather than understanding demonstrations, disruptions, civil disobedience as historic commentaries on the inadequacy of representative institutions from the point of view of those, increasing in both numbers and categories, who are marginalized, he sees them as parallel to representation, an aspect of participation of which voting is the other side. Since demonstrations may or may not be expressions of elite efforts to intervene in the political process, it is convenient for Bobbio to insist that they are merely "opinion" moulders rather than incipient expressions of alternative politics. Further, Bobbio engages in a sleight-of-hand statement: demonstrations are not forms of political action as if the mass-marches of the civil rights and anti-war movements, the student occupations of French and German universities, the massive Paris march of the left against the Algerian war in 1960 or the uprisings in Paris in 1968 were not forms of action. Bobbio's discourse shows a prejudicial side when in one paragraph he nullifies the history of the sixties, even in his own country, by the demeaning phrases that link direct action with the expression of "heady emotions", "whipped-up excitement", and so on.

However, his defense of bureaucracy is far more serious. Here Bobbio stands in a long line of socialist and progressive thought for which the state intervention is the means by which the struggle for equality becomes institutionally legitimate. Legislatures pass welfare state measures, enact occupational and health legislation, are forced to provide some minimum protections against further ecological deterioration and must, as a consequence, provide the mechanisms of enforcement and administration. These always entail the expansion of the bureaucracy which tends to promote, in its own interest, a technocratic ideology to replace the class victories to which it owes its very existence. Bobbio notes the paradox, but stubbornly insists that in advanced democratic states expertise does not replace the citizen as the sovereign power, but he cannot offer more concrete analytic arguments for the belief that technocratic domination is subject to representative institutions. His claim ultimately rests on an ethical rather than historical foundation.

Now Bobbio's dilemma reflects an admirable trait in his coherent defense of "bourgeois" democracy, his honest acknowledgement of its constraints and limits. He will not surrender popular sovereignty while admitting that it is threatened by the very successes of social-democratic struggles. Part of his problem lies in a certain realism that permeates Bobbio's discourse. For example, the increasing complexity of advanced industrial society is taken as a given framework for democratic discourse.

Surely, for Bobbio to posit direct democracy on the basis of decentralized political jurisdictions is utopian. We cannot revive the Athenian *polis* because we cannot cope with an increasingly technological culture without representative institutions, expertise and most egregiously a technical/managerial class that is profoundly anti-democratic insofar as it disdains popular sovereignty. But the hope that parliament or executive authorities which derive their legitimacy from voters who freely choose them, will be genuinely accountable to their constituents is, for Bobbio a "realistic" expectation. I submit that Bobbio's appeal to realism (for example, his flat statement that representative democracy is the only kind which exists), is a rhetorical gesture that unwittingly sidesteps the implication of his own critique of the historical development of democracy, the degree to which it departs, empirically, from the model he proposes. For Bobbio's invocation to socialists to observe the rules of the game is founded on another paradox: "where the rules of the democratic game have been observed socialism so far has not come about and does not even seem imminent" in part, according to Bobbio, because socialism has made the critique of bourgeois democracy one of the cornerstones of its program. Democracy is "subversive": "wherever it spreads, it subverts the most traditional sense of power, one so traditional it has come to be considered natural, based on the assumption that power flows downward. By conceiving power as flowing upwards, democracy is in some ways more subversive than socialism . . ." if we take the definition of socialism to mean "the transfer of ownership of the means of production from the hands of private individuals to the state",[201] in other words, the model proposed by actually existing socialist states. While this may be true, and I think it is, there are two problems here: Bobbio bases his conception of power flowing upward on the ideal type of democracy that has, by his own admission, only restricted application in even the most advanced democratic countries; and his conception of socialism is quite statist, precisely the objection of radical democratic-socialists for whom social rather than state ownership constitutes a starting point (but not the limit) of democracy. Since Bobbio cannot conceive of a practical way to achieve genuine social ownership or control, he cannot define socialism other than the ways it has been conceived by state bureaucracies, east and west. His own statism is in logical contradiction to the only reliable way that democracy can flow upward – if power is genuinely lodged at the base and representative institutions are subordinated to those that afford to popular forces the opportunities for administration typically reserved to executive and bureaucratic bodies. Under this regime a "state" does not disappear but it is radically altered both with respect to its sovereignty and to its relationship to other forms of autonomous power. We are not speaking here of some ultimate arrangement whereby all human relations are self-regulated; however desirable, this state of affairs requires a fairly long period during which we learn to live in collectivities not grounded in particular interests but have freely chosen to become individuals in the sense this term has been philosophically conceived, people able to solve problems, not by means of compromises grounded in power relations, but by reason. This situation presupposes a profound change in the nature of property, of course, but also a radical restructuring of our collective selves. And this restructuring takes both time and the transformative effects of social praxis.

In sum, there is a yawning gap between the normative assertion of the necessity of popular sovereignty and its practical definition as representative democracy. When Bobbio confronts his own use of utopian ideas, he recoils from drawing the implications of these norms for practice. For in his *Realpolitik* defense of bureaucracy, technical bases for decision-making, the cultural and political industries, as well as his devaluation of direct action as, in the main, quasi-religious catharsis, Bobbio reveals that he is engaged in little more than a polemic against the sixties, that his apologia is directed against the left, which, despite the validity of its critique of the course of bourgeois democracies has failed, in his view, to understand the necessity of the liberal state.

It is not surprising that these views have impressed many peripheral and Third World intellectuals and militants. For the sixties in Latin America were marked by efforts by the extreme left to mechanically emulate the strategy and tactics of the Cuban and Chinese revolutions, especially among far-left factions in Columbia, Uruguay, Venezuela and Bolivia and, on the other hand, a powerful effort in Chile and among some leftists in Brazil to place the question of socialism on the political agenda, and bring it about by parliamentary-democratic means. The repressive and long military dictatorships in both countries that followed leftist electoral victories did not encourage socialist revolutionary ideas. On the contrary, Marxists and socialists have been chastened by the revelation that the political culture of these countries was, at its base, dominated by authoritarian forces. Therefore, what has emerged in the eighties is nothing less than a spate of theoretical and political declarations on the left that declare the priority of representative democracy to socialism, that argue for the restoration of the liberal state as a strategic objective of the left as the best chance to secure liberties and a parliament that will ensure the right of various parties to represent their respective constituents. But, we must note that the left-wing conversions to representative democracy after two decades of revolutionary activity are dictated as much by the effects of militarism, the worldwide economic crisis and the recognition that US imperialism remains a forceful presence in the Americas capable of thwarting radical democratic movements, directly or indirectly, as it is by ideological shifts. Moreover, Latin Americans have been affected by the examples of the civil war in El Salvador, the US assault on Nicaraguan sovereignty, and by the Mexican constitutional crisis of 1988 where the United States remains perhaps the determining power in deciding the fate of these societies. Like those in Eastern Europe who seek freedom from Soviet economic and military domination, Latin Americans believe their first step to fundamental social transformation is to secure representative democracy, which has emerged as the most immediate alternative to authoritarian rule.

After the experience of really existing socialism and militarism in the periphery and semiperiphery few would argue against the proposition that one of the pillars of the liberal state, the guarantee of speech, assembly and, more widely, dissent and opposition must be considered a permanent legacy of the past. No social order which purports to be considered democratic can argue, even under conditions of hostile encirclement such as exists in Nicaragua, or as existed in the Soviet Union prior to the Second World War, that repression of these liberties is justified. While condemning the pressure brought to bear on the revolution by the United States government and its agents, radicals must be critical of the victim's refusal to depart from the historical script. The tragedy is, of course, that its periodic suspension of press freedom and other forms of political expression is often a reaction to what the state perceives to be imminent U.S. invasion and constant subversion of its institutions; the Nicaraguan government has lost a crucial opportunity to take the ideological and political initiative by defending all liberties, even for its most virulent internal enemies. What gives the socialist defense of the liberal state more weight is the unwillingness of the revolutionary left to acknowledge that freedom of political expression is a non-reversible legacy of the political philosophy of left-liberalism, since other varieties, especially the Burkean and Hobbesian traditions, are prepared to forgo these in the service of social discipline, an ideology shared by authoritarian Communist states.

Since the Nicaraguan revolution succeeded in 1979 in deposing the hated Samoza regime, it has been U.S. policy, following the sacred precepts of the Monroe doctrine, to aid, by diplomatic, economic and military means, the overthrow of the Sandanista regime. The U.S. government has done everything possible to reduce the Nicaraguan economy to a shambles by denying normal trade and diplomatic relations to the new government and by financing a group of exiles and ex-Samoza guards to conduct a long war of attrition designed, finally, to drain the new government's economic and moral resources.

The policy has been brilliantly successful in all but its ultimate aim of counter-revolutionary overthrow. The Nicaraguan economy is on its knees and the Sandanista government has lost its once-tremendous prestige among an exhausted and increasingly impoverished population. Many of the regime's left supporters have quietly retreated to the background as Nicaragua has become a garrison state. Within the United States, official policy is to label the regime a "Marxist" government (which it is not) to charge it with molesting its neighbors (it has engaged in only defensive incursions into Honduras, the base of the rebel forces) and, on this "evidence", to continue to give financial and military aid to the counter-revolution. In the face of this U.S.-sponsored terrorism, it is understandable that many on the left hesitate to criticize the Sandanistas in any way, fearing that criticism will give aid and comfort to its rightist enemies. Similarly, many on the left bracket the emergence of Solidarity in Poland from their general support for insurgent workers' movements precisely because the Reagan administration and its successor have made Solidarity an element of their cold war policy. The problem with this stance is that it reproduces the reception to Stalinism when, in the wake of the terror of the 1930's Soviet regime against the internal left opposition, the pro-Soviet left and left-liberals were silent or preferred to accept the explanations for events such as the Moscow trials from Stalin's minions. I would not want to attribute anti-communism as a political ideology entirely or even principally to this history, but those who will not acknowledge its contribution to the postwar phenomenon of a growing conservative defense of capitalist democracy among ex-leftists, have reduced the cold war to "objectivist" explanations.

Of course, I do not mean to equate the Sandanistas with the Stalinist state; the comparison made by neo-conservative discourse is scurrilous. I am, however, calling attention to the analogy, at the level of reception, of the position of many in the global left for whom the enemy of my enemy is my friend. These groups and individuals seem unable to distinguish between an unremitting defense of the right of the revolution to exist, and support for its behavior. Clearly, to defend the right to self-government has been conflated by the American right with support for regimes whose democratic record is subject to criticism. When the democratic left refuses to bare its criticism of revolutionary and socialist regimes it merely compounds the error of these regimes and condemns itself.

The burden of the history of western capitalism as well as really existing socialism is that democracy, in any meaningful sense, remains an elusive goal. Riding the Paris subway in May 1988, I was impressed by the frequent searches by police of people who looked like African immigrants to discern whether they had the proper papers; ordinary police practice in black and other minority communities in the United States consists in search and seizure practices; motorists are often stopped, their cars searched without warrants, presumably for drug possession. The American prisons are bulging with victims of an increasingly retributive criminal justice system which seems to have jettisoned, except where politically inadvisable, the rehabilitation ideology it temporarily adopted in the late sixties. But the U.S. remains a paragon of liberty in comparison to most other countries even if, in comparison to Western Europe its representative institutions are fairly narrow sites for public debate on crucial issues. In Western Europe, the loyalty of the representative to the party exceeds his/her sensitivity to constituents who were responsible for his/her election. This discrepancy is underlined by the fact that parliament is obliged to deal with national and international issues which are rarely contested in locally-based elections. There are, of course, exceptions to this rule, notably the 1988 national elections in Israel and Canada, where major national issues were really at the heart of parliamentary elections, and smaller northern European countries, particularly Sweden, where social-democratic parties are much more open to popular will than their comrades in countries such as France and Italy.

The presidential systems of France and the United States, for example, do not lend themselves to such referenda. Although there are broad ideological orientations behind media images of candidates that seem to dominate the selection process, the convergence at the ideological as well as practical plane is surely a stunning verification of the radical claim that the parties offer less and less for the voters to choose. This state of affairs demonstrates another claim of Marxist analysis: although nationalism has become a more important legitimating ideology in recent years (not only of colonial peoples, but also those that are hegemonic), the dominant tendency of economic and political relations is towards integration on a global scale, or at least for the surrender of national autonomy to regional blocs. American cultural hegemony is even more stunning in both Third World societies and Europe, east and west. These centrifugal forces may not eliminate the reality of competing elites, the dream/analysis of "organized capitalism" has never materialized; but there is little question of the closing of autonomous spaces within which politics may become truly democratic. Which makes Bobbio's discourse on democracy peculiar. He has described the reality of western democracy in utopian terms while attacking those who argue for direct participatory democracy as "unrealistic". The fact is, neither form of democracy has resulted in permanently broadening the base of participation because, despite considerable deterritorialization of industrial production, popular culture and political hegemony, abetted by the widening of the technological sensorium (the development of means of communication as a social and personal wraparound, for example), power has been increasingly linked to knowledge which is rarely, if ever subject to popular sovereignty. Knowledge is the new locus of sovereignty which forms a kind of dual power to that of the national state, which has depended upon the accumulation of physical capital for its economic and cultural viability. With the exception of Green politics, which insists that scientific knowledge and technology be subject to a public sphere of debate, traditional political parties or parliaments are not sites for such appraisal. Science and technology policy are treated as technical, not political, issues. Or when they were subject to political determination, as in France during the 1981 presidential elections, the Socialist demand was for increasing the state budget for research but did not specify, beyond industrial policy, how it should be spent. One of the reasons for this is the historic socialist and communist support for science and technology as the best hope for economic growth and their consequent refusal to enter a critical discourse on these questions. The political dynamic for democratic revitalization has come from the new social movements which have insisted not only on an upward flow of democratic power, but the creation of new arrangements that would facilitate a horizontal flow as well as widening the purview of issues subject to public debate and decision-making

Bobbio represents a tendency of political theory stuck in the vertical models of power. Horizontal power can only flourish by reconstituting local communities as powerful. This proposal entails a transfer of many decisions reserved to executive authorities, over welfare, educational, technological, international, and repressive institutions to local control as well as the transfer of power in the workplace to the producers. However, if my description of the increasing centralization of power is right, achieving direct democracy entails new arrangements in the production and distribution of goods at the regional and local level so that decision-making regarding what is produced, how it is to be produced and distributed and how much, can really come within the purview of the base community. Further it would require disaggregation of many now-centralized economic activities to accommodate the productive capacity of individual enterprises as well as regionalization for the purposes of creating an ecologically sound physical environment.

The discerning reader will already have asked how this proposal is possible, given the nature of scientifically-based technologies, the possession of which is crucial for reproducing central ownership of the means of production, whether by the state or large privately-held corporations. Obviously, the will to direct democracy or representative forms that make delegates effectively recallable, requires at least two crucial pre-rules: knowledge must be widely shared, through education and free information-flows, so that scientific and technological decisions may be made by people who possess neither capital nor credentials; and the basis of productive activity must be radically dispersed, not only to facilitate control but also on ecological grounds. For it can be easily demonstrated that especially in large countries and regions, the concentration of industry, polluting motor vehicles and population, generates unhealthy living and working conditions and has wreaked significant damage to the homeostatic relations of societies to their external physical environments. As I have argued, domination among humans is interlocked with domination of nature. For this reason, decentralization of crucial social functions is a necessary condition for the achievement of a grassroots-generated society and ecological relations that improve the quality of life.

Some of these arguments have been elaborated by others, but only a few theorists have made the link between democracy and ecology. There is, of course, a second argument that can be made for direct democracy, the normative goal of empowerment which implies recognizing that one of the crucial weaknesses of orthodox Marxism has been to privilege the struggle against exploitation over the fight to overcome alienation. For it can be argued that alienation, engendered by such developments as the concentration and centralization of capital, the emergence of the "new" urban spaces organized with a nightmarish vision of expressionist, if nct modernist abstraction (skyscrapers dotting the landscape, monoliths as living spaces, empty deserted streets even in daytime and so on), is really the problematic of late capitalism just as exploitation was crucial for the intensive regime of industrialism. Some have conceptualized this as the cultural question and this surely comprehends an important feature of the question of empowerment; but the loss of control presupposes an entire historical compromise that we have made with the search for the good life or, to be more precise, the good life has been framed in the music of the machine and its consequences. The articulation of this regime of domination with patriarchy, with exploitation and technological progress, is precisely what is at issue in the rejection of the adequacy of representative democracy. For its procedures are necessarily aggregative and do not address the everyday consequences of large social questions. For example, lacking the votes in legislative bodies to win abortion rights, American feminists have been forced to declare control over a woman's body an individual matter free of public determination in order to qualify under constitutional guarantees. This strategic judgement, as I have indicated earlier, resulted from the overwhelming evidence that, despite opinion polls which show substantial public support for abortion rights, legislative bodies have effectively blocked them. For even though the US Supreme Court has ruled that states may not deny these rights, Congress and many state legislatures have refused to appropriate funds to ensure access to abortions for poor women. This example demonstrates the structural unresponsiveness of legislatures to the popular will when party alliances prohibit them. Further it illustrates the degree to which party elites are separate interest-groups from those they purport to represent.

Which raises a final objection to exclusive or even predominant reliance for ensuring democracy by means of representative institutions. For just as it may be argued that bureaucracies tend to class formation with their own ideologies and political programs, so political elites often tend to class formation, the nature of which varies in relation to knowledge and bureaucratic hierarchies. They tend now to become fractions of the same class, even when they are plainly subordinate to capital, at least "in the last instance". In Third World countries where the various elites have combined as a class which controls, if not owns the decisive economic instruments, representative democracy which presupposes the existence of an opposition able to freely exercize civil liberties is far from realization. In western democracies, what is in question is whether elites are "delegates" rather than merely seeking the legitimacy that constituencies may confer on their programs. The presumption of delegation of authority is compatible with one of the crucial mediations of direct democracy that recognizes the validity of certain situations of representation provided it is considered a mandate for certain actions fully discussed and determined by popular assemblies. In its most uncompromising form, the control over delegates is provided by recallability, to which Bobbio replies, "By whom?". The question cannot be answered without addressing the problem of the scale of governance, upon which the form of self-regulation depends. Clearly, his objection to a mode of direct democracy that assumes the large-scale centralized jurisdictions characteristic of many urban areas is valid. But, if decentralized power is actually implemented it might be possible to restore the delegated basis of representation rather than resigning ourselves to choices between competing elites, such as is the case in the selection of enterprise committees in France and Italy, where trade union "parties" compete for votes on the basis of agitation and propaganda but rarely, especially in large enterprises, genuine delegation from a participating base.

At the root of this debate are diverging conceptions of the meaning of citizenship. For those accepting the minimalist assumptions of the liberal state, that most decisions that have effects on everyday life take place beyond the powers of any possible or given public sphere of debate and dialogue, voting is an adequate measure of participation and therefore citizenship, at least in larger jurisdictions. If one takes a more comprehensive and therefore optimistic view, democratic citizenship is intertwined with a significant restructuring of social relations so that horizontal and vertical power flows from the base of society and representative institutions, to the extent that they are a necessary outgrowth of popular assemblies which are delegated and not constituted by elites who derive a mandate from electoral victories or alliances. Obviously, the crisis of Marxism in this regard consists largely in its historic ambivalence towards the support of either representative or direct democracy, that is, its failure to adopt a thoroughly democratic ethos and political commitment, especially when as a political practice, it captures state power. Further, its traditional split between reform and revolution resulted from its antipathy to a more evolutionary conception of the path to direct popular rule. Parties which adopted the Marxist perspective regarded proposals to reorganize the basis of bourgeois citizenship within the capitalist order as disruptive and "reformist". Clearly, times have changed so that Marxism finds itself caught between its strategic commitment to the liberal state (so long as capitalism prevails) and a transitional authoritarian state that is currently in the final stages of crisis. As a result, socialists and Marxists are, more often than not, counted in the ranks of those who defend one kind of hegemony or another and those whose position on existing state forms ranges from dissent to opposition, and who are obliged to distance themselves from both Marxism and really existing socialism.

For those, like myself, whose socialism is rooted in the belief that what Negt and Kluge called, in the late sixties, a "proletarian" public sphere (or more appropriately now a popular public sphere), questions of democracy remain at the center of the emancipatory project. This project differs from really existing social democracy and Communist orthodoxies insofar as it holds to the revolutionary metaphor that social transformation entails a change, root and branch, in relation to the old order. This means, following the spirit of Ernst Bloch[202] that direct democracy is viewed as a practical utopia, the not-yet conscious of social life that is expressed, not only in the resistance to domination characteristic of shopfloor action and the refusal of students to learn the prescribed curriculum in schools but is revealed in the high divorce rates in western countries when women really do have some rights, and the anti-politics of voter abstention. Of course, resistance is not enough. Periodically, throughout history people have tried to create popular public spheres in the form of alternative schools and cooperatives, rebellious unions and voluntary associations that organize around impossible demands. Sometimes these alternative forms take a right-wing direction in part because the left is perceived by many people to be part of, and not in opposition to, the prevailing order. As the struggles in Poland and South Africa demonstrate, the will to direct democracy is not identical to liberal, social-democratic politics no matter how much these are a necessary ingredient in the struggle against authoritarianism. Perhaps only another explosion can put new democratic expression back on the political agenda. In any case, the vehemence of the arguments for representative democracy indicates that despite the nadir of this alternative movement, political theorists are still looking over their shoulders.

NOTES

176. Norberto Bobbio, *The Future of Democracy* (London and Minneapolis: Polity Press and University of Minnesota Press, 1987); *Which Socialism*, loc. cit.
177. Adam Przeworski, *Capitalism and Social Democracy* (London and New
York: Cambridge University Press, 1985).
178. Ernesto Laclau and Chantal Mouffe, *Hegemony and Socialist Strategy* (London: Verso Books, 1986).
179. Louis Althusser, "Ideology and Ideological State Apparatuses" in *Lenin and Philosophy* (London: New Left Books, 1971); Nicos Poulantzas, *State, Power, Socialism* (London, New Left Books, 1978).
180. Karl Marx and Frederich Engels, *Selected Correspondence* (Moscow: Foreign Languages Publishing House, n.d.).
181. Eduard Bernstein, *Evolutionary Socialism* (New York: Schocken Books, 1961).
182. Rosa Luxemburg, 'Social Reform and Revolution' in Dick Howard (ed.), *Selected Political Writings* (New York: Monthly Review Press, 1971).

183. For a detailed account of the movement and its relations with the Bolsheviks see Voline, *The Unknown Revolution, 1917–1921* (London and Detroit: Black and Red/Solidarity).
184. Carl Schmitt, *Crisis of Parliamentary Democracy*, translated by Ellen Kennedy (Cambridge: MIT Press, 1988), p. 59–60.
185. Ellen Kennedy, "Introduction" in Schmitt, *Crisis*, op. cit.
186. Which, of course, is the heart of republican doctrine.
187. For a classic statement of the Leninist fear of bureaucracy in the transitional state see Leon Trotsky, *The New Course* (1923).
188. For an excellent introduction to the left-communist tendency see Serge Bricanier (ed.), *Pannakoek and the Workers Councils* (St Louis: Telos Press, 1975).
189. John Maynard Keynes, *The General Theory of Employment, Interest and Money* (New York: Harcourt, Brace and World, 1969).
190. See especially C. Wright Mills, "The New Left" in *Power, Politics and People* (New York: Oxford University Press, 1963).
191. SDS, *The Port Huron Statement* (New York, 1962); James Miller, *Democracy in the Streets* (New York: Simon and Shuster, 1987). Hayden drafted the Statement, integrating sections written by others on the committee.
192. See James Miller, *Democracy in the Streets*, op. cit.
193. For a good summary of the politics of the European New Left, see George Kastiaficas, *The Imagination of the New Left: A global analysis of 1968* (Boston: South End Press, 1987).
194. For the best account of the left critique of the PCI position and of the program of the radical workers' movement in Italy, see Joann Barkan, *Visions of Emancipation* (New York: Praeger Publishers, 1984).
195. Andre Gorz, *Strategy for Labor* (Boston: Beacon Press, 1967); Serge Mallet, *The New Left* (London: Spearman Press, 1975).
196. Mario Tronti, *Ouvriers et Capital*, translated into French by Y. Moulier and G. Bezzo (Paris: Christian Bourgeois Editeur, n.d.).
197. Jean Baudrillard, *In the Shadow of Silent Majorities* (New York: Secret Agents Series, Semio-Text, 1986).
198. Bobbio, *Future of Democracy*, op. cit. p. 18.
199. See David Held, *Models of Democracy* (Palo Alto: Stanford University Press, 1987), Chapter 5.
200. Bobbio, *Future of Democracy*, op. cit.
201. Ibid.
202. See Ernst Bloch, *Principle of Hope* (3 volumes) (Cambridge: MIT Press, 1986), Volume 1.

Bibliographical Essay

This book draws from sources in economic, political, sociological, philosophical and aesthetic literature within the Marxist tradition and outside it. The bibliographical essay is a better way of discussing sources than listings because it gives the reader an annotation of what has been important in the constitution of the work.

General sources: Contemporary debates within Marxism are quintessentially involved in the interpretation of various texts of Marx and Engels to substantiate their respective positions. To grasp the various arguments in my book, the reader should explore Karl Marx, *Economic and Philosophical Manuscripts*, Marx and Engels, *The German Ideology*, volumes 1 and 3 of Marx's *Capital*, as well as the rough draft of *Capital* published under the title *Grundrisse* (New York: Vintage Books, 1973). None of these texts yields its immanent meaning to even the most discerning reader. Nor have all readers focused on the same aspects of Marx's philosophical and theoretical arguments. My point of view is that of Walter Benjamin, who asserts that we read Marx from the perspective of our "now", that is, the specific location within which the historical text derives its signification. For our time, the most celebrated and important readings of *Capital* have been those of Georg Lukács' *History and Class Consciousness* (Cambridge: MIT Press, 1971) and Louis Althusser and Etienne Balibar's *Reading Capital* (London: New Left Books, 1970). Both treat *Capital* not just as a work of political economy but as a central text for comprehending Marx's theory of history and of social transformation. Each of the two books argues in its own way for a reading that stresses Marx's categories of philosophic understanding. Lukács is looking for the absent subject in the logic of capital and the authors of *Reading Capital* stress that the absence is Marx's statement that the subject must be renounced.

Karl Korsch's *Karl Marx* (New York: Russell and Russell, 1963) argues for an interpretation of Marx in which the Principle of Historical Specification becomes the most important category of historical explanation. According to Korsch, Marx's revolution in social thought consisted in his discovery that nothing in society was immutable, that all characteristics of social relations and of individuals referred to specific historically-produced conditions. Korsch's refusal of a critical philosophical argument for the materialist interpretation of history contrasted sharply with his earlier claim that Marxism could not dispense with philosophy until the conditions to realize it, the socialist revolution, made speculative reason unnecessary.

Korsch's study of Marx, written in 1938, reflected the antinomies of Marxist thought in that particular period. On the one hand, he shared the position with Lukács that nature did not influence human societies directly and that human nature was essentially a product of the ensemble of social relations historically considered; on the other hand, he argued for the view later attributed to Engels and George Plekhanov (see especially his *Fundamental Problems of Marxism*, Chapter 6) that natural conditions, especially geography, were among the elements constituting the specificity of the mode of production. In his discussion of pre-capitalist economic formations found in the *Grundrisse* (Notebook Five, pp. 483–554), Marx's position on the natural presuppositions of production resolves itself dialectically – that is, nature is granted its autonomous moment in the metabolic relationship between the mode of production and its object. The institutions of society, the sedimented forms of social relations (family, commune, etc.) mediate nature's relation to individuals who are at once part of nature and, through their social relations, separated from it by their historical practices. *The Crisis in Historical Materialism* in this volume refuses the historicism of Lukács and Korsch but, at the same time, does not go over to Plekhanov's naturalism. For other discussions of this issue Alfred Schmidt's *Concept of Nature in Marx* (London: New Left Books, 1971) is probably the best, but Agnes Heller's Lukácsian *Theory of Needs in Marx* (London: Allison and Busby, 1975) is worth consulting, as is *Alienation and Praxis* (Austin: University of Texas Press, 1977), by Kostas Axelos.

The proliferation of recent work in the Marxist theory of class is marked by its alternate a priorism and scientism. Until recently much of the writing in this area proceeded on the orthodox assumption that the process by which capitalism may be abolished and a new society created required a specific historical agent of change. That is to say, most Marxist writings on class have posited what Anthony Giddens calls the knowledgeable subject – see his *Central Problems in Social Theory* (Berkeley: University of California Press; and London: Macmillan, 1979) – as the necessary condition for social transformation. There are at least two major controversies surrounding the question of the subject of historical change. The first is whether the working class, or some other group standing in a definite relation to ownership and control of the means of production, can be considered the appropriate historical agency in the wake of the changes – both technological and political-economic – in late capitalism. Perhaps the most celebrated work challenging this traditional Marxist conception has been Herbert Marcuse's *One Dimensional Man* (Boston: Beacon Press, 1964). For Marcuse, the question of whether the working class is now an agent of change is not theoretical, since any possible socialist society could only be brought about if there could become a self-conscious revolutionary subject. The issue is empirical: the domination of manual labor by intellectual labor; the repressive, but successful, development of capitalist rationality, as expressed quintessentially in the capacity of technology not only to deliver the goods to a wider sector of the underlying population than even Marx could imagine, but also to dominate all social relations, especially the relations of production. These conspire to render the workers a dependent variable in the new technologically-configured totality. Andre Gorz and Serge Mallet have argued that the introduction of knowledge as the new hegemonic productive force in the reproduction of capital and the relations of production has deprived the old working class of its power, but brought into existence a new working class which possessed knowledge but did not share in the possession of the means of material production or the control of the labor process. See Serge Mallet, *The New Working Class* (London: Spokesman Books, 1978) for the fullest explication of this position, and Andre Gorz, *Strategy for Labor* (Boston: Beacon Press, 1967) for the most powerful development of this concept of the new working class into a political principle of socialist strategy. In the environment of the world capitalist crisis of the 1970's and 1980's, this argument fell into considerable disfavor as Marxists of many complexions expected the old needs to reassert themselves and a radicalization of the working class to occur. Nevertheless, the debate about class was not exhausted by these differences, since both orthodox and revisionist theorists for whom history was configured by class struggles held that the working class was the class in radical chains of which Marx spoke. Its "self-consciousness" was crucial, whether called that or not. (Giddens, for example, used the rather elegant phrase "discursive consciousness" to connote the formation of the knowledgeable subject.)

In the past twenty years, a whole new side of the debate has made its way into theoretical discourse. For the various structuralist and post-structuralist writings, the debate about the working class asks the wrong questions, because of its *a priori* assumption of a subject that is not historically and structurally constituted. For Louis Althusser, Nicos Poulantzas and their school, human subjects are themselves to be explained by the specificity of the relations of production. That is, one may not posit a particular human agent without reference to the conditions under which it is constituted by a concrete social formation. There are two things to be asserted here: first, the "subject", "consciousness", etc. is not *given* prior to the conditions of its existence, which are precisely those forms of structuration that arise from the institutions of the social formation. Second, ideology, the seat of consciousness, is not itself derivative of material relations conceived as economic infrastructure. Society is a structured totality of which ideology is a set of material practices. For a seminal exposition of Althusser's view, see "Ideology and Ideological State Apparatuses" in *Lenin and Philosophy* (London: New Left Books, 1971). For Poulantzas's reading and development of this argument, see especially his *Political Power and Social Classes* (London: New Left Books, 1975) and his later work *State, Power, Socialism* (London: New Left Books, 1978). The second important contribution of these writers to the development of Marxist theory consists in their critique of the bifurcation of ideas and material forces and their insistence that ideas are material forces. The fundamental concepts are derived from what has been commonly referred to as *structuralist* linguistics which is, among other things, a theory of language in which language's historical character is subordinate to its synchronicity. That is, language is viewed as a material object, not a property of "consciousness". Thus, society is itself constituted by means of language. In turn, discourse, ideology, and the like are understood as relatively autonomous aspects of a totality of social relations of which the economic infrastructure, in the Marxist reprise, is understood as the determining force (in the last instance).

ideological roots of all scientific thought, refuses the *tendency* in this mode of social theorizing. At bottom, one may not avoid the sin of metaphysics, as Derrida himself has acknowledged (see his discussion of this issue in *The Structuralist Controversy* (Baltimore: Johns Hopkins University Press, 1967, edited by Richard Macksey and Eugenio Donato). One remains in Marxist discourse, as Sartre understood, by *engagement* in the world, that is, by commitment to praxis, to the processes of social transformation. The radical critique of all possible historical law, especially historical law which relies on an *a priori* subject, leaves open the search for the personifications of a change as a way of intervening in the present that goes beyond voluntarism. Deleuze, Derrida and Foucault are, among other things, activists in the movements of human liberation. Yet, there is no *theoretical* reason implied in their praxis. The power of Marxism remains its theory of the subject as a practical knowledgeable actor in the world.

The most interesting of all recent Marxist works to develop this argument is that of Jean-Paul Sartre, whose *Critique of Dialectical Reason* (London: New Left Books, 1976) has influenced this book in various ways. It seems to me that Sartre's long and sometimes difficult book struggles with all of the questions that have gripped all manner of Marxists in the past twenty-five years, since the crisis in Stalinism became an object of universal discussion. Sartre's work is the contemporary analogue of Marx's cryptic remark in the *18th Brumaire* concerning the dialectic between the making of human history that is always personified and the material conditions already in existence. Sartre argues that these material conditions are, in turn, made by prior generations. According to Sartre, all of these conditions, the making and the already made, are conditioned by *scarcity*, which is itself a social category. Curiously, in Ronald Aronson's *Jean-Paul Sartre: Philosopher in the World* (London: New Left Books, 1980), there is no attempt to show the relation of Sartre's philosophy to contemporary debates in French social and historical theory. For Sartre himself introduced the possibility that the subject, having been constituted by the conditions already in existence, created history through a praxis which itself was determined, but also was not predictable.

I wish to offer some remarks and references to the issues of race and sex. As I have indicated in the text, these questions are by no means comfortable within Marxist discourse. The Marxist literature on race in the United States and Caribbean has attempted to reconcile issues of race and class without notable success. Nevertheless, the British publication *Race and Class* is noteworthy for its effort to interrogate Marxism from the point of view of racial autonomy, as well as to focus a Marxist gaze upon race issues. In the text of this book I have referred to work on class and caste, particularly Olive Cromwell Cox's *Class, Caste and Race* (New York: Monthly Review Press, 1964), Louis Dumont's *Homo Hierarchicus,* and Barrington Moore's *Injustice* (White Plains: Myron Sharpe, 1978). But the psychological literature is equally important, particularly the work of Franz Fanon, whose *Wretched of the Earth* (New York: Grove Press, 1964) and *Black Skins, White Masks* (New York: Grove Press, 1967) introduced the sexual dimension into the debate around racism and capitalist social relations, and reintroduced considerations of social philosophy into the discussion, an exploration rigorously excluded by orthodox (i.e. economistic) Marxism.

Needless to say the most important, and still the most powerful, feminist statement is Simone de Beauvoir's *Second Sex,* because it has resisted the principle of historical specification to argue for the ontological significance of male domination, that is, the notion that the structuration of social life has entailed sexual inequality. This mode of analysis is continued in Shulamith Firestone's now-neglected *Dialectic of Sex,* which, despite many shortcomings, remains the best American work, and also shows the inadequacy of the subsumption of sexual questions under class categories. The most recent and interesting feminist writing is, undoubtedly, what has been termed the *New French Feminism* (Amherst: University of Massachusetts Press, 1979). Although this collection, edited by Elaine Marks, is too fragmented to give more than a superficial sample of the kind of thinking that has emanated from De Beauvoir's theoretical daughters, it is the only place in English where some of the work is collected in a single place.

The distinctive character of the work of Luce Irigaray and Helene Cixous is their successful extension of some themes in post-structuralist discourse to problems of feminism. They argue that the *principal* configuration of sexual relations is the exclusion of women from language and discourse. There is no language within which women may speak, for women are outside language. Thus, patriarchy and male supremacy are not merely institutional practices sedimented in family, school, work, and politics. The mode of existence of social relations is language, and women are the absence in the text of public discourse. They cannot find themselves in the forms of knowledge, politics, sexuality, science, etc. Thus, feminism becomes a critique of the most intimate cultural forms when it focuses upon the deep structure of human interaction. The French feminists pose the question of the viability of civilized society as such. For not only is the bourgeois claim to equality challenged at a level below its juridical expression, but the transhistorical relation of women to men is subjected to a kind of critique that makes inescapable the conclusion that women are not present in history. And, unlike those Americans who imagine that the recovery of the voices of women retrospectively may restore them to a place in civilized society, the French feminists assert the necessity for the transformation of culture *per se*.

This argument has been used widely to oppose theoretical discourse as male, the entire realm of abstraction which is held to belong to men, just as Alfred Sohn-Rethel in his *Intellectual and Manual Labor* (London: Macmillan, 1978) argues that abstraction in science and technology is entwined with domination. As radical as is the demand to transform social life at its root, the very materiality of communication, the infrastructure of all society, relies on most sweeping theoretical statements. Women have been consigned to the realm of the particular, the concrete. Men have taken hold of theory as the province by which they maintain their supremacy and reproduce patriarchal culture. Yet the requirement that all discourse be transformed as a condition of the emancipation of women, including the sediments of language in the crucial institutions of the family and the state, is the most fundamental critique extant of hierarchy in society. At the same time, the anti-theoretical bent of feminist criticism, although grounded in its critique of patriarchal scientific and technological thought, poses problems that are insoluble because they remain at the level of *critique*.

The critical literature on mass culture falls into several modes. The most original and ultimately problematic work of critical theory is *Dialectic of the Enlightenment* (New York: Seabury Press, 1972), particularly the chapter on "Enlightenment as Mass Deception". Here Max Horkheimer and Theodor Adorno sound the alarm about the effects of mechanically reproduced art. Their theory, now well known in this country, is not only that mass-audience culture is a degradation of art; such views are well known among bourgeois critics of mass-audience art as well. But the development of a technology that permits the wide dissemination of art as entertainment springs from the unintended consequences of the enlightenment. Science and technology, heralded by seventeenth- and eighteenth-century intellectuals as the means by which we may liberate ourselves from the thrall of scarcity and mysticism, has produced a new form of mystification. For the consumer of mechanically reproduced art, culture becomes a haven that relieves him of the boredom inherent in rationalized labor. But for the powers that be, culture becomes an instrument of domination. It degrades the critical faculties and makes easier the manipulation of consciousness through its fragmentation. Mass culture preys upon the libido, directing it to spurious satisfactions that are attendant upon consumerism.

Another view is promulgated in Walter Benjamin's essay "The Work of Art in the Age of Mechanical Reproduction", (in *Illuminations,* edited by Hannah Arendt, New York: Schocken Books, 1969). Here, this close friend of Adorno and of the critical theorists hopes for the democratization of art through the loss of that element which retained art as the exclusive province of the economic and intellectual elites, its auratic quality. The loss of aura prefigures the end of art as private property, according to Benjamin. In his *Baudelaire: Poet of High Capitalism* (London: New Left Books, 1974) Benjamin extends the argument to his canonical figure of high culture. As I tried to show in my essay on Foucault and Benjamin, Benjamin's nostalgia for the days of the marginality of art – when art was often marked by its obscurity in the marketplace – is sternly mediated by the oft-repeated reminder that art is produced from the refuse of everyday life, that no artist really belongs to a single audience since the sources of art are to be found in the city streets.

Perhaps the most interesting of the newer works on mass reproduction of art is made by the fledgling "science" of semiotics. Its complex roots are quite distinct from its current uses, but suffice it to say for these purposes that the theory of signs involves a complex of philosophical issues. Among its earliest proponents was the American philosopher Charles Sanders Peirce: see his *Selected Writings,* edited by Justus Buchler (New York: Dover, 1960). Charles Morris, following Peirce, has written a short, but illuminating volume, *Foundations of a Theory of Signs* (Chicago: University of Chicago Press, 1938). However, the attempt to integrate semiotics with a theory of popular culture has been pursued by French structuralism and post-structuralism. See especially Roland Barthes, *Elements of Semiology* (Boston: Beacon Press, 1970) and Umberto Eco, *A Theory of Semiotics* (Bloomington: University of Indiana Press, 1976) for two different attempts at a fundamental text suitable for the study of art. Also see Christian Metz's *Language of Cinema* (New York: Oxford University Press, 1976). For an application to advertising see Judith Williamson, *Decoding Advertisements* (London: Marion Boyars, 1978). Barthes has produced a highly original semiotic analysis of a canonical work of realist literature, Honoré de Balzac's "Sarazine" – *S/Z* (New York: Hill and Wang, 1976). The importance of this study is its attempt to demonstrate that there never was a continuous narrative, even in the era of realist hegemony, that all art is produced from a gaggle of codes, juxtaposed in various ways. Thus, Barthes makes of Balzac a writer of post-structuralist fiction, since all writing is decentered and its seamless narratives only a form of ideology.

Modern semiotics is not merely a "technique" for the close analysis of literary and other cultural texts. It is a theory of representation, an argument that art refers only to the conditions of its production which, in some instances, has a referent outside its own modalities of creation, but does not represent an external referent. Thus, together with Jacques Derrida, Barthes means semiotics to be a philosophical statement that the process of signification attaches itself to a signified more or less depending upon the context within which such activity occurs. Thus, the *signifier* has materiality and is not dependent upon some reality that is independent. The world, in short, is a complex of signifiers that, under specific conditions, is codified in various ways.

Jean Baudrillard's *For a Critique of the Political Economy of the Sign* (St Louis: Telos Press, 1981) adopts this viewpoint to critique Marxism's tendency to understand the media and other elements of "consumer society" merely as ideological objects. That is, consistent with post-structuralist aesthetics, of which Benjamin may be a precursor, he insists upon comprehending art as a form of the production of life. Further, carrying the critique of the *a priori* subject to the system of cultural objects, Baudrillard argues that there is a cultural logic that requires no specific "consciousness" or intersubjectivity to motivate it. Baudrillard is among a small group of writers, of which Jean-Joseph Goux is another representative, who have attempted a radical transformation of Marx's categories of political economy to show their culture forces and thus reverse the economism of contemporary Marxist theory.

In this regard, Henri Lefevbre stands out as a singular influence upon the new cultural critics, notwithstanding his own antipathy to the structuralist project. Lefevbre's *Everyday Life in the Modern World* (New York: Harper and Row, 1971) is part of a longer work, begun in 1947, to provide Marxism with a critique of everyday life, of which what he calls the "bureaucratic society of controlled consumption" became the cutting edge of social analysis for writers like Baudrillard (whose later work is still engaged in refusing the whole distinction between production and consumption that is still present in Lefevbre). Those wishing to explore the permutations of consumer society further will find a fine example in Guy Debord's *Society of the Spectacle* (Detroit: Black and Red, 1972), a spectacular critique of everyday life, including mass media, that does not presume that the mechanical reproduction of art has redeeming features.

Since the first edition of this book, there has appeared a large body of literature on various issues raised here. On class and stratification, particularly noteworthy are Eric Olin Wright's *Classes* (London: Verso, 1985) and Pierre Bourdieu's *Distinction* (Cambridge, Mass., Harvard University Press, 1984), especially because they take profoundly different perspectives. Wright acknowledges that class relations are mediated, but he refuses what for Bourdieu becomes a crucial element of stratification: status. For Bourdieu the category "cultural capital" is a material force with economic capital and is not principally derived from the latter. Wright clings to class as a structural category unimpeached by anything but location of an individual or group within an economic structure.

Orlando Patterson's *Slavery and Social Death* (Cambridge, Mass., Harvard University Press, 1984) is among the most significant works on the importance of racial domination in forming modern western culture since Cox's earlier work. Of course, earlier works by Eugene Genovese (*Roll, Jordan, Roll: the world the slaves made*, New York: Random House (Vintage), 1976), Herbert Gutman (*The Black*

Family in Slavery and Freedom (New York: Pantheon Books, 1979) and David Brion Davis (*Slavery and Western Culture*) are also extremely useful for comprehending race. But the singularity of Patterson's book is to have introduced theoretical categories for explaining the persistence of race, most pertinently the idea of slavery as a form of deracination, a term which has become a leading modern mechanism for perpetuating domination even when the institution of slavery is abolished, as in western societies. Patterson has integrated the economic features of racial oppression, and its cultural and discursive aspects, with a thoroughness no other writer has approached. While the eighties have been marked by a significant ebbing of new social movements, it has also been a time of reflection for writers aligned with these movements. Alden D. Morris's *Origin of the Civil Rights Movement* (New York and London: Collier Macmillan, 1984) and Nell Irvin Painter's *Standing at Armageddon* (New York: W. W. Norton & Co., 1987), are both outstanding efforts to remind us that the struggles of blacks and labor respectively are collective events not made primarily by "great" leaders, a tendency in curent historical writing exemplified by the emergence of biography as a major publishing subindustry. Theirs are not precisely "anonymous" histories since the periods covered are within the last century when documents and records of even the activities of blacks and workers' movements are readily available, at least in comparison to earlier times.

In the United States the last decade has witnessed a veritable explosion of work in women's history, feminist theory, attempts by feminist critics to construct a new canon of women's literature as well as continuity in feminist psychoanalytic theory and criticism. The British debate has made new theoretical contributions, particularly the writing of Meaghan Morris (*The Pirate's Mistress*, London: Verso, 1988), Veronica Beechey (*Unequal Work*, London: Verso, 1988), Jacqueline Rose, and the work of Jessica Benjamin (*Bonds of Love*, New York: Pantheon, 1988) whose theoretical sweep is, frankly, unusual in the American discussion, which has largely been developed in other fields, particularly literature and history. Clearly in these dark times when retribution against women by men enraged by their putative power-loss has become rampant, especially as it conjoins with the rise of conservative ideology, feminist writing takes on the character of a profound political intellectual act. And there is no more powerful discourse in social theory than feminism which, in comparison to the quality of ordinary academic contributions, appears monumental. The diversity and richness of new work on sex, gender and race provides considerable hope for the revival and reconstruction of historical materialism.

A fairly good starting point on Marxist political thought is, of course, Marx and Engels, *The Communist Manifesto* (1847), but Marx's later political and historical writings are equally valuable. Marx's *Class Struggles in France* and *The Critique of the Gotha Program* (1878) are both reflections, in different registers, on the Paris Commune. From this event, Marx developed his conception of the proletarian dictatorship as a model of socialist transition. And it is useful to consult Marx/Engels, *Selected Correspondence* (Moscow: Foreign Languages Publishing House, n.d.) because many ideas about politics and the state are contained in the letters to comrades, as well as acute assessments of the political situation in many of the countries of western Europe and the United States.

The lack of formal elaboration of Marx's own state and political theories gave the leaders of the turn of the century Socialist International little pause (Karl Kautsky's *Socialist Republic* (pamphlet, n.d.) is merely a restatement of orthodox views), except, of course, Rosa Luxemburg whose political writings (Dick Howard, ed., *Selected Political Writings*, New York: Monthly Review Press, 1971) provide a good running commentary on socialist and nationalist politics of the era prior to the First World War, and Eduard Bernstein's heretical *Evolutionary Socialism* (New York: Schocken Books, 1961) which became the occasion for Luxemburg's best polemics. However, the Russian Revolution has produced a veritable library of theory and reflection. Plekhanov's *Socialism and Political Struggle* and Lenin's 1902 pamphlet *What is to Be Done?* (in Robert C. Tucker, ed., *The Lenin Anthology*, New York: W. W. Norton & Co., 1975; Lenin's *Collected Works*, Moscow and London: Lawrence & Wishart) are good starting points concerning the position of Russian Social Democracy on the eve of the first revolution. But one should also remember that the unexpected revolutionary upsurge in 1905 produced a profound change in Lenin's conception of the revolutionary process, ideas which were articulated most forcefully in his First World War polemics, *The Renegade Kautsky*, *Imperialism* and other works. Lenin's most utopian conception, the so-called withering-away of the state in the transition to communism is found in his pamphlet *State and Revolution* (1917) which has become virtually canonical in Bolshevik–Leninist futurism and the object of more recent derision (see A. J. Polan, *Lenin and the End of Politics,* London: Methuen, 1984, for a critique of *State and Revolution's* impractical, almost rhetorical character). In the post-Bolshevik era, the Frankfurt School stands above all other neo-Marxist tendencies in developing state and political theory. Here the work of Otto Kirscheimer and Frederick Pollack stand out (see Andrew Arato and Eike Gebhardt, eds, *The Essential Frankfurt Reader* (New York: Urizen Books, 1978) for a representative sampling of their writing on state capitalism in the light of the rise of fascism in the thirties. (Another important article, Max Horkheimer's "Authoritarian State" is included in the same collection.) Franz Neumann made incalculable contributions to the development of Marxist state theory in the years before his untimely death. His classic study of Nazi Germany, *Behemoth: Structure and Practice of National Socialism 1933–44* (London: Frank Cass, 1967) and his essays published as *The Democratic and the Authoritarian State* (Glencoe, Ill.: Free Press, 1955) influenced the Institute's own work in this field. Mention should be made of the extensive Trotskyist and neo-Trotskyist literature on the Soviet Union, the rise of fascism and its consequences for western democracy, the Spanish civil war and many other aspects of inter-war politics. For Trotsky's political critiques, see especially *The New Course* (1923; London, New Park, 1972) and his *History of the Russian Revolution* (New York: Monad Press, 1976). Also *The Revolution Betrayed, What Next?* (New York: Pathfinder Press, 1973), his superb attack against so-called third-period Communist strategy in the light of Hitler's rise to power in Germany, and Max Schachtman's important *Bureaucratic Revolution* (New York: Labour Action, 1953) where he enunciates the famous thesis that Russia had, by the mid-thirties, become a state capitalist regime and the Party constituted a veritable new class. This judgement was hotly contested in Marxist circles, not the least by Trotsky himself who, until the last, defended the socialist achievement of the Soviet Union even as he excoriated its leadership.

The crisis of Marxism beginning with the 1960's, became the occasion for a new discourse on the state. The celebrated debate between Ralph Miliband and Nicos Poulantzas focused for a decade the direction of the discussion. Miliband's *The State in Capitalist*

Society (London: Quartet, 1973) and Poulantzas's *Political Power and Social Classes* (1968, English translation 1975; London: New Left Books). The issue was joined between the classical base/superstructure distinction drawn from Marx's *Preface* and upheld by Miliband, and the Althusserian conception according to which economic, political and ideological structures were relatively autonomous elements of the social formation determined only "in the last instance" by the economic. Hence, for Poulantzas the state itself is constituted by its institutions of consent as well as coercion, which, in the contemporary western capitalist context are contested terrains, while Miliband posited a more or less direct correspondence between economic and political power. Other works, notably Bob Jessop, *The Capitalist State: Marxist Theories and Meditations* (London: Martin Robertson, 1982) and Martin Carnoy, *The State and Political Theory* (Princeton: Princeton University Press, 1984), have aligned themselves on one or another side of this divide. Miliband himself, in perhaps his most important book, *Marxism and Politics* (Oxford: Oxford University Press, 1977), drew closer in the seventies to Poulantzas, without adopting the structuralist theoretical apparatus.

Until the eighties, however, the Marxist discourse on politics suffered from the overly-strong emphasis of most writers on structure. Perhaps the pioneering work of C. B. Macpherson (*The Political Theory of Possessive Individualism: Hobbes to Locke*, Oxford: Oxford University Press, 1964, *Democratic Theory: Essays in Retrieval*, Oxford: The Clarendon Press, 1973) and many other books, prefigured the revival of political philosophy among neo-Marxists. In the eighties, with the global decline of the socialist and workers' movements, the old certainties fell into disrepair. The end of communist hegemony among Marxists played a role in reviving a debate regarding agency, a discourse abetted by the emergence of the new social movements in the seventies.

Some of the democratic debate refers to the apparent stability of capitalist democracies, especially in Norberto Bobbio's *The Future of Democracy* (London and Minneapolis: Polity Press and University of Minnesota Press, 1987) and *Which Socialism?* Other contributions in this vein are Thomas Furgeson and Joel Rogers, *Democracy* (New York: Penguin Books, 1985), and Benjamin Barber, *Strong Democracy* (Barber is a left democrat, not a Marxist). For post-Marxist discussions see especially Ernesto Laclau and Chantal Mouffe, *Hegemony and Socialist Strategy* (London: Verso, 1986) and my critique, Stanley Aronowitz *Social Text* 16; also Claude Lefort, *Democracy and Political Theory* (Minneapolis: University of Minnesota Press, 1989). For a recent Marxist, i.e. Macpherson-inspired defense of radical democracy from a socialist perspective, see Anthony Arblaster, *Democracy* (New York: Polity Press, 1987). A useful survey is David Held, *Models of Democracy* (Palo Alto: Stanford University Press, 1987).

Index